DISCARD

D1713340

Methodists and the Making of America

Methodists and the Making of America

Organizing to Beat the Devil

Charles W. Ferguson

EAKIN PRESS
Austin, Texas

Originally published as *Organizing to Beat the Devil*
Copyright ▪ 1971 by Charles W. Ferguson

Library of Congress Catalog Number 73–139018

© 1983 by Charles W. Ferguson

ISBN
0-89015-424-4 Hardback
0-89015-405-8 Paperback

Printed in the United States of America
By Eakin Press, P.O. Box 23066, Austin, Texas 78735

SECOND EDITION

TO

Hannah Jane Wright and
Charles Nathaniel Newton Ferguson

Prolegomenon

With all that has been written about religion in America, slight attention has been paid to the possible effect of strong church bodies—numbering millions of members holding with some degree of intensity ideas peculiar to their faith—on various aspects of the country's culture. The aim of the Religion in America Series is to study religion as history and to examine the interplay between the contents of religious and conventional history. The task of this particular book is to present the interstitial connection between the denomination under discussion and the nation that has been its host.

There are at times striking parallels between occurrences in the story of Methodism and the story of the United States of America—as in the separation of The Methodist Episcopal Church north and south over slavery long before the States divided. The object of the present book, however, is to look beyond the obvious and to measure, whenever it is possible, and to suggest, when it is not, subtle but traceable relationships.

Quite possibly, for example, not a few of the regulatory practices of a body of people devoutly methodical affect American social habits and procedures. The combination of exuberance and statistics that belongs to the national scene, of idealism and bureaucracy, of ponderous effort and quick wit, of grandiose plans and infinite detail—all may arise out of forces of which Methodist churches in their various branches are a part, if not indeed the chief exemplar.

The current Methodist term *administrivia* illustrates an awareness of this combination within the denomination, as does the saying that the Greeks had a word for it and the Methodists have a pamphlet for it. And the omnipresent sense of legal order and parliamentary procedure is summed up in the story of the action of the official board of laymen in a local church who, upon hearing that their pastor was ill, voted thirteen to twelve to pray for him.

Because of the limits set by its purpose, the book attempts a description rather than a chronicle. It is far from comprehensive and some of the omissions will outrage those who know the epic as a whole. But the omissions, save for those that could be assigned to ignorance or faulty powers of selection, are deliberate. They have been made in deference to the main line of inquiry. A further defense of the omissions is that the full story can be found in other books, notably in *The History of American Methodism,* published in 1964 by the Abingdon Press and running to more than two thousand pages of text. In three volumes, the work is admirably researched, covers virtually every phase of the subject, and is suited to the use of either the student or the aerial observer.

Limits of purpose also determine the number of branches of Methodism here treated. Adequate literature on all branches is available to the curious, and whatever the particulars of the history of each, the several branches have common characteristics and they pose a common question: How far is aggregate Methodism responsible for the worship of methodology in American life?

The reader who is interested in this question and the implications that flow from it will find in the following pages material to explore. And it is to be hoped that he will also find provocation to examine other faiths and factors to determine their bearing on American character.

Contents

Bodies Treated in This Account

The Methodist Episcopal Church. Established 1784
The Methodist Protestant Church, 1830
The Methodist Episcopal Church, South, 1845
The Methodist Church. Formed by a reunion of The Methodist Episcopal Church, The Methodist Protestant Church, and The Methodist Episcopal Church, South, 1939
The United Methodist Church. Formed by a union of The Methodist Church with the Evangelical United Brethren Church, 1968

OTHER BODIES MENTIONED IN THE ACCOUNT

Primitive Methodists, 1792
Primitive Methodists (English), 1811
The African Methodist Episcopal Church, 1816
The African Methodist Episcopal Zion Church, 1822
The Wesleyan Methodist Church, 1843
The Free Methodist Church, 1860
The Colored Methodist Episcopal Church, 1870
(Name change to The Christian Methodist Episcopal Church, 1956)

Methodists and the Making of America

I Hidden History

Methodism is America in microcosm. You find in its story our history—vivid, convenient, and condensed, with all the glories, violence, prejudice, and aspirations that make us a peculiar people.

An English religion animated by an enthusiasm shocking to the country of its origin, Methodism overflowed the bounds of the motherland and found lodgment in the colonies shortly before the Revolution. English missionaries bearing the message of its singular and cardinal claim—that the lowliest man or woman could exercise infinite power when converted through its faith and by its ways—spread the word in the wilderness of America.

These missionaries, as well as the native preachers who rose up in their wake, operated under a system of governance unlike that of any other religious body. Built around a unit called a circuit, the system was marvelously suited to the supervising of vastness. Preachers, ordained at first only by their own devotion, rode the circuits as regularly as night followed day. At each point on their appointed rounds they preached the power of newness. They formed those who believed into groups of persons who became neighbors in a common cause. They chose a leader to watch over the group and see to it that the members met without fail once a week to cheer and refresh each other and, in lusty song and fervent prayer, to replenish their faith, keeping it radiant until the circuit rider could come again. Under the system and by their regularity the Methodists lived up to their name, which had originally been a nickname derisively applied to a band of Oxford students who insisted that all things, even ecstasy, be methodically induced.[1]

What went on in small groups of American Methodists was hardly to be noticed by men of affairs who, in the excitement of political independence, were first busy with battles and then later engaged in harvesting the fruits of victory and in seeking the proper form for a new nation to take. But there it was, this organized body of belief with a rapidly increasing number of adherents. A moment had come. Idea and circumstance had met. Tenets needed to brace and fortify men's souls for the scaling of mountains and the felling of trees and the making of peaceful settlements beyond the pale of the known were being advocated repeatedly by a band of unremitting prophets and practiced by people they left behind.

The circuits were scattered, but there was not one that was not connected with some of the others through the intermediary of the traveling preacher and none that was not indirectly in touch with, and sharply aware of, all. Drums within the forest could not have set up a more resonant scheme of communication. By means of it there was fashioned a fellowship within the body politic, a fellowship self-consciously distinct and yet unself-consciously part of the mass moving restlessly west. There came about a kind of consanguinity of temperament between the people called Methodist and the people called American.

This consanguinity was so definite that it did not have to be acknowledged. The ganglia of Methodist societies were not visible to the casual observer but their effect could be detected in retrospect. A year after the Treaty of Paris was signed in 1783 and the Revolution brought to a victorious end, the preachers in America embracing the doctrines of John Wesley, priest of the Church of England and founder of the Methodist societies in

Great Britain, drew together and organized a national church. There was nothing outwardly political about the move. The decision to separate the societies in America from the Church of England, to which they had been nominally allied, was prompted by the need to find some means by which the sacraments, particularly of baptism and communion, could be given to the thousands of Wesleyan converts residing in America.

It was a decision made on Mr. Wesley's initiative and on grounds strictly religious, his determination being to have the means of grace available to his followers in America. Unable to get the Bishop of London to ordain priests for the new land, Mr. Wesley took the responsibility himself. Although without ecclesiastical authority, acting solely on his belief in the practices of the primitive church, he ordained two laymen and consecrated Thomas Coke, who had been a clergyman in the Church of England, and authorized Coke in turn to ordain and consecrate Francis Asbury, an English lay missionary who had stayed in America during the Revolution. The two would be joint superintendents of the new church.

But Mr. Wesley had reckoned without the spirit of independence loose in the land across the sea and permeating all phases of the common life. Francis Asbury, Englishman turned American through a dozen years of residence, refused to be ordained or elevated to the post of superintendent until he had first sent a rider to summon all the preachers from their circuits and got their consent. He insisted on being elected—to the astonishment of Mr. Wesley when he heard about the matter. From their posts and far-flung outposts the preachers rode to Baltimore for a legislative meeting known as a Conference. They reached the place in sufficient numbers to make a quorum on the day before Christmas, 1784. Asbury was elected, then ordained, then consecrated.

Thus a body that called itself The Methodist Episcopal Church had come into being. It was not long in severing its ties with the Methodist connection in Great Britain, declaring itself to be its own boss and even reading Mr. Wesley's name out of the minutes

3

when he sought to exercise authority in an administrative act. As relations between the United States and Great Britain worsened in the early 1800's and there was threat of another war, the Church disposed also of Thomas Coke, asking that he no longer attempt to serve any episcopal function in the American conferences.

Formation of The Methodist Episcopal Church took place more than two years before the convention to consider a federal constitution for the United States of America assembled in Philadelphia. Government was in the air and on the ground. The Methodists had adopted from their beginnings in the colonies the Wesleyan system of circuits and of a fixed Annual Conference to make laws and draw up regulations. To a certain extent, then, they were already a government with set procedures strongly centralized when the federal union of the states was formed under the Constitution. The new union of the states, however, gave added zest to the Methodists' sense of regulation. They were now pretentiously national, their scope defined by the scope of the country, their geography limited only by national metes and bounds.

What you had in the post-Revolutionary period—in the lustrum of 1784–1789—were many people out of many lands united in a distinctly new form of central government and, at the same time, a small number of devout and earnest souls joined in a severe ecclesiastical government. There were other denominations, including the regional Puritans turned Congregationalists in New England, but there was no religious grouping so conscious of the country as a whole and so well organized in machinery to carry out regulations. It was not that the nation set a pattern of action for the Church or that the Church had any measurable influence on the national government. It was simply that the two were locked arm in arm as, beginning almost simultaneously, they faced an uncertain future.

Methodism and the United States of America being coeval, the two have been constantly under the same environment. From the early days of the nineteenth century the denomination has remained one of the biggest Protestant bodies, and it has been at all times one of the most enterprising and energetic. The complex of Methodist bodies, moreover, stands for peculiar ways of thinking and doing business. Many offshoots of the parent body have kept the word Methodist in their title and retained most of the main offices and features of the original organization. The conglomerate represents the widest possible range of population. If the majority bodies are preponderantly middle-class, all economic levels are present and accounted for in one or another of the branches, white or black. For these reasons the Methodist cultus may be presumed to have been a factor, subtle but constant, in the ecology of ideas and emotions that affect the climate of national opinion. Observation of Methodist thought and action brings with it an opportunity to examine neglected aspects of the American scene.

Observation can begin with a glance at the products and by-products that are familiar parts of that scene. What became Goodwill Industries evolved out of the remedial work of a Methodist preacher and his wife in the slums of Boston. The Salvation Army grew from the labors of a Methodist preacher and his wife in London. Both bear the Wesleyan stamp. So does Chautauqua, which started on a camp-meeting ground and projected itself into a pioneer program of adult education, brought into being the first correspondence schools, and provided entrepreneurs and agents the idea for the traveling tent shows that gave small-town life in the United States its first live contact with the performing arts. Chautauqua also provided the setting and encouragement out of which the Woman's Christian Temperance Union developed. The educational program of the temperance movement was conducted by the most prominent Methodist woman of her day, Frances E. Willard. National prohibition in the form of a constitutional amendment rapidly ratified by the states, resulted from the work of the Anti-Saloon League, a political arm of Methodist churches.

In addition to products, certain events in the unfolding Methodist story should be noted for their bearing on political events in American history. Questions arising out of the control of slavery led to a division of The Methodist Episcopal Church into branches north and south sixteen years before the formation of the Confederate States of America. The division was organically made after full-scale debate in the General Conference, which was equivalent within the Church to the Congress of the United States. Every move and most of the talk during the separation took place in public and was reported in detail, Methodists being good Americans and not shy about shouting their problems to the heavens. A separate and assertively autonomous church was formed in the South and the self-sufficiency of the South as symbolized by the success of that church was eloquently propounded during the years that preceded the demand of the South Carolina commissioners for the evacuation of Fort Sumter.

The southern and northern branches of the Church remained apart for almost a hundred years, deeply embittered by the grievous events of the Civil War and its aftermath, but the last sixty-five of those years were spent by officials of both branches in a determined effort to end the separation. And it was ended. It was ended through a full revision of the honored Methodist scheme of government, a remarkable accommodation of central authority to regional rights and sectional difficulties. The effect of the reunion cannot be traced with the same precision as that of the separation, but it proved nonetheless to be a demonstration project in reconciliation that must stand as one of the great stories of all time and that any set of enemies might well study.

Other events in the Methodist book of acts are so wide in scope and high in drama that their religious significance has been lost in political dazzle. A case in point is the settlement of the Pacific Northwest and its acquisition by the United States. In the 1830's the Methodists sent the first missionaries to that vast region, then known as the Oregon Country, stretching west from the Rockies to the Pacific and reaching south and north all the way from Spain's California to Russia's Alaska. Under treaty the region was open to settlement by both Americans and British.

6

Trappers known as Mountain Men had roamed the streams and valleys until they had well-nigh exterminated the hapless beaver. Then talk of farming the fertile parts began and the talk resounded across the land and developed into Oregon fever and Oregon Country became a promised land for Americans moving west.

The Methodist missionaries went for the purpose of converting the heathen Indians, but they found them indifferent to the kind of preaching that aroused whites. Gradually missionary efforts turned to setting up the rudiments of civilized living for the scattered settlers, and the leader of the Methodist Mission, Jason Lee, on his first trip back east carried and presented to a member of the United States Senate the first petition drawn by the settlers to ask that the laws of the United States be extended to the new territory.

In time wave upon wave of immigrants hit the Oregon Trail and spread out over Oregon Country. The sheer weight of numbers tipped the scale heavily against the British and established American sovereignty. Political action made the transfer under the emblazoned banner of Manifest Destiny and to the battle cry of Fifty-Four Forty or Fight. But the Methodists, being expansionists, were in the van of expansion and their church at this period became in essence an instrument of the state.

Religious activities, being intense, purposive, and special, are likely to be discounted, if not overlooked entirely, in the historian's swift recountal of political action. It is in politics where decisions are taken and recorded. Yet, as in the case of some of the familiar dramas of Shakespeare, the aside may be vital to the action.

What of camp meetings? Were they, as commonly presented, mere spectacles, to be noted chiefly for their extraordinary motor phenomena and their widely derided excesses? Enough data have come to light lately to show that the camp meeting was a distinct and unprecedented form of social organization. It was an innovation that introduced the isolated individual to the exhilarating experience of mass living. Uniquely American at first, it offered the opportunity for both men and women, married and unmarried, old and young, black and white, rich and poor, to form a sudden city populated by thousands, so that day and night for a season people out of loneliness dwelt together. Along with the singing, always the singing, and along with the elation of sudden inner change, the camp meeting served as a school that taught those who attended it lessons in social adjustment and community living, lessons not taught on the same scale by any other institution of the frontier.

Religion and religion alone provided the incentive, the invitation, and the auspices of these gatherings. No organization save a religious one could sponsor them, and no other interest was deep enough to maintain them, but the arrangements and conduct of the camps were secular in significance and brought to those assembled a picture of complicated neighborliness they could not have had otherwise in a sparse land. That the meetings lasted but a few days, or at most a week, speeded up adjustments and put a premium on relationships, possibly preparing those who took part for other and better encounters later.

Invented by a vagrant Presbyterian at the beginning of the 1800's, the camp meeting rocked the West and noisy news of it spread throughout the country, bringing religion to the attention of people who had forgot it or had not noticed it during the doldrums and skepticism that followed the Revolution. The Methodists, attracted by the results, took it on as an evangelistic art form and promoted it for forty years as their chief means of putting across their message to the masses. Needless to say, they organized the camp meeting, built solid campgrounds for it, hedged it with rules. Their long and advertised use of it established American revivalism and marked the shift from the importance of cultivating the small group to the technique of reaching the mass.

What were the general consequences? Was the continual practice of appealing to the emotions of the mass a service or a disservice to the nation? Did the cultivation of crowd response unduly encourage in audiences an uncritical mind and an addiction to demagoguery and theatrics?

It is bootless, although it may be a pleasant pastime, to assign cause and effect at every turn in telling the story of a religious body in its cultural setting. Many events and institutions will stand still for analysis. Ideas will not. They flow. In the Methodist ideology are ideas which may have a subterranean influence that can never be traced. One is the idea of perfection— the unique theological concept enunciated by John Wesley that the common man can not only get rid of the burden of sin by being linked with God but that he can also get beyond sin and attain perfect love for his fellows. Acceptance of the idea of perfection led to surface events as real as the slave revolts or the draft riots or the building of the Union Pacific. But what have been the imponderable effects and what will be the ultimate environmental influence of the idea must remain matters of conjecture.

The surface effects are in themselves impressive and argue for further thought. Known as The Second Blessing, the Wesleyan doctrine of perfection was freely accepted by the Methodist societies in England. It found precious little place in the American wilderness, but it remained as a doctrine, was embraced by advocates in other denominations, and before the middle of the nineteenth century returned to Methodism. After the Civil War it was openly accepted by a substantial body of believers. Some Methodists championed it and its adherents were credited with much good work among the poor. Some of the believers in due course became so intense in their convictions that they withdrew from Methodist bodies and formed a series of churches variously designated as Holiness or Pentecostal. These offshoots of Methodist doctrine now number an estimated fifteen million members throughout the world, being especially strong in South America, where they are said to be giving Communism competition of a vigorous sort because of their appeal to the lowly.

The side effects created by the idea of perfection were likewise

9

impressive. Some were aberrant, adding tall tales of scandal to the American scene and showing what may happen when an abstruse doctrine gets out of the hands of its custodians. In 1834 a young man who had studied for the ministry, John Humphrey Noyes, worked out his own comfortable theology, which included the antinomian view that a Christian could be above the mores as well as above the restrictions on morality. He announced that he had attained a state of perfection or sinlessness, and founded a society in Vermont to relay his convictions to others. He advocated free love and encouraged its practice within the society. Devoted members followed him when he was forced to flee Vermont. They later took up residence around him to found the Oneida Community in New York.

Other public expressions of perfectionism were far more socially acceptable, illustrating the variety of interpretations to which the idea was open and the scale on which it could be applied. It brought to pass after the Civil War one of the first instances of institutionalized interdenominational cooperation in our history. Various churches joined with the Methodists to form a holiness association to promote the audacious concept of perfection. The association crossed over borders usually stoutly defended and, through its machinery and efficient operation, set up a fellowship of rivals. For a while some Protestant churches had an agreed goal of endeavor under the guidance of a transcendent ideal. Camp meetings were revived, and during the days of Reconstruction offered the only natural setting wherein members of churches north and south could gather at the river of faith.

That the idea of perfection found hospitality in the United States, gained dimensions here, was carried far beyond our boundaries, as Methodism was from England, may be far more significant than any of its visible manifestations. It was not at variance with our temperament or our thought. Who is to say that it did not enter at least subtly into what men have called the American dream—a magnificent and logically untenable belief in our eventual goodness?

It is not enough merely to note the coexistence of kindred ideas and attitudes in the history of the United States and the story of Methodism, seeing that no analogy will walk on four legs. Comparatively, the treatment of women by the denomination and the nation appears to be the same. At the founding of The Methodist Episcopal Church in 1784 women were ignored, as they were in the drawing up of the Constitution of the federal government. Not until the twentieth century were they given constitutional privileges, save by some African bodies, either in Methodism or in the nation-state. The cultus and the culture agreed.

Yet Methodism has been an alembic for the crucial testing of old prejudices. Its complicated operation needed women as society grew more complex, and schemes for their use fitted well into its structure. In these circumstances women were able to prove that they had a high degree of managerial skill. For a hundred years Methodist women have been in big business. They have had an unparalleled opportunity to demonstrate—not on streets but on boards, before audiences, in offices, in local and national campaigns, at conventions and door to door. The result is a cumulative experience that gives women confidence and men pause. This experience—enlivened by a sense of mission and fortified by statistics that make it inescapable in the record of social progress—cannot fail to have some bearing on the ultimate possible acceptance of American women as full partners in national affairs.

The fact is that the epic of American Methodism touches almost every aspect of the current scene, and a recountal of it may add to the discernment with which we can ponder the phenomenon of our country. Whether it adds to our understanding or not, the story itself is engrossing. It has a touch of the familiar and much of the strange. It offers the experience of eavesdropping on the past and some of the intimacy of theater-in-the-round. It is a drama of man's inner thoughts made vocal. There is in it a good deal of nostalgia and some redintegration, of having been there and here before. There is suspense and there is promise.

II Hail to the Chief

It was but a month after General George Washington took the oath of office as first President of the new United States of America in April 1789 that he consented to receive a delegation from a new religious body called The Methodist Episcopal Church.

Word of the wish of the Methodists to visit the President reached him at the presidential mansion in New York City, a massive three-story house on Pearl and Cherry Streets, which served both as an office and a residence.

The President was setting precedents carefully, one of them being that he would receive callers but not pay visits. And those received must be chosen judiciously. Worthy of the President's time were groups wishing to pay their respects and bespeak their allegiance to the concept of the independent political union of which he was the head. Two weeks before the Methodist appointment the German Lutheran Congregations in and around Philadelphia had presented an address of allegiance. The Presbyterians had drawn up one in their first General Assembly.[1] Other groups, religious and secular and of sundry hues, would follow, including the Society of the Cincinnati, an alumni body comprising officers of the Continental Army.

Some would come out of display, the Cincinnati among them. The President was of their number. They could not be refused an audience, but in the public eye at the time the Cincinnati stood for the aristocratic and elite elements that some citizens said were trying to rule the country. Not so the Methodists. They represented quite ordinary people—but organized and, by all reports, growing like a young boy. That they accepted the new order and had voted to wish it well showed a sign of promise. Although numbering only fifty-seven thousand in a population of three million, their significance was not to be overlooked.[2]

In 1784 they had set themselves up as a body of believers independent of their founder, John Wesley, a fervent priest of the Church of England, whose zeal had overleaped the bounds of formal religion and had attracted the devotion mostly of the middle and lower classes of English society. It was still a question of how independent The Methodist Episcopal Church would remain. Mr. Wesley, although he stood hardly more than five feet, was a powerful man and his influence far-reaching. A person of piety and of unquenchable confidence in matters of religion, he had meddled in politics during the days before the American Revolution and had made some statements which were, to say the least, unhappy.

In the early days of agitation for better treatment of the Colonies, Mr. Wesley had shown sympathy for the American cause, writing to Lord North, the king's chief minister at the time, that he thought the colonists were "an oppressed people asking nothing more than their legal rights." As open rebellion approached, however, Mr. Wesley changed his tune and his stance, persuaded by the arguments of his friend, Dr. Samuel Johnson, who in 1775 published a pamphlet entitled *Taxation No Tyranny*. To Dr. Johnson the Americans, considering the way they were behaving, should be regarded as a race of convicts and "should be thankful for anything we allow them short of hanging."

A prodigious and eclectic reader and a masterful condenser, Mr. Wesley had a way of taking the works of authors and issuing them under his own name if he thought the act would do the people good. He took the Johnson diatribe, extracted what he considered the best arguments, toned it down and presented it to his followers under the conciliatory title of *A Calm Address to Our American Colonies*.³ It was received in America with something less than favor—and with the net effect that the people called Methodists came to be regarded as opposed to the cause of independence. That all but one of the missionaries Mr. Wesley had sent out to the Colonies returned to Great Britain upon the outbreak of hostilities heightened the notion that Methodists, whatever guise they wore, were Loyalists. Had they changed?

Four weeks after the inauguration of George Washington The Methodist Episcopal Church held its Annual Conference in New York and not far from the presidential mansion. The Annual Conference, involving far more than a group of men conferring, was the term used to describe the official governing body of the Methodist societies. It comprised the preachers. They came together at stated intervals to transact the business of the various societies that made up the fellowship as a whole. Whatever this body did could be taken as the official action of the new denomination that now boldly called itself a church. In England the Methodists were part of the Church of England. In the Colonies their place of meeting was a chapel at best, and the term *church* was reserved for whatever might be the established church of a particular colony. But since 1784 the Methodists had said they were a church.

The place where the Annual Conference met in 1789, John Street Church, had earlier been called Wesley Chapel. It was built in 1768, of rough stone faced with plaster, pointedly and modestly resembling a residence, complete with fireplace and chimney in one corner. There were benches without backs and at the rear there was a balcony that could be reached by a ladder and could hold an overflow crowd.⁴

During the Revolution, with New York occupied by the British, no preacher had been appointed to Wesley Chapel. The chapel, however, had been allowed to remain open. The morning worship hour was given over to a service for Hessian troops, but a Methodist society, numbering almost two hundred, met Sunday evenings, with acceptable preachers taking turns in the pulpit. Most of those who belonged were loyal to the British government. After the war Loyalists cleared out of the city and membership in what was constituted as the John Street Church dropped to sixty.[5] The appointed preacher in charge was John Dickins, an Englishman by birth who had spent most of his time during the Revolution traveling and preaching in Virginia and North Carolina. Dickins was a man of more than ordinary education for a Methodist, being versed in Greek and Latin and mathematics. He had been at Eton. His preaching attracted wide attention and his flock was a large and growing one when the 1789 Conference assembled.

On the first day Francis Asbury, one of the two bishops of the new body, suggested that it might be proper "for us, as a church, to present a congratulatory address to General Washington in which should be imbodied our approbation of the Constitution, and professing our allegiance to the government." The suggestion came from a logical source. One of the early missionaries sent out to America, Asbury had moved restlessly and unceasingly among the young societies, preaching, exhorting, leaving dedicated groups to carry on the work he commenced. He had not returned to his homeland when war broke out, and during the Revolution his position had been equivocal at best. Because of his prominence and leadership, he endured more than his share of the obloquy that attached to being a Methodist. He had been forced to go into hiding at first, and all during the hostilities his travel was restricted. And having his travel restricted was the worst fate that could possibly have befallen Francis Asbury. He was by nature a ceaseless itinerant.

Gradually it became clear to the Americans that the central and controlling interest of Asbury was Methodism, not political action. Of the *Calm Address* Asbury said plainly, "I am truly sorry that the venerable man ever dipped into the politics of America." He went on shrewdly to note that the *Calm Address* simply showed how loyal Mr. Wesley was to the government under which he lived: "Had he been a subject of America no doubt he would have been as zealous an advocate of the American cause."[6] Once the war was over, Asbury had turned again heartily to the cause of Methodism and he had been the chief architect in showing how the societies could be built into a church. Although Bishop Asbury had not himself signed the oath of allegiance to the new government, he was present now to pledge the cooperation of the whole body of believers he represented.

The other bishop of the young Church, Thomas Coke, stood in marked contrast to his colleague and showed the scope of opinion and background within the bonds. Coke was a small and learned Welshman who had been a fellow of Jesus College, Oxford, and held a degree of doctor of laws from that institution. He was still a British subject, loyal by oath to George III. Known colloquially as the dapper doctor, he had been on American shores only four years. In England he had been closely associated with Mr. Wesley during the days when the leader of the Methodists was denouncing the colonists as rebels. He was linked in faith with the founder of the societies and shared fervently his views on moral issues, among them the business of slavery. Knowing that Mr. Wesley considered American slavery "the vilest that ever saw the sun," he could not let the subject alone and went about preaching on it far and wide, to the approval of some and the outrage of others.

It was the subject of slavery that had brought the two leaders together with George Washington long before the occasion of their congratulatory address, and it was at the instigation of Bishop Coke that the meeting had come about. Preaching in Virginia in 1785, soon after the formation of The Methodist Episcopal Church, the Welshman had urged every preacher to circulate a petition to the General Assembly of that state, praying that it make the emancipation of slaves legal. In his diligence Bishop Coke, along with Bishop Asbury, made bold to call upon George Washington, entreating him as a distinguished Virginian to sign the petition and lend his influence to the cause. The General received the visitors very politely, by Coke's testimony, and asked them to dine. He declined to sign, noting that the Act would be inappropriate because he was a member of the assembly, but he assured the Methodists that he shared their sentiments and that he would support the measure sought by the petition if it came to a hearing.[7]

Nothing had come of the petition, and now the matter between the Methodists and the new national government was not slavery but greetings. Yet even greetings called for a careful consideration of procedure. The fact that the building where the Conference was in session had been a chapel for Hessians and Loyalists raised some delicate questions. If the President casually received a delegation coming from this church, it would seem that he was overlooking background which patriotic New Yorkers did not. There must be some indication that there had been a political change of heart in Methodists close at hand.

To make clear that the American Wesleyans were American, leaders of the Conference chose Major Thomas Morrell, a preacher who had served on General Washington's staff, to act as go-between, to call on the President in advance, and to arrange the ceremonial occasion. Morrell was as American as they could make them at that time. He had raised a company at the beginning of the Revolution, engaged in a number of daring expeditions and had been wounded in the breast at the battle of Flatbush Heights. Before his wounds had fully healed, he had been made a major. His mother had been converted under the preaching of Philip Embury, the first Methodist to preach in New York. Morrell had not come into the fold until the war was over, but he too came in by the accepted method of conversion, and then he had become a preacher.[8]

With Bishops Asbury and Coke, with John Dickins, pastor of the John Street Church, and with Major Morrell, retired, the Methodist delegation was well rounded and suited admirably to the purpose. The President received his visitors gravely. They stood respectfully before his desk and the President stood tall behind the desk and listened with thoughtful eye while Asbury read the prepared salutation in what Morrell later described as a most thoughtful manner. It began:

Sir: We, the bishops of The Methodist-Episcopal Church, humbly beg leave, in the name of our society collectively in these United States, to express to you the warm feelings of our hearts, and our sincere congratulations, on your appointment to the presidentship of these states. We are conscious from the signal proofs you have already given, that you are a friend of mankind; and under this established idea, place as full a confidence in your wisdom and integrity, for the preservation of those civil and religious liberties which have been transmitted to us by the providence of God, and the glorious revolution, as we believe, ought to be reposed in man.[9]

It was a somewhat cagey and qualified prolegomenon, with proper ascription of man's good fortune to Providence, but it did bring in "the glorious revolution." It was a signal that something new was beginning. The address reminded the President that God was "the source of every blessing, and particularly the most excellent constitution of these states, which is at present the admiration of the world, and may in the future become its great exemplar for imitation." It assured him also of fervent Methodist prayers "that God Almighty may endue you with all the graces and gifts of His Holy Spirit, that may enable you to fill up your important station to His glory, the good of His church, the happiness and prosperity of the United States, and the welfare of mankind."

In that order.

The President delivered his reply, according to Morrell, with fluency and animation. He read a thoughtfully worded statement he had had time to compose after studying the advance copy of the Methodist message Morrell had brought him four days before the appointed meeting. It was a case of preplanning as well as preparation. Nothing was to be left to the hazards of informality. By sending their sentiments ahead of time the Methodists had in a sense organized the occasion. It was only courteous to let the President know what would be said so that his reply could be couched in fitting terms. There was thus a meeting of purpose as well as words. The Methodists would remind the President of his reliance on a higher power, of which they were in some measure custodians, and the President's purpose was to remind the Methodist dignitaries that they were part of the United States.

It would be his function, President Washington said, "to contribute whatever may be in my power toward the civil and religious liberties of the American people." He made it plain that he trusted the people of every denomination who demeaned themselves as good citizens and promised that he would "strive to prove a faithful and impartial patron of genuine vital religion." He thanked the Methodists in particular for the fact that they were going to pray for him and closed by saying, "I likewise implore the Divine benediction on yourselves and your religious community."

The meeting ended in pleasantries and the Methodists took their leave, going out into the bracing late spring air of New York. They had had their say and they would return now to their Conference, where a number of rules and regulations looking to the welfare of the Church were the order of the day. One rule had to do with slavery, a subject that continued to agitate the conscience of the preachers. At the time of the founding Conference, meeting during the Christmas season of 1784, the preachers had voiced their determination "to extirpate this abomination from among us." They had decided that all Methodists must free their slaves within twelve months. Those who did not like the rule could withdraw voluntarily from the societies; but those who stayed in and failed to obey would be expelled.

It was strenuous action, inspired in no small part by Bishop Coke. The preachers meant business, but they reckoned without the fact that the great part of Methodist strength lay in the

South and in states where laws forbade emancipation. The expulsion rule was suspended five months after it was made, and no firm position on the holding of slaves had been taken since. Now in 1789 the Conference in John Street merely forbade "the buying and selling of men, women and children, with an intention to enslave them." There was to be among Methodists no traffic in flesh. But there was no rule against holding slaves. It had disappeared.

It was time to be practical. The Methodists were the fastest growing religious body in a new society and nothing must stunt their growth. Their vigor was an American vigor, whatever their origins, and their beliefs, based on intense faith in the power of the individual, were in harmony with the demands of an expanding country with infinite horizons. America and Methodism might become partners in destiny.

III Autonomy above All

The visit of the delegates to the President occasioned quite a little comment in New York. Criticism centered around the fact that Coke had signed the pledge of allegiance while yet a subject of King George III. Did this mean perhaps that being a Methodist was more important than being British? Or would there not be a divided loyalty and a conflict of interest?

Questions of this sort might agitate the minds of those who continued to look upon the never-ending involutions of British intrigue. Others might regard the statement of the Methodists as a ploy or as a mystery which time would unravel and resolve. Still others, however, took the address of allegiance calmly and as a matter of course. The *New York Packet* noted it to be "affectionate and respectful" and construed it as a sign that the Methodists as a whole "were warmly attached to the Constitution and the government. . . ."[1]

Beyond the news and comment and gossip lay certain residual facts which made the pledge offered by the Methodists and its acceptance by the President logical to those who were reflective. The country needed the support of every kind of variety of person, group, and influence, especially any offering faith and inspiration. The President had shown a historian's appreciation of religion, seeing it as an abstraction in action. Prominent in his inaugural address were the statements: "No people can be bound to acknowledge and adore the invisible hand which conducts the affairs of man more than the people of the United States. Every step by which they have advanced to the character of an independent nation seems to have been distinguished by some act of providential agency."

Obviously encouragement must be given to religious bodies which would implore and might invoke the divine favor. The President, however, was not a man to keep his head in the clouds. He combined the transcendent and the down-to-earth in a remarkable way. As a gentleman farmer George Washington had introduced the mule into America in 1785, developing a fine strain through careful breeding, and planters around Mount Vernon had found the hybrid ideally suited to long, hard, steady work.[2] There was long, hard work ahead for the people of the United States and it had to be steadily done. There would be need for both mules and Methodists.

Methodist societies on American shores, during the two decades before the formation of the Republic, had already demonstrated certain qualities which any helmsman of a ship of state could well reckon.

For one thing, they had a capacity for steering, too. The very word "govern" came from Latin and Greek words meaning to steer, and the Methodists had a veritable passion for government, for processes and endeavors designed to regulate human affairs by means of law. It was not idle, or to be overlooked, that they began as a small body of believers in Oxford, England, who were so severe and habitual in the practices of both devotion and charity that less serious students derisively dubbed them Methodists. And it was a matter of record that the Wesleyan societies had brought into being, two years before the Constitutional Convention met in Philadelphia, a government of their own, national in scope and ambition, strongly central in power but diffused in authority and brilliantly suited to the needs of a population ever on the move.

Anyone who had any doubt about the usefulness of the Methodist love of legalized order and constitutionality could consult the preparations for and the minutes of the meetings at which The Methodist Episcopal Church was formed.

The year was 1784.

The time was Christmas Eve Day.

The place was Baltimore.

The scene was the Lovely Lane Chapel, lying near the center of the town.

There had been called an irregular, extraordinary, almost an emergency gathering of the preachers, possibly eighty in all, who made up the itinerancy of the Methodist connection in the United States. The Annual Conference, the function of which it was to handle matters vitally affecting the brethren, was not scheduled to convene until the following June. But a message of serious concern to the societies had come from Mr. Wesley and, in the ruling opinion of his assistant in America, Francis Asbury, it could not be settled without getting the circuit riders together. The decision to summon them from their widely scattered circuits was not taken until mid-November 1784, and the earliest possible date for them to reach Baltimore in any numbers was deemed to be the day before Christmas. It had taken news of the Declaration of Independence a month to travel from Philadelphia to Charleston.[3] Hard riding would be required not only to cover the distances but also to reach and fetch the preachers. The majority of the Methodists were in remote rural areas of Virginia, including its western reaches, the Carolinas, Georgia, and Pennsylvania.

Chosen to carry the tidings of the special gathering of the itinerants as fast as ever he could was one of their number, a Marylander, Freeborn Garrettson. As sturdy as his given name suggested, there was much about the man to make the choice a happy and successful one. In some of his experiences he paralleled his fellows and in others he outstripped them. He had been converted, after a frivolous and aimless youth, under Methodist preaching. He had entered the ministry of the societies at the age of twenty-three, renouncing the world and obeying the edicts of a stringent conscience. Son of a prosperous planter, he inherited slaves, and after his conversion he had stood in the midst of his household at family prayer and declared the slaves belonging to Freeborn Garrettson to be free.[4]

Nor was his conscience limited to the ethics of slavery. He was opposed to war. He refused military service and he refused also to take oaths of loyalty when they were demanded of him by the states in which he traveled. He was often stoned, beaten with clubs, and jailed, yet from the time he entered the ministry of the Methodists in 1775 until nine years later, when he was given his mission as messenger, Freeborn continued to preach without interruptions save those imposed by persecutions. In 1781 he had traveled five thousand miles and delivered five hundred sermons. Much of his work had been in the South.

If any man could find the preachers and bring them in for decision-making, it was Freeborn Garrettson, tough, resilient, a man of sternest purpose. Added to his fitness also was a sense of drama and an understanding of the essence of the message he had to convey. He was on more than an errand. He was a Methodist and a preacher and he knew the importance of what was to be put before his fellow itinerants when they reached Baltimore. A friend and intimate of Francis Asbury since the beginning days of the Revolution, when he visited with the leader of the societies during his period of gloom and forced seclusion, Garrettson was privy to the decision Asbury had reached and the reasons for it.

The proposal to be laid before the preachers was not less than that they pass judgment on a request, even an order, sent across the waters by Mr. Wesley. The request would not be acceded to, or the order obeyed if it were to be interpreted as an order, until the traveling members of the fellowship, meeting as a Conference body, agreed that it should be.

It was exciting news to be carried far and wide. Up to this point members of the societies had been loyal members of the Church of England, merely more intense in their beliefs and more spirited in their actions than were their unregenerated companions. For the ceremonies of their faith, including baptism and communion, Methodists were to attend services of the Church of England. Now that this church had been discredited by the separation of the states from Great Britain and disestablished by the laws of the states and a new body—the Protestant Episcopal Church—was being formed to take its place, where were the Methodists to turn? Should they perhaps cast their lot with the new Protestant Episcopal Church?

Mr. Wesley thought not, and his word ran like law among the Methodist societies, whether in Great Britain or in the states that had been Colonies. The founder had suddenly decided that the Wesleyans in America should have a connection of their own and he had drawn up papers and prepared an order of service for them to follow. He had given papers and forms to Dr. Thomas Coke, having first laid hands on him in an unprecedented move and consecrating him to be superintendent of work in the United States and authorizing him to bestow upon Francis Asbury the same rights and privileges.

The action had come to pass after much prayer and fasting and careful scrutiny of the Scriptures, as well as a study of the reflections of those versed in church history, and it seemed simple to the man who had full power to do as he pleased in all things Methodist. But Mr. Wesley and Dr. Coke both had reckoned without Francis Asbury. Dr. Coke found nothing amiss in kneeling before Mr. Wesley and allowing himself to be consecrated a superintendent to serve across the sea, but Asbury knew something about procedures in a self-consciously self-governing land. He had no intention of kneeling obediently and having hands laid on him as a part of a new religious body until the men who made up that body chose him to be their superintendent. Ordination could follow but it must not precede the preachers' choice. The itinerants of the country as a whole, north and south, must come to Baltimore and show the world and Mr. Wesley who ruled the societies.

This was the significance of the message Freeborn Garrettson

27

bore and explained as he set out posthaste for far places. What was at issue and at stake was purely a matter of government, of determining the seat of authority, of vesting responsibility. Religion was involved, yes, because the sacraments were religious ceremonies. But the main thing was rights, not rites. Who was to decide and determine? Who had the right to manage the affairs of the societies adhering to the principles of Mr. Wesley in the land of a people who, as he put it, had been "so strangely made free"? And how could this right be protected and guaranteed?

Of course there was more in the background, vivid detail that any good messenger and storyteller could use to hook the interest of his hearers. It could be noted, for example, that Dr. Coke had presumed rather too easily on his acceptance in America. In company with Richard Whatcoat and Thomas Vasey, two lay preachers Mr. Wesley had ordained for service in the States, Dr. Coke had arrived in New York at the beginning of November 1784. There John Dickins received the men amiably and approved the plan as it was unfolded to him. Dickins felt sure that the preachers would approve the new arrangement, startling though it was, and urged Dr. Coke to make it public as soon as possible.[5]

Likewise people in Philadelphia saw the merits of what Mr. Wesley had in mind. Even Episcopalians, distraught over their own problems of organization, gave their informal nod when Dr. Coke preached at St. Paul's, being invited by the rector, and then described the plan.

Thus encouraged, the British preachers borrowed horses in Philadelphia and pushed on to Dover, Delaware, where they came to rest at the Philip Barratt homestead. Until his death shortly before the arrival of Coke and his companions, Judge Barratt had been a staunch Methodist leader in Delaware and a warm friend and protector of Francis Asbury. The judge had contributed liberally to build a preaching house nearby. Measuring forty-two by forty-eight feet, it was built of brick, stood two stories high, and it had a vestry. When it was being built in

1780 the fortunes of the Wesleyans were at low tide and it had seemed ridiculously big, prompting the remark in the neighborhood that even a corncrib would hold all the Methodists after the Revolution.⁶ But Barratt's Chapel had been built and put to good use both as a meeting place and a showpiece.

The preachers told the Widow Barratt that they would like to meet as many members of the societies as could be assembled the following Sunday. So great was the press of people who came to hear the English preachers that November Sunday morning that the chapel was hardly big enough to hold even the Methodists in the immediate vicinity.

It seemed that everybody was there. Everybody except Asbury. He had been away on a preaching mission and he arrived at Barratt's Chapel after the service had begun, taking his place quietly at the back of the congregation, where he could find standing room only. When Dr. Coke had finished preaching there was a solemn pause and a deep silence. Asbury made his way through the crowd. He "ascended the pulpit and, without making himself known by words, clasped the doctor in his arms and accosted him with the holy salutation of primitive Christianity." The other preachers, so stories ran, were melted in tears. It was further said that the whole assembly caught the glowing emotion, as if struck with a shock of heavenly electricity, and there was no one present who was not crying at the display of Wesleyan fellowship.⁷

The service went on, however, and Asbury still had no word with the visitors. There followed the sacrament of the Lord's Supper, the Wesleyan name for Holy Communion. Asbury was astonished to see Whatcoat take the cup and pass it to the communicants. Here was an Englishman doing in a Methodist chapel precisely what Mr. Wesley had forbidden his preachers to do, and Asbury, obedient to the wishes of the founder, had sought to prevent.

After the service Dr. Coke and the other preacher had Sunday dinner at the Widow Barratt's, about a mile from the chapel. Here Asbury got for the first time the full impact of the message from England and he was shocked when he first "learned the intention of these my brethren in coming to this country." He admitted somewhat dubiously later in his journal, "It maybe be of God." Present with Asbury and the English preachers at the Sunday dinner were other preachers from round about, including Freeborn Garrettson. These had come together at the invitation of Asbury and they constituted a council to consider whatever matter of importance the messengers from Mr. Wesley might have to communicate to the Americans. Following a private conversation between Coke and Asbury, the preachers of the council Asbury had formed were invited in and asked to debate whether a Conference of all the preachers should be called. They debated the matter thoroughly and decided unanimously that no step as remarkable as the one Mr. Wesley had proposed should be accepted without the final consent of all the preachers.

It turned out also that Dr. Coke had himself been taken aback when in February of 1784 Mr. Wesley had called him to City Road Chapel in London and there disclosed his plan and purpose for the American societies. That a man of the founder's sense of propriety and strict regard for the rules and structure of the Church of England should think that he could actually ordain another member of the Anglican clergy to an order tantamount to that of a bishop had seemed to the learned young doctor incredible. He had asked time in which to think the problem over before he could agree to be a party to the plan. Mr. Wesley, however, had not been much disturbed by the doctor's hesitancy. In July he divulged his idea to a selected group of British Methodist preachers. According to the report of one itinerant present, James Pawson, the preachers to a man opposed the scheme. "But," Pawson added, "I plainly saw that it would be done, as Mr. Wesley's mind was quite made up."[8]

Dr. Coke had at last been persuaded. It was hard to stand up to Mr. Wesley's views, much less change his mind. Besides, he was acting out of absolute necessity. Anglican bishops he approached refused to cooperate by ordaining Methodists for the

States, where there were thousands of faithful men and women, whose hearts had been changed, left without the means of grace. So Mr. Wesley had taken the unprecedented step, convinced that he was acting in the light of the precedents and practices of the early Church. His action caused consternation in England. His younger brother Charles, although best known for the marching songs he wrote for the Methodists, was even more of a High Churchman than his brother. Charles Wesley was scandalized and dashed off an apt quatrain:

> How easy now are Bishops made
> At man or woman's whim!
> Wesley his hands on Coke hath laid,
> But who laid hands on *him*?[9]

These were among the antecedents of the meeting at Barratt's Chapel and the postprandial session at the home of the Widow Barratt. There were many strange elements in the story and not all of them could be sorted out, but there was at least one certainty and that was the fact that the men on the circuits would have to agree before the plan from England could be put into effect. A country which had made a business of rejecting distant authority and was bent on the regulation of its own affairs, would need all the experience it could get in the practice of government.

Once the decision to call the Conference had been made that Sunday afternoon, Freeborn Garrettson was immediately dispatched. He was, as Dr. Coke expressed it, "sent off, like an arrow, from North to South. . . ." He was directed to send messengers to the right and left while on his ride, and to gather all the preachers together in Baltimore.

With simple Christian modesty Freeborn later reported, "My dear Master enabled me to ride about twelve hundred miles in about six weeks." He added, "A tedious journey I had, preaching going and coming constantly."[10]

Jesse Lee, the first historian of American Methodism, noted

that Garrettson's inveterate love of preaching slowed him on his mission. He failed to get his message to some who were entitled to attend the Baltimore conference.[11] Even so, Garrettson reached all the preachers save those in western Pennsylvania. The men summoned responded, forsaking their rounds and setting out over the foul roads and unbridged streams to the place their leaders had chosen—there to settle the way the scattered societies should be organized and governed.

There would be much to think about as they rode along. It was a time of preparation. The season was Advent.

IV Conference Is King

The day before Christmas 1784 fell on a Friday. The ground round about Baltimore was covered with a heavy frost as Francis Asbury and the British preachers left their lodgings at Perry Hall, an estate about twelve miles distant, and rode through the chill morning air to Baltimore's Lovely Lane Chapel.

The chapel, only ten years old, had been refitted for the impending sessions. A gallery had been put in to accommodate visitors who might want to observe the proceedings. A stove had been installed.[1] Preachers coming from far away would have a modicum of comfort denied members of the local society regularly meeting in the chapel. Some of the rude benches had backs pegged on to them and thus were made to resemble pews, although Mr. Wesley had once laid down the explicit rule: "Let there be no pews and *no backs* to the seats."[2] Subtle changes were taking place, as if in anticipation of momentous ones to follow.

Francis Asbury had been busily in charge of arrangements since Freeborn Garrettson began his ride. He had sent the three delegates from the founder out on preaching missions, not only for the good their ministrations might do the members of the societies but also in order that the circuit riders might have the

33

opportunity of sizing up and of being prepared to act on the proposal they brought. Nothing was to be imposed, not even superintendents. The journey by Dr. Coke had, by some reports, covered eight hundred miles, and the impression he made had not been altogether good. Thomas Ware, a preacher on the Eastern Shore of Maryland, noted, "His stature, his complexion and his voice, were those of a woman rather than those of a man; and his manners were too courtly for me. . . ." Before they parted, however, Ware found many qualities in Coke to admire and no longer marveled at his selection by Mr. Wesley.[3]

The preaching missions were only part of the masonry work done to lay foundations for the special Conference. Still searching his soul, Asbury had spent a day in late November fasting and praying. Then he had noted in his journal that the preachers and the people seemed to be much pleased with his projected plan and added, "I am myself led to think it is of the Lord." For a solid week before the Conference, Asbury was closeted at Perry Hall with the men from Britain. There were ample space and auspicious circumstances. The mansion had been built by Henry Dorsey Gough. It was a center of social life for the well-to-do, Gough being one of the wealthiest men in the region. But he was also devout and his home was open at all times to preachers and members of Methodist societies.[4]

At Perry Hall, Asbury and his colleagues drew up over days and nights of work an agenda of questions and possible answers that would fit the proceedings into the vise of order. The occasion was fraught with history and there was no precedent for the decisions to be taken. It was a moment of genesis and creation, not one to be treated lightly. The principle that men were not to govern without the consent of the governed was familiar but now the time had come to put it into operation in the forming of a church whose challenge and mission were as big as a continent.

The Conference was scheduled to convene at ten in the morning and at ten sharp the meeting came to hushed order. It was a strange and solemn assembly. The preachers, although most of them were from the backwoods, were in knee breeches. The hats they carried had broad brims and low crowns. The clothes were black as dirges and cast a spell of gloom over the room, somewhat relieved by the youth of the faces gathered. Of the sixty itinerants who turned up before the Conference ended, almost all were in their twenties.[5] Even the leaders looked young. Coke was thirty-seven and Asbury was thirty-nine.

Dr. Coke presided, as was fitting. He was Mr. Wesley's representative and he read the good man's letter addressed affectionately "To the Brethren in America." The plan of making the brethren in America a separately constituted church was then laid before the Conference, where it was analyzed rather than debated. There is little in the records to indicate what public opposition was voiced or what choices were considered. We do know from the writings of a young itinerant who had just been taken into full connection with his fellows that there were some misgivings. Thomas Haskins had studied law before entering the itinerancy. He was a thinking man, not merely a talker. He stood high in the estimation of Asbury and some attention was bound to be paid to his views.

These views were in sum that the societies ought to think a long time before cutting the cord with the body of their origin, the Church of England or its successor. The very day that Dr. Coke appeared at the service held in Barratt's Chapel, Samuel Seabury, a clergyman of the Church of England who had remained loyal to the British during the Revolution, got himself consecrated by nonjuring prelates in Scotland. It was now certain that the continuing episcopate claimed and held by the Church of England would have legitimacy in the United States of America and that an episcopal church could be organized among the Americans. Energetic steps to this end had already been taken and Haskins suggested that action on Mr. Wesley's plan be deferred until the next regular Annual Conference of the Methodists, when it could have mature deliberation and when clergymen of the church to which the Methodists claimed to be dutiful sons and daughters might also be present to discuss

35

ways and means of ordination. It seemed not within the hoops of logic that societies which Mr. Wesley had forbidden to make themselves a separate ecclesiastical entity in Britain should be encouraged to do so in America and given a tacit tie with the English Church through means that were casual and dubious. Mr. Wesley might be fully convinced of the propriety of his doings, but the church of which he was a clergyman was not, and a separation accomplished without an apostolic priesthood, properly transmitted, might or could cause permanent harm.[6]

Haskins brought his reasoned view to the Conference in written form and stood ready to oppose the plan laid before the preachers. But it was not a time for debate or opposition or obstruction but rather for agreement, for sealing, for bonding. The American preachers had got what they wanted. They had been called in, consulted, acknowledged, their wishes asked. Unanimously they voted the first day to adopt the plan. In so doing they established a new church and the next order of business was to name it.

The name chosen was of both immediate and abiding significance. Of course the word Methodist had to be in the title. And now that a body of believers had been duly and legally constituted, it could be called a church. Methodist Church it would be. But what else? The word *episcopal* was in the air—a sign in the sky. It designated a form of church government wherein there were definite orders of ability and authority, as there were in the Church of England, the same being that of deacon, then elder, then bishop. The essential of the system was that it provided for guiding supervision, for an arrangement whereby those who managed the church body could see the task as a whole, could oversee, could speak from the peak. Mr. Wesley had appointed superintendents. As one of the members of the Conference put it, "the plan of general superintendency was a species of Episcopacy." So the full title chosen by the Conference was implicit in the plan which had been sent across the waters. The name would be The Methodist Episcopal Church. It was credited to John Dickins, a man whose learning and genial disposition combined to lift him high in the esteem of the Conference as a whole. A motion to make the name official was put forward and carried without a dissenting voice.[7]

Certainly the name was a happy one at the hour it struck, and it settled and fixed one matter that had for several years troubled the minds of the itinerants. There had been a threat that the Methodist societies in America might adopt a presbyterian form of government, might in fact end up as the Methodist Presbyterian Church. In the presbyterian form of government there were no orders; the preachers were of equal rank, being all elders or presbyters, the word *presbyter* coming from the Greek word for elder. A presbytery was made up of a body of elders who constituted their own authority by declaring it. Authority was derived from the group and not, as in the episcopal form, transmitted through a succession of ordinations.

The possibility that Methodism might be presbyterian had been sharply posed by defiant action taken at an Annual Conference held at Broken Back Church in Fluvanna County, Virginia, May 18, 1779. Discussion of the sacraments had been the burden of the sessions. A majority of the eighteen preachers present voted to form a presbytery of four who would have the right to ordain each other and then in turn to ordain as many of the preachers who wished to administer the sacraments.

The decision taken at Broken Back threatened to break the back of Methodism in America. Asbury had been outraged. Because of restrictions placed on his travel, he had not been present at the Conference which created that thing so unnatural to Methodism, a presbytery. He commenced early in 1780 a series of letters designed to persuade his errant brothers in Virginia that they had overstepped their bounds. His aim was to heal, to join sentiments back together again, to avoid any open breach over a question as sacred at the sacraments.

Asbury's conciliatory approach had not been sanctioned by his brethren in the North, who were incensed at what they called secession in the South. They did decide, however, that Asbury and a committee be dispatched to Virginia to tell the recalcitrants to stop administering the sacraments like Baptists and other dissenting groups. Mr. Wesley had been careful at all times to keep Methodists from appearing to be dissenters. They were aroused and inspired regulars. With all their zeal, they were members of a system, making a complex of many units, and no unit must be allowed to take over and govern.

The Southerners received the committee from the North in a called Conference at Manakintown, Virginia. They made it clear from the outset that the Lord had greatly blessed the work of the presbytery during the year that it had been in force and they saw no reason why they should give over and desist from practices that had brought so much good to the societies. Deliberations were undertaken, however, and Asbury, who had a talent for compromise and a greater talent for knowing when to use it, put forward the proposal that the Virginians suspend their system of authority until Mr. Wesley could be consulted and there could be a general meeting of the preachers in Baltimore to resolve the question.[8]

The proposal had been accepted and an open breach averted, but the best that had been achieved was a state of suspension and this afforded no atmosphere in which to conduct vigorously the Lord's work. Asbury saw the "spreading fire of division" in Virginia. Obviously Mr. Wesley's decision and ordinations had not come a moment too soon. Its psychological effect had been tremendous and now that the Conference meeting in Baltimore had accepted it officially, and The Methodist Episcopal Church existed, the most moot matter of government had been handled and the time had come for the ceremonies.

In a word, Francis Asbury was ready to be ordained on the conditions he had set. Proceedings of the Conference had moved swiftly and the vital matter it had been called to decide handled promptly. Some of the preachers were late getting in from distant points, but they were carefully briefed as they arrived, the business done before their arrival recapitulated, and their sanction secured. All were in accord. There was no need to delay beyond Christmas Day the laying on of hands, especially seeing that it would have to be done by degrees. Asbury was but a layman and he was now to be a superintendent. On December 25 he was made a deacon in the ceremony Mr. Wesley had prescribed. On December 26 he was ordained an elder, and the following day he was elevated to the highest office in the newly created church.

The consecration of the Englishman who had chosen to become an American, principles and all, provided a scene of solemn beauty, a welcome interruption in the earnest talk of the brethren, and a life-size picture they could carry back to their circuits. They saw hands laid in love upon the head of a leader they had come to respect through the hardships he had shared with them. It was as if they saw him receive from on high confirmation of what they knew to be his worth. However unacceptable or casual might be the authority for his ordination by the standards of established church bodies, their fellow was at the moment and for a moment at one with all good men who had gone before. There was a presence. Something, of only a sublime sentiment, was transmitted to him and through him.

Considering that in the ceremony there was to be funneled through Asbury so much that was distilled out of the past and might be channeled in the future, it was fitting that there should be present like a ray of light among the preachers dressed in sepulchral black a figure arrayed in robes of white. He was of another culture and another faith, yet he was a friend and he was there to join the service of consecration, a symbol that the new church had in it many elements for the making of a new land and that it was hospitable to elements that it did not wholly embrace.

The man in white was German. Philip William Otterbein had been ordained in the German Reformed Church before coming to America as a missionary in 1752, but he had been far from satisfied with the temper of his religious life. While serving a church near Lancaster, Pennsylvania, he underwent an experience not unlike a Methodist conversion, and he was from then on warmly attached to the Wesleyan societies and he became a firm friend of Francis Asbury. There was a habitual precision and deference to routine in Methodism that appealed mightily to the German mind. Otterbein had admired the discipline of the societies and, by Asbury's testimony, agreed to imitate Methodist methods as far as possible—even while he preached in their native tongue to some of the masses of Germans coming to America at the time. Asbury regarded Otterbein as a father in Christ and often consulted him. It was natural that this tall and stately German preacher should at Asbury's request take part in the ceremonies at Lovely Lane, one hand placed on the head of the new superintendent, as an old print shows, and the other holding an open book at his side.[9]

The Christmas Conference lasted a week. In addition to the consecration of Asbury, there were ordinations of a dozen other preachers to perform the sacraments now duly authorized. There was preaching three times a day—morning, noon, and afternoon—with Dr. Coke holding the pulpit at noon every one of the seven days. And there were business sessions enough to make firm the resolutions of the young Church. A ritual was adopted, the same being an edited and abridged form of the order of service used in the Church of England. Other items came up as well, including the question of what could be done to extirpate slavery.

Then the sessions of the Conference came to a close and the itinerants went back to their appointed rounds. In many respects they were stronger men and better equipped than they were when they came. They were not only refreshed by much inspiration and good preaching and the chance to swap yarns and sleep several nights running in the same house. But now they also had the assurance of a status they had not enjoyed before. They had been made rulers of a sort, having shown their ability to take decisive action, by making their corporate selfhood firm, putting it on record, and staking it out with metes and bounds. Under their deliberations a church had been born and this church was now in their care. But most of all they had the means of caring for it. That means was the Conference, the nursery of small and growing freedoms. The Conference was their government, the law of the land of the circuits and forests and swollen streams and bare preaching houses. Wherever they went they would be aware of the government of the world of which they were a part.

The power the preachers took unto themselves at the time of the Christmas Conference astonished Mr. Wesley. He was not prepared for it, and the enormity of what the Americans had done came home to him only gradually. As Dr. Coke gently put it, Mr. Wesley "did not intend, I think, that an entire separation should take place."[10]

In 1787 Coke and Asbury had issued a revised edition of the *Discipline of the Methodist Episcopal Church,* the title given the book of rules and regulations governing the conduct of business, and in this edition the word "superintendent" was changed to "bishop." Mr. Wesley's indignation resounded all the way across the Atlantic. In English practice a bishop was a prince who sat with the Lords in the seat of government. He mingled with those who occupied positions of secular authority and he held office at the appointment of the head of state, the king. Mr. Wesley wrote to Asbury: "How can you, how dare you suffer yourself to be called a Bishop? I shudder, I start at the very thought! Men may call me a knave or a fool, a rascal, scoundrel and I am content, but they shall never by my consent call me a Bishop! For my sake, for God's sake, for Christ's sake, put an end to all this!"[11]

How could anyone explain to the founder of the Methodist societies that a bishop laboring intimately among the flocks in America, affording pastoral care to the preachers, was not the same as a fat prelate in Great Britain? There was no explaining. One could only say with the gentle Richard Whatcoat, "Why should I throw myself into the sea to calm the wind?" The truth is that the Christmas Conference set in motion forces that in hardly more than two years' time left The Methodist Episcopal Church with hardly a vermiform connection with the founder. Out of pious and filial deference to the great man

41

the Christmas Conference had given him this pledge: "During the life of the Rev. Mr. Wesley we acknowledge ourselves his sons in the gospel, ready in matters of church government to obey his commands."[12] But when Mr. Wesley acted on this assurance he realized how far the preachers had departed from him. He wrote to Dr. Coke and told him that he wanted a general conference of the preachers in America called. He named the date and the place where the meeting was to be held, as well as told the preachers what to do: Mr. Whatcoat was to be made a superintendent.

Dr. Coke, who was abroad at the time, put through the changes as ordered—much to the disgust of the itinerants. They obediently met but by the time they arrived at the Conference, on May 11, 1787, they were so much up in arms that they rescinded the agreement of 1784 in which they had promised to obey Mr. Wesley.[13] For good measure they voted to omit reference to his name from the minutes. And they did not consent to Whatcoat's elevation. There was no possible oversight this time. The Conference refused. An itinerant named James O'Kelly led the opposition, saying that Mr. Wesley's candidate was too old (he was fifty) and that, moreover, he was "a stranger in the wilderness of America."[14]

There was no place among the leaders of The Methodist Episcopal Church for those who were strangers in the wilderness of America.

V When the West Began

On the last Friday of May in 1783 there appeared a fetching advertisement in the *Pennsylvania Evening Post*, the only daily newspaper published in the United States at the time. The heading read: "A Light Waggon." The message was bold, inviting, and clear: "The subscriber begs leave to inform the public, that he has furnished himself with a neat light waggon, a pair of excellent horses, which he will hire to go to any part of the continent. Any person wanting such, shall be immediately waited upon by applying at his livery stable in Moravian alley. MICHAEL DENNISON."[1]

". . . to go to any part of the continent . . ."

The word *continent* had limited scope. It designated merely the area embraced by the states that had banded together to fight the Revolution, as may be seen in the fact that the army, the Congress, and the currency were referred to as Continental. But continent was a big word and a distant word and it had snow on its peak, and it summoned. The announcement in the Philadelphia paper showed that America had begun to move. Its peoples rippled like muscles under the loose skin of government. Men harkened to the call of the West, the bourn from which few travelers returned, and those who did return brought tidings and pictures of wonder.

Nor was it only the lure of land that had begun to lead migrants across the mountains. Conditions in the States were dismal and held slight promise of improvement. The eloquent idealism that pictured a brave free world to follow the Revolution had vanished and left thirteen sovereign and separate states with jealously guarded boundaries and rights and customs. The effect of the recent British occupation could be seen in burned towns and villages and it could be felt in the bereavement of families. One out of every forty of the inhabitants of the states had suffered death or injury. People were restless and fugitive. During one month 123 advertisements for runaway wives appeared in the newspapers.[2] Men had touchy honor and were quick to defend it with the gun. Intemperance was on the increase and so was the number of distilleries to take lucrative advantage of the thirst for rum.

Moreover, the country was impoverished. Inflation had made Continental currency meaningless and in time a laughingstock and then a disaster. The very army that had been raised to win the Revolution was itself approaching a rebellion, and only the courage and the timely intervention of General Washington prevented mutiny. Thinking was under the influence of the French and France was moving toward a revolution of its own.

Old-line churches along the seaboard were dead and empty, having given over their facilities and exhortations to the cause of Independence. The goal attained, their clergy found little left to say. It was a period of suspended hope when a whole mass turned its body and face in a new direction. A moment had come when time and space were one. The West was a region. It was also an idea and a period, forever beginning.

The West and Methodism were simultaneous. Their time had come at the same time. Yet the two were not identical. People moved beyond the Alleghenies like water released, eagerly or under compulsion. The preachers moved under a system. Unique to Wesleyans, the system was called the itinerancy. In the itinerancy preachers did not itinerate on their own initiative or wander about like friars. They went where they were sent. They were assigned, ordered, told where to go, how long to stay, where to go next when the time came to establish another circuit. The preacher had his appointed rounds and he held at a different point some sort of service every day of the week and two or three times on Sunday. You knew the day and the hour when the preacher would appear.

To the fringe of civilization where "church bells were seldom heard and religious observances were so rare as to be holidays," the itinerancy of The Methodist Episcopal Church brought regularity, a methodical procedure for distributing religious ideas. In many areas there were no local churches of other faiths well enough set up to call pastors. Ministers of other persuasions, particularly the Baptists, were lured by the vastness, individually consecrated, called by God if not by congregations, as fiery in faith as the Wesleyans. But they lacked the facilities and the connections the itinerancy afforded and they lacked the experience of learning as they went, of sharing what they learned through Conference gatherings at stated intervals.

In short, the Methodists were well equipped during the late 1700's to move forward in their regular and systematic way along the two roads that led to the new world. These roads, both built decades earlier for military reasons, linked the East with the Ohio at Pittsburgh and offered the hardy, the determined, and the enterprising a chance to move cattle and household goods across the Alleghenies. One was 110 miles long. It was known as Braddock's Road. Part of it had been built as early as 1752 by a land development company. It had been extended and improved by Colonel Washington of Virginia. In 1755 it had been carried to the waters of the Monongahela at the time of General Edward Braddock's hapless mission against the French. The mission was a failure but the road to defeat remained to become a thoroughfare for migrants moving from Virginia and Maryland to settle in unsettled regions.

45

The other passage was known as Forbes Road. It lay to the north, having its starting point in Pennsylvania. It too was named for a British general, John Forbes, sent out three years after Braddock's defeat to reduce Fort Duquesne and oust the French. Taken ill before he could fairly launch his campaign, General Forbes had left most of the arrangements to a subaltern, Colonel Henry Bouquet. Largely under Bouquet's influence and against the opposition of Colonel Washington and other Virginians, it was decided that the new campaign would not follow Braddock's Road. The route chosen for the Forbes Road turned out to be 197 miles long, but the clearing and construction of it had gone on at a pace hard for the eyes to believe, the job being completed in less than six months from the time of its start in July of 1758. Working parties numbering fourteen hundred men heaved at the task, carried out now and then under French and Indian attacks.[3] There must have been Romans among the British or British who had learned their skills from Rome. Stone arch bridges were part of the passage and they were so well erected that they continue in use under heavy modern traffic more than two hundred years later.

Braddock's Road was only twelve feet wide, whereas Forbes Road, running through the rugged wilderness of western Pennsylvania, was twenty-five feet across, which meant that wagons could pass or that one party could go around another that might have paused for rest or repairs.

Over both these roads there took place a migration the like of which had not been seen before. In the early years of the nineteenth century Bishop Asbury exclaimed, "It is wonderful to see how Braddock's Road is crowded with wagons and pack horses carrying families and their household stuff westward. . . ."[4] The two roads converged on the village of Pittsburgh, bringing settlers from both north and south to the site of what the French had called Duquesne. Through one Pennsylvania village near Pittsburgh 236 wagons and six hundred merino sheep passed in one day. "All America," said a European observer, "seems to be breaking up and moving westward."[5]

The Ohio was the West. The word *frontier* was French and the frontier was where the French had been. Also the word *frontier* derived from an Old French word meaning "forehead." It described by implication the way men faced, the direction and point toward which they set their faces.

Certainly the frontier was not a straight line, or any line at all, or a clearly defined boundary. If followed roughly, very roughly, the Ohio, which had its headwaters around Fort Niagara and ran four hundred miles north and south, or as near north and south as a river could, making a crescent at Fort Pitt and then flowing majestically on for another four hundred miles before turning toward the Mississippi. Settlers were not supposed to cross the Ohio, lest they further vex the red man, and there were fitful efforts made by the confederation of the United States of America to keep the settlers where the government said they belonged. But the efforts were bootless. The patrols were weak, poorly paid, and lacking conviction for the task assigned them. They might watch the logical crossing places, but there was nothing logical about the people who came to the bank of the river. They might cross anywhere and, most likely, where they were least expected.[6]

The swashbuckling frontiersman represented the idea of freedom at its ultimate. It was not the freedom of books or essays or of political theory. It was the freedom of raw and bloody fact. The hero of the marches in the period following the Revolution was an ideal to be envied by many who stayed on the eastern seaboard or in the seats of respectability. But if he was an ideal he was no model. Dale Van Every in *Ark of Empire* describes him as a person who was

rude, uncouth, violent, greedy, cynical and brutal. He was a poor workman, a bad farmer and a disorderly citizen. . . . His love of fighting for its own sake inclined him when his enemies were out of reach to turn with equal gusto on his friends. His scorn of authority extended to disrespect for his own elected officers and made him a completely

47

undependable soldier. His own extreme self-will led him to conclude that all men were governed primarily by self-interest. Much of his personal conduct was marked by a barbarity to rival any Indian's. He decorated his buckskins with beads and fringes, wore a breechclout, took scalps, and in his callous aping of savage behavior recoiled only at painting his face and burning prisoners. . . .[7]

There he was, a child of nature and a holy terror, a primitive with a gun and on the loose. In a way, the society of the day owed a debt to him. He served en masse and through his love of the wilds as a buffer against the Indians and in consequence he made less perilous than they might have been otherwise the lives of many who disapproved his ways.

The frontier and the approaches to it were populated by others besides leatherstocking characters. There was a respectable contingent made up of ordinary folks who wanted mainly a better lot, who moved in families, who were glad for modest decencies to sweeten a hard life.

Out of old records and recollections Harriette Simpson Arnow in *Seedtime on the Cumberland* has given us a mural in words of ordinary people on the frontier. They "gathered in little groups, squatting, whittling, chewing tobacco, talking, their voices carrying echoes of their lives in other countries. They had smells of leather and horse sweat, baking cornbread, wood smoke, black homemade powder with the sting of burning sulphur; sight of flickering flames, the bobbing world beyond a horse's ears . . . ; and all the sounds as familiar as some tune of Watts, the rush of white water, a gun in the woods that was like a falling tree, horseshoes on hard rock, and always night after night the howling of wolves and the hooting of owls. . . ."[8]

Occasionally pastimes were rough, as in watching the antics of a just-skinned wolf. Dress could be picturesque and add to the excitement of doing nothing but watching other people. Pantaloons were worn to save stockings and "a hunter diked out in a waistcoat with sleeves, a pair of pantaloons, and a large red and worsted sash, had a dash and an air of derring-do his wife in her long-tailed, full-skirted two-piece, brightened only with an apron and often set off with a cap, could never match."[9]

The stillness of forests and open spaces induced in people of the frontier a fondness for the sound of the human voice. "They sang much, whistled, talked a very great deal, had many rhymes, riddles and tongue twisters." Boys were adept at imitating the sounds of birds and animals. They could have the sport of waking a family at midnight by crowing the way a rooster crows at dawn, and they could in the woods make noises that might attract animals to the waiting hunter.

Food was a daily problem. One historian tells us that in many cases pioneer families cloyed of animal food, almost loathed it, though it was of excellent quality. There was no yearning for fleshpots. What the heart and stomach longed for was bread. Meal was often old and full of weevils by the time it reached the home. It took three years for the average settler to get his own field cleared and into full production and meanwhile he was at the mercy of merchants and had to take what he could get.[10]

It was a world of transported emotions, needs, appetites, longings, and hopes that had to be transplanted in a new and often inhospitable soil. The craving for companionship determined the character of play as definitely as it affected religious expression on the frontier. In games and dances the young acted out their desires in a fashion staid adults approved with a smile. The games paired the young off. Couples became mates for the duration of a game. Kissing was a main feature, either as an aim or as a reward. The dance most popular was the Virginia reel with its "hilarious running sets." Boy met girl. They were partners in the dance. The swinging of partners, the fast swapping of partners on command and rhythms that stirred the innards, looks that told epics, the hasty encounters and contacts, making a moment last an hour—all these things had their place and their effect. Always there was music and the convenient means of making it. Instruments were small and could be carried. These included fiddles, zithers, mouth organs, banjos, and guitars.[11] Mostly they were strings, tying impulses and memories in a bundle to be carried home again.

There was, they say, some sexual irregularity. But the family was the unit and marrying and giving in marriage went gaily on. Life was a mixture, as elsewhere. There was gaiety and it relieved the grimness but the grimness was the leitmotif, returning like a dirge.

Along the frontier death by violence was common, and not less horrible because it was to be expected. When a person heard that another was dead, he did not ask the cause. He asked, "How did he get killed?"[12] Indians watched the waters and, being worked up to a high pitch of fury by the great tide of whites pouring into their hunting grounds, were determined to seize and kill as many intruders as possible. Some whites had gone over to their side and were their allies. The Indians had worked out with them a decoy to lure hapless travelers to shore. A white man would pretend distress and call upon those passing in boats for help. If they answered the call, they would be done to death.

James B. Finley, an early Methodist preacher, tells of his boyhood experience in passing down the Ohio with his family. Only a few months before the Finley party set out a family by the name of Orr had all been killed when they answered a white man's call. The Finley group was too wise to fall for this deception, but it posted men with guns in the lead boat and sentinels at the helm and stern of each boat night and day, lest Indians they saw along the shore come out in canoes and attack. The boats passed unmolested, however, and came at last to land at a place called Limestone in Kentucky.

The Finleys did not tarry long in Limestone but moved on to Washington in Mason County. Indians stole almost all the horses in the village the first winter, so that farmers were hardly able to carry on their business in the spring, rich in cane as Kentucky proved to be. White spies disguised as braves ranged constantly between the settlements and the Ohio, from Limestone to Big Sandy, "yet the Indians would come in undiscovered and kill our friends and steal our horses."[13]

The town gradually achieved a precarious security based on vigilance. The rudiments of government appeared in answer to necessity and to deal with new problems as they arose. Kentucky became a state not long after the Finleys arrived and the legislature passed laws intended for the common good. One was a law against the practices of vagrants and criminals from other states who took refuge in the land of Boone. When any person was found to be without employment he was taken up and, after having been advertised for ten days, he was sold to the highest bidder, who would put him to work for two or three months, the term depending on the sentence given him by the local magistrate.[14]

In some respects and in some places the great stretches beyond the Ohio began gradually to take on the semblance of a civilization. Although settlements were widely scattered, the very presence of great numbers of people in new areas made order a matter of common concern. By 1800 as many as thirty thousand persons had poured into Kentucky. The census showed a population of 887,331 in the country classified as Western. They were in families, for more than a third of the total were children under ten.[15] There had to be found ways and means by which families could live together in a measure of harmony, protected against the baser elements of the new land, not to mention outraged Indians.

Government would help. The new federal system was operating under the most excellent Constitution which, as the Methodist delegates had assured President Washington, was the admiration of the world. It has done a hard job well. Wisdom was present in its councils and imagination was present too in the minds of the men who guided it. They had plans and dreams for widening the new government's influence and of organizing the areas still beyond its control. A committee of which Thomas Jefferson was chairman had met and drawn up plans for the

Territory northwest of the Ohio River. Under Jefferson's influence, historians suspect, the committee had even given names to some of the states to be formed: Michigania, Cherronesus, Sylvania, Assenisipia, Metropotamia, and Polipsia. Nine other states had been carved out but not named.[16]

For all the plans of the people in the federal government, however, the division of the West from the East was real, as real as the towering mountains that separated the two sections. General George Washington had perceived and had stated the threat that the vast differences between the two regions might lead the West to form a nation of its own. In the dank winter of the Christmas Conference, immediately after surrendering his commission as commander in chief, he had set out to inspect the lands that lay toward the Ohio. He had realized that as the settlements to the west grew more populous, as they were bound to, the settlers would grow more self-reliant, that their leaders might find the Mississippi their natural outlet and see their advantages with the Spaniards in New Orleans, or even with the British in Canada, rather than with the almost inaccessible eastern seaboard. "The western settlers," he had declared, "stand as it were on a pivot. The touch of a feather would turn them any way."[17]

There had not been the political separation Washington had thought possible, but there still remained two decades later a gigantic physical separation of peoples with a common temperament and heritage. To join the young and growing West with the remote East would require more than government. There would have to be another link at another level to give people in their daily lives some feeling of common purpose.

Not by any means alone, but along with other groupings and especially with their inescapable system, the Methodists would help to provide connective tissue between the two sections. What they did might not affect the fortunes of the new nation but it could affect its character.

VI Vow of Obedience

The Methodists preached a democratic gospel while under a monarchical form of government. So says the discerning American church historian William Warren Sweet. Certainly the government had many of the aspects of a monarchy during the rule of Francis Asbury from 1784 until near the time of his death in 1816. In the formative years of The Methodist Episcopal Church he made every appointment of every preacher and he did it without consulting anyone. As far as lawmaking and constitutional procedures were concerned, authority rested with the Conferences. But as far as determining where preachers went throughout the ever-widening territory of the connection, it was the bishop in the person of Asbury who made the decisions and saw that no one else did.

As other bishops were elected and as the traveling preachers became more assertive of their rights, the government shifted from monarchy to polity, a form defined by Aristotle as one in which the people as a whole govern, but indirectly. Among Methodists an aristocracy comprising both bishops and preachers made the decisions but the people of the churches had the right to accept or reject these decisions.

Polity was a mixed arrangement ideally suited to the circumstances of the frontier. It was a continuous reminder of authority theoretically exercised in behalf of the whole communion. Baptists and Presbyterians cooperated in area associations, but among them ultimate power reposed in local congregations, whereas among Methodists authority was vested in a national body which supervised the work of every unit. Even deeds to local church property were held by the central governing body. With this mingling of the national and the local, polity was government made visible to the rank and file. It revealed what people, under an engendered idealism, would stand for in the way of regulation, even in frontier conditions, where lawlessness appeared natural and was at times a vogue.

The conspicuous growth of The Methodist Episcopal Church during the decades following its formation in 1784 made it easy to associate success with system. In 1773, when the first Conference was held, there were ten preachers, nine of them English, and 1160 members. But by the time of the death of Bishop Asbury in 1816 there were 695 preachers and 214,235 members. The population of America increased 36 percent between 1800 and 1810 but Methodist membership increased 168 percent. From one member among every 2050 Americans in 1771 the Methodists in 1816 numbered one member for every 39 Americans.[1] The Methodists were, thanks to their expansive impulses and the itinerancy, so widely distributed as to seem ubiquitous. Moving south and away from scenes of conflict during the Revolution and west as soon as the Revolution ended, they were here, there, and everywhere, and particularly strong in sections where the population was sparse.

Hence polity could be seen and studied throughout the length and breadth of a growing nation. Members and nonmembers alike knew the routine and its rigidity and how the circuits had invariable priority, no matter what hardship might be worked on the preacher. The idea was to get the right man in the right place. The better the man the more subordinate he might be to the authority of the bishop, who had full and final voice in determining where a man might serve best. In no case were considerations of the preacher's health or comfort to enter into the decision. Often the preachers winced but they went.

Etched poignantly in the minds of his brethren was the transfer of Samuel Parker, one of the most brilliant of the western preachers, from Illinois to Mississippi. Parker was a preacher of rare powers, among them a power of song that carried over into his sermons. He had a voice of unusual melody and was excelled by few if any in the ability to sing. Crowds came to hear him sing and remained to hear him preach, enraptured by the tonal quality that poured forth. An old German once cried out after hearing him, "Mine Gott, vot an outcome dis Barker has got!"

Parker was first heard in Kentucky and Ohio and then sent in 1809 to preside over the work of the Methodists in Illinois, Indiana, and Missouri. Under the music of his preaching, membership in the territory grew from 382 to 2000 during the next few years. At the age of thirty-nine, Parker felt secure enough in his work to take unto himself a wife. Prospects were good. But at a meeting of the Conference in Cincinnati in 1819 the bishops decided that new territory was to be opened up in Mississippi and that the man for the needed job was Samuel Parker. That he was by now in delicate health and the post to which he was to be sent lay in unhealthy environs, that his wife "would be torn from the embraces of her friends," that an infant son would make the trip with great hazard, mattered not at all.

An audible wave of sympathy swept the Conference when the appointment was read out, and when the Parkers left Illinois in the spring the parting scene touched all who witnessed it. The infant son died on the journey. Parker finally reached his destination, enfeebled by fatigue, and without the strength left to do the work assigned him.[2]

But the system remained intact, fortified as it was by years of hardship endured by men who, with unfailing willingness and devotion, had gone where they were ordered. At times venturesome men with more daring than the rest would volunteer for distant and impossible posts, but they went with the consent of the bishop and they stayed in touch with the Conference to which they were assigned. Tobias Gibson was a young Southerner born in South Carolina and living in Georgia. He had inherited wealth which he forsook and renounced at the time of his conversion, entering the Georgia Conference in the twenty-second year of his age. He traveled large circuits at the expense of his health until 1799 when he volunteered for service in the Mississippi Valley. He rode alone on horseback through wilderness stretches until he reached the Cumberland River.

There Gibson sold his horse and bought a canoe and paddled more than six hundred miles to his destination at Natchez— eighteen years before Mississippi became a Territory. He began to preach in an outpost four hundred miles from the nearest Methodist society. He found the need greater than he could meet singlehanded and, preaching along the way as he went, made four trips of six hundred miles each in an effort to get more workers from the Western Conference. Some workers joined him and Gibson continued his labors until 1804 when he died of lingering consumption. But word of his work spread and he became one of the early legendary folk characters of the itinerancy whose endurance was not that of a frail body but of an unconquerable soul.[3]

Arteries of the Methodist organism were the circuits. The term *circuit* was Methodist in origin, and riding circuits regularly was a part of the English heritage. The word *station* was used to designate a church with enough members to support a pastor. Stations were found in big towns and cities. Circuits were made up of smaller societies near a station or of scattered units in rural areas meeting at designated preaching places. These might be friendly farmhouses, commodious barns, carpenter shops, courthouses, taverns, warehouses.[4] The genius or singularity of the arrangement was that each of these places would be visited at least once a month at an appointed hour by a Methodist circuit rider. Some circuits were under the care of a single preacher, but two ministers might be appointed to each circuit,

56

one an older man with experience and a younger man of zeal, a kind of apprentice who worked with the older man and under his supervision, even though he might occasionally have appointments of his own.

Once every three months the preachers, young and old, of a number of circuits would foregather to have a quarterly conference to hear reports of progress and to refresh each other. These quarterly conferences were under the presidency of a presiding elder. The office of presiding elder evolved in the development of the American church and it was an American innovation. At the Christmas Conference it was not thought proper or fitting to have each and every preacher running around administering the sacraments. Only elders were given the authority. This limitation meant that those who could administer the sacraments needed to be distributed throughout the connection and that they had to travel on their own appointed rounds. Seeing that they were widely distributed and constantly on the move, they were given the added task of checking up on the work of the preachers in the districts they covered. There was thus established by both act and practice a further level of supervision to check the labors of those who rode the circuits.

It was in this way that every local group, whether church or society in or around New York or in the remote areas of Mississippi, was tied in with The Methodist Episcopal Church as a whole. The order of responsibility was from circuit rider to presiding elder to ,bishop, and the bishop appointed the presiding elders and told them what districts they would serve.

At the time the Church was formed Francis Asbury had insisted that the Conference was supreme. Once the itinerancy under the Church was in action, he assumed command. Thomas Coke was not an administrator. Besides, he was in and out of the country and, as a British subject, had little influence among the preachers. Richard Whatcoat was finally elected bishop in 1800, but he did not assert his gentle nature in the episcopal office and did not interfere with appointments. William McKendree was the first American to be elected bishop and he insisted on studying the appointments Asbury made and in consulting the presiding elders about the justness and wisdom of these appointments before they were read out. But McKendree was not made a bishop until 1808, so that for the first twenty-three years of The Methodist Episcopal Church the itinerancy was a gigantic chessboard on which Asbury made all the moves, with only occasional opposition from some of the preachers.

It was one of those strange circumstances in the history of institutions where it was the man who shaped destiny. Bishop Asbury determined the character of the early American Methodism, and he was a man of anomalies and contradictions. Although he never took the oath of allegiance to the new Republic, he was an ardent American. Although he insisted on the consent of his fellows in the itinerancy before he allowed himself to be ordained, once he was made a superintendent he wore the vestments of an Anglican bishop when circumstances allowed. Although he knew the woods and the ways of the wilderness, he sought to keep the preachers in knee breeches and spoke out against long trousers when they began to appear.[5]

In the matter of vestments and knee breeches he stopped pressing his views, bowing before the fact of change. In the matter of itinerating he did not. It was deep in his blood and in his bones. Hardly had the Christmas Conference come to a close when he set out through a snowstorm on a fifty-mile journey to reach a point where he thought preaching was needed. He crossed the Alleghenies sixty-two times, and by a careful reckoning of the records it was estimated that he rode horseback, all told, 275,000 miles. He summed up his feelings with the cry, "Live or die, I must ride!" Only toward the end of his days did he consent to use a carriage, and then when he was too weak to sit his horse.[6]

From the time of his arrival as a Methodist missionary to the Colonies in 1771 he was convinced that the preachers ought to move about, lest they become sluggish and the people suffer neglect. There was need of "a circulation of preachers to avoid partiality and popularity." He was perplexed and vexed over the tendency of the preachers to allow themselves to be shut up in places of comfort. "I am fixed to the Methodist plan," he said. "My brethren seem unwilling to leave the cities, but I think I will show them the way." He did. He made an exploratory trip from New York into Westchester the last of November after his arrival in late October. Early in January of 1772 he was on the road again, breasting the cold and snow, to extend the good work beyond New Rochelle. He preached in Mamaroneck and Rye and then switched back and crossed the ice-laden Hudson to preach at New City. The trip almost did him in. He was attacked by a soreness of throat that kept him in bed for seven days. It was feared that he might strangle. He could neither eat nor drink without great pain. But he was raised up again and moved immediately southward to Philadelphia, Maryland, and Virginia.[7]

This was the man who set the pace of early Methodism in America. Combined with his pious restlessness in the cause was a solemnity and solidity which gained the confidence of his fellows. They referred to him affectionately as Father Asbury and records remain that describe him as venerable before he had reached the age of forty. Five feet nine in height, he somehow had a commanding presence, a dignity that inspired deference. He was aware of the importance of clothes and his extraordinarily neat attire set a good example. He had long brown hair and a quiet voice that created an atmosphere of peace, and only the searching gaze of the man in face-to-face encounter gave any notion of the fire and fiber within. He had "steel-blue eyes so penetrating that few could withstand them as they glinted under the slightly falling eyelids."[8]

Among the preachers, who accepted Asbury as bishop and fully entitled to appoint them to their circuits or stations, there was also an awareness of the way in which his love of America mingled with his love of Methodism. This mingling bespoke a background in which the practical and the mystical were joined. The father of Francis Asbury was English, the mother Welsh.

The father was a farmer and a gardener employed by wealthy families not far from Birmingham in Staffordshire, England. His work kept him down-to-earth. The Welsh mother was under a spell of depression during the early boyhood years of Francis, having lost her only daughter in infancy. She spent her days in reading and prayer. At length she found "justifying grace and pardoning mercy" and became a source of strength to the distressed of spirit in her neighborhood, being hospitable to persons who came to discuss religion and often holding simple religious ceremonies in her home.

Francis had been sent early to a schoolmaster and he had begun to read the Bible between the ages of seven and eight, taking great pleasure in the historical part of it. But the schoolmaster, Asbury said later, was a great churl and beat him cruelly. The man's severity filled the boy with such a dread that any activity was preferable to schooling. At thirteen he decided that he could bear the torment no longer and he got a job at a forge near his home. The master of the forge treated him more like a son than an apprentice and he was free to grow and develop at his own pace.

His pace was speeded up two years later when one of John Wesley's itinerants stirred his mind and imagination and reached his soul. Still working as an apprentice at the forge, young Francis began holding prayer meetings in his own and nearby communities. Before he was eighteen he was licensed to preach on trial, which he did most acceptably. The people listened "wondering and weeping." He preached not only on Sunday but four or five times after-hours during the week. When he was twenty-one he was accepted into the full Wesleyan connection of preachers and began to itinerate on circuits in various parts of England. He stayed at his assignments for four years, all the while on his rounds making a scrupulous study of the doctrines laid down by Mr. Wesley and of the stringent and binding rules that held the societies together.[9]

English Methodism offered Francis Asbury everything but scope. He had his eye on far horizons, as was plain when, at

the Annual Conference held in Bristol in 1771, he responded to
Mr. Wesley's announcement, "Our brethren in America call loud
for help." Without a moment's hesitancy the young man volunteered his services, made haste to prepare for the voyage. In
company with Richard Wright, another preacher, Asbury set sail
from Bristol on September 4, less than a month after his twenty-
sixth birthday.

Not until October 27 did the ship on which he took passage
reach Philadelphia. As at last the young preacher approached
the great land mass before him, he was touched by an emotion
for which he was not prepared. Whether out of relief after the
long passage or from some deep missionary motive, Asbury felt
a sudden magnetic attraction of the land he had volunteered
to serve. "When I came near the American shore," he said,
"My very heart melted within me." This was where he belonged. "I feel that God is here," he noted in his journal.[10]

To Asbury's love of Wesleyanism and the souls it might save
was now added a love for the field of his chosen labor. In
time the two affections grew together and commended him to his
brothers, then bound him to them. He never left the American
shore. By the time it became plain that the Colonies would
rebel against the motherland other missionaries named by Mr.
Wesley began to return home, including Thomas Rankin, an
authoritarian disciplinarian Mr. Wesley had sent out in 1772
and placed in charge of Methodism in the Colonies. In the
winter of 1777–1778 Rankin went to Philadelphia, then held by
the British, quietly returned, left for Britain, urging the other
missionaries to follow him and to return as priests of the Church
of England when the rebellion ended.

But Asbury remained, held in the toils of the land that appealed to him and of people who might need him. Then came
temptation to try him sorely. One other English missionary was
still left, George Shadford, his close friend and a man of such
heartiness and good humor that he could cheer the lowest. And
he came to call when Asbury was at his lowest, in hiding at the
home of friends. Should the two part? What would Shadford do?

If he left should Asbury accompany him? Surely Shadford's decision would have its effect.

An eloquent and persuasive talker, George Shadford had been more effective than most of the other English missionaries in attracting converts. Mr. Wesley had observed his talents and knew how they would match the mountains across the sea. When he was ready to embark the founder had written: "I let you loose, George, on the great continent of America. Publish your message in the open face of the sun and do all the good you can."[11] The preacher had followed the founder's injunction and fulfilled the high hopes set for him. His theater of operations had been Maryland and Virginia until his message was drowned by drums and guns. He had been threatened with arrest in Virginia. Turning north in the dead of winter, he had nearly perished in a snowstorm, and in Maryland he had found the same hostility he had encountered in Virginia.

In discouraging circumstances the two English missionaries met. Asbury was at the house of Judge Thomas White in Kent County, Delaware. Judge White was not at the time a Methodist but His Honor's hospitable nature and his feeling for justice had led him to provide the unpopular Asbury a place of refuge and to permit other Methodists to visit him in secret. Suspicion was rife among the neighbors at the time of Shadford's visit and the preachers were concealed in nearby woods. Judge White would take their meals to them. The arrangements were supposed to be hidden from the servants but the servants knew what was going on well enough to aid the deception by telling the neighbors that "the master goes through the woods to feed his swamp robbins."

Two men with common convictions and a single aim in life, though differing widely by temperament, must decide whether they would go or stay. Shadford was better suited by far than Asbury to preach as one crying in the wilderness to a violent people. He had grown up with pleasures and had an innate sense of the depravity of man without conversion. As a youth he was given to "wrestling, running, leaping, playing football, and dancing, at which he excelled." Restless and unresolved, he had joined the British army while in England, but he had found no peace in war. The only thing that had impressed him was a sermon by a Methodist preacher, who spoke earnestly and without a book or notes, person to person. Shadford had been suddenly smitten by a conviction of sin. A Methodist society had been formed in the town where he lived and Shadford joined. Soon he was exhorting and soon after he was licensed to preach and itinerate in the regular Wesleyan connection.

Shadford and Asbury discussed their plight at length and then agreed to fix a time when the matter would be decided. On the morrow they would fast and pray the livelong day and then announce to each other what the Lord directed. They did, but when they addressed each other after their prayers, Shadford announced that he had been told to return to England. "One of us must be in error," said Asbury. "Not necessarily so," said Shadford. "I may have a call to go and you to stay."[12]

Shortly after Shadford had left, Asbury had written in his journal: "I was under some heaviness of mind. But it was no wonder: three thousand miles from home—my friends have left me—and I am considered by some an enemy of the country —every day liable to be seized by violence and abused. However, all this is a trifle to suffer for Christ and the salvation of souls. Lord, stand by me!"[13]

Home was England. The friends who had left were English. When he spoke of America it was "the country" and not "my country." Yet he had stayed and the Lord had stood by him. He watched and cautiously waited, keeping his eye on the American cause and the fortunes of war. In due course he wrote to Rankin that in his opinion the Americans would become a free and independent nation. He added that he was much knit in affection to many of them and that "Methodist preachers had a great work to do under God in this country." The letter had luckily fallen into the hands of American army officers, some said by design, and its tone and contents noted. There had followed a change in the attitude of the military toward him.

The governor of Delaware, already lenient, relaxed further the restrictions that had been imposed on travel. The young preacher to whom movement meant so much was now free to stretch his horse's legs a bit and make preaching missions within the state.[14]

The letter had marked the turning point. There was less and less doubt where the interests of Francis Asbury lay. Methodism and its methods mattered supremely to him, and America was the place where he would exercise his concern. Practices and habits apparent before could now be given some continuity.

In addition to stressing the importance of movement, Francis Asbury had also shown all along a strong belief in the importance of the Wesleyan principle that everything must be done decently and in order. No preacher was to step out of bounds and do what he thought best, regardless of how much good he might accomplish. He must remain obedient to authority. From the beginning he had frowned sternly upon any threat of independent action among the preachers. He was no less diligent in his insistence upon conformity than he was in keeping the preachers on the move.

One preacher in the days before the Revolution met every requirement for an itinerant, save one. He ignored authority. He denied it rather than defied it. His name was Robert Strawbridge and his field was in the South. He caused no trouble by overt acts, stirred no dissension. He simply would not be regulated. He showed thereby in his attitude a complete lack of comprehension of the fact that Wesleyanism was a system. Asbury in turn found the man incomprehensible.

At first glance Robert Strawbridge seemed the ideal itinerant. He had undergone the experience of conversion on one of Mr. Wesley's visits to Ireland. A native of Drummer's Nave, near Carrick on Shannon, he commenced at once to preach. Whether he was licensed by the Wesleyans or simply took to the roads out of exuberance is not clear. But it is clear that to him preaching was a natural act. He did it wherever he went. When he married he married a Methodist woman, and when in 1759 he emigrated with her and their children, he preached on shipboard. He preached from the moment his restless feet touched colonial soil and continued to preach when he settled on Sam's Creek, near Baltimore.[15]

Strawbridge had another mark of the worthy itinerant—an ability to organize the people he converted. Near his home he set up a small group of believers. He started another in a brother settler's house not far away and then merged the two groups into a society. Later he built a log meetinghouse, with holes sawed out for a door and windows. It wasn't much but it was a place for gathering and showed that Strawbridge had a gift for sequence and growth.[16]

His zeal was unexcelled and outran his interest in his own welfare and that of his family. His wife understood patiently and shifted for herself and her children as well as she could while Strawbridge was on his rounds, which was almost always. Finally he raised the question, "Who will keep the wolf from my own door while I am seeking after lost sheep?" The neighbors, admiring his self-sacrifice, agreed to look after his small farm without charge.[17]

It was a timely act of Christian charity, for the travels of Strawbridge on horseback took him unto all parts of Maryland, then into Delaware, Pennsylvania, and Virginia. Everywhere he went he preached "with an ardour and fluency which surprised his hearers and drew them in multitudes to his rustic assemblies." Many were his converts, and among them were young men who, touched by the wand of his intense faith, became preachers themselves. One was Richard Owings, the first native American to become a member of the traveling fellowship of Wesleyan preachers in America.

Wave after wave of influence went out from Strawbridge and his extraordinary powers had to be acknowledged. He could lay claim to holding the first Methodist meeting on these shores, having commenced his work in 1760, or six years before Philip Embury preached in New York. But with all his grace and grit, Strawbridge somehow did not belong to the Methodist connection. He worked with those around him and beneath him but he would have no truck with those above him. He not only preached and formed societies but he also baptized his converts, appointed preachers, and to the consternation of the missionaries from England, administered the sacrament of Holy Communion.

"What strange infatuation attends that man!" wrote Asbury in his bewilderment. "Why will he run before Providence?" Four years of patient effort went into the attempt to make Strawbridge keep up his good work but mend his ways. They came to naught. There was nothing to do but to exclude him from the fold, valuable as he undoubtedly was in getting results and much as the Wesleyans admired results. His name appeared on the Conference roster in 1775 but not again thereafter, although he lived and preached until his death in 1781.

The rejection of the recalcitrant may have been a lesson to Strawbridge, though there is no sign that he took the discipline to heart. It was certainly a lesson to Asbury as a man learning the ways of administration. It demonstrated that on occasion forceful action had to be taken at the top. Obedience was an irrefragable operating principle in Methodism. Men in the ranks did what they must for the good of the order and the good of the order was to be sought and maintained at all costs. This being the case, the exercise of firm authority, even if called arbitrary, was essential.

There is much to suggest that Asbury was discomfited by the role he assumed as manager of the whole itinerant system after The Methodist Episcopal Church was formed. He said, "I sit on a joyless height, a pinnacle of power, too high to sit secure and unenvied . . . ," adding, ". . . too high to sit secure without divine aid."[18] There was always the divine cause to invoke, but there was also the management of human affairs that had to be considered. Of his dealings with the founder, Asbury is reported to have said, "Mr. Wesley and I are like Caesar and Pompey: he will bear no equal and I will bear no superior."[19]

Some early Methodist decisions were taken through Asbury's convictions and influence rather than through definite acts of the will or pen. What was to be done about the Germans? Should they be taken into the Methodist connection? Besides Philip Otterbein, who had helped to ordain Asbury, others were in close fellowship with Asbury and his preachers. One was Martin Boehm, who now and then accompanied Asbury on his rounds and was allowed to preach whenever there were persons present who could understand German. But the bishop knew that the language was a barrier to organization and that his preachers had enough to do without having to learn German. Consequently the Germans, determined to be Methodists, organized themselves without benefit of Methodist clergy. They formed in 1789 a church known as the United Brethren in Christ, and they adopted Methodist polity and discipline at almost every point.

What was in effect Asbury's administrative decision not to incorporate the German-speaking Wesleyans in the American connection stood for almost two hundred years before it was changed. At the time it was made it simply helped toward the smooth operation of the itinerant system, which was Bishop Asbury's chief passion. Under the system Americans throughout the United States and its territories were presented with the graphic claims of religion. They were presented also with the claims of regulation and social control. The preachers were out there with their urgent messages but behind the preaching was the system, and it offered one and all a chance to observe government in action.

VII Where a Few Were Gathered Together

The small group, close-knit, comprising a dozen or more of the faithful, was the essential of early Methodism in America.

A circuit rider jogging his rounds in sparsely settled territory might find only a few persons at some lonely spot who wanted to become Methodists. If so, he called them together and formed what the Wesleyans called a class. The class was straight out of the *Discipline,* a fixed group with severe rules and regulations. It was put under the command of a leader chosen by the itinerant. The leader met with the class each week, chastened and chided the members in matters of faith and conduct. Admission to the class meeting was granted only to those holding a white ticket, issued quarterly by the preacher and validated by the leader. Records of attendance were scrupulously kept. Three successive absences without ill health or other good reason meant that the ticket would not be reissued.

As the preacher went on to the next point of his circuit he left the professing Methodists combined in a unit where the members could regularly support each other's faith and grow in grace. In the early days of his ministry Mr. Wesley had said, "I am more and more convinced that the devil himself desires nothing more than this, that the people in any place should be half-awakened and then left themselves to fall asleep again." Methodists on the circuits would not be allowed to languish or cool off. They had the means of remaining steadfast.

The class was instituted by Mr. Wesley in 1743, so that by the time The Methodist Episcopal Church was formed there had been almost four decades of group experience among Wesleyans. If there were enough Methodists in any one place to form a society, the itinerant immediately broke the society up into classes of twelve to fifteen members. The class was the thing. In every gathering of Methodists, in stations or on circuits, there were groups who met without fail at regularly appointed times. Judging by the general statistics of membership in 1810 there could not have been fewer than fourteen thousand weekly class meetings going on in the United States and its territories.

In strictness, regularity, continuity, and cohesion, the class meeting was unlike any arrangement made by any other denomination on the frontier. It bottled and preserved zeal that, considering the emotionalism of the preachers, might otherwise have been scattered to the winds or dumped into the rivers.

In an economy that needed occasions for neighborliness, the group offered the distraught and lonely individual a habitat. Wade Crawford Barclay cites the class meeting as one of the ways the Methodists promoted close fellowship on the frontier. It helped to develop a sense of community in public life, breaking down the abstract into the specific and the close-at-home. As Barclay reminds us, Cavalier and Roundhead, New Englander and Southerner, Yorker and Eastern Shore, Teuton and Celt came together repeatedly in these meetings and in groups small enough for the members to get acquainted and to become conscious of being "part of the new democratic community which was America."[1]

The nature of the class meeting depended on the character of the leader, and among the multiplied thousands of laymen who led the groups in their discussions there could not have been uniform skill or tact. It was partly for this reason that the itinerant on his rounds would meet with as many of the classes as possible and size up their spiritual state, thus forming his opinion of the leader. The itinerant did it also because the intimate give-and-take of the group was more satisfying than the regular service in which he did all the talking. Asbury as a bishop tried to arrange his schedule to meet with classes wherever he went.

It was, however, the local leader, who, meeting with the class over a period of years, set the tone. The fact that many of the leaders held their posts for life indicates that they must have done a good job and learned as they went the techniques of group conversation. The authors of *The Story of Methodism* reconstruct a class meeting which shows the leader at his functional best. Testimony and confession were voluntary and it was up to the leader to find how each member could be induced to put forward what was on his mind and say what might be good for his own soul.[2]

Twelve persons "having the form and seeking the power of godliness" are seated in a circle of chairs. In the center of the room is a plain table and on it is the leader's Bible. The leader is a shoemaker who has not stuck strictly to his last but has turned aside enough to consider the vagaries of human nature. To begin the meeting he pitches the tune of hymn sung fervently by all. Prayer follows, petitioning God to be present to open the hearts of all, to expose the inmost thoughts and imaginings, and to inspire all to new heights of living. The leader next reads a passage of Scripture and makes pointed comment on it.

Now comes the time when he turns to the members. He asks a young man from a nearby farm how it has been that week with his soul. The young man replies haltingly that all has gone well. The leader wants to know more. "No wrestlings with temptation?" "Yes." "Did that old temper rise up again?" "Yes." "And did you win the victory?" "Yes, thank God." "Hallelujah! Go on as you are and one day the crown incorruptible will be yours."

It took all kinds to make a class. The leader turned next to a woman of spirit who had no hesitation in her replies. "Sister Lee, has the Lord been your support this week?" She rises and speaks volubly and rapturously, pouring out a record of spiritual blessings in rich profusion, concluding, "The blessing of God is upon me. By Him this week I have been kept from temptation. Life has become a song and a way of glory! Praise His name!" The group is thrilled by her fervor and shows its approval by shouts of "Amen!" and "Glory to God!" But the leader asks, "So you feel this has been a week of nothing but spiritual triumph, sister?" Upon being assured that it has been all glory, he asks one or two further questions and then comments sagely, "Well, Sister Lee, how happy you must be! And how happy your husband must be!"

There is a pause and there is a chill in the room. Her husband is not a Methodist; he is a reprobate, and the members of the class have heard rumors that he might be a better man if conditions at home were better. Sister Lee's eyes flash but she says nothing, and the leader persists, "Doesn't your husband rejoice with you?" "Him!" The woman can hold in no longer. "Why, that worthless scamp, he came home the other night and found me singing a hymn tune. 'Ha!' he says, 'more religion, is it?' At once I saw that he was fixing to make sport of me, so I flung a mop at his head, and he's been quiet since then."

There are a few further remarks by the leader and then he passes on to the next member, "leaving Sister Lee glowing with a sense of such victories as she has really won, but with a lively appreciation of the heights yet to be surmounted."

Some class leaders and some preachers acting as leaders, taking advantage of their position, turned their role into that of a prosecutor and were harsh to the point of tyranny. Stephen Beggs tells of one William Cravens, who made a practice of meeting classes at the places of his appointment. He used the rough and ready tactics of the West. He would ask each member about strong drink. Those who confessed that they drank and would not promise total abstinence he would direct to sit apart from the group and then he would hold a prayer meeting in their behalf. If they had not reformed by the time of his next visit he turned them out of the church. He had his own special areas of morality, and in these areas his righteous condemnation knew no bounds. Once he dealt with two men who wanted to become preachers and sought recommendation for admission on trial. But both had deficiencies, and Beggs heard Cravens say that he "would as soon hear a Negro play a banjo or a raccoon squeal as to hear a negro-holder and a petty lawyer preach." Then he turned to the two men described and said, "How dare you lay your dirty hands on this sacred book?"[3]

Such tactics belonged to the ranter in the pulpit rather than to the class leader. With all their occasional irregularities and the excesses of some who were supposed to lead them, the classes formed an integral part of Methodism, superbly adapted to conditions in broad new America. They were another example of the prophetic foresight of the founder and carried out the purpose for which they had originally been formed. Mr. Wesley wanted to be sure "that the feeble and the lonely would be sheltered and cheered."

The class meetings had grown out of Mr. Wesley's quick-witted improvement and adaptation of an idea put forward by a member of the Bristol society. The society there had fallen into debt and a member suggested that it be divided into groups of about twelve, that each group be placed under a leader who would be responsible for the collection of a penny a week from each member. If some members could not pay as much as a penny, the leader would make up the deficit.

The idea seemed sound to Mr. Wesley and the man offered to visit a group weekly and to be responsible for their contribution. When he began his rounds he discovered that, besides not paying their part, some of the members were not living as they ought. Immediately Mr. Wesley turned the class meeting into more than a money-raising device.[4] Classes were set up throughout the Wesleyan connection in England and class leaders were instructed to inquire into the spiritual state of the members. Some of the disorderly members uncovered in the process of forming the sessions were rejected; others reformed. Mr. Wesley fixed the new group idea into the structure of the societies,

73

arranged for there to be regional meetings of class leaders and then, for good measure, called all the class leaders in England together and addressed them on their duties in conducting Christian conversation.[5]

For all the statistics of growth it piled up in its formative years, Methodism was not a mass religious movement. Rather it was a movement sustained at the community level by groups—small constitutent bodies—which helped to relate the individual to the mass. The group formed a habitat in which the nurture of the individual was natural. To cultivate and conserve aspiration and good impulses became the object of regular and repeated sessions. Later strong organizations with the same aim would emerge, their shape determined by changes in the larger society of which the Church was a part. Sunday schools grew up, as did a league of youth named Epworth after the birthplace of John Wesley. Various other agencies followed as the Church became institutionalized, but all avowed as their concern the cultivation of the individual in his various relationships. Schools and leagues had their roots in the soil of the class meeting and in the habit of nourishing the good intentions that sprouted best in an atmosphere of neighborliness, whether in towns bulging into cities or on the frontier.

In addition to the class there was another group known as the band. Its aim originally had been to promote the cultivation of the soul and the development of the inner life. The design was to afford a place which would separate those who wanted to become deeply religious and to move toward Christian perfection from those who were content to be morally upright and respectable. The band offered a graduate course in piety, and members were to be chosen from the more earnest and serious members of the classes, those most acquainted with each other and able to discuss each other's souls in intimacy and candor. Those admitted to a band had to answer eleven searching questions, including:

IX. Consider, do you desire that we should tell you whatsoever we think, whatsoever we fear, whatsoever we hear, concerning you?

74

X. Do you desire that in doing this we should come as close as possible, that we should cut to the quick and search your heart to the bottom?[6]

A band comprised not more than six persons. Married men met separately from married women. Unmarried men and unmarried women formed different bands. No holds were barred in wrestling with the spirit. The leader was expected to "speak his own state first, and then to ask the rest in order, as many and as searching questions as may be, concerning their state, sins, and temptations."

The band idea was taken over with appropriate zeal by American Methodism. The first *Discipline* had explicit and detailed instructions for the conduct of band meetings—more instructions in fact, than for class meetings. Bishop Asbury and other leaders hailed the bands and there were strenuous efforts to get them afoot. But the bands had their day and ceased to be. By 1844 references to the bands no longer appeared in the *Discipline*.[7]

The band presumed too much on American capacity for introspection. The Methodists represented people on the go, busy with the gospel of getting on, felling trees, moving goods, improvement of themselves on a broad scale. Among the bands, almost by prearrangement and design, the sins of the flesh got more attention than the interest justified and possibly became a bore. There lingered among the Methodists a puritan regard for woman as temptation. But temperament and location both helped to modify the view of woman as temptress. Among the activist Methodist settlers women were workers, companions in calico and not crinoline, a factor that may have made it hard for the bands to drum up and keep alive preoccupation with sex by means of a series of lay Protestant confessionals.

The class dealt with the common interests of men and women in their work and in community life. It touched the needs of ordinary men and women who did not want to make a profession or performance out of goodness. But, whatever their relative merits, they were both groups conducted as an essential part of

ORGANIZING TO BEAT THE DEVIL

the real ritual of the Church, and they helped to stamp the group image on Methodism and provide an early clinical experience in group effort and democratic thinking.

The classes and bands also did a full share of developing leaders. Their leaders made up a level of the lower hierarchy of the Church by means of which the control of the itinerants could be reflected, emulated, duplicated, and appreciated. They completed the Methodist process of control and supervision and revealed that due process and decency and order and regulation and government by rules were not matters merely grafted on to the structure but were in fact an expression of the inner soul of Methodism.

The scheme by which the Church operated worked from the bottom up as well as from the top down. It worked, as one writer put it, through a series of concentric circles. The class leaders and band leaders formed one. The exhorters constituted another. They were men licensed by the officials of a local society to speak or pray on appropriate occasions—when given permission by the itinerant. A shade above the office of the exhorter was that of the local preacher. He, like the exhorter, was of lay status and earned his keep by secular pursuits, but he was licensed by the society to preach in the absence of the regular itinerant and actually allowed to ride a circuit when the circuit rider was attending an Annual Conference.

The local preacher was called local to distinguish him from the traveling preachers, who alone constituted the governing body of the Church as a whole and who were responsible only to the governing body which they constituted. Above the traveling preachers were the presiding elders, who visited local churches and preached in them four times a year and held quarterly conferences and got reports from traveling preachers. Above the traveling preachers and presiding elders were the bishops, overseeing all.

At every post up and down the line was a superintendent or foreman to look after those in his charge. There was thus organic and interstitial, as well as mechanical, connection between local leaders on the one hand and the bishops and the Conference on the other. By this arrangement the Methodists put forth and established in a restless and lawless new country a substantial set of guidelines, a series of orderly procedures conspicuous to all. Government supervised from afar but to a certain extent administered locally was a demonstration of the system. And the effect was psychological as well as instructive because, through the class, Methodism emphasized the small group as the true cell and center of a vast corporate body.

VIII The Circuit Riders: What Manner of Men?

"The Methodists preached a message to the common man and used the common man to preach it."[1]

This summary statement helps to explain why the preaching and personalities of the itinerants appealed to the mobile masses of Americans about to shape themselves into a complex society. Many if not all of the circuit riders were untutored and virtually all were uncultured. What they lacked commended them to their hearers as much as what they offered. On every level except the moral they confronted the migrants as equals.

The Presbyterians were for a while every whit as ranging and venturesome as the Methodists in the West, and some of their preachers were as free-swinging. But in time the congregations of that persuasion made it plain that they wanted an educated ministry and a religion with a measure of intellectual content.[2] They got what they wanted, but many on the frontier did not want close-reasoned theology. They craved companionship and warmth. These qualities the circuit riders had outside the pulpit, and in the pulpit they made up in color what they lacked in content.

They had, among other things, a flair for the dramatic and

79

an opportunity to use it. The circuit, with its regular schedule of stops, was in some respects collateral to the traveling minstrel. One-night stands gave the men a chance to know their lines well, to preach the same sermon over and over again, to refine and perfect gestures, and to study the effect on an audience of tone and facial expression. Not infrequently they supplied the only vital or convincing drama in a culture that was without theater or opera.

Very early the itinerants began to build a tradition of the theatrical and the picturesque. Shortly after the first Methodist society was organized in New York there appeared one Sunday morning in the rented room where the society met a British officer in full regimentals, complete with side sword and a green patch over his right eye, showing that he was no summer soldier. He took his place quietly among the members and listened to young Philip Embury, a tradesman and the first man to assume the role of preacher among the Methodists who had come from Great Britain to New York.

The presence of the officer distracted the small congregation. In England soldiers had broken up Methodist meetings. There was further concern, too. The year was 1766. There had been tension that year over the quartering of British soldiers in New York and there had been clashes and scenes of violence not far away. At the end of the service, however, the officer put the minds of the Methodists at ease. He strode forward to the make-shift pulpit and introduced himself as Captain Thomas Webb of the king's service but explained that he was "also a soldier of the Cross and a spiritual son of John Wesley."[3]

The announcement was enough to validate him, and his speaking ability was enough to establish him. Before long Captain Webb was preaching in uniform regularly to the New York society and he attracted such numbers that the meeting room would not hold them all and it was necessary to rent a sail loft in William Street to accommodate those who came to hear him. He preached with both vehemence and pathos and his gestures combined submission and command. As an opening gesture he would take his sword from his side as he commenced and lay it with a flourish across the pulpit while he addressed the pious and the curious. His delivery was that of thunder, now a harsh and terrifying clap and then a distant rumble, amiable but ominous. It is said that "all saw the warrior in his face and heard the evangelist in his voice, under which they trembled, wept and fell." John Wesley had described Webb as a man of fire. John Adams, who was to hear him later, noted that "the old soldier was one of the most fluent, eloquent men I ever heard. He reaches the imagination and touches the passions."[4]

The preaching of the captain gave the Methodists a hearty send-off in New York. The rigging loft, for all its spaciousness and height, proved to be small for the growing society. There were enough members to deserve a meetinghouse, and it was Captain Webb, a good man on the streets as well as in the pulpit, who led the way in building it. He made a subscription of thirty pounds, which was a third more than that of any other member, then lent the society three hundred pounds. Later he went around the city drumming up funds, touching the high and the low, so that the list of donors contained some of the best names, including those of the Livingstons and the Stuyvesants.[5] Lots on John Street were purchased and the preaching house, christened Wesley Chapel, was erected. Philip Embury supervised the construction and worked on the job as a carpenter. On October 30, 1768, two years after the first class of Methodists was formed, Embury preached the dedicatory sermon from a pulpit built with his own hands.

As the occasion showed, the captain could gracefully step aside, and there was a place in the societies for the quiet and the steady as exemplified by Embury. But it was the picturesque and the flamboyant who supplied the diet deficiency for the colonials and the early Americans. Some eccentrics too spectacular to maintain their connection with the other itinerants were drawn into the fold and left their imprint after they departed, increasing the public appetite for the unusual in the Methodist pulpit. Lorenzo Dow of Connecticut once stood up before a congregation and announced with the voice of a stentor that he had the latest authentic news from hell.

James Axley, a man of multiple talents and diligent in a variety of good works, used ventriloquism in the pulpit and engaged in a colloquy with an imaginary apologist seated at the rear of the congregation. Axley felt that his fellow preachers were beginning to imitate the world and should be called to task. Once at a Conference he addressed himself to the subject. The man at the back was made to say that some Methodist ministers dressed fashionably and acted the dandy. With his own strong voice Axley denied the charge, but the straw man said, "Well, sir, if you won't take my word for it, just look at those preachers in the pulpit behind you." The preacher obediently turned and looked at his brethren who, sure enough, were dressed fit to kill. Axley turned sadly to the man at the back and concluded in a subdued tone, "If you please, sir, we'll drop the subject."[6]

Benjamin Abbott was an early son of thunder who had power to an exceptional degree. His fellow itinerates hailed him as "one of the wonders of America—no man's copy. He was frequently remarkably eloquent, sometimes overwhelmingly so. . . ." And he could be eloquent without opening his mouth. An eyewitness described the manner of his preaching. He would stand silent in the pulpit, look round the congregation, his eye piercing every breast. Then he would say, "Lord, begin the work; Lord, begin the work *now;* Lord, begin the work just *there!*" He would point the sword of his finger straight at a member of the crowd. On the occasion reported, the man singled out, standing as an idle onlooker by the side of a tree, "fell immediately as if he had been shot, and cried aloud for mercy."[7]

Even the best actors might turn up in the smallest or least expected place. The size of the circuits kept the preachers on the go. On Ohio circuit James Finley rode twenty-five places where he regularly preached. It took four weeks to make the rounds, the circuit being in parts of five counties. On another circuit later Finley had to preach thirty-two times on every round.

He was obliged to look as closely as possible after the needs of more than a thousand members, preaching to them or meeting with them at homes in small groups.[8]

The size of the circuits also created in the itinerants both reverence and disdain for distance, a sort of mixed feeling and a way of thinking that was akin to the moods of people they reached. The exposure to the elements made them elementary and matter-of-fact as well as expansive in their approach, and the unceasing motion, little relieved by repose, gave rhythm to their speech. It was a normal response to the stimuli of the great outdoors in a land that was almost all outdoors. One of the most eloquent of the early preachers, Henry B. Bascom, declared that a room contracted his thoughts. He could think better under the sky and stars, and those who heard him rejoiced that his style had not been cramped by the law of the schools.[9]

Travel put the preachers where the people lived and made informal meetings with settlers easy. The repeated statement that no matter how far out and to what remote corner settlers went they were sure to find a Methodist parson there ahead of them grew into a jocular legend. But there was enough basis in fact to give it foundation. Richmond Nolley, an itinerant who endured incredible hardships to find new fields where the need was sore, particularly looking after the care and spiritual instruction of the children in the wilds, once came upon a man unpacking his wagon while his wife was busy around the fire. "What!" exclaimed the settler when he heard the salutation and turned to see the garb of his visitor, "Another Methodist preacher! Have you found us already?" The settler said he had left Virginia and Georgia to escape the Methodists. His wife and daughter had joined the Church and he was sure that in the upper stretches of the Tombigbee River he would be shut of Methodist preachers. Nolley suggested that he had better make peace with the preachers because there would be Methodists in both heaven and hell.[10]

With virtually no home of their own the preachers were at home in every home. They preferred as hosts people of their own persuasion, but they were adept and adaptable if they met up in their rounds with deists or those who were distinctly inhospitable. Once Axley turned up at an isolated home near nightfall. It was a house with servants and plenty of room, but the lady of the house made it clear that she would not take the stranger in. He could warm his bones for a while and then seek shelter elsewhere. The preacher sat in front of the fire. He began to think of the glad day when he would have an eternal home and would not have forever to move on. The thought reminded him of the Lord and he began with great naturalness to sing songs of praise and gratitude. It was said that all who heard Axley sing became his friends. Hardly had he finished his third hymn when the lady called the groom and told him to take the preacher's horse to the stable. "And feed him well!" one of the daughters of the household called out.[11]

In homes where they were expected or came as regular visitors, their coming was looked forward to with pleasure. They were companionable in cabins—it was their natural habitation when they were indoors at all. They were genial, hearty, optimistic. They brought news and gossip, good stories, and tales of Indian adventures. Henry Smith, an early stalwart of the Ohio area, made record of how remarkably kind and sociable he found the people: "Many pleasant hours we spent together by the side of our large log fires in our log cabins, conversing on various subjects; but religion was generally our delightful theme." He goes on from the vantage point of years to remark that "some of us smoked the pipe with them, but we really thought there was no harm in that, for we had no anti-tobacco societies among us then."[12]

The preachers lived where the people lived; they preached where the people lived as well. They knew the linings and crevices of the hearts of their hearers. They were enough acquainted with the sins and weaknesses of their fellows to draw a bead on sin. Many had known the ways of the world in some detail before they commenced preaching. William McKendree had a particularly psychic sense of what men did and regretted. He had served in the commissary department of the Continental army and had been present at the surrender of Cornwallis. He was converted in 1787 and the next year was received on trial in the itinerancy. He advanced rapidly and in 1799 was sent west to supervise work in Kentucky and adjoining states. Here his eye picked up the sin of extortion as one that most needed to be condemned. Men of low conscience would take advantage of settlers coming with their bread-hungry families into Kentucky.

McKendree addressed himself to the matter directly in one of his sermons, describing the hapless citizen who has moved to "your fine country to become your neighbor and your fellow-citizen. . . . But you sell him your corn at double price, and the corn, when it is only fifty cents to the bushel, you ask a dollar; ah! and receive it too of the poor man who has to grapple with misfortunes to support his family!" The preacher went on, pressing home his point until a man in the congregation could stand it no longer but rose and called out, "If I did sell my corn for a dollar a bushel I gave them six months to pay it in." Although McKendree calmly assured the protestor that the sermon had not been addressed exclusively to him, there was in Methodist preaching a ringing personal note and those who listened had no trouble in making their own applications on the principle, often gleefully cited, that a hit dog hollers.[13]

Circuit riders were physical men, and their preaching in gesture and tone was bound to take on some of the character of the world and the people they knew. It had in it flash floods, falling trees, mountain torrents, thunder and lightning, the call of birds, the darkness of the forests, the howl of wolves, the threat of panthers, the cries of lost men, the jog of horses. The preachers were men apart by virtue of their convictions but they were not set apart by priesthood or privilege. They were at one in body and emotion with those on the frontier.

There was in them at times an awareness of Samsonian strength. A touch of the American pride in size can be seen from an entry in the journal of Jesse Lee, a man of such heartiness that, though a Virginian, he spread the warmth of Methodism through icy New England. Lee noted that, after finishing the business of the Conference in 1799, he and three other Methodist preachers went to a nearby grocery store to weigh. He tipped the scales at 259 pounds. Seely Bunn weighed 252; Thomas Lucas, 245; and Thomas F. Sergent, 220. The total, Lee noted with some satisfaction, came to 976 pounds—"a wonderful weight for four Methodist preachers, and all of us travel on horseback."[14] Another robust itinerant who rode circuits in Ohio, Michigan, and Illinois was James Gilruth, and he was so big that he needed two horses to carry him on his journeys, riding them alternately and allowing the nag who showed signs of weariness or exhaustion to follow along behind.[15]

The preachers along the frontier trails and in the backwoods where meetings were infrequent did not let manners interfere with the Lord's work. Nor did they stand on decorum or appeal to the law if their meetings were disturbed. James Havens, known as the Napoleon of Methodism in eastern Indiana, had a reputation far and wide as a man of strength whose muscle was equal to his preaching. Stephen R. Beggs, who wrote an engaging history of the West, once saw Havens take hold of a ruffian who was making a disturbance at the altar. Seizing the disturber by the back of the neck, Havens turned him literally heels over head and threw him to the floor. When the man still looked as if he might be unruly, the preacher held him so fast that the man was almost strangled.[16]

James Finley did not hesitate to seize disturbers at his meetings, shake them until their teeth rattled, and pitch them out a window or door. In time rioters would quail before Finley, a contemporary assures us, but only when they threatened trouble. For all his disciplined violence, "his heart was most genial, his discourses full of pathos and his friendships the most tender and lasting."[17]

Being closely identified with the settlers in manner of living and in emotions, the circuit riders found a ready response on the frontier to the essential idea they carried. This idea was summed up in and centered around the word *conversion*. The preachers

86

one and all had a transmissible experience to offer the lonely and the fearful and the displaced. This experience, repeatedly and visibly confirmed through their ministrations and the meetings they held, demonstrated that the meanest man and the ugliest woman might become heroic and serene. The change came about through an act of free will which put the incomplete person directly in touch with God. The result was a transformation of inner feeling and outward conduct. The result was also and always an improvement notable enough to be seen by family and neighbors. When a person was converted he became better—better by all standards—and he became a cooperative member of the community. The preachers made miracles every day—miracles for all practical purposes. "Horsethieves stopped stealing. Wife-beaters turned into affectionate husbands. Highwaymen," as Barclay points out, "who made their living by assaults on emigrant wagons turned from violence to peaceful pursuits."

Problems became solutions and there was hope of happiness even in the wilderness. The idea of conversion offered people regularly the prospect of change and newness, of forever beginning. It was religious in origin and auspices, but it was also practical, and the implications it loosed on the frontier were momentous. Man joined with the Infinite had infinite strength and there was no limit to what he might accomplish. Those who were converted were more than conquerors. Quite ordinary men and women in a strange and primitive environment found themselves in touch with a remarkable source of power, a power that not only sustained them in their trials but also elevated their faith to a point where nothing seemed impossible.

Other denominations offered the God-man idea but not in a form that afforded men and women in motion confidence in the divine origin of their abilities and possibilities, a religious base for individual worth. As Calvinism, with its corollary of predestination, filtered down to the frontier in standard Presbyterian preaching it had much in it that carried forward the old Puritan approach to salvation, interpreting sinners in the hands of an angry God. Often the result was a kind of horrorscope predicting man to be a victim of the forces of destiny. God was God. Man was worm. God was all-mighty and all there was to it. In His inscrutable wisdom He had chosen from the foundation of the earth those to be saved. It would be well to act as if chosen, and the better the life the better the chance: good conduct might be a sign you were among the elect.

The thought that God was all in all and that man was in God's hands could console the lonely heart and ease the troubled mind lost in the woods of the world. There is a destiny that shapes our ends, and it is well to believe that we are guided and to leave the major decisions and directions to the all-encompassing Mind. There comes from this view at its best the joy of belonging to the vast, the exhilaration of being a part of the universe.

Lacking in this view, however, was any real encouragement to believe in the partnership of God and man. A religion that stressed the overwhelming power of God led to reflection. Methodism, with its stress on the freedom of man's will to be joined to God's will, led to action. It offered an activist faith in a kinetic culture. Under the doctrine preached by the itinerants man could make his own destiny. The limits of it need be set only by his willingness to put the power of God to work. Because circuit riders in a land of frontiers regularly reached outlying areas not cultivated as assiduously by Baptists, conversion became a hallmark of Methodism. Other groups offered it but the Methodists advertised it and dramatized it as the religious version of rags to riches. The various stages of the experience had been surveyed by John Wesley and drawn up and laid down like a trustworthy map. The first stop the prospective Christian could reach over rugged terrain was the point where he was convicted of sin, declared guilty by his own heart, made painfully aware of his utter worthlessness without God. This might take some tough travel but he would come in time to a point where he had a sudden and mystical awareness that the burden of sin had been lifted from his soul. There followed a hilltop fulfillment which brought a rejoicing not uncommonly expressed in shouts.

Then came the peaceful valley, bringing with it the certainty that the spirit of God and the spirit of the convert were united and both bore witness to the new creation that had taken place.

To adapt and suit the theology of a learned Oxford don to the mood and living arrangements of the thousands of persons scattered along the American frontier was no mean task. Yet the circuit riders proved equal to it. They did it by endless variations on a theme by Mr. Wesley, by keeping the emphasis at all times on the main stages of the pilgrim's progress, and by teaching songs that put the message across in rhymes and verse, which, put to familiar melodies, could and did emphasize the cardinal tenets of the faith even more repetitiously than the sermons.

Much of Methodist theology was written to be sung. John Wesley put some of his sentiments in verse. His brother Charles put practically every sentiment he ever had in verse or doggerel. Before his pen was stilled he composed more than six thousand religious poems, some with a dozen verses, and in some verse of most if not all of them he stressed the decisiveness of the conversion transformation, as in:

> He breaks the power of canceled sin,
>   He sets the prisoner free;
> His blood can make the foulest clean;
>   His blood availed for me.

Religious songs were written to be read and memorized and carried in the mind as well as to be used in meetings. Books were scarce. Songs often had to be lined, read out a line at a time, and then sung. Great importance was attached to the words and they reinforced, both when lined and when put to melody, the central ideas of the sermon. There were no hymnals with music and words on the same page. The singing Methodists put the words to whatever tune most of the crowd knew, and usually this was a folk tune.

At times the combination of words and music made a perfect unit and got fixed enough in the ear of the pioneer to bring nostalgia to the aid of faith. A case in point was "Amazing Grace," which lost none of its force, no matter how often it was repeated. Hymnodists believe the tune to be a variant of an old tune called "Loving Lamb." At any rate, the words were put to a folk melody, and once they were sung to that melody could not be sung to any other. There is a slow cadence to it that makes you rock on your feet as you sing it and a lilt to the high notes that calls the soul to peaks beyond the shoddy limitations of this world. Sung without an accompaniment it can make you swoon. Sung by a great crowd of people it could melt the hardest heart and the rocks around to boot.

The sound of "Amazing Grace" had a life of its own, but put to the words of John Newton, a vagabond, a deserter from the British navy, a soldier of fortune and a slave trader, who ultimately found peace, it served as one of the most graphic illustrations imaginable of the experience of conversion, beginning:

> Amazing grace! how sweet the sound,
> That saved a wretch like me!
> I once was lost, but now am found,
> Was blind, but now I see.[18]

Under Methodist preaching on the frontier or in sparsely settled areas, conversion was a public ceremony set to music. The experience almost invariably began in an assembly and it was usually consummated in the presence of singing witnesses. It was a form of folk opera in religion when conflicts within were acted out antiphonally. To the convert and the earnest itinerant it was vastly more and not to be thought of as symbolic at all. But the preachers, with amazing vitality to match amazing grace, and with their sense of drama, knew how to encourage, direct, and assist the physical manifestations of what went on within. And they were by nature and physique equipped to take part in what went on. Their voices amplified their convictions. They spoke with a freedom born of distance from the restraints of urban areas, where some of the sophisticated looked upon

Methodists with contempt and held them up to scorn for their rampant enthusiasm.

Preachers among the pioneers shouted, banged and thumped Bibles, and walked as they talked in the pulpit. Their gestures were often as big and wide as their circuits and took on the dimensions of the space of which they were a living part. One preacher testified that the greatest kindness he received on his rounds was from a good woman who would regularly sew up the seams of his coat around the armpits. That's where he busted his seams—and would again.

Considering that the itinerants were muscular, it is not surprising that they got muscular responses from their hearers even before the days of the great camp meetings. Converts "were born strong into the Kingdom and entered it shouting." Beggs tells of an old Revolutionary soldier who had been standing on the outskirts of a crowd at an open-air service. Pretty soon "he came running to the altar crying at the top of his voice, 'Quarter! Quarter! I have never heard such cannonading as this. I yield! I yield!'"[19]

In the wilds the circuit riders did not deliver ethical homilies or make tactful suggestions about conduct. In the pulpit, for all their geniality outside, they were either-or men. Their minds were fixed in opposites. There were no compromises to be suffered. On the point of right living their dispositions were as impersonal as a steel trap, with jaws that closed at once on any sign of sin. They helped to fix, as much as the Baptists, polarity in American mental habits. Choice was imperative. The nature of man was evil, his tendencies vile, his motives base. But if he would heed the message and follow the methods laid down for the act of conversion, man could be changed in the twinkling of an eye into a person who would be good and might become perfect. There was hope and optimism in the direst threats the preachers delivered.

Their aim was always the creation of a new man, one who had not been there before, decent, godly, and kindly. They enjoyed the gymnastics of religious zeal and did nothing to stay the antics of those who were born shouting into the Kingdom. But they were sage enough to allow for variations in temperament. Some might be born again quietly and still become great. They had always to reckon with this possibility, for there had not been anything compulsive or physically strenuous about the momentous experience John Wesley underwent on May 24, 1738, at a prayer meeting near Aldersgate in London. There, he reported, he had felt his heart strangely warmed. It was a quiet event, as became a highly disciplined priest of the Church of England who for years had been influenced by members of a pietist German brotherhood known as the Moravians.

Yet of the change wrought, both John Wesley and those around him were immediately aware. Friends and acquaintances were startled. One woman wrote in great agitation to Samuel Wesley, telling him how his brother John had come to her house and, after her husband had finished reading a sermon to a few people assembled there, stood up and told the people that five days before he had not been a Christian any more than he had been in that room five days before. Then, according to the woman, he had added that "the way for them all to be Christians was to believe, and own that they were not now Christians."[20]

Within days after the Aldersgate meeting John Wesley left on a pilgrimage to Herrnhut, near Dresden, seat and center of the Moravian fellowship. Upon his return to London he began preaching to those he deemed in greatest need. To the condemned felons in Newgate he records that he offered "a free salvation" and to a gathering in the Bear Yard he preached "repentance and remission of sins."

What happened to Mr. Wesley could not properly be put down as the conversion of a hardened sinner, although the dimensions of change were such that many later construed it to be. There had been a quickening, a deepening, an enrichment, a shaking of the soul. Strict observance of rules for holy living, even over and beyond that required in holy orders, did not make a Christian. The moral was plain. No matter who you were or where you were, you were not even eligible for the good life unless your heart had been changed.

Out of the strength of this conviction had come the Methodist societies in England, made up of and led by artisans and tradesmen and wives and farmers, all born anew and given dignity by following the prescription Mr. Wesley had written. Man might become great through the grace of God. Man and not God was to make the decision that started the process of change. In Britain the blessed assurance of man's worth had wrought wonders. According to William Lecky in *The History of England in the Eighteenth Century,* Wesleyanism saved England from the bloodshed of revolution.[21] It accomplished social change through an idea. As Bishop William T. Watkins stated the matter: "Every man was declared to be a potential son of God and 'the wretched that crawl the earth' were invited to become the actual sons of God." Under this proclamation the masses of England threw off their fatalistic view of life. "For Methodism there was no rabble."[22]

It was out of this robust heritage of confidence in what the individual might become that the itinerants preached as the settlers moved west. It was the kerygma of rebirth, a proclamation of strength to men who had faith to move mountains. The religion that resulted was personal—intensely so, accepting the environment as inevitable. Daily living exacted the full energy of the settler. To change circumstances was not his lot. Rather he needed the power to rise above.

IX Poverty Leads to Chastity

It was fitting that men of God be poor in an economy of scarcity and struggle. The itinerants knew it and poverty became their lot. They lived in what was an almost ostentatious penury, which identified them with the common run of the people they served and at the same time dramatized them as men who might have had wealth (for they were observed to be highly competent) if they had not renounced the spangles of the world and chosen the better part.

In brief, itinerant poverty was an act of esprit de corps—an austerity assumed and proclaimed by the governing body of the Church. It was designed and legislated by that body. At the Christmas Conference the itinerants had voted that each and every one of them would receive an annual allowance of twenty-four pounds, payable in Pennsylvania currency and amounting to sixty-four dollars in Continental currency. To this provision the Conference very firmly added in the minutes the line: *And No More.* There was to be no rank of office in the matter of money. All members of the Conference—including the superintendents who were in effect bishops and the presiding elders who were empowered to go about administering the sacraments—were to receive exactly the same amount as the far-off circuit rider. *And No More.* The word *salary* was avoided. Allowances were allowed, but it was prescribed that the preacher take his stipend only if he found himself in actual need. No fees or gifts for wedding ceremonies were to be received and, later, when they were permitted, such gifts were placed in the hands of a steward to be divided equally among the members of the Conference.[1]

It came to pass, then, that every man who was accepted in the Methodist ministry took a virtual vow of poverty. He dissociated himself from the lure and hope of worldly gain, from the motives that prompted other men. Preachers of other denominations might supplement their measly income by weekday work, but the Methodists had their rounds to ride and were daily on full-time duty in the Lord's work. A few here and there peddled merchandise as they went, but they were looked at askance, regarded as deviants and not models. Some tried to carry on farming or business ventures, but the added labor exhausted them, and congregations complained that they had given way to a craving for riches.

Evidence of poverty as evidence of dedication was important to the brotherhood partly because of the stern Wesleyan views of wealth. Money—in whatever amount a man happened to have —was not to be saved or hoarded or even invested but given away, as soon as it touched the palm, to those in need. In the days of newness shortly after his conversion Mr. Wesley had made a covenant with his workers: "If I leave behind me ten pounds above my debts and my books, or what may happen to be due on account of them—you and all mankind bear witness to me that I died a thief and a robber."

The record of the founder spoke for itself. His life income from books was tremendous, amounting to between thirty thousand and forty thousand pounds in a day when a horse could be bought in England for ten pounds. Yet he never abandoned his frugality or moderated his generosity. His behavior furnished vivid incidents to bear on the attitude of the preachers in England and America. In 1776, when the British Treasury was hard pressed, the accountant general noted from his records that a successful author had not declared his silver as the law required. Accordingly the accountant general wrote Mr. Wesley:

> Reverend Sir: As the commissioners cannot doubt that you have plate for which you have hitherto neglected to make an entry, they have directed me to send you the above copy of the Lords' order, and to inform you that they expect you forthwith to make due entry of all your plate. . . .

The accountant general got an immediate answer:

> Sir: I have two silver tea-spoons in London and two at Bristol. This is all the plate I have at present; and I shall not buy any more while so many around me want bread. I am, sir, your most humble servant, John Wesley.[2]

Poverty among the preachers led to a preoccupation with plainness and an insistence that frills and worldly displays must be scrupulously guarded against. The extent to which objection went may be seen in the case of James Kelsey, a Georgia preacher, who was brought up before the quarterly conference on the charge of wearing gold spectacles. The presiding elder refused to heed the critics and reprimand Kelsey, but there was a good deal of commotion over the matter and one woman who sided with the man in the gold spectacles noted in her diary, "I am almost ashamed of it."[3]

Plainness might be an affectation, but there was rarely any need to affect impecuniosity. Itinerants might impose on the hospitality of members, or even deists, as they moved about their circuits. Bed and board was not a major item in the budget—and this fact had apparently been calculated when the allowance given the preachers was granted. But there were certain items for which cash on the barrelhead was needed and often the preachers did not have it. Their allowances might not be paid. In his collection of documents on frontier Methodism,

William Warren Sweet presents an item showing that on a Texas circuit the standard question was asked at a quarterly conference, "What was the collection for the preachers?" The answer written into the minutes was, "Nothing."

Even if the preacher got what money was coming to him he might not get it on time or when it was most necessary to have it. At the General Conference of 1800 the annual allowance was raised from sixty-four to eighty dollars but the itinerant was required to keep a strict account of all that he received and hand back to his Annual Conference any monies over his stipulated allowance. With all his close reckoning he could not tell ahead of time what he might count on and he had to scrimp and scrounge as best he could.

Clothing was one item for which cash was needed. Jacob Young, an early itinerant in Kentucky, discovered as one winter approached that his shoes were nearly worn out and his old cloak too thin for the oncoming winter. He was at his wits' end. "But man's distress is God's opportunity," he observed. "A strange lady came at the right time and handed me a dollar. Solomon Goss gave me four or five dollars. Some other friends, unknown to me, gave me a few dollars more. I went out and bought me a pair of shoes, a piece of heavy cloth, and employed Miss Thankful West to make me an overcoat for one dollar. By the time my garments were all in order, my money was all gone."[4]

A preacher might need clothes and a horse at the same time. Many itinerants in New England walked, but in other parts of the country, and especially in the West, distances made the horse essential—a perpetual necessity, as one preacher sadly put it. When William Burke, a western itinerant who was never deterred by distance, had to buy a horse costing him nearly a hundred dollars, the drain left him nothing for raiment. "However," Burke reported, "I economized in every possible way. I borrowed a blanket and wore it instead of a greatcoat through the winter, and by that means paid my debts."[5]

Prices of saddle horses differed in various localities but usually a good horse cost an itinerant a year's allowance. What's more, the circuit riders did not get the mileage out of their mounts that men did who stayed in one place and could give the animals steady care. Horses' lives were shortened by traveling in all kinds of weather, often over unfavorable roads or no roads at all. One itinerant, George Brown, wore out eight horses in two years—and this in the comparatively settled country of Maryland and Virginia. Each horse was replaced at great sacrifice and at his own personal expense, being a continuous drain on his meager allowance and keeping him in debt. The comparative value of horses and clothes can be seen in the comment of Thomas Ware, who in 1797 went to east Tennessee: "I set out for my field of labor poorly clad and nearly penniless, but happy in God. In the Holston country there was but little money and clothing was very dear. My coat was worn through at the elbows; and I had not a whole undergarment left; and as for boots, I had none. But my health was good, and I was finely mounted. . . ."[6]

Possessions were not to stand in the way of the commitment to spread the Good News. In 1790 Bishop Asbury crossed the mountains into Tennessee and reported, "I found the poor preachers indifferently clad, with emaciated bodies, and subject to hard fare; yet I hope they are rich in faith." They had to be. On their shabby garments they wore the badge of poverty, and any satisfaction or pleasure they got out of life, besides occasional casual and easygoing visits in the cabins, had to come from the discharge of duty, from adherence to the mores and precepts of their order. Obedience led them to their hardscrabble circuits, where indigence was their allotted lot, and poverty involved indirectly if not forthrightly a vow of chastity. The preachers could not afford to get married.

There had been some agitation, started in the days before the Christmas Conference, about an allowance for wives. There were men in the societies who objected, "thinking it unreasonable that they should raise money for a woman they never saw." The matter rested until the Church was formally organized and then it had been provided that the wives of preachers already married should receive $64.00 a year and that each child under six would be allowed $16.00 annually, and a child of six or over, up to the age of eleven, would receive $21.33 per year. The provision for the children was not pleasing when it was referred to the societies, however, and it was dropped.[7] If the preachers insisted on marrying they were not to be encouraged to procreate. They could shift for themselves and stretch their stipend as best they might, for marriage was frowned on in enough ways to make it almost forbidden. It was understood that "to marry is to locate." To locate meant that the itinerant would no longer itinerate. He would be allowed to preach and exercise certain functions of the ministry under the direction of the preacher in charge of the place where he settled down, but he would lose his status and his voice in the governing body of the Church.

As more and more stations began to be established there was some hope that a man might be appointed to a church in a large town or city and not have to travel a circuit. Then he could perhaps marry. The prospect here was slim, however, and Asbury made the point clear by the wry comment that preachers who aspired to being in a station would "have to wait, or stretch their loves." Asbury himself was as celibate as an abbot and remained so all his life. Coke married in 1809 at the age of fifty-two, but was in England when he did, and he wrote Asbury at the time he conveyed the news that he did not intend to come back to the United States. The distasteful intelligence that his British coadjutor had taken the marriage vow, "forsaking all other," set the American bishop off on some bitter reflections. In his journal he observed: "Marriage is honorable in all—but to me it is a ceremony awful as death. Well may it be so, when I calculate that we have lost the traveling labors of two hundred of the best men in America, or the world, by marriage and consequent location."[8]

The Church was the thing and marriage was a threat. The preachers got the point. In spite of the two hundred excellent men Asbury complained of having lost to the marriage bed, most of the preachers accepted the unwritten but not unspoken policy of celibacy. In the Virginia Conference the year of Coke's mar-

riage and Asbury's comment there were eighty-four preachers. Of
this number only three were married. Presiding with Asbury was
William McKendree, the first American to be elected a Methodist
bishop. He had been elevated the year before, and he was a
bachelor.[9]

Lingering in the English background of the Methodist societies
in the United States was always the influence of Mr. Wesley, and
he had advised his preachers against marriage. He had gone
against his own advice and married at the age of forty-seven,
but the act had been a mistake which he rued to his dying day.
The marriage had confirmed both his theories and his convictions. The woman he married, a widow, had not only proved
to be a vixen who tormented the little man unmercifully when
he was at home, and was said to have dragged him around the
room by his hair, but she also sorely interfered with his itinerating. In time she went away and Mr. Wesley went on with his
travels. The lady died a few years after the separation but Mr.
Wesley had learned of her death only after it was too late to
go to her funeral.[10] Accounts of the whole affair trail off into
obscurity. She is represented to have been a Mrs. Vazeille,
spelled in enough different ways to make her a proofreader's
nightmare. Usually she appears in print without a first name, although just to mix you up further, one index item gives it as
Mary.

Now and then, in the face of bad example and good advice,
a traveling preacher rebelled and took unto himself a wife. William Burke of Virginia did. He was a pioneer preacher and he
was also a pioneer in testing the metes and bounds of the
Methodist system. He had first established himself as sound on
the doctrine, obedient to the commands of those who gave him
hard missions, and on a par in poverty with the most improvident
of his colleagues. There was nothing irregular about this earnest
Virginian, and for this reason his defiance in marrying caused all
the more consternation among officials and his fellows.

Burke's youth was spent in riotous living. He was vain and
entered "into all the amusements of his day." But at the age of

twenty he underwent a spectacular conversion and was licensed to exhort. Then he learned his power. "I had a voice like thunder and there was a fire in my bones," he reported in his autobiography. "The dry bones of those in the meeting place began to tremble. Sinners began to leave the house; the fire was too warm for them."[11]

In 1791 the young preacher was dispatched to organize a desolate circuit four hundred miles around the Holston Mountains of Tennessee. There were more Indians than Methodists on it, but he sat his saddle and stayed his rounds. He traveled often at night to avoid Indians. Once a group of Baptists, just ahead of a party escorting Burke on the way to meet and protect Bishop Asbury, was scalped. There were times, though, when Burke would travel a hundred miles without the sight of a single house or human being, even an Indian.

It was in the midst of such hazards and loneliness that Burke decided to marry. He got the consent of the woman he loved, and he did not ask the consent of anyone else. But he could not escape being conscious of what it would mean "to travel with what the people and the preachers called the incumbrance of a wife." Later his fears were justified: ". . . everything was thrown in my way to discourage me." Although he longed to go the even tenor of his way and demonstrate that marriage need not turn a preacher into a sloth, criticism hounded him wherever he turned. At the first Conference after his marriage his character came under examination. Bishop Asbury did not defend him outright but he did remind the preachers of Burke's accomplishments as a debater who could take the hide of his opponents. Thus the married itinerant escaped actual censure, but later Burke's presiding elder advised him to locate, saying that the people would not support a married preacher.

This prediction proved to be more truth than piety. Each new circuit brought fresh frustrations. At one place he found the prejudice so stern that he could find no home, Methodist or otherwise, "for love or money," where he might board his wife if she followed him to his circuit. Undaunted, Burke set about cutting logs for a cabin. Within a few weeks he had a snug room ready for his wife—aided in the project by friends who were willing to help in a strenuous enterprise even if they were not willing to give a woman married to a preacher bed and board.

Burke labored, all told, for twenty-six years in Virginia, Kentucky, Tennessee, and Ohio, and his long-suffering wife went whither he went, patiently adjusting herself to whatever degree of prejudice showed itself, acting always with a dignity that could have been no handicap to the preacher. He tells us that she wrought with her own hands, paid her board when he could not build her a cabin, and clothed herself.[12] But the game was hopeless and at last Burke took supernumerary relations, which meant that he stopped itinerating but continued to hold membership in the Conference. Still the preachers would not let him be. He was charged with having once treated his presiding elder with contempt. There was no record in the minutes of the incident which led to the charge. Nonetheless Burke was suspended. Two years later he was expelled from the Conference on the grounds that he continued to administer the sacraments while suspended. He became postmaster of Cincinnati and held the position for twenty-eight years. Meanwhile he remained faithful to his church as a layman, and the General Conference of 1836, after years of investigation, cleared him of early charges and restored his name to the minutes.[13]

By 1836 times had changed and a preacher could marry without risk of great penalty or constant harassment. In the early days, however, it remained a rule "almost as inexorable as death" that no preacher should marry until he had completed at least four years of traveling the circuit. Even when restrictions eased, the preacher owed the first allegiance of his conscience to the Church and not to his wife. Burke in retrospect was mindful of this point and wrote with a touch of pride, "I lost but one single appointment in consequence of my marriage."

Women who might be approached with proposals by preachers needed to understand clearly where the main interest of their men lay. Mad Lorenzo Dow, who had all the traits of the itinerant to an exaggerated and eccentric degree, fell semi-madly in love with a young woman called Peggy. He proposed just before going off on one of his endless preaching missions, telling her plainly that if she found no one she liked better, if she would be willing to give him up twelve months out of thirteen or three years out of four, would never tell him not to go to his appointment, he would be willing to marry her, but added: "If you should stand in my way I should pray God to remove you."[14]

Dow never had to ask God to remove his Peggy. She married him and stayed with him to the bitter end of his tumultuous career, never complaining, ever faithful to his cause. In common with other women who successfully married Methodist preachers, she knew she must not stand in the way of the Lord's work. Once Philip Gatch, an early faithful whose province lay in and around New Jersey, was about to set off on a trip that would keep him absent longer than usual. To his dismay, just before taking horse, he found his wife's arm bleeding where it had been pierced by a spindle. The injury was so serious that he thought he ought not to leave. Sister Gatch did not think any such of a thing. Firmly she insisted that he go on and fill his appointments. He went. To him there was nothing harsh in his actions or to her anything sacrificial in hers. His wife's heart was in his work, he tells us, and records, "We parted in peace and when I returned we met in love."[15]

X The Stern Discipline

The itinerancy constituted a highly selective and exclusive religious fraternity, convinced that it knew what was best for the people and was competent to carry it out. Along with personal traits in common, the preachers had also corporate characteristics. They regarded themselves as peculiar, chosen, set apart, destined, partners of the Most High. They formed an elite class, the members of which associated freely and familiarly with the concourse of believers and yet at moments of decision withdrew into themselves and into the involutions of their own procedures.

Not a little of their sense of singularity derived from a sense of mission. The feeling of being divinely appointed for a lofty purpose belongs to the psychology of most religious groupings. In the case of The Methodist Episcopal Church the feeling was proclaimed by the hierarchy itself and it was given continuity by repeated emphasis in Conference gatherings and transmitted to the membership through layers of authority.

The mission had been stated and accepted officially at the Christmas Conference. The question had been raised, in the Methodist manner of keeping minutes, "What may we reasonably believe to be God's design in raising up Methodist preachers?" And the answer had been voted and written into the minutes:

"To reform the continent and spread scriptural holiness over the land." The covenant lay between God and the preachers. The mission that summoned them was stupendous, and the very dimensions of it justified, nay demanded, the exclusion of all of lesser frame and faith.

That the body which stated and accepted the assignment of the reform of the continent and the spreading of scriptural holiness over the land was small in number added to its intensity. It was normal to fear that others who had not caught the vision in the same way would not be as dedicated as the preachers were for the task at hand, even though they might be thoroughly devoted.

Women proved their loyalty to the cause by serving as daughters of Dorcas, by long-suffering and patience, by freeing preachers from some of the concerns and chores of daily life. They were excluded, however, from the deliberations and inner ceremonies of the lodge that comprised the initiated itinerants. Excluded also were the local preachers, although they were but a shade below the traveling preachers in rank. Likewise laymen were vouchsafed no part in the government, however fervent or faithful they might be in the role of stewards or class leaders. Those not in the fold during the early and formative years of American Methodism were by no means rejected or purposely barred. They were simply not admitted. It seemed only natural that men who organized the Church should constitute the Church.

There were no Africans among the voting itinerants, although some of the Africans were, by the testimony of the whites, masters of homiletics and forensics. One was Harry Hosier, known as "Black Harry"—or as "Harry, a black." He served as groom to Asbury and often accompanied the bishop and other itinerants on their rounds. Dr. Benjamin Rush called Black Harry "the greatest orator in America." Bishop Coke, whose travels were not confined to the United States, said, "I believe he is one of the best preachers in the world."[1] Occasionally, Asbury lent Hosier to Coke, who noted with a touch of shrewdness in his journal,

"Sometimes I publish him to preach at candlelight," explaining that the blacks could better attend service at that time and that the whites would be sure to stay and hear the sermon.

Small, utterly black, keen of eye, and quick of speech, the inspired groom caught the ear of every audience. Many were the times he preached for Asbury, who said that he would rather hear Harry preach than to hear himself. In time the preaching of the black became a legend. It is said that the first reference to Methodism in the New York press came about through the preaching of Harry Hosier.[2]

A story (doubtless apocryphal) has it that some visitors once came to a service Asbury was to address but there was such a press of people that they could not get inside the door. Listening outside, they were delighted to hear such eloquence and whispered their admiration to others standing near. "That is not the Bishop," they were told. "That is the Bishop's servant." To which the strangers politely replied, "If such be the servant, what must the master be!"[3]

Competence was not in itself the criterion for admission to the itinerancy. The mores, as in rules of race, had to be respected, lest prospective converts be alienated, but beyond the mores the standard was mystical. It required proven dedication, inner zeal, the witness of the spirit—an experience expected of all Methodist converts but raised to the nth degree among those who pledged the energies of their whole being to the Lord's work. Standing shoulder to shoulder in periodic Conferences and moving together in daily performance, the preachers gave each other strength, forming a kind of communion of saints in the wilderness.

The steady recognition of purpose common to their task created among the itinerants a sense of separateness, of being set apart, even from the main body of believers. Certain outward symbols indicated this separateness. In a day when there were few pictures to feed the visual man the symbols supplied a picture quality in pioneer life. To begin with, Methodist preachers were mounted. For more than a thousand active years, since the days of the Crusades and chivalry, men on horseback had enjoyed a peculiar and romantic association—one significant of power and command. From ancient times man and horse had been joined in story, picture, and legend. Classical mythology summed up the vision in the creature called the centaur, half man, half horse. The centaur expressed a strange belief that came back easily and on slight provocation. It is said that when the Indians of Mexico for the first time saw men riding horses after the beasts had been landed from Santo Domingo they thought that man and horse were part of the same body.

Out of a confluence of circumstances flowing from the past, Methodists could be associated with mythology and heraldry. In the more immediate past the saddle horse had been a military creature, notably observed in battles, and giving man an advantage over his foe. In the United States after the Revolution he became a Methodist creature and the preachers were the Lord's Horsemen—not that only Methodists rode horses, but that virtually all their preachers outside of New England were mounted.

The dress of the preachers was another distinctive feature. With allowance made for slight variations in periods and localities, the garb of the itinerant amounted to a uniform. It was marked at first by a black round-breasted coat, a long vest with corners cut off, short breeches and long stockings. Later the straight-breasted black coat came in, with full-length trousers.[4] In 1833 a resolution offered in the Illinois Conference "to require a straight coat of ministers was approved by a vote of nearly two to one." Simplicity was the shibboleth. Acceptance of the broadcloth of the Methodist clergy meant a renunciation in raiment. One of the notables of the early Methodist Church, Nathan Bangs, was converted in 1800 at the age of twenty and immediately had the ruffles taken from his shirt and the long cue from his hair. He had been a fashionably dressed schoolteacher but he could not be at one with his brethren if he wore fancies.[5]

The head of the preacher had chief attention. Hair was

turned back from about midway between the forehead and the crown and was allowed to grow down to the shoulders. The hat was flat-crowned and had a broad brim. The importance of the hat to the man of the late eighteenth and early nineteenth centuries can hardly be measured, whether it was the *chapeau bras* of the officer or the coonskin cap of the woodsman and hunter. In the case of the Methodist preachers the broad-brimmed and low-crowned felt hat marked him for quick identification.

The horse and the hair and the hat were but outward indexes of the camaraderie of the traveling preachers, a camaraderie inspired and blessed by dedication but also cemented by hardship and shared risks. Only the young and the hardy could risk the hazards of the itinerancy, and even among them death took a high toll. Almost half the preachers who died before 1800 were under thirty years of age at the time of their death, and up to 1844 approximately half died before reaching the age of thirty-three. Of the first 672 preachers whose records were kept in full, two-thirds died before they were able to render twelve years of service.[6] It became a solemn and impressive custom (still honored in every part of the world) to open each Annual Conference with Charles Wesley's searching hymn "And Are We Yet Alive?" On paper it is a mild hymn, recounting the vicissitudes that have befallen the brethren since they last assembled. Sung by five hundred preachers, gathered after long separation, it has the rousing spirit of a drinking song. Its tones are weighted with memories handed down and enhanced along the way.

One would assume that those engaged in a calling with such depletions would seek recruits and try to build up the ranks. But the religious order known as the itinerancy sternly kept its standards high enough to form a barrier against the casuals who could not prove their faith at every step of their path to the door. It was hard to get into the itinerancy and harder still to stay in it. From 1773 to 1806 there were 251 preachers admitted on trial who were not admitted into the full connection.[7] Of the

650 preachers who had joined the itinerancy by the opening of the nineteenth century, about 500 had not been able to stand the gaff and had had to locate.[8]

Those accepted into the brotherhood found themselves constantly under surveillance. The system provided in precise detail for procedures to be followed in the event of any breach of conduct. A rumor or a breath of scandal was cause enough to have an itinerant hauled before his peers and examined and cross-examined. In a word, the preachers were subject to trials as well as tribulations, and the trials were of their own making, scrupulously conducted, with voluminous records kept. Fixed court action carried out by the preachers policed the brotherhood, sustaining the demand for exemplary behavior and providing the means by which men not a credit to the profession could be expelled.

Trials were numerous, decisions definite. Out of a total of 2468 preachers admitted to the connection between 1769 and 1828, a total of 57 were expelled.[9] At the Christmas Conference of 1784, when the Church was formalized, the preachers, foreseeing the need of keeping their ranks pure and undefiled, prescribed for themselves an annual examination of character and conduct, known as the passing of character. It took place at each Annual Conference, behind closed doors. The name of each traveling preacher was called and any improper conduct rumored or reported could be brought to the attention of the assembly. If charges serious enough to constitute an accusation were brought, a trial was arranged. At the Annual Conference also cases appealed from the quarterly conferences were reviewed by committees of nine, who read the records and might also call further witnesses. The decision of the Annual Conference, acting on the report of the trial committee, was final and led to exoneration, suspension, or expulsion.

The preacher had to be above reproach and exemplary in conduct because part of his duty was to look to the behavior of Methodists in his charge. The Church was early sensitive to the wildness of the West and realized that special rules needed to be drawn up to guard against old sins in new form. The *Discipline,* issued every four years, showed a national awareness of what people were up to and preachers should guard against. It sketched changing patterns of wrongdoing. The *Discipline* of 1808 spoke out on wicked land deals and manipulations. Rules were to be enforced "fully and strenuously against all frauds, and particularly against dishonest insolvencies, suffering none to remain in our society, on any account, who are found guilty of any fraud." Methodists should avoid the very appearance of evils or association with those who might have evil intent. Warning was issued against receiving bribes from political candidates and the circuit riders were to advise Methodists "to discountenance all treats given by candidates before or at elections."[10]

There followed a score of explicit items to be avoided by those who would flee from the wrath to come. These included the buying and selling of goods on which duty had not been paid, taking unlawful interest, and *"the using of many words in buying or selling."* Small things made big sins in Methodist morality, and the rules laid down for the preachers and members alike were not casual suggestions. They were part of the law of the Lord and if the preachers and members did not observe them they were to be punished, and they could not be punished without a trial that proved the error of their ways. As William Warren Sweet describes the circumstances: "Sin was a fact which could not be dealt with lightly. It had to be faced realistically and just punishment meted out. . . . Where there were rumors abroad that some Methodist had violated a church precept, it was almost certain that the accused would come up for trial."[11] A preacher charged with an offense or rumored to be guilty of misconduct would be summoned by the presiding elder to come before a committee named to hear the case. If he were found guilty, he would be suspended until the next Annual Conference, at which time the case was reviewed or tried again.

The preachers saw the need to keep their flocks distinct and intact, to preserve them as leaven. Martin Ruter, superintendent of the Texas Mission, which opened in 1837, stated the situation in writing to one of his fellow preachers: "In a new land, having so little piety, there is a great danger of receiving improper members and of fixing the standards of faithfulness too low." There would be many who would not be "prepared to lead the cross-bearing life."[12]

To winnow the chaff, laymen as well as preachers were subjected to trials before committees appointed to hear the charges against them. These charges might allege infringement of rules laid down in the *Discipline* or conduct considered inappropriate in the light of these rules. One of the leading Methodist laymen of Ohio, Samuel Williams, joined with other citizens in organizing a Fourth of July celebration. He went further and proposed a toast—to be drunk with water—in honor of liberty, civil and religious. To his brethren on the Hockhocking Circuit such behavior seemed unseemly. The committee who heard his case was unanimous in agreeing "that the attending of barbacues and Drinking of toasts on the 4 of July is contrary to the Sperit of Christianity and cannot be don to the glory of God." For his breach of Christian propriety Williams was expelled.[13]

Conduct unbecoming a gentleman was doubly unbecoming a preacher. While Peter Cartwright was a presiding elder in Illinois he had to deal with the case of the Reverend Thomas W. Jones, who had engaged to marry Eliza H. Miles. During the fall of 1849 Jones wrote Miss Miles a number of letters, showing a dwindling affection, and on October 27 he wrote that his mind was so deranged that he had forgot that he had "ever made any appointment for the consummation." Troubles continued to multiply. He was worried about money and wondered if the father of Miss Miles might offer any assistance. The Lord might be hedging up their way, he said, and he would have to wait on the guidance of Providence. As late as December 1 Brother Jones wrote that he still had hopes. By January, however, he was married to another lady.

Within a few days after learning of the offending preacher's defection, Miss Miles laid the letters in the lap of her pastor, who wrote to Cartwright as presiding elder, telling of the Excitement Created and the Conversation about the Matter, saying that there ought to be an investigation and adding "for if this charge is true, what will be thought of us?"

The committee appointed heard the evidence and read the letters. Two of the members concluded that the conduct of Jones was highly censurable but not bad enough "to exclude him from the Kingdom of grace and glory." A third member dissented. At the next Annual Conference the trial committee reversed the majority opinion of the local court and Jones was suspended. He had been guilty of a breach of the marriage contract and would no longer command the instant respect of his fellows or the people.[14]

There was little privacy left the preachers, and if they strayed even tentatively they were sure to be detected as culprits. The fullness of the trials reminded them of this fact. One case involved A. G. Meacham of Shelbyville, Illinois, a doctor as well as a preacher, who seems to have thought of himself as having more bedside rights and privileges than most. But in May 1839 William Nichols charged him with immoral conduct, specifying that he had tried twice to get in bed with Malinda Nichols, daughter of the accuser.

The record of the testimony and questions and answers runs for pages and shows that none of the parties involved was to be left unspared. The committee decided that the charge was sustained. They had to admit with a chaste sense of justice that the specification of the first night was proved but that there was reasonable doubt about the second night. Nonetheless, one night was enough. Meacham was suspended until the next Annual Conference, whereupon he sat down and wrote the officials of the Conference, confessing openly his immorality and high imprudence "for making two attempts with wicked intention at illicit intercourse." For good measure he went on to admit that he had also made two attempts with another young woman, Elizabeth Sawyer of Wabash Grove. When the trial was over and the confession signed and news of it bruited, not only the Methodists but the whole community had a peeping view of human nature as seen from one angle. Any Methodist preacher with lingering hankering for woman flesh had his warning.[15]

The case of the Reverend W. B. Mark was not without its touching aspects, as his confession shows. He wrote the bishops and the members of the Illinois Annual Conference to be held in 1836: "Oft have I looked forward to the session of the Annual Conference as a kind of Jubilee." It was about the only fun preachers could have. But Mark had had another kind. He had been found guilty of having unlawful intercourse with Mrs. Eve Whitney. In his letter he laments that he had not strictly observed his ordination vow and very considerately adds that he is making full confession in order "that my case may not consume time and obtrude upon the more pleasant duties of the conference. . . ." Certainly it would have been time-consuming and embarrassing to hash over the details of his case. He admitted that he had been indiscreet with Mrs. Eve Whitney. He had committed an even greater indiscretion by giving Brother Whitney his earthly all to keep the matter from becoming a scandal. His earthly all had been a thousand dollars, paid with the understanding "upon the positive condition and Solemn promise that it should be kept a profound Secret." Brother Whitney had not kept his pledge. Whether he was tried for blackmail is not a matter of available record, but Brother Mark was out and the itinerants had rid their ranks of one more person whose sin had brought disgrace upon the brotherhood.[16]

Cases of fornication and adultery attracted the most attention, but sex was not the only form that sin took. Whatever sin impaired public confidence in the clergy and gave the itinerancy a bad name provoked action as quickly as the sin of lust. Occasionally bad apples got into the barrel, in spite of every stern precaution. In 1857 Peter Cartwright brought seven charges against the Reverend D. J. Snow, and he might have added an eighth—that of general cussedness.

Among other things, Snow had contracted a debt with a widow, failed to pay it, and tried to defraud her out of the amount borrowed. In addition, he was charged with having lied about other transactions and, to cap his obloquy, had said that Cartwright had called another preacher "a damned son of a bitch." The charges against Snow were sustained, and he was suspended from all ministerial functions for a year.[17]

The trials were protective, intended to keep the order above reproach and not to exact any retribution. The itinerants had their ideals and their assignment and the person who did not share their fervor was not to continue in their favor. Misconduct was but a sign that the preacher did not understand the purity of the itinerancy and its commitment. Punishment of any grave offense could be left to the civil authorities, but a breach of conduct short of crime must be considered as seriously by the brotherhood as a lawless act would be by the state.

Through the Conference system the itinerancy had the standard order of procedure by which severe rules could be enforced. There was also in the system, with its integrated levels, means by which discipline of the membership of the churches could be carried out—and for a time it was. But as membership spiraled and Methodist doctrines became more widely popular in their appeal to the citizens of a fast-growing nation, the itinerants found strong regulations harder and harder to administer. They did seek to keep alive and extend from themselves to the whole body of believers some of the peculiarity of Methodist practices. In the General Conference of 1796 the preachers assembled declared: "We do not prohibit our people from marrying persons who are not of our society, provided such persons have the form and are seeking the power of godliness; but if they marry persons who do not come up to this description, we shall be obliged to purge our society of them. . . ."[18]

The position taken was reaffirmed when the question came up eight years later, but the action taken was hardly more than the expression of a resolute wish and there is scant evidence that the admonition was widely heeded. By the early 1800's

The Methodist Episcopal Church was in process of change. Wesleyanism had begun as a sect, that is to say, as a religious society with distinct tenets of faith and conduct erected as standards for admission. *Religion in the Struggle for Power* by J. Milton Yinger cites the Quakers as the classic example of a sect and the Moravians as another. There was no modification of the tenets to accommodate or attract those outside the fold.[19]

The Wesleyans in England at first had been highly selective and had admitted into fellowship only those who had undergone conversion and could show evidence of it in conduct. The Methodists, however, had not been content to remain a sect. There was among them a peculiar evangelistic zeal that made them want to share the wealth of their experience, first in England and then overseas. The establishment of a separate body in America and its expansion among all sorts and conditions of men led to a measure of compromise and accommodation in the regulation of the membership, as was shown in such ways as the lifting of prohibitions that had at first been placed on owning and selling slaves. The success of the Church as an instrument in the winning of souls came to be recognized as more important than the exactions placed on membership, with the result that subtly and by degrees Methodism in the United States, by the Yinger standard, became a church and ceased to be a sect.

Yet the Wesleyan ethic continued among the traveling preachers and they in time constituted the sect. Both through dedication and through circumstances created by an unwieldy growth of membership the itinerants turned more and more attention to themselves and formed a tight coterie, confident that the members of the Conference were entitled to arrive at vital decisions affecting the whole Church by the authority of a majority acting within a tiny minority.

What would be the effect in the long run of such a governing body? Would it run afoul in its own efficiency? Were there, in the very nature of Methodist polity, although it had evolved naturally, weaknesses that could in time lead to disorder and disunion?

There were reflective men within the connection who felt that this dire result might come about. In less than a decade after The Methodist Episcopal Church was founded there were stirrings of protest against the aristocracy of the itinerancy, but the effects of this protest could be stayed for a spell because the West was still out there and there was an immense and assigned task for the preachers to accomplish. The prospects of growth and development looked good, especially at the opening up of a bright new century. There was tumultuous excitement on the frontier. A series of great revival meetings began, sweeping men by the thousands into the Kingdom. Decisions that had to do with the structure of the Church could wait. The promise of growth through the conversion of men en masse and by the wholesale was at hand.

XI Frolic of Faith: Camp Meetings

During the early 1800's there occurred in the groves and forests of America a succession of religious festivals called variously the Great Revival in the West, the Kentucky Revival, and the Scotch-Irish Revival.

In terms of masses involved, methods used, and fellowship generated, these festivals knew no precedent. They were reminiscent of the Great Awakening, a series of revivals in colonial days under the preaching of Jonathan Edwards and George Whitefield, a Methodist and a close companion of John Wesley from the days of the Holy Club and the man who had persuaded Mr. Wesley to leave the pulpit and preach to people in the fields.[1] The western assemblies had precedents, but they also had new and striking elements that added both to the appeal and excitement. They brought together people of all ages, male and female, mostly white but with some black, and let them dwell together as neighbors day and night, sometimes for a week in seasons when the weather was good. The gatherings gave rise to a widely used technical term to distinguish them from earlier revivals: camp meeting was the term, and it described a religious assembly on a given day at an appointed place, announced well in advance, with the understanding that as many persons as possible would congregate with bedding and provisions, fully prepared to stay until the closing song.

To the joy of coming together in a vast concourse of people the advance notice added the lure of anticipation, of planning the trip, of looking forward to new adventures—and these among friendly strangers. Children would find new playmates and new games, possibly learn fresh mischief. Men would brag and talk big at a safe distance from the scene of their stories. Even pinched and bedraggled wives would get a change in setting for their unrelenting routines. Young people brought the glances that back home they took to dances and there would at least be chances to touch if only in some brief encounter. No matter how earnest their purpose in coming, those who came would be in a holiday mood on arrival, busy with make-ready and make-do, the very act of laying out the camp yoking them to others in a camaraderie that thrilled the marrow.

Religion provided the setting for these great gatherings, and only religion could lend sanction to what took place. It transformed pleasure into a virtue. The people who reached the grounds had traveled long distances from remote cabins or scrawny villages and they found themselves in a city with neighbors as close as the next tent and with milling and marching thousands to join with in the frolic of faith. The very numbers brought exhilaration to lonely souls, many of whom had not been in a crowd before.

There was no body-count to tell the size of the crowds until the Methodists later adopted the camp meetings as one of their methods and began to report statistics. Estimates by observers, however, indicated that the average assembly would draw five thousand to ten thousand. At the largest of all there were said to be twenty-five thousand. Depopulated areas round about gave a more reliable clue to how the meetings drew. "Age snatched his crutch, Youth forgot his pastime, the laborer quitted his task." So ran a saying of the period. "The crops were forgotten, the cabins were deserted, and in large settlements there did not remain one soul."[2]

The fact that settlers could travel long distances safely and leave their holdings at home unprotected was enough to give a special note of gaiety to the rustic gatherings. For the first time since the beginning of the movement west the settlers were free to make journeys with only normal hazards and hardships along rutty roads and over scratchy trails. Indians no longer lurked in the woods. Only a few years before the period of the first camp meetings two treaties had guaranteed a period of peace. This blessing had been visited upon the land through the energetic efforts of soldiers and politicians. It had not come from on high, and yet there would appear to be almost a note of providential planning in it.

Mad Anthony Wayne had defeated the Northwest Indians at the battle of Fallen Timbers and had negotiated in 1795 with twelve of the tribes the Treaty of Greenville, named after the Ohio fort from which Wayne had conducted his campaign. By this treaty the Indians ceded vast areas of land to the whites in southern and western Ohio. A definite boundary had been established to mark off Indian territory and to establish sections in which the whites would not be attacked. A second treaty, negotiated with Great Britain through the patient offices of John Jay, further extended the safety area of the whites. One provision of the Jay Treaty was that the British agreed to quit six forts they had continued to hold in United States territory after the Revolution. From these forts the British had been able to supply the Indians for forays against the encroaching whites. Obedient to the Jay Treaty, the forts were evacuated in 1796, and the settlers no longer had to reckon constantly with the chance of Indian attacks. In brief, settlers could go and come and they could assemble. The result was that those who reached the camp-meeting sites were living at a time of what one historian of the West describes as hysterical thankfulness.[3]

Other circumstances helped to create, in the region where the revivals commenced, a fitting and plausible background for the excitement that followed. The inveterate lawlessness of parts of Kentucky invited the wrath of God as surely as did Sodom and Gomorrah. Logan County, in particular, had become such a refuge for scoundrels that it was known far and wide as Rogues' Harbor, offering hospice to murderers, horse thieves, highway robbers, runaway indentured servants, and other assorted fugitives who had come to the place to lose their identity. Rogues' Harbor called for an avenging broom wielded by the servants of the Lord, no less, to clean the place of putridity and filth.

Then, too, there was present in Kentucky and Tennessee at the time a considerable contingent commonly and colloquially called Scotch-Irish. They were lowland Scots originally and they were dubbed Irish because they had settled in Northern Ireland as part of a colonizing project James I had started at the same time settlers went to Virginia. They had found conditions in Northern Ireland intolerable and early in the eighteenth century they had begun migrating in droves to America.

The Scots-Irish were men and women of smoldering intensity, long apostate from the faith of their forebears. Whatever the degree or nature of their wickedness, they were haunted one and all by the memory of conscience. In their blood ran both the Teutonic and the Celtic strains, "combining the shrewd practical common sense and intelligent purpose of the Teuton with the strong emotionalism of the Celt." Both common sense and emotion showed them the error of their ways as they drifted in the dereliction of the frontier. They had come to live more and more in what they knew to be open violation of that "stern but strongly ethical religion in which they and their forefathers who followed Knox and Calvin had been reared."[4]

The time had come and now was when men of conscience and of no conscience at all would confront the claims of the Lord. These claims were brought and laid like a subpoena before the residents of Logan County, Kentucky, during the last years of the eighteenth century by a man of terrifying visage and thundering voice. He was a Scots-Irish Presbyterian preacher named James McGready. "His person was not prepossessing," a contemporary tells us, "nor his appearance interesting, except his remarkable gravity, and small piercing eyes. His coarse, tremulous voice excited in me the idea of something unearthly.

His gestures were the reverse of elegance. Everything appeared by him forgotten but the salvation of souls."[5]

Here was a Scourge of God to outdo an Attila. McGready preached a doctrine repugnant to his orthodox Presbyterian brothers but familiar and heart-warming to the Methodists. He stressed conversion and the new birth and knowing exactly when it came. He added an emphasis of his own out of the Puritan harshness of Jonathan Edwards and his description of sinners in the hands of an angry God. McGready spared no man's feelings. He "sounded forth clear and strong and terrible in fearful denunciation . . . of impenitent sinners." The fiery prophet and the evil-doers of Rogues' Harbor could understand each other. McGready brought the message of demand. The choice was *this* or *that*. Clean up your rotten life or go to hell. Extremes met and became means. There was no purgatory of in-between. Rogues must repent. And to the apostasy of the Scots-Irish he addressed himself with equal vigor, calling down on them everlasting doom if they did not change their ways.

Born in western Pennsylvania around 1758, McGready was a creature of the frontier. He had been brought up in the Carolinas. His rough-hewn gospel bore no resemblance to the pious aristocracy of the Calvinists. The man was no theologian, anyway, but a moralist with religious fervor and with the conviction that men needed religion to live straight. His method was to bang their heads together and make them think. In the Carolinas he was accused of "running people distracted and diverting them from their necessary vocations." Opposition mounted until enemies tore away and burned his pulpit and sent him a threatening letter written in blood.[6]

In 1796 he had accepted a call from three small churches in Logan County, Kentucky. He was received well, finding there some of the hearers he had impressed in the early days of his preaching. They knew the severity of his intent and aided him as he went about carrying it out. He wanted a flaming revival of religion that would ignite the county and sweep on to other sections of the country. For McGready was more than a mere preacher. He was an evangelist, a man who thought in masses. The Lord worked best in a crowd. Nothing short of an earth-shaking event would suffice to turn a wicked and willful country toward the Kingdom.

With impassioned preaching McGready combined personal visits to the faithful, pledging them to pray every Saturday evening and to devote the third Saturday of each month for a whole year to prayer and fasting that the Holy Spirit might visit Logan County and the world with a great awakening. It took almost a year of waiting on the Lord before a revival did come to one of the points on his circuit, the Gasper River congregation. Enthusiasm ran high, showing what could be done, but there was opposition and coldness, doubtless inspired by the Devil but expressing itself in the work of a staid Presbyterian minister who went about sowing seeds of sobriety.

It was nearly three years before the fire fell again. Then in June 1800 an awakening shook the Red River Church, where some five hundred persons turned up for services that continued from Friday through Monday. Crowds overflowed the building. Emotions were intense and some remarkable physical responses began to appear. Many swooned and fell under the impact of the preaching and exhorting. One preacher who had come as an observer got caught up in the excitement and went through the house "shouting and exhorting with all possible ecstasy and energy and the floor was soon covered with the slain."[7]

Still the camp meeting had not appeared. Only one man had brought provisions in his wagon. The rest had had to shift for themselves or beg or forage in the surrounding countryside. Obviously, the time had come to pitch for larger crowds, and McGready knew the moment. He announced a meeting to be held at the Gasper River Church the last week of July. For more than a month news of the coming event spread up the creeks and down the hollows. People were invited to come and bring their grub and bedding and stay for the duration. They responded, flocking to the grounds around the church from as far as a hundred miles away, starved for companionship in a society of isolated settlements, lured by the prospect of an anything-goes religion.

Gasper River was the setting of the first camp meeting, and for instituting the institution James McGready gets full and un-challenged credit. Thirteen wagons loaded with people and provisions turned up. The next month twenty-two wagons came to a meeting at the Muddy River Church, while many others came on foot, "provided for encamping." One meeting followed and emulated and improved on the one before. The largest and most spectacular was held at Cane Ridge, Bourbon County, in August 1801. It began on Friday and continued for six days and nights. For two days before it opened the roads approaching Cane Ridge were filled with wagons and carriages and with men and women on horseback and walking. A visitor who arrived on Saturday gave his sister in Philadelphia a word picture she could understand: "I first proceeded to count the waggons containing families, with their provisions, camp equipage, &c, to the number of 147. At 11 o'clock the quantity of ground occupied by horses, waggons, etc, was about the same size as the Square between Market, Chestnut, Second and Third streets of Philadelphia."[8]

While the meeting at Cane Ridge was a joint enterprise of the Presbyterians and the Methodists, and a number of preachers cooperated, its planning was chiefly the work of Barton W. Stone, who in his youth had been converted under the early evangelistic work of James McGready. Stone had studied the meetings of McGready and caught some of his inspiration. For Cane Ridge he had sent out invitations urging people in Tennessee and Ohio, as well as from all parts of Kentucky, to attend.

The whole series of meetings that spread through Kentucky and Tennessee between 1800 and 1805 cannot be dissociated from James McGready and men of like mind and power. These men could take pride that Providence had attended and used them, for there had come to pass a gigantic event which caught and held the gaze of people throughout the United States and in Europe. A sweeping revival of religion had been long a consummation devoutly prayed for. Around 1796, Christians in both Europe and America had "united in a quarterly concert of prayer for a revival of religion in the world and for a more general propagation of the gospel. In the Presbyterian church, the year 1796 was marked beyond all others by official calls to fasting and prayer by presbyteries, synods, and the General Assembly for the outpouring of the Holy Spirit. A large number of congregations in western Pennsylvania had drawn up written convenants to pray for a revival."[9]

Until Gasper River the petitions and covenants appeared to have been in vain. Sporadic and intermittent revivals had broken out here and there but not with the contagion required to make a movement. Then, as if in answer to world prayer, the second great awakening had begun in Kentucky, where you would least expect it. It had begun also at a time when it was least to be expected. The apathy and coldness in the churches since the Revolution were matched and echoed by indifference outside the churches and the scorn of the lawless. Antireligious views provoked by the French deists and dramatized by the aggressive atheism of the French Revolution were widespread. Nothing big was happening in religion, nothing to rate public attention. The camp meetings made the headlines. Writers from all over the country and from abroad came to see and hear. What they wrote was often derisive, dealing with the frenzy and the excesses, but it made the news and got attention where there had not been attention before.

The Kentucky Revival spread the idea and ideas of religion to a section starved for social life and sentiment and it tied the two together and helped to make religion a part of the norm. In spite of the staunch efforts of the Presbyterian, Baptist, and Methodist preachers, the West in the early 1800's lacked the apparatus and the occasions of faith. The revivals exposed the settlers to views and teachings they had forgot and that they needed to be reminded of frequently if they were to remember them at all. In a sparsely settled land, but one growing more populous, and now at peace so that people could congregate, the camp meeting offered a vehicle by which religious ideas could travel, and travel fast, from one section to the other. It gave sections divided at least a modicum of experience in common.

XII Released by the Lord

The early camp meetings formed a sluice through which an incredible abundance of energy flowed—from out of history and social circumstance, from out there, from God knows where. They belonged to a particular time, and yet there was much of the immemorial in them. They linked the people of the West with the rites of ancient times and identified them with the devout of other and of unheard-of faiths. The setting was druidic. The word *druid* comes from an early English word for oak. The religion of the Celts belonged to the forests and its priests and wise men were of the forest, performed their ceremonies in groves. The association between the camp meetings and the ceremonies of the Druids was not conscious, much less acknowledged, but it may have been part of a deeply repeated religious experience.

Was there some consanguinity with England that went back thousands of years before the days of John Wesley? The camp meeting could be said to be a peculiar American institution, suited only to the singular circumstances of the land of its origin. Yet Mad Lorenzo Dow and his beloved Peggy took it to urban England, where it had no business being at all, and it caused so much excitement that it split the Wesleyan Methodist connection there asunder. Officially the Wesleyan Conference declared, so soon after the days of Mr. Wesley, that open-air preaching to the poor and uneducated was a thing "highly improper in England." Nonetheless the English adaptation of the camp meeting went forward. Two British Methodists, Hugh Bourne, a layman, and William Cleves, a local preacher, were expelled from the connection when they continued to hold open-air revivals. A considerable following joined them in their enthusiasm and formed the Primitive Methodist Church. It became in time the largest grouping of Methodists outside the connection. At revivals held in England, Scotland, Ireland, and Wales the Primitives sang American camp-meeting songs and other spirited tunes of their own devising. Their singing and their antics caused them to be called Ranters.[1]

Further basic and primitive qualities that tied the pioneers in with the religions of mankind could be noted. Those who took part in the western revivals cannot fail to have known through their familiarity with the Old Testament that the holy places of the early Hebrews were holy spaces. Jehovah dwelt outdoors. He was a God of hills and streams, deserts and wilderness until priesthoods put him indoors for their convenience. In the outdoor revivals of the West people were once again worshiping in space. God had a natural setting. There was a mysterious psychic connection between men and women on the frontier making peace with their Maker and the wandering Jews of the days of Moses and Aaron. It was a fellowship that broke all barriers of time.

Strange uniting factors were at work, not only drawing people together in vast crowds from wide distances but also encouraging them to step across barriers that bristled with intensity or had become fixed by long custom. Often the scene suggested a great cathedral with pillars of trees, medieval in its effect, but in the main the camp meeting offered a church without doors or formalities. Men and women of all persuasions took part. A Methodist preacher, John McGee, had helped James McGready, a Presbyterian, conduct his first stirring revival. As time passed and the number of assemblies increased, Presbyterian, Baptist, and Methodist preachers worked side by side, and McGready was able to exclaim triumphantly "that bigotry and prejudice have received a death wound . . . Presbyterians and Methodists love one another."[2]

The future of interdenominational harmony looked rosy during the first surge of the meetings. Enthusiasm for a new method and the excitement of bringing great numbers into the fold at once made rivalries for the once unimportant. There was promise of a wider brotherhood among believers. In the sacramental services which were a feature of the meetings, the Baptists would withdraw for their closed fellowship, but the Methodists and Presbyterians would hold communion at a common altar.

One of the first sights to catch the eye of a voluble observer at Cane Ridge was that of an assembly of black people being exhorted by a man of their own color, "some of whom appeared deeply convicted and others converted." There was room for all on the grounds under the stars. In both slaveholding and non-slaveholding states and territories blacks were allowed to attend the meetings, setting up their own camp behind the preacher's rostrum. Often in the excitement, increased by the presence of the blacks, the services of the two groups flowed together, and Charles A. Johnson in his study of the frontier camp meeting tells us that later, when the section for slaves was separated by a plank partition, the barrier was torn down on the final meeting day and the two peoples joined in a song festival and marching ceremony.[3]

The camp meetings permitted and even encouraged attitudes and acts that had not been permitted before. The indulgence granted women had no precedent in religious circles. There had been protracted outdoor gatherings at the time of the Revolution, such as those conducted by a Baptist preacher named John Waller, and they bore certain similarities to those that came later. But the earlier gatherings had been for men only. In the book of rules drawn up by Waller, women were not allowed to enter the grounds from an hour before sunset

until an hour after sunrise.⁴ When the all-day-and-all-night affairs got under way at the time of Cane Ridge, however,
women were welcome on equal terms with men.

True, they were separated in the main assemblies by a rail
and sometimes by a fence. But they were not separated in
experience. They were invited to get religion along with the
men, and once the women were in the process of getting it,
you couldn't tell them to stay in their places and behave themselves and act like ladies. You couldn't police posture. Women
"in their frantic agitations" sometimes "unconsciously tore open
their bosoms and assumed indelicate attitudes." One writer tells
us that women threw themselves on the ground in suggestive
positions, that they treated clothes as an encumbrance, and that
under the ecstasy induced by the circumstances they hugged
and kissed everyone within reach.⁵

Under the intense and vibrant emotions sanctioned, the camp
meetings in an uncanny way forecast change in behavior patterns and societal forms. The informal cities they created in a
completely rural environment adumbrated, in fact demonstrated,
some of the problems of urban life. Bring a lot of people of
all ages and both sexes into a marked enclosure and you have
vexations and delights that you didn't have before. Propinquity
led to familiarity and access led to sex adventures that shocked
the proper, alarmed camp leaders, and armed the critics, who
knew and said that such things were bound to happen.

Cane Ridge, setting of the biggest assembly, was the scene
of the most immoralities. After the Saturday evening service
six men were found lying under a preaching stand with a
woman who did not have religion of the sort that was being
preached and practiced. The next evening a couple was caught
in the act of adultery.⁶ What went on outside the grounds and
around the edges was nobody's business and impossible to
control. Often, some leaders charged, these goings-on were designed to discredit the services and give the meetings a bad
name. The unprecedented crowds drew to the borders of the
unfenced enclosures harpies, hustlers, whores, hangers-on, riffraff,

whiskey peddlers. Other peddlers slyly bent on legitimate gain entered the camps, mingling with the folks, plying whatever trade they had. Book agents offered their wares, and barbers and bootblacks their services. It was heaven for anybody who wanted to make a fast "buck," the name given a dollar because the buck's skin is larger than the doe's. Sometimes the preachers would announce the professional interests of the converts, one saying that there was a man present who desired to pull teeth. An observer reported that he had seen a man bustling from tent to tent, passing out printed notices of a headache remedy.[7]

The very size of the crowds attracted larger crowds. The meetings also had the added lure of dumfounding physical demonstrations. Spectators came to see individuals shaken as if by an elemental force and turned into something other than ordinary human beings. Not only did men and women get religion; they had convulsions, were changed outwardly as well as within.

There had been religious frenzy and tales of frenzy before— as at the time of the First Crusade. But now there was no foe but the Devil within to attack, no tomb to be rescued from the infidel, no immediate goal for concerted action. On the frontier everything was intensely individual, and there was no way for deeply stirred emotion to vent itself save through strenuous muscular response.

The motor phenomena attending the early camp meetings were, as one solemn social scientist confesses, unearthly and inexplicable enough to awe even the sophisticated mind. An analyst would be hard put to explain the practice of holy barking, unless he speculated that the victim was a reincarnated werewolf. A person would drop to his all fours and run around snapping and growling and making gutteral sounds similar to the barking of a dog. Some barked in the manner of a mastiff so long that they became hoarse and sounded more than ever like a mastiff.

Other breeds were also represented. A preacher in lower Kentucky reported that "it was common to see people barking

like a flock of spaniels on their way to meeting." They might
remain quiet for a while at meeting and then "start up suddenly
in a fit of barking, rush out, roam around, and in a short time
come barking and foaming back."[8] The barking mania affected
children in particular, and among them may have been a form
of mischievous mimicry. But it was not confined to children. It
was said to be not uncommon to see numbers of men gathered
about a tree, barking, yelping, "treeing the devil."

The manifestations of persons enduring the duress of terrible
emotions were naturally influenced by the images of their daily
experience or of the experience of the period. The revivals sprang
up not long after the Revolution and immediately after warfare
with the Indians, when death by gunshot was common. Most
casually accepted of the remarkable behavior during the early
meetings was the act of falling as though struck down in battle.
The nomenclature of the meetings in songs and in preaching was
military. Preachers "poured hot shot into Satan's ranks." Men
were mowed down by cannon fire. The grounds would be covered with the slain. Figures of speech stressed the victims as
casualties of combat, of sudden death, for the attacks came on
swiftly. A man or woman might be listening to the exhortations
of the preacher and in an instant fall to the ground and lie there
to all appearances lifeless for fifteen minutes to six or eight or
ten hours. A witness at Cane Ridge claims to have seen as many
as eight hundred struck down. Falling became so commonplace
that it caused no interruption of the service, "save as it became
necessary to remove those who fell to a place of safety where
they would not be trampled upon." There they "were laid out
like so many corpses."[9]

There was plenty of time to study the symptoms of the
slain and there were enough cases to provide the curious with
a basis for clinical analysis. For some there was no warning
before the fall, with others the fall was preceded by a tremor
or a prickly sensation in the hands and feet. "The heart swells,
liking to burst the body; occasions shortness and quickness of
breath," one witness said. Whether warned or not, the victims

fell to the ground helpless, "convulsed through their whole frame as if in the agonies of death." An apparently breathless and motionless state followed. Barton W. Stone, who engineered the giant meeting at Cane Ridge, wrote: "The pulse becomes weak and they draw a difficult breath about once a minute; in some instances their extremities become cold, and pulsations, and all signs of life forsake them for nearly an hour." Then they might again show signs of life—"by a deep groan or piercing shriek or by a prayer for mercy fervently uttered."[10] Afterward they might continue to lie motionless for hours, the man or woman smitten having made known as a rule the wish to be stretched out on his or her back.

Not all who fell lay supine. "Some talked, but could not move. Some, shrieking in agony, bounded about like a live fish out of water. Many lay down and rolled over and over for hours at a time. Others rushed wildly over the stumps and benches, and then plunged, shouting 'Lost! Lost!' into the forest."[11] One who fell occasioned the great solicitude on the part of those not at the moment affected. They would swarm around the fallen, "laughing, leaping, sobbing, shouting, swooning." A preacher who kept a diary said: "If the assembly were languid, a few shrieks and one or two instances of falling would quickly arouse them, and as far in either direction as the people could see or hear, others would be caught in the contagion and would likewise fall. . . ."[12]

The oral response to the experience of falling and of emerging from it showed wide variety. Some would lie silent without moving the lips and then, according to Stone, "rise, shouting deliverance." Others, after lying for a while, began to "speak in an astonishing manner as to length of time, matter, and loudness of voice. Some of the most powerful sermons I have heard from mortals," said one observer, "come from persons on the above description, unable to help themselves. Some have spoken almost without cessation for the space of five hours, and some parts of the time so loud that they might be heard for the distance of a mile."[13] Preachers would have to suspend their own exhortations until those coming out of the coma of faith had delivered their messages from the upper world.

All who came out of the deep world of falling testified that they had felt no bodily pain from any source, either from striking obstacles as they fell or from forms of torture tried experimentally on them while they were under. A wide range of response, however, marked the inner experience of those who fell. Some said that "they had the entire use of their reason and reflection, and, when recovered, they could relate everything that had been said or done to them." Others "had seen visions, heard unspeakable words, smelled fragrant odors, and had a delightful singing in the breast."

Violent physical reactions to the excitement of the revivals increased as they spread to an ever wider region on the frontier. In Tennessee appeared a new exercise that was dubbed the jerks. At first it was mild, confined to a spasmodic jerking of the forearm at short intervals, but its intensity grew with the spread of the meetings, and in time jerking "affected every muscle, nerve, and tendon in the body."

Whoever was smitten went out of control, whether incorrigible sinner or eager seeker. "Nothing could better represent this strange and unaccountable operation," said one eyewitness,

> than for one to goad another, alternately on every side with a piece of red-hot iron. The exercise commonly began in the head which would fly backward and forward, and from side to side with a quick jolt which the person would naturally labor to suppress but in vain, and the more any one labored to stay himself and be sober the more he staggered and the more rapidly his twitches increased. . . . Sometimes the head would be twitched right and left to a half round with such velocity that not a feature could be discovered, but the face appeared as much behind as before, and in the quick progressive jerk, it would seem as if the person was transmuted into some other species of creature.[14]

Peter Cartwright said that he had seen as many as five hundred persons jerking at one time. Those who thought the agitation ridiculous would in turn be seized in the manner of a man trying not to stutter in the presence of a stutterer. The exercise was most prominent at the forest revivals but it had a way of getting beyond the meetings. A Presbyterian preacher of the day heard that a neighboring congregation was afflicted and he went to remonstrate. He was "seized himself while addressing them, and upon returning home communicated the malady to his own people assembled to hear the report of his visit."[15]

Most convincing was the contagious effect on those who merely visited the camps out of curiosity or to deride. Proud young gentlemen and young ladies, "dressed in their silks, jewelry, and prunella, from top to toe," would turn up and it amused Cartwright to see them suddenly take the jerks. "The first jerk or so you would see their fine bonnets, caps and combs fly and so sudden would be the jerking of the head that their long loose hair would crack almost as loud as a waggoner's whip."[16]

As in the case of falling, those shaking with the jerks under the conviction of sin often reported inner tranquillity during the spells. Some told an interviewer that they had experienced the happiest moments of their lives. It was a point the casual visitor would overlook, being beguiled by the physical phenomena that marked the meetings. Outward violence could be accompanied by inward peace, and the tremendous commotion of the outdoor gatherings had, under pioneer circumstances, a chastening and exhilarating effect on the inward man. In a way that seemed incomprehensible to many, but perhaps in the only way possible at the time, the roaring camp meetings of the early 1800's induced reflection, examination, assessment of self, a reverent recognition of the inscrutable.

James B. Finley visited Cane Ridge when he was a young man of twenty—and for no reason but to gape. He had no interest in religion. He was given to games, would fight at the drop of a hat and often did, took a dram now and then, and rousted when he pleased. The spectacle of the meeting impressed him not at all at first, save for the noise, which he thought must be like the roar of Niagara Falls. There were more than a thousand shouting at once and the sound carried for miles. When he arrived and looked around he felt that he was in "a vast sea of human beings, which seemed to be agitated as if by a storm." Some of the people were singing, others praying, some crying for mercy "in the most piteous accents." Soon he began to comprehend that "a strange supernatural power seemed to pervade the mass of mind there collected. While witnessing these scenes, a peculiarly-strange sensation, such as I had never felt before, came over me. My heart beat tumultuously, my knees trembled, my lips quivered, and I felt as though I must fall to the ground."

Finding himself about to be overwhelmed, Finley fled to the woods and there tried to man up his courage. After a while he returned to the scene of the excitement, "the waves of which, if possible, had risen higher. The same awful feeling came over me," he records. He stepped up on a log, where he could get a better view. The scene that presented itself was indescribable. "At one time I saw at least 500 swept down in a moment, as if a battery of a thousand guns had opened up on them, and then immediately followed shrieks and shouts that rent the very heavens. I fled into the woods a second time, and wished I had stayed home."

On his second flight to the woods Finley manned up his courage with alcohol, but the dram he took did not help. He did not return to the campgrounds but walked alone until dark, when he crawled under the hay in a barn and spent a miserable night. Next morning he told the friend who had ridden in with him that he wanted to quit the place and head for home. They rode in silence until toward the end of the day, when Finley burst into tears, lamenting and repenting his unguided and sinful life. He wept through the night and at dawn went deeper into the woods to pray. His conversion followed, and later he got the call to preach.[17]

136

Finley's experience suggested that, in assessing the meetings, men had to reckon with the post-hypnotic effects as well as the conversions that took place on the campgrounds. After the Great Revival in the West the Baptists added ten thousand members to their rolls and the Methodists a like number. To outsiders, what caught the eye were the symptoms of disorder, but to the devout these symptoms were accompanied by a harvest of results, and the results argued that the camp meetings were good and of God. In the West the prophets of the Lord had harkened to the experience of Elijah. A great and strong wind had rent the mountains and did break in pieces the rocks, but the Lord was not in the wind, nor in the earthquake or in the fire that followed. But often there had followed these great convulsions a still small voice, and men had to admit that the Lord was in the still, small voice of inner change.

XIII The Meetings Come to Order

"My continual cry to the presiding elders is order, order, good order. All things must be arranged temporally and spiritually like a well disciplined army."[1]

So spoke Bishop Asbury when he heard the tiding of the Great Revival in the West. The meetings were unruly, attended by too much that was muscular. But they had unleashed a power for good not heard of before, and they were not to be dismissed or opposed but brought under control. The bishop watched and encouraged the meetings from the outset. After the Kentucky Revival had spent its first force around 1805 and the effect threatened to evaporate, gone with the wind that had swept the frontier, The Methodist Episcopal Church captured much of the energy that had been generated and put it into well-built conduits. It appropriated a religious form of proven appeal and worked the main features of it into a kind of mobile ark to go along with the people as they moved west. It imposed stern rules and regulations, enforced propriety where there had been laxity before, and made the spruced-up camp meeting a chief instrument of its program of expansion.

For almost four decades after 1805 the Methodists were the only denomination to use the camp meeting extensively and regularly. The Baptists, although put off by the extravagances, exhibited fervid interest, but they lacked the national organization to give continuity to a campaign and their efforts were bound to be local and spasmodic. The Congregationalists showed no interest in a form that appealed to the multitude; rather they looked with scorn upon its antics and theatrics. Although Presbyterian preachers aroused the first interest and carried the revival to its climax, they were distinctly irregular and atypical, not to say freakish, as Presbyterians. Revivalism among the masses was no natural part of the Presbyterian system. The Synod of Kentucky, ruling body of the region where the camp meetings started, looked with official horror on the preachers who took part. These preachers were members of the Cumberland Presbytery, governing agency of the immediate area, and when the Presbytery later relaxed some of its educational requirements for the ministry, the Synod of Kentucky first censured the lower body and then in 1806 dissolved it. Four years later the Cumberland Presbytery withdrew from the general body of Presbyterians and set up an independent church.[2]

Among the Methodists there had not been so much as a murmur of misgiving about the camp meetings. They were familiar with some of the phenomena that appeared in the gatherings in the groves. Falling was one. They had in their own revivals and sometimes in ordinary services seen men and women sink to the floor and lose consciousness under the stress of religious experience. There had been occasions on which an entire congregation had fallen. Not a few of the itinerants active during the time of the Kentucky Revival had been smitten. William Burke, who was supervising the work of Methodism in parts of Kentucky during the early 1800's, had fallen senseless to the floor at the time of his conversion and knew nothing until he found himself on his feet giving glory to God "in loudest strains."[3] The Methodists were not strangers to passion in religion and not at all disinclined to prod the emotions deliberately in the hope of breaking through a man's protective hide of indifference. Mr. Wesley had called the prodding heart-work, and critics in England had charged his workers with being energumens.[4]

The noise of the camp meetings and the joys of fellowship offered drew people to a religious service who would never darken the door of a church or chapel. The unregenerate would, out of curiosity if no better reason, attend the meetings in the open air. Once on the grounds the preachers could confront them with the penalties of godless living. Otherwise they would not be touched at all. Disorders might accompany the meetings, but the good would be likely to outweigh the bad, and the thing to do from the Methodist point of view was to forestall the disorders, not abandon the gatherings simply because they had a few bad features.

Two months after James McGready held his first camp meeting, Bishop Asbury and William McKendree, presiding elder over a wide domain in Kentucky, took part in an outdoor revival held by Presbyterians on Drake's Creek in Tennessee. Both men were mightily impressed. Not long afterward McKendree united his forces with the Presbyterians who were trying out the new form of service, cooperating to the extent of helping to form joint committees to make camp regulations and select speakers. For a while he even suspended the required and unalterable class meetings and the regular operation of the itinerant system in order that full attention might be given to the sessions in the forest.[5]

Asbury, being a bishop, was in an even better position to promote the new form. In January 1801, three months after he had seen his first revival in a sylvan setting, he noted news from New York, Pennsylvania, Maryland, Delaware, and Vermont "of a work of God equal to that in Cumberland." He began a series of newsletters to the itinerants in which he hailed the meeting as "a pleasing, growing prospect." His enthusiasm waxed as he heard reports of results. He saw the new type of revival as a remarkable means of harvesting humans, saying: "God has given us hundreds in 1800, why not thousands in 1801, yea, why not a million if we had faith? Lord, increase our faith."[6]

The bishop referred to the outdoor revivals as field fighting and as fishing with a large net. He rode herd on his preachers and presiding elders, urging them to report the camp meetings held in the course of a year, "the numbers attending, souls professing converting grace, days of continuance." In 1806 the presiding elders of Delaware planned to have one hundred days of camp meetings during the year. They were able to tell him, however, of not 100 but of 150 days and nights in the woods and a total of 5368 converted. Everywhere interest grew, fanned by the bellows of the bishop. He wrote Coke that he hoped the year 1810 would bring as many as six hundred outdoor revivals, adding in a kind of ecstasy of expectation suited to the spirit of the gatherings he praised: "Campmeetings, campmeetings, Oh Glory, Glory!"[7]

Such was the incoherent exuberance of an administrator mild in manner and dignified in demeanor. He was caught up in the excitement as much as any convert. He made it his business to move the new form east and have it tried out near cities. Not long after Cane Ridge the bishop expressed the wish that the Baltimore preachers "hold one out in the plain south of town, and let the people come with their tents, wagons, provisions. . . . Let them keep at it night and day."[8] He did not hesitate to give specific instructions and stage directions. The towns and cities were very dead, he reported, and it was necessary to use extraordinary means to reach them. There must be great crowds before the law of averages went into effect and at least some could be rescued from their waywardness.

Embodying the norms of Methodism, Bishop Asbury combined orderliness with zeal, carrying both the torch and the T square. If the camp meetings were to become Methodist, they would have to become methodistic, strict in form and reliable in plan and structure. Father Asbury did his best to have the camp meeting incorporated in the chart of the Church, so that preachers would actually be required to hold outdoor revivals as a part of their work. He did not succeed but he did manage to have camp meetings held in conjunction with conferences—the last quarterly conference of the year, which met in the spring and the Annual Conferences, which met in the summer. The arrangement was not altogether popular, as the journals of some of the preachers show. One, Benjamin Lakin, had some acid comments to make about sleeping in the woods at the Annual Conference when he looked forward to a few decencies and amenities and a chance to sleep in a good bed several nights running at the yearly meeting of the preachers.

The four-day period was standardized. Meetings ran from Friday afternoon or evening until Monday. People got readily accustomed to the routine. It was said that "the good people go to camp meetings on Friday, backsliders Saturday, rowdies Saturday night, and gentlemen and lady sinners on Sunday."[9] So schemed were the services that the preaching was not only scheduled but graded by the time the speaker was put up. Those who led the opening services on Friday night were known to be third-rate platform performers. You knew that the preachers who took the 8 A.M. service next day would be better, but not the best. It was understood that those who spoke at 11 o'clock would be the "intellectual Samsons" of the encamped gathering. Plans went even further: "Work schedules were arranged in shifts so that some of the preachers slept while others labored in the pulpit. Leaders took their places at the speaker's stand, the exhorters were strategically located in the audience, and aids to the penitents stood waiting at the altar."[10]

Even before the meetings became highly regulated, there had been a gradual tidying up of circumstances, and for one of the most notable improvements an itinerant could claim credit. This was the establishment of the Mourners' Bench. Mourner was the name given by Methodists to penitents, persons who were convicted of sin and willing to talk over the state of their souls but not ready to make the decision that would turn them into true converts. Before the day of the Mourners' Bench workers would move through the congregation and seek out penitents. A reflective Methodist itinerant named Valentine Cook got the idea of setting up a rough and rude altar at the front of the meeting place. All who were willing to take the first step toward the Kingdom were invited to come forward and signify their willingness to be waited upon by the workers.[11] It was a convenient arrangement for those who were smitten but had not lost consciousness, and it did much to lend some order to the services without restraining or confining the mourners. It helped also by encouraging prospects to take definite and purposive steps forward and toward the preacher and the altar, a place of decision. Getting people to move in the right direction was essential to the success of any evangelistic meeting.

Rules for policing the premises as well as ordering the services were clearly drawn and widely distributed. Again the hand of Asbury could be seen at work. He warned the leaders of the meetings to be "as wise as serpents" and not to let any scandal or impropriety mark the proceedings. The rules were printed and distributed at the first service and, for good measure, read by preachers or laymen. In some cases they were even sent out well in advance, posted prominently on trees along the roads that led to the camp sites. The wayfaring man, even though he be a fool, knew what to expect. One critic of the Methodists' "peculiar love of legislation" poked fun at them for converting trees into "lettered pillars . . . inscribed with the twelve tables of the camp code."[12]

Once drawn, the rules were as fixed as the laws of the Medes and Persians. The all-night meetings of the earlier days, when worshipers took over after the preachers had gone to bed, were forbidden. There was a curfew at ten, although the word, taking its meaning from a medieval practice of putting out the fires at a fixed hour, did not apply. The fires and candles and torches were left burning to light the grounds. There was a watch to see that strangers did not stay in the encampment, that women were not allowed to stray from the grounds after dark. Guards with identifying armbands and carrying, at Bishop Asbury's suggestion, white peeled rods, roamed the camp after others had gone to bed. Candles were kept burning inside tents. Darkness was not allowed. In short, those who attended a

Methodist camp meeting had to shape up. One foreign visitor had to admit that, even though there might be a slip now and then, the Methodists contended with all their strength against irregularities.

They stabilized the camp meeting further by housing part of the sites. Tabernacles appeared in the wilderness. As early as 1809 Bishop Asbury began to take thought of the morrow and to urge permanence. It was progress in the making. He laid out plans as detailed as a blueprint. You could see them grow in the great man's mind as he suggested first that there be a good floor, strong benches, a partition "to continue the customary separation of the men and the women." There should be sides to a height of about five feet. And then, come to think of it, there might as well be a roof to keep the floor dry and to prevent the ground under it from getting damp.[13] It was the start of a building program that went on for years and led to some elaborate establishments, as at Ocean Grove and Asbury Park, New Jersey, and on a spit of land poking out into Lake Chautauqua, New York.

In time the camp meeting under Methodist auspices became so respectable that some of the petty sins of affluence began to appear—and to be freely commented upon. Women were putting on airs with food, competing in such things as cakes, preserves, chickens, and hams. It was pointed out that, once the camps were well set up, women spent a good deal of time preparing food while services were going on, getting ready for the noon meal instead of listening to the preacher. To curb extravagance and preoccupation with food one editor counseled simplicity and the preparation of as much food as possible before leaving home, so that the rich and poor might not be separated by their fare.[14]

For all the restraining influences and fancy developments, the camp meetings under new auspices retained much of their original magnetism. They drew crowds. People mingled in the mass. Boy met girl. Men swapped yarns and horses. Women exchanged recipes and confidences. The devout felt the effulgence of faith. Singing lifted heart and spirit. "Amazing Grace" was enough to raise any tabernacle roof. Preachers and exhorters still called men to repentance. Methodists were shouters and great cries might come from the congregation, either out of sheer ecstasy in the middle of a service or in moments of deliverance at the altar.

It all made for drama and companionship. The meetings, widely heralded and well attended, so that a crowd of under a thousand was considered paltry, kept the Lord in business and put religion on a par with politics in excitement. Now and then occurred some elemental event that seemed to serve almost as an accompaniment and to remind scoffers that they had better reckon with the Almighty. In 1811 and 1812 earthquakes shook the frontier like a terrier. The Mississippi River region had more than a thousand shocks and tremors. Chasms opened up and houses cracked and chimneys tumbled. The quakes struck terror to the hearts of sinners and brought them flocking to the churches. An Indiana itinerant gleefully reported that he had seen some men converted "whose conversion I had been in the habit of regarding as almost as hopeless as the conversion of the devil himself."[15] In the Miami district of Ohio Methodist membership doubled in the single year of 1812.

When the earth stopped shaking, backsliding almost canceled out the gains, and in the long run the camp meetings were more effective than earthquakes. As the movable feast of the American West they bestowed manna upon the godly and the ungodly alike. Along with the direct benefits conveyed to those who found newness of life, the meetings afforded all who came, whether to scoff or pray, a school for the study and practice of the rudiments of community living. Each camp created an intricate interplay of social forces requiring techniques of social control. The aim was peaceful intercourse and the lessons learned were in local government and in the regulation of local affairs. These lessons were not enough to civilize a pioneer people on the move, but they were all the area of the frontier had to offer, and the government and societal experience gained cannot have failed to establish certain values to be remembered. The meetings gave remote and rural people a medium they could not otherwise have fashioned to govern themselves. To the government of self they added the invitation to self-government.

The design and layout of the camps picture for us a high degree of social planning and comprehension.[16] There were three patterns—that of a rectangle, an open horseshoe, and a circle. The circle was the most mystical and the most popular. Whatever the shape, the outer rim of the camp was formed by wagons, with the horses stationed behind them. Next came a row of tents of every color and description, some improvised out of blankets and sacks, some tautly made. There might be as many as two hundred tents. In front of the tents and on the edge of the open-air auditorium were the campfires.

The campfires illuminated the space where the people assembled and they were supplemented by lanterns and flickering candles hung in trees around the clearing. There were also flaming elevated tripods for light and many worshipers carried pine-cone torches as they marched in procession or walked to visit other tents. Rules provided that one person stay and guard the tent at all times. In front of each tent was a large pail of water. How well fire was kept under wraps may be seen from the fact that only one frontier campground was devastated —the encampment on Carter's Valley Circuit, Tennessee, in 1833.[17]

The details of planning, foresight, and management shown in the camp meetings were remarkable against a background of firmly individual emphasis in religion. Salvation was presented as personal, not generic. Religion was for men and women, not for society or government. One of the admonitions given those who attended the meetings was to avoid talking politics. Vexing social problems belonged to the environment, to be accepted like the vagaries of weather. Naturally, the reiterated insistence of the preachers on conduct as the true measure of religion raised the moral tone of the west country and helped toward better citizenship by means of making better men. But there was no stress on man's indissoluble connection with the social order of which Methodism was a part and to which it was a party. Along with the shouting there were great silences—on the status of women, the lot of slaves, the uses of violence, the property rights of the Indian.

The Indian himself, if regarded as other than a menace or an abatis, was looked upon as a potential convert, fair game for missionary enterprise. There was poetic and religious justice, in the fact that the first Methodist missionary to the Indians was a Negro.

John Stewart was a free-born Virginia mulatto whose parents claimed to be mixed with Indian blood. They abandoned him in childhood and moved to Tennessee. Later, in an effort to follow after them, he found his way to Marietta, Ohio, where he fell among bad companions, drinking himself into insensibility and illness until, his credit cut off, he sobered up and got a job. One evening as he passed down a street he heard in a house the voice of singing and prayer. He ventured in and, after screwing up his courage, made known his state. It was a Methodist prayer meeting. Stewart attended frequently. He was subsequently converted under Methodist preaching and joined the church. By degrees and under a strange compulsion he decided that he must become a missionary to the Indians. His first approach met with indifference and then hostility until he took out his hymnbook and began to sing and charmed his listeners into perfect silence, broken only by the words "Sing more!" each time he ended a hymn.[18]

It was a beginning that led to his mission among the Wyandots who, living close to the whites and mixing with the most vicious, fell into degrading vices. Stewart met with more than a measure of success. The response he got led indirectly to the founding by the Methodists of their Missionary Society in 1820, the extension of widespread Indian work, and the introduction of camp meetings among Indian tribes.

Some of these meetings were attended for a time with the jerks and falling and frenzies that had marked the early revivals among the whites. Over the years, however, the testimony of white visitors presented the grove gatherings of the Indians as sedate, even serene, a genial powwow with the Medicine Man in the Sky. In southwest Mississippi Choctaws were incorporated in camp meetings by Jacob Young, and later enjoyed some encampments on their own. But the Choctaws were among the tribes wrenched from their lands and pushed west during the Indian removal ordered by Andrew Jackson.

It was well that some Indians with the proper attitude share the white Methodist institution of the camp meeting, but there was no protest on the part of the Church when a government violated their lands. The religion of the camp meetings continued to be strictly personal and the methods by which it was preached also kept the weight of emphasis on the personal. The essence and genius of the method arose out of the conviction that the individual could be reached in the mass and through the mass, best brought to terms with himself in a crowd. The intimacy of the mass, and the ease with which the crowd under the spell of induced emotion could be led to a single conclusion, carried over from the early Kentucky revivals into what were by comparison sophisticated gatherings under dignified auspices.

At first the Methodists struck a balance between the camp meetings and the class meetings. In this combination the mini and the mass joined. But when camp assemblies became a sustaining feature in Methodist practice, group meetings subsided and fell gradually into disuse. Many undetermined factors may have entered into the change, but the fact is that the growth of mass efforts during the years before 1805 and 1844 coincided with a shrinking of group activities. Methodism moved toward the mass rather than the group as the primary form in society. It set the norm that the individual mind could be swayed and changed through dramatic exhortation and set the stage for the intensely personal appeal in politics as well as evangelism. In this happening the camp meeting had a stellar part. The modern gifted evangelist addressing huge crowds in Madison Square Garden, his words and visage carried to millions

ORGANIZING TO BEAT THE DEVIL

by television, is aided by the tradition started and continued in the camp meeting.

The enduring emphasis placed on personal conduct was further publicized by a characteristic conviction in Methodist preaching, namely, save the soul and you save all. Not exclusively, but most emphatically, the Methodists believed that good people made a nation good. The more converts the sooner, the better. Numbers counted. Let the good outnumber the bad. This was the basis of hope. It was a simple idea, it seemed logical, and it would not die. That systems and political arrangements and the ghosts of dead postulates bear mightily on the welfare of a society was not even a theory, much less a conviction, at the time of the camp meetings, either when they were brash and young or when they were mature. On the primacy of the individual, Methodist doctrine and American temperament agreed. To Americans the way lay west, where it would be possible for every man to achieve the impossible. Methodists and non-Methodists both had their eyes on virgin land, the distant but immediate, remote but urgent, the ever-beckoning West. Men would move and Methodism would supply the philosophy.

XIV The Methodists Take Oregon

In the late summer of 1831 there appeared in the frontier town of St. Louis four Indians from that vast region of the Far West known as the Oregon Country. They had come all the way to see the white man's wigwam, but what they wanted most, they explained, was to learn the truth about the white man's God and to take back with them copies of the Bible for the instruction of their people.

So the story went. No two accounts have the same details, and there seems to be no doubt that the story was embroidered in many retellings. But there is good evidence that the Indians actually turned up. The embroidery was on whole cloth. The romantic design given it came from Methodist imagination and the wish to be needed and sought in far parts.

Oregon was the vague name given the immense map of land and rivers beyond the Rockies, stretching west all the way to the Pacific and reaching from Mexico's California in the south to Russia's Alaska in the north. It was a never-never land inhabited only by game and Indians and visited by trappers in their relentless slaughter of beavers. No one owned Oregon. Under a treaty drawn in 1818, and renewed for an indefinite period in 1827, citizens of both the United States and Great Britain were free to move in and settle if they wished. For all practical purposes, Oregon was unclaimed land in a land where land was the answer to every question.

The visit of the Indians, then, was not to be treated casually. Methodism had already proved itself to be a religion with scope enough to embrace a continent. It had spanned the Atlantic, planted itself up and down the eastern seaboard, organized itself in Baltimore, and moved ever westward. The movement had its scouts and explorers as well as preachers who rode fixed circuits. Nothing daunted their faith. Protestant worship was forbidden by law in Mexico, but the law had not prevented William Stevenson of the Missouri Conference from pushing out beyond Arkansas into Texas as early as 1815 when it was part of Mexico.[1]

Another trail blazer, Jesse Walker, had brought Wesleyanism to St. Louis in 1818, the year the first steamboat reached the place. Walker, a Virginian born and bred, had discovered the West through the outreach of Methodist missions. As a lad in the Old Dominion he had sampled the Baptists and the Presbyterians, but they did not suit his restless spirit. He sought out a Methodist meeting and decided that the religion proclaimed and practiced there was just right. He was licensed to preach. By 1804 he had a circuit and in 1806 he accompanied William McKendree to Illinois to spy out the land for the Lord. He found it good, went back to pack his family and establish a new home in the West.

Jesse Walker was a man Illinois could not long contain. He was forever on the move. Another preacher of the day declared that wherever he went Walker had been there ahead of him. St. Louis seemed to Walker a good and strategic spot at which to start a church. Situated near the confluence of the Missouri River and the Mississippi, the town was a place of beginnings. Perched above the Mississippi on a limestone bluff forty feet high and two miles long, it was the starting point for most of the expeditions into the western country. It was also the place where the people from the East headed when they headed west. Many of these were Methodists.

By the end of his first year Jesse Walker had built a small preaching house with side galleries and with pews borrowed from the Episcopalians, who had no minister at the time. He had a membership of seventy and a flourishing school for poor children. So established was Methodism in St. Louis in 1822 that the Missouri Annual Conference held its sessions there. The Conference was meeting in St. Louis again when the Indians arrived and it was within the logic of circumstances that General William Clark, superintendent of Indian affairs for the tribes of all the Missouri River country, should refer the strange request from the Far West to the Methodists as well as the Jesuits.[2]

Present also in St. Louis during the stay of the Indians was another Walker—this one William Walker, an educated half-breed Wyandot, who had worked with John Stewart. William Walker also served as a go-between in handling the affairs of the Wyandots with the United States government. He had come to St. Louis to confer with General Clark. In the course of their talk the general told Walker that there were three Flathead chiefs in his house and asked Walker if he would like to see them. A fourth, General Clark said, had died a few days before, and the three remaining were quite sick. Walker visited the Indians in an adjoining room, having heard of the tribe before and being at first more curious about the shape of their head than the state of the souls. He drew a pen sketch of one head, showing how the forehead had been flattened or leveled by pressure on the cranium in infancy.

General Clark told William Walker that on his journey to the Pacific Northwest in 1804–1806 he and Meriwether Lewis had made friends among the Nez Percé and the Flathead tribes and that the four Indians had traveled from beyond the Rockies to see him, being in a deep quandary. A white man in their country had informed them that the Indian mode of worshiping the Supreme Being was radically wrong. The white man had told them further that "the white people away toward the rising of the sun had been put in possession of the true mode of worshiping the Great Spirit. They had a book containing directions on how to conduct themselves in order to enjoy his favor. . . ."³

It was to learn this mode of worship and the favor it brought that the Indian chiefs had been deputed to call upon their friend and father, General Clark, who had assured them that what the white man had said was true. The general had done his best to give the Indians a succinct history of mankind as the Christians saw it.

The chiefs had seemed pleased—rewarded for their journey and satisfied in their great quest. But the journey had sorely taxed their health and strength. Walker learned on a later visit that a second of the chiefs had died in St. Louis and that the two remaining Indians, although not well, had set out for their native land. No one heard of them afterward and it was presumed that they died on the way back to the Oregon Country.

The story haunted William Walker, especially in view of the fact that there was no sign that the chiefs, earnest inquirers though they were, ever reached their tribes with the truth. Months after the happening, not being able to get the vivid implications off his mind, Walker sat down and wrote an account of the matter to a generous New York merchant, Gabriel P. Disosway, a tried and true Methodist who had become friendly with Walker when in 1820 the Missionary Society was formed as a result of John Stewart's work with the Wyandots.

Disosway caught the drama of unfilled need at once. He took the letter Walker had written and the sketch he had drawn and sent them on to a leading Methodist organ, *The Christian Advocate and Journal,* enclosing also a letter of his own to say that missionaries ought to be sent to the Flatheads to tell them what their tribesmen had come so far to find out. These "extraordinary inquirers after the truth" should not be disappointed. The Walker letter, according to a recent research report by Ray A. Billington of the Huntington Library, was reprinted in virtually every religious magazine and newspaper in the United States and "echoed in pulpits with glowing pleas for the 'Wise Men from the West' who had tramped 2000 miles in quest of the Holy Word. They were pictured as pausing in St. Louis to utter a last pathetic message: 'We are going back the long, long trail to our people. When we tell them, after one more snow, in the big council that we did not bring back the Book, no word will be spoken by our old men, nor by our young braves. One by one they will rise up and go out in silence. Our people will die in darkness. . . .' "[4]

The letter was published during a period of dreadful conscience in Methodist circles over Indian affairs. The forced removal of Indian tribes from lands east of the Mississippi, lands guaranteed by successive treaties, was implacably in progress. In the North the removal had been accomplished, to all appearances, peacefully, but in the South among the Cherokees, the Creeks, and the Choctaws, it was encountering stern resistance that engendered cruelty and barbarity on the part of the whites.

Methodist missionaries stood by the Indians, defended their rights, went along the trail west with the hapless victims, making the Indians' lot their own. Officially, however, The Methodist Episcopal Church ignored the removal. The Annual Conferences of the South made no protest against the injustice done and expressed no sympathy for the suffering that followed. The Tennessee Conference even went so far as to dissociate itself from the activities of the missionaries in supporting the Indians— on the grounds that church and state must be kept separate.[5]

There was nothing in the background to make the Church set itself in opposition to the actions of the United States government. In 1830 Congress had authorized the Indian removal and it was part of the law of the land. Yet, as the devotion of the missionaries showed, there were individual Methodists sorely troubled and deeply disturbed by this official indignity that climaxed the consistent mistreatment of the red man.

Prominent leaders in the Church found themselves aglow over

the news from St. Louis. Among them was Dr. Wilbur Fisk, president of Wesleyan University at Middletown, Connecticut. When the *Advocate* reached the Fisk home his wife tells us that he came to her with the paper and, explaining that he did not even have time to sit down, read the story to her and, having finished reading, said, "My dear wife, we will have a mission there." Within *one half hour* (the italics were hers) Fisk had a letter in the post office to the man he was convinced would be best suited to head the mission, a former student of his named Jason Lee. The next day Fisk began to raise funds and between seven hundred and eight hundred dollars were collected in Middletown alone.[6]

By mid-April of 1833 the Board of the Missionary Society recommended the establishment of a mission among the Flathead Indians. It remained now only to find the ideal person to serve as head. According to the specifications Fisk had set in his mind, this man must be unencumbered with a family and possess the spirit of a martyr. He and those who accompanied him must live among the Indians, "learn their language, preach Christ to them and, as the way opens, introduce schools, agriculture, and the arts of civilized life."[7]

Fisk was sure, as he had told his wife the night he read the *Advocate*, that Jason Lee was the one man for the job. He was, to begin with, a stalwart fellow, standing six foot three, and of iron constitution. He had spent his boyhood on the farm and in the forests. He could chop a cord of maple wood in two hours. As a woodsman he had managed gangs of men and knew how to command. He had been born in Stanstead, Canada, but his forebears were of irreproachable English and American stock with a good record in the American Revolution. At twenty-three Jason had undergone a genuine Methodist conversion. A few years after his conversion he had felt the call to preach.

Having had scant schooling in his early youth, Lee left Stanstead and entered Wilbraham Wesleyan Academy at Wilbraham, Massachusetts, to equip himself better for the ministry. Here he had come under the tutelage of Wilbur Fisk, this being in the days before Fisk went on to Wesleyan. Lee applied himself to his studies with such diligence and showed such leadership that he was enlisted by Fisk to help with the instruction of other students. Later Lee returned to Canada and offered himself as a missionary to the Indians of Canada, but the appointment had not come through when he received Fisk's letter asking if he might be available for the Oregon mission. In June 1833 the Missionary Board made the appointment and Bishop Elijah Hedding ordained Lee, a young man of thirty-one by now, purposely for the task at hand.

Difficulties, multiplied by distance, presented themselves at once. A year after his appointment Jason Lee had not yet reached St. Louis, the starting point of the journey west, but his party had been on the way almost all of the time and they had covered a lot of ground. With his nephew Daniel Lee as his assistant and with Cyrus Shepard recruited as a teacher, Jason had made many stops and at every stop he found missionary zeal; if he didn't, he aroused it. Standing tall in the pulpit, given a thoughtful mien by a slight stoop, Lee conveyed to the Methodists within the sound of his voice a sense of being united and steadfast in a consecrated enterprise.

Leaving New York in January 1834 the missionaries stopped for meetings in Philadelphia, Baltimore, Washington, and Pittsburgh before heading down the Ohio to Cincinnati and then on to St. Louis. There they had a rendezvous with Nathaniel Wyeth, a Boston merchant and adventurer who was assembling a party of rough and ready fellows for an overland trip to the Oregon Country. It was Wyeth's second trip to the Far West, although he was but thirty. The Lees had met him in Cambridge the year before on his return from his first visit to Oregon. He had brought back with him two Indian boys, who had made a deep impression on white audiences, being of far western tribes, both Flatheads. With Flatheads in common, it seemed only natural that the missionaries and Wyeth should join forces. Wyeth knew the route and not a little about the country which was their destination.[8]

There are reports that Wyeth was not pleased to have the missionaries in his company. He was a man with a purpose but not a man with a mission. He was bent on business, hard bent. A shrewd Yankee, he had demonstrated the rewards of enterprise by shipping ice from New England to the West Indies, and he had a habit of looking for gain in far-off places. Before his first journey he had formed a joint stock company to set up trapping and supplying operations in Oregon and to catch and process salmon. On that journey many of his men had deserted, his supply ship had been wrecked, and he had been able to put into effect none of his plans.

Now, however, with fresh Boston money and rich in confidence, Wyeth was ready to start again, convinced that Oregon would sooner or later yield the secrets of its wealth to the diligent and the brave. He was a man of practical fanaticism, a dreamer who carried his dreams in saddlebags and on pack horses. His first contagion of what men called Oregon fever had been contracted from a New England schoolteacher, Hall Jackson Kelley, who through his fiery and eloquent writings had become known as the Prophet of Oregon. Kelley was a fanatic of words and his words had the power to turn men's faces toward the land of his dreams. But he was bookish, not a colonizer or a prospector or a settler, and Wyeth, after a period of adulation, had left Kelley's inspiration to one side and had gone off on his own. He was no theorist but a man on horseback, heading west.

It was with Wyeth and his secular band, bent on gain, that the missionaries set off from St. Louis. The party numbered seventy. There were traders, hunters, trappers, two Philadelphia scientists, Thomas Nuttall and John K. Townsend, and there were 250 horses. It took eighty-eight days to make the trek. There were Indians along the route but they were not Flatheads. They were Indians who had taken on some of the white men's ways. At appointed stopping places they would at night shoot guns in wild abandon for the sheer pleasure that the noise gave and ride their horses around the edges of the camp with such whoops and yells that the milder members of the party were terrified, the camps being turned into bedlam, as one of the scientists wrote in his diary.[9]

Jason Lee reached Oregon with his sense of mission undiminished. After all, it was the Flatheads he had come to serve. In the quietness of the joy that comes at the end of an endless journey he wrote Fisk: "There are now twenty Indians within six feet of me. . . . Who, *who* will volunteer to come out and sound the trumpet of salvation among them? May God in his mercy thrust out some who will not count their lives dear unto themselves but spend them in the service of the Red Men."[10] Lee's first silent encounter with the idealized red man was the most satisfactory he was to enjoy. When he started sounding the trumpet of salvation he found that it fell on deaf or indifferent ears. "It is rather my opinion," he wrote after one of his early efforts, "that it is easier to convert a tribe of Indians at a missionary meeting than it is in the wilderness."[11] Their eagerness for the white man's God was not anywhere in evidence.

Conditions in the Oregon Country were far more complex than they had seemed to the Missionary Society and to Jason Lee on the way out. While it had been agreed by treaty that settlers from the United States and Great Britain could both enter the region, it was also tacitly understood—and plainly seen by anyone who visited the place—that the northern section was under the suzerainty of the British, who exercised control over the economic life of the area through the Hudson's Bay Company. The permeating operations of the Company turned Oregon into a society that had tissues and nerves—a state that belied the appearance of vast and vacant land.

The strength of the Company's influence had been increased in 1824 when a gentle and percipient fellow named John McLoughlin had been made its chief factor. Born in Quebec, he had come to the region as a physician for an earlier business operation, had turned trader, and had worked his way up the ladder of Hudson's Bay Company. Known to the Indians as the White-headed Eagle, McLoughlin was a man of commanding presence and great composure who set an example of good manners hard to overlook or to cope with. He had shown great ability, although his methods often puzzled the directors of the Company, in keeping peace and quiet among the Indians and in keeping to a minimum the competition of American trappers who invaded his territory. His master strategy was courtesy. Whatever his aims, whether they were as clear and pure as they seemed to grateful visitors or as devious as some critics claimed, he was invariably and skillfully kind.[12]

Dr. McLoughlin was standing on the shore of the mighty Columbia to greet the missionaries when they arrived by way of a Hudson's Bay barge he had sent to meet them and deliver them to his headquarters, Fort Vancouver. Located near the junction of the Columbia and the Willamette, a placid river flowing through a fertile valley that lay to the south, Fort Vancouver was more of a storehouse for goods than it was a bastion. It was a place of certain hospice for all who came to the Oregon Country. The chief factor made the missionaries at home in the fort and, when their supplies arrived a few days later, provided them with horses and guides that they might find the best location for their mission station.

It was through talks with Dr. McLoughlin that Jason Lee and his cohorts began to discern some of the complexities that lay ahead. The Flatheads were in the hills, driven there by enemies. They were not assembled in tribal centers for the convenience of those who had come to convert them. McLoughlin stressed that to do good to the Indians the missionaries "must establish themselves where they could collect them around them; teach them first to cultivate the ground and live more comfortably than they do by hunting, and as they do this, teach them religion. . . ."[13]

The good doctor had good reason to give Lee and his men good advice. The Company was obligated by its royal license to improve the Indians and here were dedicated men who had come to Oregon for the purpose. They bespoke a determined interest and, in this respect, they were the first missionaries. They had back of them a highly organized and well-to-do church, the fastest growing in the States. They paid the region a compliment of respect by being there. Five years before, a scout for the American Board of Commissioners for Foreign Missions had turned in a chill report, advising the board that Oregon savages had no promise, that missionaries could not survive among them. Now here was a party of missionaries with supplies and contacts—eager, energetic, and holding close ties with the world beyond the Rockies.

The area chosen for the Methodist mission was south of Fort Vancouver. It was rich prairie land. On his first journey to Oregon, Nathaniel Wyeth had visited the country round about and had said in his journal, "I have never seen country of equal beauty except the Kansas country." He had found families of retired Hudson's Bay Company people living there, and had declared, from seeing the yield of the gardens, that if Oregon was to be colonized, this was the place to begin.[14]

For the site of the mission house the Lees selected a spot near a grove of oak and fir trees on the east bank of the Willamette, hard by a stretch of prairie two miles long and half a mile wide. There the party set to work like pioneers to finish the house before the rainy season set in. There was not a carpenter in the party and yet the whole building had to be put up piece by piece from green trees split and hewed by hand. It took four weeks to put together a structure thirty-two feet long and eighteen wide, a story and a half high. The next spring thirty acres of the nearby prairie land were plowed and fenced and seeded, Dr. McLoughlin furnishing the seed and oxen. Farming also took time, but the soil was fertile and the crops good. The yield was enough to supply food for the missionaries and there was enough left to feed Indian children who came to the mission.

The first children came in the winter after the first spring. They were three, two boys and a girl. They were naked, filthy, and plastered with vermin. They were accepted, cleansed, and clothed. Others came, and before long Cyrus Shepard started a

161

school. Most of the Indians were opposed to having their children attend and the enrollment was made up largely of homeless waifs, two of whom had come a distance of two hundred miles. In 1836 the school consisted of nineteen Indians and half-breeds and by October of that year it had grown to fifty-three. They were a rag, tag, and bobtail lot, described as "the poorest, frailest, lowest specimens of our common humanity."[15]

Not to Shepard, though. The clue to the man's character was in his name. His gentleness endeared him to his associates and made him a leader of his flock. There being many Indian dialects, he set about teaching his charges in English. This made the learning process slow, but he was much rewarded by the speed with which his waifs caught on and the amount they were able to grasp. As the pupils were fed, clothed, and taught, they were given English names, usually those of prominent Methodists such as Wilbur Fisk and Elijah Hedding. It was a happy house for all its difficulties as long as Shepard lived, but in late 1839 he got a scrofulous infection. His leg had to be amputated and he did not long survive the operation.

Jason Lee's letters to Fisk show that he early had to acknowledge the failure of his mission when it came to making converts among the Indians. Eighteen months after he arrived in the Columbia region he wrote: "The truth is we have no evidence that we have been instrumental in the conversion of one soul since crossing the Mountains. . . ." This confession was painful to make and a man of Lee's resourcefulness could not accept it as final. It rather suggested that, having examined the task before him, he saw that the emphasis of the mission must be shifted. The Indian's physical lot mattered. Even on this point he was discouraged but hope welled in him like a mountain spring. "We are doing little directly yet to benefit the Indians," he had written earlier, "but we trust that we are laying the foundation for extensive usefulness in the future."[16]

There was not much besides the school to give the mission a sense of mission. Nearby Indians let it be known that they expected to be paid for attending worship.[17] Older Indians stayed to themselves in the hills, almost ceremoniously indifferent to the men who had come to save them, unwilling to change their ways with either the soul or the soil. To reach them at all long journeys were required. Temporals, including coming and going, seemed to take an increasing amount of time and Jason Lee saw that he must have more help. He wrote the Missionary Society that, if they would supply laymen to attend to the temporals, he and his associates would gladly attend to the spirituals.

The Society responded handsomely, sending in 1836 a physician and a blacksmith with their families, a carpenter, and two female schoolteachers, along with household furniture, and about twenty boxes of clothing of various sorts and sizes, as well as agricultural and mechanical implements and surgical instruments. The trip was made by way of Hawaii, where there was a delay of four months while waiting for a connecting ship, so that the party did not arrive until almost a year after it left New York. At Fort Vancouver the new contingent met with the same hospitality Dr. McLoughlin had shown before, being kept there as guests of the Company for a week. In January 1837 a third group of missionaries sailed from Boston and arrived in September of the same year. One of them became the wife of Jason Lee.

With an augmented staff Jason Lee was ready to expand his program. A nearby tribe, hitherto neglected perhaps because of their closeness, were systematically visited in their lodges. Religious meetings were held and a preaching house built. Due efforts were made to persuade the Indians to cultivate the soil and to build comfortable houses to live in. The efforts all along the line, however, proved vain, and after a year the stepped-up labors were abandoned.

It was hard for Jason Lee to explain to his Board at a great distance and in laborious letters what was going on in the hollow and echoing vastness called Oregon. Indians were becoming obsolete. They were dying out where they were not driven out. Their curve was down. Even if they had been in

163

the ascendancy, it was clear from the experience of the missionaries that the unyielding indifference of the red man would not lend itself to treatment. On the other hand, every sign and token on the far horizons showed that the white men would soon be pouring in.

Not a few factors contributed to the growth of settlements and the promise of more. Wagons were one. By clever and continued experiments men found that wheels˙could be used in the mountains. In 1827 General William H. Ashley, member of a St. Louis firm engaged in trapping, sent a howitzer through the South Pass, a broad valley cutting across the Rocky Mountains at an elevation of 7550 feet, proving that wheels were feasible over a greater distance on the journey to Oregon than any had supposed before.[18] Three years later a caravan including ten five-mule-team heavy wagons carrying eighteen hundred pounds each went all the way through the pass. Later Benjamin Louis Eylalie de Bonneville, a West Point graduate who had become interested in the fur trade while stationed on the frontier, took twenty light wagons carrying two years' supplies for a party of more than a hundred men through the pass to the Green River and added another 271 miles to the developing road of access.[19]

It was plainer by the year that a great migration was possible. Within the Oregon Country events were taking place which showed that settlers would fare increasingly well in this world's goods. In 1837 a herd of 650 head of cattle driven from California reached the Willamette Valley. Mrs. Jason Lee wrote joyously to her brother in the East about what the cattle would mean—milk and butter for all. The arrival of the cattle increased the independence of the settlers, who had up to then relied on Hudson's Bay Company for such cattle as they could get. Overland commerce with the outside world was one more sign pointing to the successful settlement of Oregon Country by the whites.[20]

About this time a federal agent in the person of Lieutenant William J. Slacum arrived in Oregon on a fact-finding expedition.

He was entertained at the mission and Lee helped him draw up a petition asking that the protection of the United States be extended to Oregon.[21] Obviously some preparation must be made to provide settlers with conditions under which they could decently live. There were marvelous economic opportunities, there was plenty for all and wealth for some, but there was not even a semblance of government to protect and regulate business transactions. If a man staked out a piece of land there was no place where he could register his claim. If a settler died there was no place to probate his will. Absent were the ordinary procedures whereby the adjoining United States of America handled the affairs of its citizens.

The Settlers' Petition by its very name bespoke the moral concern of resident American whites over the future of the region. The signers declared: "We flatter ourselves that we are the germ of a great state, and are anxious to give an early tone to the moral and intellectual character of its citizens." They cited "strong inducements for the Government of the United States to take formal and speedy possession." Notable among these inducements was the power of the federal government to keep out the riffraff and all the undesirable elements likely to pour into a new country, such as renegades from the Rocky Mountains, "the profligate deserted seamen from Polynesia, and the unprincipled sharpers from Spanish America." The petitioners stated flatly what they took for granted: "The territory must populate. The Congress of the United States must say by whom." The choice was between the scum named and "our hardy and enterprising pioneers."[22]

In the same month that the Settlers' Petition was signed Jason Lee decided to go east and plead the cause of the Willamette Mission to his Board. He could report in person on activities almost as easily as he could by long-winded handwritten accounts. Besides, funds were needed for the work and it would be possible not only to present specific needs but to help raise the money by appearing before church gatherings.

Accordingly he set off, the Settlers' Petition in a little trunk strapped to his horse's side. He stopped at Fort Walla Walla long enough to visit with Dr. and Mrs. Marcus Whitman, who in 1836 had established a Congregational mission to the Indians there. What he picked up from the Whitmans and from a nearby post presided over by other Congregational missionaries, the Henry H. Spaldings, did nothing to reassure him about the prospect of converting the red man to the white man's way of life. The natives under the Spaldings were of a better grade than those along the Willamette, he reported in a letter to his nephew, Daniel Lee, but they were still trouble; "the truth is they are *Indians.*" He warned his nephew and those at the post to use a firm hand with their charges, noting that the Whitmans and Spaldings had thought it proper to let the Indians feel the lash when they deserved it.[23]

Only a sense of urgency and a feeling of high purpose could have led Lee to make the long and grueling trip across the country at this particular time. He had married one of the teachers who had come out in 1837. His wife was about to become a mother. Should he wait until the child was born? Like a good Methodist preacher's wife, Anna Lee put his mind at rest: "If you think it your duty to go, go," she said to her husband, "for I did not marry you to hinder you but rather to aid in the performance of your duty."

The effect he had along the way seemed to justify his plan and timing. Not lacking a gift for the theatrical, Jason Lee took in tow three Indian lads of the tribe he had gone forth to convert. These lads offered tangible evidence of the original intent of his mission and reminded audiences that the Indians were still out there. Their behavior brought home to audiences the feeling that some good had been accomplished. They were pliant and decorous and fitted well into the services the missionary held.

A preacher of the day tells of the impression Lee and his Indians made at the 1838 Annual Conference in Alton, Illinois. While the Conference was in the midst of business Lee stepped dramatically before his brethren. His appearance brought the

Conference to an awed standstill. "His long exposure to sun and rain, camping out nights, all pressing upon him amid his untiring labors, were as so many chapters of untold suffering; and yet, in his countenance, there was a heavenly resignation. . . . Our astonishment was increased when he introduced as his traveling companions natives from the tribe of Flathead Indians." The young men, the recording preacher thought, had made considerable progress in learning, as was evident from their demeanor. They had beautiful voices and sang several Methodist hymns in their own language.[24]

The scene was repeated wherever a congregation assembled. Jason Lee took seven months to reach New York. Word overtook him in Kansas that his wife had died in childbirth and that the baby, a boy, had died a few days later. The news increased the sadness and resignation of his countenance and deepened the sympathy with which he was heard. Everywhere he went he preached the gospel of Oregon. He presented his case to the Missionary Board, and when it agreed to his request for a program of massive aid, he set off preaching again, touching conferences in New England, churches in New York, Philadelphia, Baltimore, and Virginia.

In Washington, Lee laid the Settlers' Petition on the desk of U. S. Senator Lewis Fields Linn of Missouri. No solon could have been more hospitable to the appeal of Oregonians for United States protection than this ardent advocate of expansionism. Linn placed the matter before the Senate. Nothing came of the move but the petition was printed and got some attention.

In virtually every other respect Jason Lee's trip was a triumph. He had found response at every turn and often unexpectedly. Visiting one of his old friends from Wilbraham Academy he learned of a fine young woman, Lucy Thompson, who had made a spirited missionary appeal to her classmates in her valedictory address. "I must know that lady!" Lee exclaimed. An introduction was arranged, correspondence followed, and the two were married in July of 1839.

By autumn plans were complete for the return to Oregon,

and the arrangements offered eloquent testimony to what Lee had accomplished. With his help, the Methodists had raised enough money and had enough conviction about the Oregon mission to charter a new three-masted sailing vessel, copper-fastened, christened the *Lausanne,* to make the voyage around Cape Horn and to Oregon by way of Honolulu, transporting Lee and his new wife and a great body of missionaries, along with cargo, which included a tombstone the chief of the mission had purchased for his first wife.

The passenger list numbered fifty-one, all pledged to the Oregon cause, all engaged, as Lee put it, "to obligate themselves to remain in our service for ten years unless released." The *Lausanne* carried the largest single missionary contingent that had ever been sent out, and as it stood ready to start its twenty-two-thousand-mile voyage it attracted the attention of the press. In New York the *Journal of Commerce* noted that the sailing of the vessel was an important event, "whether considered in its religious or political bearings," adding: "Among other things, it will expedite the settlement of the Territory."[25]

Oregon wasn't even a Territory. It was in effect foreign country and critics observed that the passengers on the *Lausanne* were colonists, intended to establish further American holdings in the western lands between California and Alaska. The charge was scotched by the Missionary Society, and it was apparent to all but the critics that the aims of those making the voyage were strictly religious. Certainly the Methodists went to work with zeal and a right good will once the *Lausanne* reached Fort Vancouver and the entire party had been made to feel at home by the incurably cordial Dr. McLoughlin.

Jason Lee was ready and prepared to expand again. Outpost missions were set up and some of these were visited regularly. Now and then there were spiritual rewards, some indication of effect. At one place an Indian said, "All white men we have seen before came to take our beavers; none ever came to instruct us. We are glad to see you." Obviously the missionaries had a wholesome social influence in a wild and unorganized country.

They provided the rites of marriage and baptism and burial, gave the rudiments of education and promoted temperance and family life. All these blessings, however, were better suited to the needs of the white man than to the red man.

By the very shape of circumstances the missionaries—through such enterprises as setting up a school for white children and building the first Methodist church on the West Coast, and near it a white parsonage with green shutters—began to shift the weight of their emphasis more and more on the needs of the settlers. By 1840 the number was conspicuous, as Jason Lee had foreseen it would be. A visitor to the Willamette Valley that year found about 120 farms tilled by five hundred settlers, producing thirty-five thousand bushels of wheat yearly.[26] Two other mission stations were opened up by the Lees and they became centers for settlers rather than for Indians.

Along the trails to Oregon a combined hegira and odyssey had commenced. Over these trails and shortcuts and experimental routes passed wagons loaded with household goods and hopes. Oregon was a goal for families. Adventurers went to Texas and California, but Oregon was a place of homes. Talk of free and fertile land and friendly climate made families on the edge of the old frontier want to get up and go. Letters to the newspapers, the resonant writings of Hall Jackson Kelley, who never made good as a colonizer but could arouse even a statue to want to wander, spread interest. On Jason Lee's fund-raising tours he had spoken to forty thousand persons, all under respectable Methodist auspices and all susceptible to the urge to move.[27]

Not merely those who went or wanted to go to Oregon had their fancies inflamed. Stay-at-homes caught the fever and sometimes were the most delirious of all. The Oregon question ceased to be a sleepy subject for diplomats. It became an issue, which is to say that it became a matter of controversy, and it found popular expression in a fighting phrase: Fifty-Four Forty or Fight. The phrase was coined in 1844 by William Allen, then governor of Ohio. It was caught up and repeated by expansionist

Democrats, and before long settlers moving toward Oregon began painting the words *Fifty-Four Forty* on their wagons. It was an earnest expression of their expectation to have free access to the whole of the Oregon Country.

Allen's alliterative allusion to the dispute with Great Britain bundled history, geography, and American policy up into five words. Fifty-four forty was the parallel, running just below Alaska, that the United States and the United Kingdom had agreed would mark the northern boundary of what was called Oregon. The forty-ninth parallel marked the rest of the border between the United States and Canada. The cry of Fifty-four Forty or Fight served popular notice on His Majesty's government that the United States laid claim to all land up to Fifty-four Forty and would go to war to back its claim.

In thoughts, words, and acts Jason Lee was ahead of trends and unabashedly at the center of gathering events. A supple and resilient man, deeply conscientious, his motives were above reproach. Religious hope and aspiration were back of everything he did, yet he faced in the tasks that confronted him a confluence of forces long and vigorously in the making. Lee was not powerless in the grip of these forces. He was part of them, helped to make them. He was an American and a Methodist and, for all his zeal, intensely practical in his approach. The net result of the actions of the man and the play of circumstances was a program to convey to an alien territory the benefits of white New England culture. America and Methodism were mystically joined. In the fall of 1843 he wrote: "On one point I have not the shadow of a doubt, viz., that the growth and spread, and rise, and glory and triumph of Methodism in the Willamette Valley is destined to be commensurate with the growth and rise and prosperity of our now infant, but flourishing and rapidly increasing settlement, for such is the adaptation of Oregon's soil to the genius of Methodism and such fruit as she has already produced in this country that I am persuaded she is destined to flourish here. . . ."[28]

Lee dealt in futures. His gifted imagination was aloft when

he wrote these lines. Methodism was not flourishing in Oregon at the time. With all the people on his augmented staff, he was having personnel and administrative problems. Not unlike other fervent fellows, Jason Lee was too busy to get anything done. Nothing would stay put. By the time he had returned to his base after some long journey to put the Indians at rest or to visit an outpost, some new crisis had developed. The Indians, for all practical purposes, had to be neglected, but they could not be neglected without repeated efforts to save them. When neglected they grew hostile or demanded gifts of peace.

Whatever sally Lee made seemed doomed to failure. He set up a manual training school for Indian boys, but a contagion broke out among the pupils. Many died. Others ran away or were removed by their parents. The ranks of the missionaries were depleted by sickness. Death stalked the staff. Lee's second wife died, leaving him an infant daughter. Discouraged, some of the missionaries resigned and returned home, telling the Missionary Board bluntly that Lee was not qualified for the task committed to him. These criticisms took their toll of confidence and before long (or as soon as was possible with the slowness of the mails) inquiries reached Lee, expressing concern over what had happened to thousands of good Methodist dollars. Correspondence between Lee and the Board showed that not a few of the problems had to do with the handling of money and the care of the physical properties of the mission, there not being much else that could be seen or worried about at a distance. Before he left Oregon Jason Lee had heard that he would be called home. In Hawaii the news was grimly confirmed, and to it a missionary resting there at the time added the shocking intelligence that, without waiting to hear Lee's explanations, the Board had superseded him as Oregon mission superintendent. His successor was already on his way. It was all the more necessary now that he reach New York by the fastest possible means.

There was a small schooner leaving for Mexico the next day, having room for only one passenger. Lee left his daughter in the care of friends, made his will, and took the schooner, which landed him more than a month later on the coast of Mexico. He crossed Mexico by a conveyance known as a diligence, an uncovered stagecoach pulled by eight horses and mules, traveling over rough cobblestones convict labor had laid. From Vera Cruz he took the first mail packet to New Orleans. There he boarded an upriver steamboat for a twelve-day journey to Pittsburgh. Crossing the Alleghenies by stage, he reached New York five months after he left Oregon.[29]

The General Conference of The Methodist Episcopal Church was meeting in New York. But the year was 1844 and the business of the Conference was taken up almost entirely with the case of Bishop James O. Andrew and the right and propriety of a bishop to own slaves. There was no time for the Board to hear the plaintive plea of a deprived missionary.

Later, in June, there was. Lee gave a good and matter-of-fact account of himself and his dealings. After days of hearings the Board affectionately dismissed all charges against him, and the man had at least the satisfaction of knowing that his work had not been unappreciated if it had not been sufficiently understood. Deeply hurt but loyal to the last, Jason Lee even offered to go back to the mission in a subordinate position. But the treasurer was adamant. There were no funds available for more missionaries in Oregon.

It is doubtful if he could have made the trip again. Jason Lee was a man whose force was spent. He was emaciated and his clothes hung loosely around his great frame. True, the old fire was there and it flared up when he preached. At the meeting of the New England Conference in 1844 he "powerfully and successfully advocated the claims of the Oregon Mission." The Conference named him agent for the Oregon Institute, the new name given the Indian Mission Manual Labor School he had founded. He planned to spend two years or more in the East raising money for the institute. Then he would return to Oregon. His health failed rapidly, however, and he started back to Stanstead. In March of 1845 he died in the place of his birth, his mind unimpaired to the last, though speech failed him. As best those at his bedside could determine, his thoughts were in Oregon.[30]

James Knox Polk was in the White House. Expansionist Democrats had put him in office and Fifty-Four Forty or Fight had been their slogan. In his inaugural address and in his first annual message to Congress Polk had insisted on possessing the whole of Oregon, to which, he said, the title of the United States was "clear and unquestionable." In April of 1845 Congress authorized the President to give Great Britain notice that the Joint Occupation Treaty would be terminated. Negotiations to settle the boundary began and, after a year of tugging, a compromise was reached, blessed by Britain's genial disinclination to go to war over the northern boundary of the Oregon Country. Polk, realizing that the American case had been overstated, sheepishly agreed to accept the continuation of the forty-ninth parallel as the border, and the insistence on Fifty-Four Forty was dropped. Expansionists were outraged, but at least and at last the United States had come to possess most of the land which two nations had claimed.

Another fighting phrase rang out during the period of the new westward expansion: Manifest Destiny. It was used first by the editor of *The Democratic Review* in the summer of 1845 when John L. O'Sullivan spoke of "our manifest destiny to overspread the continent allotted by Providence for the free development of our yearly multiplying millions."

Religion had become allied with politics in purpose, and now the hallowed terms of religion sounded loud and clear in political exhortations. Oregon was the beginning. Possession of the area had come about in no small part through settlements headed by the Methodist mission and through the strong and determined leadership of Jason Lee, the missionary. The Methodists had led the van. It was something to think about, this union of church and state in the march of a new nation.

XV The Mischief Begins

The golden age of American Methodism endured until 1830, although signs of tarnish appeared earlier. Whether The Methodist Episcopal Church could remain successfully national and not split into smithereens of factions was a problem that was posed before the beginning of the nineteenth century. It came up first when a local society pitted itself against the authority of Bishop Asbury and asserted its right to choose its own preacher purely because of his power and personality. It was a case of arrant congregationalism. Not only must the local church not be allowed to call preachers, but it was also important not to let any one man, however colorful or spectacular, get the impression that he could have a following of his own.

The trouble had its origin under remote and freakish circumstances. In 1786 John Wesley ordained one William Hammett, a man of great persuasive powers and personal charm. He was intended as a missionary for Newfoundland, an area outside the bailiwick of the American Methodists. Hammett set sail with Bishop Coke, intending for Newfoundland, but the weather lay in wait and before the voyage was done the good ship on which Coke and Hammett sailed was driven to a spot more than a thousand miles from its destination. The two bedraggled missionaries landed at Antigua in the West Indies, where Hammett began to preach with a right good will and so ably that in due time he had built up a congregation of seven hundred members. Pressing on to Kingston in Jamaica, he met with no less success but the penalty was greater, the English of the place falling upon the Methodists with such venom and vigor that the good man's life was in danger and he was forced to stand guard over the preaching house lest it be leveled. The exactions bore heavily upon his health and when Bishop Coke returned to the Indies in 1791 he found Hammett scarcely able to stand. A physician advised that the bishop take the preacher to America in order that the climate there, not to mention the people, might be kinder, and restore his health.[1]

The two men again took to the waters, but the waters again were not kind, and after a deplorable passage toward South Carolina, the ship was wrecked at Edisto, a point twenty-eight miles southwest of Charleston. However, the men escaped the clutches of the deep and made their way by land and luck to the city, where Bishop Asbury was holding a meeting of the clergy round about. Both Coke and Hammett preached before the assembled preachers and to a large gathering of local Methodists. Hammett's effect was instant and it became lasting. Without ado and with gusto and in the very presence of Asbury, the bishop who made it his business to attend to all appointments, the members of the Methodist society asked that Hammett be made their pastor. The request, as Asbury noted in his journal, "was a thing quite new amongst Methodists," and he appropriately ignored it and appointed another preacher to the post, leaving town after he had taken the action and with no explanation save the example of his own decision. Later he did explain to the Charleston society that he had overruled their wish because Hammett was "unknown, a foreigner, and did not acknowledge the authority of, nor join in connection with, the American Conference."[2]

Hammett took the wishes of the Charleston society quite seriously, however, and, armed with urgent petitions from the membership, overtook Asbury on the road back to Philadelphia and roundly besought him for the appointment. Needless to say he did not get it, but in a conversation, of which no record was kept, Hammett got the impression that Asbury would take further action later. In fact, Hammett claimed that Asbury yielded to the appointment as they talked but had later written Charleston to say that the appointment was null and void.[3]

The whole episode was most unpleasant and it had an unhappy ending. William Hammett detached a host of the Charleston members from their Methodist moorings and lured them into a congregation of his own, establishing The Primitive Methodist Church—before a church of the same name was formed in England. The choice of name by Hammett bore out the nature of his protest, for the primitive church of early Christian days was governed by elders or presbyters and it was not ridden by the authority of bishops. Hammett made the most of language at every turn and he must have had a wonderful way with words. But there came a time when words ran away with him. He issued a series of pamphlets in which he assailed Coke and Asbury as tyrants. He spoke out lustily for religious liberty and against "rigid unscriptural episcopacy."

Other societies accepting his views sprang up in North and South Carolina and in Georgia. Hammett grew more and more vituperative and personal, going so far as to call Coke a murderer.[4] His tactics did not make for success and after Hammett's death in 1803 the Primitive Methodists proved a rope of sand; those grains that remained were washed back into The Methodist Episcopal Church or into protest ripples that had been set in motion meanwhile.

The rise and fall of Hammett occasioned some concern in officialdom. It was disturbing but not serious. Charleston was reachable but far away, not within the active circle of Methodism. And the occurrence had involved a local society emerging into church status; it did not involve the relation of a preacher to a Conference. Quite the contrary. The fact that Hammett had no Conference standing and posed no question before the Conference made Asbury's administrative task simple.

The protest of a preacher in full connection was another matter, and it was a very serious matter if he chose the Conference body with which to lodge his protest. This made it legal and constitutional and it meant that whatever reform was proposed had to be dealt with officially. It was this background of procedure that made the case of James O'Kelly of high significance when it came before The Methodist Episcopal Church in 1792. O'Kelly was not only in good standing; he was a distinguished fellow in Virginia, where he hailed from and where he had imbibed certain republican principles, as they were called at that time—notions that the people should have some say in the management of their homely affairs, even in the church. He had the temper and temperament of the Scots-Irish as well as the liberal views of the post-Revolutionary era. He had religion and he had ideas. And, seeing that he was a Methodist, his ideas had to do with the way that the affairs of the Methodist preachers (not laymen) were managed.

What distressed O'Kelly at the outset of his campaign of reform was the same thing that distressed Hammett—the power of Asbury to move preachers around, doing it quite arbitrarily, it would seem, and yet always with the justification that the moves he made men make were for the good of the Church and of needy souls. O'Kelly warned the bishop in a letter as early as 1790 that if he did not voluntarily suspend his episcopal office for a year O'Kelly would use his influence against him.[5] Asbury knew and respected O'Kelly and bore him affection, and he knew that O'Kelly was a warmhearted and zealous fellow, that he would make no mean foe, once aroused, and that his magnetism would draw support from the other preachers.

Bishop Asbury, however, was not enough impressed to change his ways. It was the power of appointment that Asbury guarded most closely, as he had in the case of Hammett. He refused to consult with Coke on the stationing of preachers, even when Coke was around.

It was against the authority of Asbury that James O'Kelly directed his shafts. But he was too clever and too Methodist to make his attack seem personal. He called for a broad program of reform and agitated for it with the earnestness of a bee, darting here and there to gather the pollen of protest. He wanted to abolish the council of chosen leaders which had been instituted by Asbury—a kind of executive committee with powers to act between Conferences. In its stead he proposed a general conference with powers of legislation. The plea for this move he put forward under the by no means winsome announcement that he favored "the abolition of arbitrary aristocracy." He would also have the presiding elders of the several districts nominated by the preachers within the districts—not appointed by the bishop, as they were at the time.

The most daring of the propositions O'Kelly put forward touched on the right of the preachers to appeal to their fellows if they did not like or approve the post to which the bishop had appointed them. His resolution stated "that if any preacher felt himself aggrieved or oppressed by the appointment made by the bishop, he should have the privilege of appealing to the Conference, which should consider and finally determine the matter."

The resolution set off a debate that rocked the Conference and then rocked the Church. Asbury discreetly absented himself and Coke presided. Even the cultivated Welshman had to admit that the disputation was carried out on a very high level, but it occasioned no little heat and lasted for days—and nights. When the vote was taken the motion lost and James O'Kelly walked out, accompanied by four other preachers who had championed his cause, among them William McKendree, one of the most promising men in the connection. The men walked twelve miles that night to the farm where they had left their horses, and then, to all intents and appearances, they rode out of Methodism.[6]

McKendree did not. O'Kelly did. He lingered several days in and around Baltimore, and it was thought that the brethren might affect a reconciliation between him and Asbury, especially seeing that Asbury made every effort to treat him well. But the efforts to bring together two persons with antipodal points of view were vain, and soon O'Kelly had organized a band of followers into what he called The Republican Methodist Church. The new body went so far as to allow laymen some rights and it firmly provided for an equality of preachers, getting rid of what he called the Ecclesiastical Monarchy of the older church.[7]

For a while the Republican Methodists prospered as the green bay tree. Estimates were that the new body took away as much as a fifth of the membership of The Methodist Episcopal Church. More to the point is the fact that it distributed far and wide the recusant republican ideas of James O'Kelly. In the border counties between Virginia and North Carolina the O'Kelly influence was particularly strong. So intense was the interest that "families were rent asunder, brother was opposed to brother, parents and children were moved against each other, warm friends became open enemies, and the claims of Christian love were forgotten in the disputes about church government." Jesse Lee, the first American Methodist historian and a witness to some of the scenes, lamented, "It was enough to make the saints of God weep, between the porch and the altar, and that both day and night, to see how the Lord's people was carried away captive by the division."[8]

O'Kelly stirred and stimulated and agitated better than he organized. He had convictions but he lacked the orderly mind that would keep reins on men trained as circuit riders and, under a burst of sudden freedom, were pulling in all directions. Before long he gave up even the semblance of organization and dispatched with any discipline save "the pure Word of God"—as interpreted by O'Kelly. The name of The Republican Methodist Church was changed to the Christian Church and by degrees faded into the landscape of other denominations and sects.

O'Kelly's ideas did not fade. They were like sugar spilled on a floor—always underfoot, gristly and irritating and noisy and still there after all sorts of energetic efforts to get rid of it and

right when you thought you had. Of course The Methodist Episcopal Church survived the body blows O'Kelly dealt it and the
mass withdrawals his republican proposals had caused. Outwardly there were no signs of immediate change. In fact,
there was a tightening sense of structure, a feeling that more
and more eventualities must be met by laws. But, as Asbury
confided in his journal after the night O'Kelly had walked out
on his brothers, "The mischief has begun." The forms which
O'Kelly had urged upon the Church would have to be considered again and again, and there would hardly be a gathering
of the elders where the vibrant and molesting spirit of O'Kelly
was not present.

Meanwhile Francis Asbury was still in the saddle, commanding, trying to be everywhere and very nearly succeeding. He
was becoming almost as much of an institution as the Church
he served, an incarnation of the episcopal ideal, worthy of heroic
emulation by younger men. You had the Church and you had
Asbury. Most of the time the two coincided, but when they
did not it was Asbury of flesh and blood who was ascendant.
O'Kelly was the only official who had opposed him publicly
and forthrightly, calling his authority and the exercise of it into
question. With O'Kelly out of the way, there was at the moment
none to rival him or to threaten the diminution of his office.

Certainly Richard Whatcoat, at last elected a bishop ostensibly of equal rank with Asbury, presented no challenge. Until
he died quietly, as he did everything else, Whatcoat continued
to work in the vineyard as Asbury's vintner. A gentle, benevolent,
bewildered fellow, Whatcoat had been from the first content to
play second fiddle with the same patience he brought to the
ordinary hardships of the itinerancy. He did not seek status.
There were other pleasures. One was preaching. Whatcoat was
not much of a preacher, but he enjoyed preaching. Once he
said to a congregation after he had preached an hour, "I have
forgotten my text and I imagine you have too. So I will take
another one now." He did and preached another hour.[9]

What mattered to Richard Whatcoat was not administration

but the life within the soul, and the light cast by his own soul can still somehow be glimpsed through the shadows of his obscurity. It takes all kinds, and Whatcoat, who never quite made it in Methodism and caused no stink or stir, touched the lives of those who touched his. One who spoke of him at the time of his death said, "I think I may safely say if ever I knew one who came up to St. James' description of a perfect man—one who bridled his tongue and kept in subjection his whole body—that man was Bishop Whatcoat."[10]

Bishop Coke was another matter, and he might well have become a rival if circumstances and Asbury combined had not prevented it. He was not accepted by Asbury as a coadjutor. He was not consulted on appointments, and he was made sensitive of his position, writing plaintively from abroad to various Annual Conferences and offering to preside over their deliberations but saying plainly that he would not come in the role of "a mere preacher." To these offers he got no response. His status had been equivocal from the start, what with his remaining staunchly British and flitting back and forth across the waters, turning up at odd times and after shipwrecks, as in the case where he brought another alien to American shores in the regrettable person of William Hammett. He spent all-told less than three years in America. He was devout and dedicated, a preacher of logic and fluency, but he lacked thunder and lightning and the power to smite the sinner to the floor. The brethren in the New World seemed to have accepted him as a kind of heirloom, a period piece out of the Wesleyan past, more quaint than necessary.

The factor that finally weighted American Methodist opinion against Thomas Coke was secular politics. During the early 1800's tensions tightened between the United States and Great Britain. There were those who said that Britain in its high and mighty way disregarded the very existence of the United States, much less its rights. Preoccupied with the war against Napoleon and in sore need of manpower for the navy, the British adopted a policy of seizing and searching American vessels on the theory that these vessels might be carrying British deserters. The policy brought back the bile of bad memories, and when it was put into force by a British frigate outside the three-mile limit, it brought fury. An American ship of the line was hailed by a British vessel appropriately called the *Leopard*. The captain of the American ship dared refuse the right of search, and the *Leopard* pounced. Three Americans were killed and eighteen wounded.

Obviously, the British had not learned their lesson or had not been chastened enough by the earlier War of Independence and would have to be taught again that they could not trifle with the Americans. It was sad but it was so. And it meant that, in the light of the suspicions that had fallen upon the Methodists in the earlier conflict, it was no time to have a British bishop presiding over American Methodist bodies or associated with the Church in any way. At the General Conference of 1808, Coke was disposed of in a footnote to the minutes. He was not present to speak for himself. Nor was there such that he could have said in the situation of the hour. The Conference noted that he resided in Europe. The delegates were very polite about the whole business and explained that their action had come at the request of the British Conference. Then they stated explicitly: "He is not to exercise the office of superintendent among us, in the United States, until he be recalled by the General Conference, or by all the Annual Conferences respectively."[11]

Thomas Coke, the last living link with Wesleyan Methodism, Whatcoat being at rest in his grave, was now free to spread the gospel in all climes save those of the United States. He was hurt but not daunted. His scheme of operations simply took on more scope—and this time without the handicap of having to drop in on his American brethren. Coke chose India. It was far way, and the populous and heathen country, with all its crawling problems, had long held a special appeal for his soul. When he proposed the mission, the British Methodists demurred because of his age, he being at the time nearly seventy. Moreover, the cost—in the neighborhood of £6000—was far beyond their slender Wesleyan means. Coke assured his British brethren that his life and his health were his own and that he would finance the journey out of his own means.[12] He had always paid his way, not taxing any church body for his keep or passages. He had inherited money and had come by more of it through a good marriage. He was willing to devote whatever he possessed to the worthy cause of reaching souls.

With six selected missionaries, and with a printing press in the hold of the ship, Coke set sail in early 1814, happy at the prospect of what lay beyond the sun on India's coral strand. The voyage would give him time to write. He had published a history of the West Indies in three octavo volumes, an extended commentary on the Bible in six volumes, and a book that related occurrences in Europe to Bible prophecy. Here was a chance for the rover to have a little peace for further reflection. Nothing like a sea voyage to catch up on unwritten books. Besides, there were good companions on shipboard for the discussion of Christian subjects and obligations. And no Americans to worry about.

The learned missioner almost completed the passage to India, but the long leisure was too much for his Methodist soul. Within a few days of the time to land, he felt unwell and retired to his cabin to rest. The next morning, when he did not rise at his accustomed hour of 5:30, a servant entered Coke's cabin and found him dead.[13]

XVI Reform with a Vengeance

New times, new faces, new heroes, preferably American. The same session of the General Conference that disposed of Thomas Coke saw the election of the first native-born American bishop in the commanding person of William McKendree. Standing nearly six feet tall, McKendree had "black hair, dark blue eyes, Roman nose, and high cheekbones." These features gave him "almost an Indian appearance, mitigated by his exceptionally fair complexion."

The man's background was as impressive and native as his appearance. Six years after Yorktown, he was converted in his thirtieth year under the preaching of a revivalist named John Easter. A few months after his conversion his father confronted him with the question, "William, has not the Lord called you to preach the gospel?" Once when the son lay ill the father had prayed for him and the Lord had given him the assurance that the son would live to preach. Young McKendree apparently felt no disposition to keep a pledge his father had made for him, but soon he fell ill again. He was visited by John Easter, whose preaching had set him on the upward path. Easter urged the young man to enter the ministry, and he did, although not without misgivings about his course and doubts about the strength of his faith. By the second year of his preaching, however, he felt better, in no small part, he said, because of the gentle manner Asbury had with young preachers.[1]

McKendree's progress after the first hurdle was rapid. Asbury's abilities included a competence to spot and encourage men who would best advance the cause which was entwined around his heart. He spotted McKendree. There had been a time when he might have thought that he misjudged. McKendree drifted away with O'Kelly, to whom he had long been devoted. That McKendree sent the bishop a formal letter of resignation from the Conference showed the seriousness of the breach. But Asbury made possible an interview and then invited the dissident to ride the rounds with him and judge for himself whether the charges and insinuations heard in the O'Kelly debate were well founded. McKendree became convinced that they were not. Travel with the greatest traveler of them all changed his mind and he ended up on Asbury's side and, for good measure, made an assiduous study of the structure of The Methodist Episcopal Church, coming sturdily to the conclusion that it was not only in harmony with the primitive church but that it also had adapted itself superbly to the peculiar circumstances which it confronted.[2]

By 1801 Brother McKendree had acquitted himself so well as a presiding elder in Virginia that Asbury sent him to supervise the work of all of the societies in the vast and expanding West. There were some twenty-five hundred members under his care. He took charge of the work in Ohio, Kentucky, Tennessee, western Virginia, and part of Illinois. In this region it was said that he acted admirably as Asbury's major general, keeping all forces in line, plugging gaps where the weak had fallen, and pushing forward the penetration of Methodist contingents.

While rallying the troops and carrying out the charges, the major general kept his personal life in tune with the best standards of the itinerancy. It was his wont to preach and travel almost every day. His records, which were above reproach, showed that in one period of eleven months, he rested only eight days. His questing was equaled by his frugality. He kept tabs on all gifts of clothing and miscellaneous donations from 1799 to 1804 inclusive. For the year ending October 1, 1801, he received for the first three months only three dollars, and for the second quarter, two dollars. During his first year in the West he received twenty dollars, which, students say, must have been less than it cost him to travel from Virginia to Tennessee.[3]

The western area had become a conference by 1809, having nearly fifteen thousand members, divided into five districts. McKendree was presiding elder of only one, but he was the moving spirit and acknowledged leader of the area. The membership had almost doubled since the year of the O'Kelly schism, and the church was growing the way it was supposed to grow. There was also a kind of territorial integrity about the West. It represented the new and expanding force in Methodism and those associated with it had a characteristic vigor and a kind of down-to-earth and backwoods glory about them that was identified with honesty and rough-hewn uprightness. It was a different world from the effete East. But Methodism was big enough in spirit at the time to accommodate East and West and to afford some kind of bridge between them.

The twain met at the General Conference of 1808 when William McKendree was asked to preach. Some of the relatively cultured itinerants of the eastern area got a chance to see what the new type of Methodist in the West was like, and one, Nathan Bangs, a New Englander and Canadian by upbringing, was shocked when he saw McKendree. Bangs could hardly believe his ears when he heard that McKendree had been asked to preach or his eyes when he saw the man enter the pulpit and stand up to address a house that was full to the overflowing. McKendree was sunburned and dressed in ordinary clothes, "with a red flannel shirt which showed a very large space between his vest and his small-clothes." He appeared "more like a backwoodsman than a minister of the Gospel," Bangs observed. "I was mortified," he added, "that such a looking man should have been appointed to preach on such an important occasion."

Bangs was all the more mortified when McKendree stammered through his prayer and then stood before the congregation, at first almost at a loss for words. Then a magnetism seemed to emanate from him to all parts of the house. "He was absorbed in the interest of his subject; his voice rose gradually until it sounded like a trumpet. The effect was overwhelming. . . . The house rang with irrepressible responses; many hearers fell prostrate to the floor. An athletic man sitting by my side fell as if shot by a cannon-ball. . . . Such an astonishing effect, so sudden and overpowering, I seldom or never saw before." Bangs ends his account by saying that there was "a halo of glory around the preacher's head."[4]

Asbury was present and proud and he noted when McKendree had finished, "That sermon will make him a bishop." It did. Up to that time sentiment seemed to be in favor of Jesse Lee, strongly popular with the brethren, but when the roll was called McKendree and his red flannel shirt were elevated to the episcopacy and with the act came a new element in the Methodism of the day.

McKendree chose to be as much of a bishop as his senior in office. When the two men were present at a Conference he joined his colleague in presiding as if the move were the most natural in the world. What's more, he began to take amazing initiative in a most delicate area—that of appointments. Asbury made the list of appointments, telling every preacher where he was next to serve, but McKendree insisted on seeing it and he made such changes as he thought necessary after consulting the presiding elder of the district.[5] Asbury suffered as best he could this extraordinary procedure of making decisions based on the views of subordinates. He showed his distaste by not attending the meetings McKendree held to discuss appointments with the presiding elders, but he bore up, if with increasing gloom.

There were good reasons for Asbury's acceptance of the new

arrangements. One was the vigor and assertiveness of McKendree. Asbury could take the measure of any man and, as a contemporary pointed out, in McKendree he found his match. Too, McKendree, while a Virginian, represented the West through his amazing accomplishments there, and the West represented the real spread of Methodism, its conquering power. With a new region in the Church, one of great geographical spread, it was no longer possible for Asbury to claim to act as general superintendent. The Church had outgrown him. Now even Asbury must admit that there were others on whom the cause depended.

Asbury's declining health was also a disquieting factor and led to his reluctant acceptance of change. The Prophet of the Long Road was coming to its end. In 1814 he suffered an attack of inflammatory rheumatism. In the summer of that year he wrote in his journal: "I look back upon a martyr's life of toil, and privation, and pain; and I am ready for a martyr's death." His continued compulsion to travel made it appear that he was seeking a martyr's death. Friends in Philadelphia bought him a light carriage. It was quite a comedown for a great horseman, but at least he was still mobile. He crossed the Alleghenies again and moved down into the South. By now he was too weak to stand in the pulpit, though his will to preach remained. Often he would have to be carried from the carriage into the church and set upon a table at the front. From the table he would preach with great earnestness and solemnity for more than an hour.

During March 1816 Francis Asbury began his last trek. The General Conference was to assemble in Baltimore and he must attend. He reached Richmond on March 24 and there he preached once more. By the following Sunday he had reached Spottsylvania and he was so ill that friends asked to be allowed to call a doctor. Asbury knew, however, that the end had come and there was no use to waste money on professional services. He was frugal to the last. It was fitting that there be a religious service, even though he could not conduct it. They had one in the house where he lay. Friends conducted it and when it was done, the bishop asked with his waning strength if it would not be well to have a mite collection; this was the collection he regularly took in behalf of needy preachers. He was in the Church and in church to the last. That afternoon he died peacefully in his sleep, just past the biblical allotment of three score years and ten, almost as if he had rounded out and filled his years by appointment, as he had so many other missions. When his body reached Baltimore it was laid to rest, after an elaborate burial service, in a crypt under the pulpit of the Eutaw Street Methodist Church.[6]

The death of Asbury could not but seem to be well timed. The forces looking to the reform of the Church and the curtailing of the power of the office of bishop could not much longer be held in check. The sentiments James O'Kelly had loosed upon the land had become more and more vocal. They were still lodged in the minds of earnest and conscientious men. Freeborn Garrettson had not joined O'Kelly in his schism. He had held back from any overt division of the Church, but he had been on O'Kelly's side in the debate of 1792, and he had not ceased to advocate a "moderate episcopacy." He disliked the very term *bishop* and continued to use the old term *superintendent* as a form of reference and address. Garrettson felt that bishops, whatever they were called, ought to be made responsible to the Annual Conferences they served and not left to float at large.[7]

The early esteem in which Garrettson had been held enhanced through the years and made his influence great. He had extended Methodism into Westchester County, New York, and well beyond while a presiding elder and he had twelve young men and true in his charge. He had the prestige of piety and he had good connections besides, having married Catherine Livingston, sister of Robert Livingston, who had administered the oath of office to George Washington. Garrettson died two years after Asbury and was not alive to take part in the controversy that swept the Church, but his clearly expressed views indicated that the reforms he advocated were not the passing fancies of a few agitators.

The cause of reform was also assisted by a spreading spirit of democratic inclinations in politics. Religious ideas had become secular and, accepted and reinforced in political practices, they returned to haunt the Christian fold. It was an interesting round-about and the implications were hard to escape. Cardinal among the ideas that had won wide acceptance was the belief in the infinite worth of the individual. That the Lord God Himself was actually concerned with the welfare of an individual was a theological affirmation ignored by those who did not embrace religion, but religion, by repeated insistence, made the idea familiar and even the most secular minds acted on its implications. Politicians recognized and made obeisance to its corollary—a belief in the right of the common man, one without official position, to have some voice in the regulation of affairs touching or circumscribing his daily life.

The very structure and nature of the new United States government acknowledged this corollary and those who had the privilege of citizenship responded to whatever opportunities it offered. They had the right to elect those who represented them in the lower house of the national government and in their state legislatures. They had at least the theoretical right to elect the President and the indirect right to choose United States senators through their legislatures.

Such rights duly—and, in the case of some elections, dramatically—exercised by citizens of the state were not granted to citizens of The Methodist Episcopal Church. It was this irony that vexed the reformers who began to urge fundamental changes in the structure of the Church. As Methodism grew in membership, control of both polity and policy continued to be vested in a minority showing no disposition to grant any but itinerants a voice in the management. As membership reached mass dimensions, the governing minority became smaller and smaller in proportion to the Church as a whole. It was necessary to form a national church body made up of delegates. The exclusiveness of itinerants was in no way modified but rather sharpened by this arrangement. Preachers were to rule The Methodist Episcopal Church—preachers and bishops, who were also preachers.

The first delegated General Conference met in 1812. It was based on a constitution drawn four years before and approved by the Annual Conferences meanwhile. Delegates were empowered to speak for the Church and to make laws and to change laws by following a strict and narrow legislative path. The constitution was hedged by a body of restrictive rules, one of them providing that the episcopal form of government was not to be changed, any more than the basic doctrines of the Church were to be revoked or altered.

Membership of the General Conference was made up of traveling preachers chosen by other traveling preachers in good standing. Pointedly it was provided that bishops might serve as presiding officers but were not qualified to sit as members of the governing body. No constitutional provision was made whereby the vast membership of the Church could express its views, save through preachers as delegates. Ignored were local preachers, laymen and laywomen, and class leaders. The national hierarchy was well defined and fixed.

Or so it seemed. However, all the discussion and airing of difficulties that had taken place during the drawing up and adoption of the constitution left many of the preachers and more of the laymen determined in the direction of democratic change. Some of the proposals put forward, such as one that would allow the election of presiding elders by the preachers, had been ruled against by not being accepted. The very rigidity and written-in immutability of the new constitution invited the mood of reform.

Modest proposals continued to be put forward designed to broaden the membership of the Conferences. One was a proposal to admit local preachers. These men were reported to have been uneasy and restless in the South after the O'Kelly disaffection and the stern warning printed in the *Discipline* that in the future those who sowed dissension in the societies would be expelled. Even so, they manned up their courage to petition the General Conference in 1816 for admission. The petition was more plaintive than effective. It was turned down, although the local preachers outnumbered the itinerants three to one. Four years later the local preachers got permission to sit in on the deliberations of the General Conference—but only as spectators.

Meanwhile another agitation had been gathering force and dust like a whirlwind and it mounted in fury until it became a twister. This agitation looked to the election of presiding elders. The disturbance caused must have seemed quaint and meaningless to members of other denominations. Later leaders of the Episcopalians and Presbyterians volunteered to mediate the internecine dispute that grew out of the presiding elder issue.[8] Their offers were declined, and it may be just as well, for only those who knew the Methodist temper enough to understand what was at stake—and were willing to be burned at it—could have made any sense out of the controversy.

The rule creating the office in 1792 had said plainly that presiding elders were to be chosen, stationed, and changed by the bishop. But the office grew in importance as the Church expanded and those who held it were in effect head men in their areas and enjoyed power as intermediaries, being the link and channel between the plain preacher and the man at the top. The position took on more distinction when Bishop McKendree began to consult presiding elders about the wisdom and propriety of appointments. Meeting with the bishop, these men formed a committee that came to be known as the cabinet. The term had a parliamentary and political ring and added to the prestige of the consultants. To those who made it their business to foster reform it seemed that the bishop should not continue to hold such power as the right to appoint presiding elders. Men in such important posts ought to be elected by the preachers whose work they served and directed.

The matter reached the first of a series of climaxes at the meeting of the General Conference of 1820. The sessions were held at Baltimore in the Eutaw Street Methodist Church, eighty-nine delegates assembling in the presence of three bishops. In a sense there were four bishops, says one astute Methodist historian, for Francis Asbury was there too, "his body lying beneath the pulpit and his ideas about episcopal sovereignty filling the house."[9] If he was there, what he saw and heard must have disturbed him mightily. Sixty of the delegates had indicated that they were prepared to support the new method of naming the supervising elders, and in the second week of the Conference a motion to this effect was put forward. The question was debated for two days. Speeches were long, tempers were short. A compromise was proposed, namely, that the bishops nominate three times the number of presiding elders needed but that the Annual Conferences choose by ballot the appropriate number. A conciliation committee took the compromise and added the provision that the elected elders be made the advisers of the bishop in stationing preachers. This measure sailed through by a majority of 61 to 25 and a weighty burden seemed to have been lifted with a minimum of travail.

But no. While the committee on conciliation was at work, the delegates busied themselves with one of the main tasks of the Conference, that of choosing a new bishop, one sorely needed in the harvest fields of the expanding Church. On the first ballot they named Joshua Soule, D.D., a man from Maine with a high brow and a mind that delighted in the letter of the law and in the pleasures of procedure. He was as legal as a leatherbound book and the constitution of the Church engaged his fancies as well as his energies. It was Soule who had drawn up the constitution for a delegated General Conference. He had every traditional qualification of an itinerant. He had been licensed to preach at seventeen and at twenty-three had been appointed presiding elder of the Maine district.

Perhaps it was because he thought the bishop had shown wisdom when he had made young Soule a presiding elder, or perhaps it was because Soule could not stand the thought of anything not already in the constitution. Whatever the reason, the very afternoon the General Conference passed the motion to elect and give the right of counsel to presiding elders, Dr. Soule wrote the bishops a letter to say that he could not possibly accept the office of bishop under such a limitation of power as the resolution imposed. He had been elected, his letter declared, "under the constitution and government of the Methodist Episcopal Church unimpaired." Then, the very day of his election, the Conference had gone and changed the rules. Soule said he could not act under the rules that day made.

The letter was a blow that rocked the Conference, coming as it did from the great legalist and being utterly unexpected. Nobody knew what to do and everybody did everything. Bishop McKendree read the letter to the delegates, along with one of his own declaring the measure about presiding elders unconstitutional, but the delegates paid little attention. He announced that Soule would be consecrated bishop nine days later but many members of the Conference announced privately that he would not unless he gave an explanation of his conduct meanwhile. So the issue of the power of the bishop versus the preachers was acted out as well as acted upon. A motion to postpone the consecration of the new bishop ended in a roadblock tie of 43 to 43.

Facing so much hostility and still unwaveringly convinced under God that he was right, Soule resigned. Nor could anything be done to make him withdraw his resignation. That night an overwrought delegate ("a dark-lantern manipulator," as one critic called him) went around and gathered enough signatures to get before the Conference the next morning a resolution to suspend for four years the new rule on the election of presiding elders.[10] The resolution was debated all day. Some of the delegates had absented themselves or gone home, thinking the battle was over. The resolution carried on the vote of the delegates who remained, and it was now thought that Soule might consent to serve in the office to which he had been elected. He would not. The Conference accepted his resignation and adjourned in confusion. Bishop Asbury had once written, "Religion will do great things, but it does not make Solomons."

The debate had just begun. Shields were locked. Not only was the structure of the Church threatened. Its spirit was in turmoil. Tempers must be allowed to quiet. Conciliation was in order. A new publication had been authorized, *The Methodist Magazine*. Nathan Bangs was named as its editor and he announced, in view of the acerbity of the debate at the Conference, that he would not print anything of a "controversial character, lest it disturb the peace and harmony of the Church." There was no peace and harmony at the moment, thanks to the ferocity of the disputants, but Bangs, who was no opponent of reform, may have hoped that some would return. Without a forum the furore over reform might die down before the General Conference met again in 1824.

Instead it increased during the interval—and through the medium of the printed word. Denied the regular church press, the reformers turned to a series of tracts and pamphlets and they let go also through a new and stentorian publication founded by a layman, William S. Stockton, and somewhat elaborately called the *Wesleyan Repository and Religious Intelligencer*. It was a forum of reform in which the mild schemes that seemed wild to the conservatives were aired and propounded: lay representation, election of presiding elders, the seating of local preachers in Annual Conferences, moderating the episcopacy, instituting more lenient means of constitutional change—the items that were familiar and a few that were not.

What happened was a sort of replay of the Reformation in miniature, touching issues of authority that had been raised by earlier Protestant stalwarts. Each writer used a nom de plume (rather a nom de guerre) for reasons of prudence, lest his views bring penalties from the establishment. It is fascinating to see the pen names chosen, some reeking and reminiscent of earlier and sterner men's battles with the pen. One signed himself Martin Luther, Jr., another Zwingli. Still another went back to Eusebius for his guise, and one gave his contribution a militant cast by proclaiming that he was Cincinnatus.[11] Some of those who took up the staves and cudgels were men of stature within the connection and, as time passed and excitement heightened, they shed the skins of anonymity and came forth boldly, their names adding weight to their opinions.

One was the respected Irishman, Alexander McCaine. His parents had intended him for the priesthood of the Roman Catholic Church, but he had been converted in America under the preaching of that fugitive Englishman, William Hammett. The young man began preaching in Charleston and, whatever Asbury might have thought of his problems created by Hammett, he had taken a fancy to McCaine and had chosen him as a traveling companion, encouraging him also in the paths of literature. He was appointed by the bishop to compile a commentary on the Scriptures, which he commenced but did not finish. He had a reputation for clear and forceful prose and for caustic wit and there was an audience waiting when he chose to bring out in 1827 his searching book on *The History and Mystery of the Methodist Episcopacy.*

The leader in the reformation movement and the preacher most outspoken in advocating change was Nicholas Snethen, a man without schooling but not without learning. He had a lively interest in, and at least an elementary knowledge of, Greek, Latin, and French, and his mind roamed in history and poked around in the physical sciences. With all his intellectual hankering he had as much of an interest in ways and means as any Methodist and his main interest was in securing lay representation. He also favored any reform which would lessen the authority of the bishops and he championed the cause of electing presiding elders. In the debate at the General Conference of 1812 he had gone so far as to say that he would not again appear on the floor of any General Conference unless he was sent there by a vote of the laity as well as of the preachers.

Snethen did not appear again at a General Conference but his reputation was such that his absence had to be noticed. While living in Georgetown, D.C., he had been chaplain of the

House of Representatives and had the ear and fellowship of distinguished men of the day. His precarious health had enabled him to withdraw from the regular itinerancy from time to time and to lead a far more normal life than his fellow preachers. During the gathering storm over the elders, and while he was writing vigorously in support of new laws, he lived on a farm in Maryland, "well stocked with a number of slaves," until he was able to find a way to free them legally. Snethen, with his other abilities, had a superb manner of speaking. Asbury called him the Silver Trumpet.

There had been some thought that the views expressed on paper would start enough action to push reform measures through the General Conference of 1824. But the *Wesleyan Repository* never got more than five hundred subscribers, for all its superb diatribe, and there was little momentum to carry over measures from the session four years before. The Constitutionalists, as the party of the bishops was called, had gained strength. Joshua Soule was elected bishop again and this time accepted. When finally a motion to make the office of presiding elders elective was put before the delegates, it was debated all day on Aldersgate Day, the anniversary of John Wesley's deep religious experience. It was brought to a vote and passed—but only by 63 to 62 not by the necessary two-thirds.

Division yawned now like a chasm and it was purely a question of how deep and wide it would be. After the General Conference adjourned, a strategy committee of the reformers met. Unlike O'Kelly, they knew how to organize step by step. They decided to issue a periodical, forty pages of it, entitled *Mutual Rights* and to have the first issue ready in August. They addressed a circular to the whole Church. And, unforgivably, they agreed to form societies all through the Church to spread views on reform and to invite an interchange of views.

This was rebellion. The theses were on the door. Bands known as Union Societies appeared. By the end of 1827 there were twenty-four in twelve states. The reaction to this uprising was sure and swift. Trials and expulsions of preachers and members began. The distribution of subversive literature caused the greatest offense. In April of 1827 the Baltimore Annual Conference brought to trial one of its members, Dennis B. Dorsey, and charged him with "having actively engaged in the circulation of an improper periodical work." While the matter of the charge was under attention it was discovered that another preacher, William C. Poole, was circulating reform pamphlets in the very room where the Conference was being held. A motion quickly made and carried put a stop to the mischief, and then the forward Brother Poole asked if the pamphlets could be left on the secretary's table. It took another motion to prevent this audacious act.

The cases of Dorsey and Poole came to trial and a documented recountal of their various activities in impugning Methodism laid before their brothers. The two were not only read out of the Conference but expelled from the Church. Snethen warned in alarm that "your turn, my turn, may come next." His *Address to the Friends of Reform* sounded the cry: "I call upon you by every sacred name to resist this inquisitorial power, this attempt to renew in America, the old, the exploded principle of torture, this monstrous outrage on the principles of civil and religious liberty. . . ."[12]

Explusions continued to take place, sometimes wholesale, throughout the connection. Those expelled and those who sympathized with them joined in forming a body called Associate Methodist Reformers in January 1828, and a General Convention of Reformers laid before the General Conference of The Methodist Episcopal Church in May of that year a circular of grievances, seeking redress for their highhanded treatment. The General Conference gravely offered to take the mourners back into the fold if they proved to be mourners by being willing to discontinue *Mutual Rights* and disband the societies within the Church. These conditions increased the popularity of the Reformers immensely and before long they were ready to organize.

By 1830 they had formed a separate body, The Methodist Protestant Church, which drew whole congregations intact from the parent connection and doubled the membership of the new body annually for the first few years. More than 100,000 members supported the Reform contention that Methodism could assume a republican form. The new body rejected the episcopacy *and* presiding elders. Even class leaders were elected by the classes. The General Conference was made up of an equal number of preachers and laymen. One of the rules of the new body was that "no preachers or member should be expelled for disseminating matters of opinion alone."[13]

In doctrine The Methodist Protestant Church adhered to the selected Articles of Religion Mr. Wesley had sent over. On race and gender and age the new church had nothing new to say. Suffrage in deliberative bodies and eligibility to honored offices were restricted to white preachers and male members twenty-one or over.

XVII Half Slave and Half Free

The commotion over reform and the withdrawals left The Methodist Episcopal Church unsettled but unchastened, confident that its structure was "firmly supported by the hand of heaven." That the Church had survived dissent was taken as further evidence of the fact that it was the instrument of God's purpose. Survival deepened the conviction that the preachers should guard their institution as the ark of the covenant, keep it intact, preserve it from harm and for service. If the Church went to pieces, chaos would ensue. If it could be preserved, good would eventuate. The problem was that simple and that complex. A kind of hypostasis took place in which the ecclesia had more than corporeal reality. The Church was sacrosanct and the preachers were its custodians.

Matters had reached a point, however, where the attitude of the preachers toward the church they governed had a sharp bearing on their attitude toward social issues that were beginning more and more to haunt the conscience of the land. A devout regard for the form of government became paramount in all deliberations. The nature of the government of the Church, being wholly episcopal and sacerdotal, without lay elements, affected every official statement made and every position taken on such grievous subjects as the African and his enslavement. The real problem was not the autocracy which the reformers wanted to reform out of respect for democratic principles. It was that a church managed only by preachers and bishops was not representative and could not speak for persons less fervent.

Not until the Methodists formed an ecclesia did the subject of African slavery begin to be handled by administrative compromise. In the first days of Methodist activity among the colonists, freed slaves were licensed to preach, if not accepted into full connection. Meanwhile treatment of the Africans within the societies followed the prevailing pattern of patronizing kindness shown by other denominations. Methodists north and south welcomed Africans, bond and free. The society founded under the preaching of Philip Embury in New York had a slave as one of its members. So did the society set up by Robert Strawbridge in Maryland. After 1786, when a distinction was made in the reports of membership on the basis of color, it was found that the number of whites and blacks was often about equal. One district of Maryland had in its boundaries 505 white and 342 African members.[1]

Souls were neither black nor white. The preachers, obeying the color bar wherever it appeared in a slave society, preached the same doctrine to the Africans that they preached to the Americans. The central idea of Wesleyan preaching was that the lowly were infinite.

Under this kind of preaching and thinking, the soul became as real as a bone. The soul was an amazing conceit to begin with, not commonly accepted, but the Wesleyans accepted it, took off from it, addressed themselves to it, made its existence seem indubitable—and universal. All God's children had a soul, and the only problem was to find it and save it. The sternly enforced prejudices of the whites might cause Africans to sit apart, but their worth as creatures of God was asserted in class meetings and preaching services while it was denied by merchants of flesh and those who stood to profit by the sale of human beings.

Once you admitted and asserted that the African had a soul, you were bound to think that his body ought not to be held in bondage. For the very idea of soul was a deep and disturbing concept. The word had a long and honored history and was invariably and inextricably associated with religion and magic. It appeared in Old English as *sawol*, deriving from the Teutonic *saiwalo*, meaning that which is related to lake or sea. The spirits of the departed, the part left that was eternal, were thought to dwell on lakes after death. The word appeared in English as early as 1450 and was in fairly common use by the middle of the sixteenth century. Always it described the essence, an indestructible entity apart from the body, and of such strength that it survived the body. It was this indestructible essence the early Methodist preachers in America said the slave had in common with the king.

In the early and difficult days before and during the Revolution the fervor and lean-mindedness of the itinerants gave Methodism many of the features of a sect—a body more concerned with belief and ethics than with popular acceptance. The preachers spoke for themselves, not ex cathedra. The 1780 Conference met at Baltimore to report more on losses than gains and to assess the state of the societies. It was a dark hour for the new nation. Charleston had fallen in the worst American defeat of the war and the British were marching up the Atlantic seaboard. The prospect of an American victory had faded.

The Methodists met as recusants and suspects, an alien group in a country at war with the country of their origin. It was no time to tell the United States how to run its affairs or to speak out on moral issues. But the preachers spoke out against slavery. The vote was on an advisory resolution, not one that required obedience, but it stated plainly that traveling preachers were not to hold slaves.[2] It was a slim victory for humanitarianism but it showed a twitch of conscience and set an example that others might follow. Local preachers were not mentioned, however, and when slaveholders among them heard of the resolution they had little disposition to follow the example set.

Four years later the societies were organized as a church and the preachers assumed the responsibility of speaking for the church they had organized. The Christmas Conference declared that every member must free his slaves within twelve months. There was no equivocation and there was to be Methodist thoroughness in carrying out the order. Each preacher was to keep a journal in which he wrote down the names and ages of slaves belonging to masters on his circuit. Every person who did not comply with the rules should "have liberty quietly to withdraw from our Society within twelve months succeeding the Notice as given aforesaid." It was further prescribed that in the future no person holding slaves should be admitted to membership until he complied with the rules concerning slavery. The preachers wanted to make it clear, they said, that they viewed slavery as "contrary to the Golden Law of God."[3]

The preachers could hardly have made their views clearer or more emphatic in the minutes or to the world. But the local preachers and the members did not hold the same views expressed by the Conference. The dichotomy created by the claim of the preachers to represent the whole revealed the weakness of the Church. Petitions for the suspension of the rules against slavery appeared almost at once. They mounted as attempts were made to enforce the rules. The preachers could speak for God but not for local preachers or laymen. Slaves were property and useful in the South, where most of the members lived. Slavery was legal. Let the preachers preach the simple gospel but not meddle in politics and try to press on citizens what should be left to the government.

Six months after the rules were made they were suspended— in spite of Bishop Coke's insistence that they remain in force. It was, in point of fact, Bishop Coke's insistence that hastened their suspension. The preaching tour he had set out on after the Christmas Conference had not been a popular one. He called for emancipation and urged upon Methodists strict adherence to the new law of the new church. Here was the dapper doctor, fresh out of an England which Americans remembered for high-handedness and condescension as well as enmity, telling them, now members of an independent church, what to do. Their leader, Francis Asbury, would not be dictated to even by John Wesley; they would not be dictated to by Thomas Coke, especially on the subject of slavery. It could not escape their notice that the slaves on American shores had been set there by English traders.

The suspension of the rules against slavery was a blow to Coke, but it did not perturb Francis Asbury. He spoke only once on the subject of slavery and then whimsically. By his own statement, work for the amelioration in the treatment and condition of slaves would produce more practical good to the Africans than any attempt at their emancipation. The ceaseless itinerant, the Prophet of the Long Road, asked: "What is the personal liberty of the African, which he may abuse, to the salvation of his soul! How may it be compared?"[4]

With the two superintendents of the newly formed church at the antipodes of opinion on the African and slavery, the stage was set for the future, complete with scenery. It was not that the two were at odds or in opposition. They were not in the same hemisphere. They thought in different ways, each from a different set of values. They posed between them all the problems of the decades to come. Coke, having a terrible awareness of his world and a firm belief in the efficacy of faith, thought that a religious body should uncompromisingly hold up its view to the world, that none might doubt that it took its gospel to heart and would put it to work for the good of all. To such a man there could be no coexistence between Methodism and slavery.

Asbury believed that the function of the Church was to preach, to confront men with their sins, convict them of those sins, and show them the way to a new life. Results would follow renewal. And that men might be changed and through them society be transformed, the Church as the agency of salvation must be kept alive and in working order. Forms of dissension that threatened the Church threatened the welfare of man's soul. On the importance of soul both Dr. Coke and Father Asbury could agree. And that is what made them both Methodists.

After the Christmas Conference The Methodist Episcopal Church made no further pronouncement on slavery, busying itself rather with the expansion of its membership and the consolidation of its numerical gains out over the wide territory opening up to the West. The issue engendered too much caterwauling and bitterness.

The dangers of discussing slavery, even mentioning it, were increased enormously after 1793 when on the West Indian island of Hispaniola 500,000 African slaves got their freedom. They were not given it. They got it. They got it by rebellion and bloodshed and they slaughtered or forced the flight of forty thousand whites in the process. They did it under the leadership of a freed slave who became a black dictator. His name was François Dominique Toussaint, who was so swift at finding holes in the ranks of the enemy that he was given the name L'Ouverture, meaning opening. He liked the compliment and he adopted the name Toussiant L'Ouverture, making it synonymous with the terror of the black rebel. As Balzac remarked, there is nothing more terrible than the revolt of sheep, and the triumph of enslaved men over their masters put brash hopes and aspirations in the minds of flocks throughout the world.

Refugees from the West Indian rebellion arrived during the 1790's in Charleston, Norfolk, Baltimore and Richmond, adding vivid touches of gore to the news that had already frozen the hearts of slaveowners. There was talk, too, that these refugees might be agents of the French sent to sow the seeds of revolution among the slaves of America. Word of the triumph of the blacks of the West Indies was passed along to the slaves in America at their hush-meetings, and caused unwholesome excitement. Guards in the South were stepped up, patrols increased, church services among the slaves forbidden unless they were held in the open and unless whites could be present, it having been long suspected that it was in religious meetings that plots of insurrection were hatched. Round went the fervent cry, "May God preserve us from the fate of San Domingo."[5]

It looked as if God would not. The triumph of Toussiant L'Ouverture was followed in the United States by a succession of more than 250 slave revolts that lasted over half a century.[6] The first notable and well-planned conspiracy was detected in 1800. The insurrection failed, largely because torrential rains made the rendezvous of the blacks impossible, but the details uncovered chilled the blood because they were so thorough and showed such precision. Crude swords and bayonets, as well as about five hundred bullets were made through the spring. A thousand slaves with weapons agreed to meet at a given spot and fall upon the whites in the night. The whole scheme was under the direction of a slave called Gabriel, belonging to Thomas H. Prosser of Henrico County, Virginia. Gabriel was a twenty-four-year-old giant described as "a fellow of courage and intellect above his rank." Not the least frightening aspect of the uprising was the fact that it had been kept a dark secret for months, even though a thousand had been in on the plot. Who could tell what else might be brewing? And was it possible that the plotters had been given help by whites? It came to light that Methodists, Quakers, and Frenchmen were to be spared if the armed slaves carried out their designs.[7]

Revolts followed one after another, with each serving as a model for the next. Measures to guard against the terror set in motion were enough to divert the military from being employed against the British in South Carolina, Virginia, and the Louisiana Territory during the War of 1812. In 1814 there were protests in Virginia against calls for service in the militia "on account of apprehension of Negro insurrection." Many in the Louisiana Territory protested that they would not "serve a tour of duty and leave their families to be plundered and butchered by the Negroes."[8]

The period of slave revolts was a season of numerical growth for The Methodist Episcopal Church. Membership increased through an access of population in the North, as well as through evangelistic efforts, and for the first time northern members outnumbered southern. But the Church still considered itself national in scope and spirit, and it behooved the leaders to keep off the agenda as much as possible a subject that threatened to divide the country on territorial lines. It was a time to concentrate on unity and not let the issue of slavery wreck the edifice that had been so carefully built.

The spirit of Asbury, not that of Coke, prevailed. Yet the spirit of Coke could not be banished. It was the two of them and the fact of their differences that made up Methodism. And in time the fervor for the gospel that possessed them both began to lead many Methodist preachers to see and believe that, regardless of questions touching the sanctity of the Church, slavery was sin and ought to be abolished. It was not enough to save the African's immortal soul and give him Christian dignity in his chains; nor was it enough to strive for the amelioration of his wretched condition. If there was good and evil, as Methodists sternly reminded sinners, then slavery was evil and freedom was good.

The preacher who at last forced the itinerants to confront the slavery issue had been converted in a camp meeting, and for the greater part of his itinerant life he was a flaming evangelist who set whole districts on fire with his exhortations, who held revivals that were described as "overwhelming pentecostal seasons." He rejoiced in the name of Orange Scott and he came from Vermont, having been born there in 1800, the same year that brought Nat Turner into the world. Scott was cut to the pattern of the conventional circuit rider. He had given no thought to religion before his conversion. At twenty-one he had had only thirteen months of schooling. But there was a place for him in the structure of the Church. He was made a class leader and licensed to preach within twelve months after his conversion. He worked at a job for ten dollars a month, six days a week. But he found time to hold meetings after hours and before returning to the farmhouse of his parents late at night. In 1821 he began to itinerate, not on horseback but on foot, carrying saddlebags over his shoulder, filled with his few possessions, including a Bible and a hymnbook. The circuit to which he was assigned was two hundred miles around and had thirty appointed stops where he held meetings.

By 1834 he was presiding elder of the Providence district, having declined an offer to become pastor of the largest and wealthiest Congregational church in Rhode Island, saying that he preferred to hold on to the even tenor of his way as a Methodist preacher. While at Providence he began his advocacy of abolition, arousing the ire of some of the distinguished men of the connection. Not deterred, he subscribed to and circulated one hundred copies of William Lloyd Garrison's *Liberator,* spoke and wrote on every occasion, urging his church body to condemn and destroy slavery.[9]

Scott headed the New England delegation to the General Conference of 1836, meeting at Cincinnati. An antislavery convention was in session there at the same time. Word of what the abolitionists at the convention were saying about smug preachers and their indifference to human welfare—although it was not fit to hear, much less print—got to the ears of the Conference. When two delegates, in spite of insults to Methodist integrity and leaders, had the audacity to visit the convention, a motion to censure the two was introduced on the Conference floor.

It fell to Orange Scott to speak in defense of the two who had publicly identified themselves with the antislavery movement. He took the task gladly and performed it eloquently. But when a vote was taken the censure was passed by a vote of 120 to 14. That year Scott was removed from the Providence district and stationed in Lowell, Massachusetts. He began his work with a powerful revival meeting and hundreds of new converts were swept into the fold. Soon thereafter his health made it necessary for him to give over his pastoral duties for a year, but he drummed up enough energy to lecture and write widely against slavery.

Here was a hard man to tape or predict. By 1839 Scott was back in the preaching business and, just to show that the elements of ethics and evangelism belonged together, he celebrated his return to the pastorate with a whopping revival meeting that stirred the territory round about. Reinstated in the New England Conference, he was sent again in 1840 as a delegate to the General Conference, this time meeting in Baltimore.

Now Scott took the initiative. He made an earnest plea that the Conference act against slavery. It was a stirring session. Five new Annual Conferences had been added to the Church, showing how its growth and expansion continued. There was even less disposition than there had been four years before at Cincinnati to have the governors of the Church come out with a firm statement on slavery. Instead the Conference gave the preponderance of its time to matters relating to polity and paid no real attention to Scott or to any of the memorials asking for a revival of the rules about slavery.

Plainly there was no chance to make The Methodist Episcopal Church an ally in the cause of abolition and Scott left the meeting of the Conference a disappointed but convinced man. He wrote to the Methodist paper in Boston, *Zion's Herald*, a summary of his views and ended it with the words, "There is, therefore, no alternative but to submit to things as they are or secede." The next year Orange Scott withdrew from The Methodist Episcopal Church.

But he withdrew only to found another Methodist church. Polity was in his blood. A sense of both ethics and structure were deep inside him. Believing that the Methodists should take a firm and forthright stand on slavery, he helped to set up one that would. The Wesleyan Methodist Connection of America was organized at a convention held in Utica, New York, in the late spring of 1843. Excluded from membership were those who held slaves, bought or sold slaves, or claimed that it was right to do so. A year after the new body was formed the membership had grown to fifteen thousand.

Orange Scott was elected president of the Wesleyan Methodist

Connection but declined to accept the office. Untutored but fascinated by books, he became book agent through the few remaining years of his life. It was said that Methodists died well, and Scott was no exception. He died in peace and in the faith. There was no bitterness in his bones. His convictions had stirred up the snakes of controversy and there might be many to excoriate him. He did not believe it. He died with insight into the fellowship of which he was a member. On his deathbed he said, "When I am gone my old friends in the M. E. Church will remember me with kindness, sympathy, and love."

The withdrawal of thousands of members and the formation of still another church had no visible effect on the attitude of the governing preachers of the parent body. The Methodist Episcopal Church moved straight forward between its blinders, keeping time to its stately procedure, oblivious of all but methods, toward the moment of greatest crisis and ultimate separation.

Meanwhile the preachers and their flocks both could take some satisfaction in the fact that if they neglected the subject of African slavery they had not neglected the African. For all their invidious practices of pushing the African aside into undesirable parts of meetinghouses and treating him as a nuisance and as a subspecies of Christian, the Methodists continued to preach to the African, to organize him, to give him what they considered to be the benefits and inspiration of their religion. In some respects the response of the African and the use he made of the Wesleyan faith was the finest tribute to Methodism and the surest proof of its appeal to the common man in America as well as in Britain. And, as it turned out, even the rudeness of the whites in the Church had a benign effect because it put the African on his own. Prejudice ousted him from white congregations, made him want to rid himself of white patronage and show what he could do if he ran the show himself.

The case of Richard Allen and of what eventuated from his work as one of the founders of The African Methodist Episcopal Church illustrates the point as if it were a picture drawn to order. Allen was born in 1760. The circumstances of his early life were better than most slaves had reason to expect. His master and that of his parents was a leading Philadelphia lawyer, a kind and indulgent fellow, Benjamin Chew, who lived in "a fine house on South Third Street." But the life of both master and slave was uncertain. Chew fell into financial difficulties and sold the Allen family, including four children, to a man named Stokely in Delaware. There Richard worked with his parents and brother as a field hand.

At seventeen he was converted. The experience seems to have been as vivid and profound as that of any white itinerant and not dissimilar. It was followed by a profound sense of change and by the fixed routine which Methodism prepared for him. He began to attend class meetings. These were held in the woods, and it was forbidden for slaves to assemble unless there was a white man present. Even with all the restrictions and limitations, however, Richard Allen did well. He developed a desire to learn to read. And he redoubled his efforts for Stokely, the man to whom his family had been sold. Allen was intent on showing that Methodists could outwork all others. His diligence brought its reward. When he asked Stokely if he could bring the Methodist meetings indoors—into the kitchen of the big house—the request was granted. Later the Methodists moved into the parlor and some of the most exciting and dramatic preachers of the day, including Freeborn Garrettson, conducted the services.[10]

In due course Stokely gave Richard and his brother a chance to buy their freedom—for sixty pounds in gold and silver currency or two thousand dollars in Continental currency. In time they accumulated the money, although how is by no means clear, and they were on their own. Being free and being freed were different matters. The lot of the freed slave was not a happy one. Richard and his brother picked up pittances by cutting cordwood at first and then Richard got a job in a brickyard. Whatever else he did, he kept preaching on Sundays and at nights. He roamed, an itinerant without appointed rounds but with the spirit of urgency. He also worked as a helper, along with Black Harry, to white circuit riders who were forever on their rounds.

The two had every chance to learn the ways and methods of these wilderness organizers. It is said that both of them were present at the Christmas Conference—not as members, of course, but they may well have been admitted as observers. How much Allen impressed Asbury may be seen from the fact that the bishop asked him to accompany him on a trip through the South. Allen declined, uncertain what would happen to him as a freed slave in a slave region if he fell ill. It was part of his burden not to be a burden. He was resolved not to be in debt to or at the mercy of the whites. He was at pains "not to be chargeable to the connection," and whenever he ran out of money to keep him moving as a preacher he stopped and went to work until he could accumulate enough funds to preach again.[11]

Methodism appealed mightily to Africans. Its central doctrines, repeated endlessly in sermon and song, assured them both of their possible worth, through God's concern with the human soul, black or white. The class meetings offered regular fellowship. Although the services seemed informal, the order of service was that of the Church of England and vestiges of the old ritual remained to lend drama to the great matters of life and death that church worship addressed itself to. And the Methodists were a singing people. Their tunes had many a strong beat, a cadence to which the body could move in song. The hymns released the imagination and in both words and music encouraged improvisation—rhythmic talks with the Lord. And of course the hand clapping, shouting enthusiasm of the Methodists under pentecostal fire formed another basis for attraction. Methodists and Africans had much in common, which made all the more ridiculous the terrible importance the whites attached to the single difference in the color of the skin.

The more the African gained in stature and experience, the more he came to resent the white stress on using skin as a basis of judging the whole man. Some three thousand Africans had fought with the American armies in the War of Independence.[12] Africans had acquitted themselves well also in other departments of the common life. Yet white prejudice began to increase after the Santo Domingo insurrection. The word *Negro*—from the Spanish word for black—was beginning to replace *African* as a term to describe those of dark skin.

For all the shoddy treatment they received, the colored people couldn't be kept away from Methodism. By 1796, Africans made up a fifth of the whole membership of the Methodists in America,[13] and such men as the talented and devoted Richard Allen were willing to endure the harsh regulations for the privilege of preaching and spreading the good word among his fellow countrymen. Allen had returned to Philadelphia and accommodated himself to the schedule of St. George's Methodist Church. Africans were allowed to have their own service provided it came at hours that would not interfere with regular preaching. Allen preached first at five o'clock in the morning; then, as interest increased, in the afternoon; then at all times of any Sunday when the whites were not using the church. Those he converted joined St. George's and the statistical picture of the church improved impressively.

But Allen was not satisfied. He felt that his people ought to have a place of their own in which to worship. His proposal that such a place be erected met with a combination of indifference and opposition, although quarters at St. George's were getting crowded as more and more Africans were admitted. Then the church officials stopped the special services for the colored. Allen was sorely disappointed but more firmly convinced than ever that his people should have a church. Not as hangers-on or nuisances, but as people conscious of their own abilities, they should be allowed to have their own church.

The decision was taken at last by the Africans and on the basis of one exceptionally rude act. St. George's installed a gallery and on the first Sunday it was used, Allen and Absalom Jones, another African preacher, arrived with a band of worshipers and were told that they had to sit in the gallery. They went upstairs and toward seats. At that moment the preacher started a prayer and Allen and Jones and the others knelt. An usher took Jones, however, and tried to raise him from his knees, saying that the Africans could not kneel there. Jones told the usher, a trustee, "Wait until the prayer is over and I will get up and trouble you no more." Another usher was summoned and the two tried to remove Jones and another African. By this time prayer was over and the band of colored worshipers, after a brief consultation, left the church in a body, and, as Allen said in later recollections, "they were no more plagued with us in the church."

The occurrence led to the founding ultimately of the first of several national churches for the nonwhite, and these churches were as Methodist as Richard Allen. Also they gave the Negro under religious auspices the first firm assurance that he could undertake and carry through great projects on his own initiative.

The beginnings were fraught with frustration. Those who walked out of St. George's were united in conviction but not in purpose. On their own and free to organize for the first time, they had little notion of what to do but came to the sound conclusion that what they must do first was to form a self-improvement association. This they did under the banner of the Free African Society, with dues and regular attendance on meetings required and with the provision that drunkards or disorderly persons were not allowed. They looked after widows and children and in general encouraged each other and learned the rudiments of managing a society.

Both Allen and Absalom Jones were in on the organization, although Allen was discouraged and withdrew after a year because the Society had made no mention of religion. When in 1790 the Society did decide to build a church, Allen, while not readmitted, did all he could to help and was given the honor of turning the first spade of earth when ground was broken. What Allen was really interested in, however, was the form of organization the church would take. At a meeting to discuss the matter, only he and Jones favored the Methodist Church as a model. All the others wanted to follow the Church of England, then taking shape as the Protestant Episcopal Church.

Now Allen parted company again. "I informed them that I

could not be anything but a Methodist," he said. "All other denominations preached are so high flown that we are not able to comprehend their doctrine."[14] Allen got his church later. He took over an old blacksmith shop and transformed it, converted it, and called it Bethel, Hebrew word for House of God. At first it was affiliated with St. George's and was ostensibly under the white ministers of that church. However, in 1799 Asbury ordained Allen, the first Negro in America to be ordained, and Bethel gradually but fully detached itself from the parent church and became independent.

Other African Methodist churches rose up in several cities—prompted in their formation by a desire for independence and abetted in their purpose by the discourtesies and snobbishness of white churches and conferences. In Baltimore, both at Strawberry Lane and Lovely Lane, African members were allowed to sit only in the balconies and to take the sacrament after the whites had been served. Smarting under the arrangement, African Methodists began meeting in rented halls. A leader among them was a man as remarkable and distinguished in appearance and eloquence as Richard Allen. This man was Daniel Coker, whose freedom had been purchased with the aid of a Methodist layman. He too had been ordained by Asbury.

In 1816 Allen and Coker were responsible for drawing together representatives from societies in Baltimore and Philadelphia and other cities to form The African Methodist Episcopal Church.[15] In polity and doctrine the African body followed The Methodist Episcopal Church, though it made some provisions of its own when it held its first General Conference in 1820. One was that fellowship would be denied to slaveholders. Its policy of expansion had the zeal and outreach of the white parent church. For example, it moved west rapidly and when it lost ground in South Carolina in 1822 it made up for the losses by sending missionaries beyond the Alleghenies.

New York witnessed similar withdrawals from the white establishment, beginning with the incorporation in 1799 of what its charter termed the African Methodist Church (called Zion

Church) in the city of New York. The charter provided that its board of trustees would be African or their descendants. African control of church property marked a distinct and self-conscious departure from precedent. The trustees found a suitable site and the cornerstone was laid for what the Africans proudly described as "the first church edifice built expressly for the people of color in New York."

With all their proclaimed independence in property and their hope for more of it, officials and worshipers in Zion Church relied on The Methodist Episcopal Church for sacraments. They sought ordinations from white conferences but without success' until in 1822 when William Stillwell and two other white preachers who had withdrawn from The Methodist Episcopal Church ordained various elders in Zion. The ordinations and the conference at which they took place marked the beginning of The African Methodist Episcopal Zion Church.[16] Hope of being constituted a separate conference in the white connection continued for a while and then faded and the Zionists achieved a selfhood and held it. Growth was not as rapid as it was in The African Methodist Episcopal Church, but it took place, so that by the third decade of the nineteenth century you had two national Methodist bodies managed entirely by Africans.

One of the sublime ironies of the grim years before the Civil War is that Methodism failed officially to set its face against slavery and yet provided the means by which hundreds of thousands of Africans, given a chance of sorts through the Church, could prove the worth that Methodist doctrine attributed to them. What other national institution in the dreadful night of slavery told the African that he had value and gave him the lessons in organization to prove it?

XVIII A Church Divides a Nation

On the first day of May 1844, hardly more than a year after the organization of the antislavery Methodists under Orange Scott, the 1844 session of the General Conference of The Methodist Episcopal Church met in the city of New York, a place chilly and remote from the South and the West, impersonal and, in atmosphere, unsuited to a religious band made up of firebrands and evangelists and fanatically earnest men, many of them in outlandish attire. Not a few of the 178 delegates had been on their weary way for weeks, carrying well-worn valises and small trunks, coming by slow stages, river steamers, coastwise vessels. Others had reached the scene by steam cars, some on horseback or on foot, all wending toward the metropolis.

Head of the Indiana delegation, Matthew Simpson, had left Greencastle on March 20 in a three-horse wagon carrying his wife and children, along with other preachers, including Edward R. Ames, who was being talked of as a bishop. Simpson's diary records that "the air was cold, occasionally filled with falling snow, and the roads were excessively muddy." The first day the party made twenty-six miles. The next day they added twenty-nine. On the third, after traveling two miles, Ames missed his carpetbag and time was lost while the wagoner went back to try to find it. In due course the party took a train from Columbus to Madison and then a steamer to Cincinnati. Simpson arrived in New York the day before the opening of the Conference on the first day of May.[1]

Delegates gathering from every quarter had a chance to talk as they rode along or as they stopped at some point of rendezvous or to visit friends. Not a little of the talk was ominous gossip that created a mood of dread. The subject of slavery got into every conversation or else was pointedly avoided and was present all the more. A slaveholder's convention had met at Annapolis and demanded stringent revision of the slave laws, so that the lot of slaves, many of them Methodists, might be increasingly miserable in the future. Many felt that the Orange Scott separation required a positive stand on abolition lest more preachers and members leave the Church in droves. Most chilling of all was a piece of news everyone knew, although it was not official: There was to be present among those who attended the General Conference a bishop who owned slaves.

Such a thing had not happened before and there were those who said that it must not happen now. Certainly the news posed the problem of slavery in a way that offered no escape. Whatever business the Conference might attend, the hidden agenda was the case of Bishop James Osgood Andrew of Georgia.

Proceedings began in dignified, orderly, and routine way on a Wednesday morning at nine. In the chair was Bishop Joshua Soule, the stern and rock-bound New England author of the constitution of the delegated General Conference. There was a hint of the rumble of trouble ahead and delegates could see the lines being drawn even in the generalities of the bishop's address. He paid a paean to the episcopacy and stressed the importance of evangelistic efforts in defining what the Church could do for people of color, saying that this work was to the glory of the preachers. Then he added, "But to raise them up to equal civil rights and privileges is not within our power. Let us not labor in vain and spend our strength for naught."[2]

All went quietly through Thursday, but on Friday the Annual Conference of which Orange Scott had been a member brought forward a petition against slavery. There were vocal protests that slavery was not a suitable subject for a General Conference, but the delegates accepted the petition and the chair was ordered to appoint a Committee on Slavery to receive any other memorials on the subject. The following Tuesday real trouble began. It came on the appeal of Francis Harding, a preacher who had been suspended by the Baltimore Conference for refusing to free certain slaves he had come to own through his marriage. Harding appealed the decision and asked the General Conference to reverse it.

The debate touched off lasted for four days. Harding contended that the slaves belonged to his wife, not to him, that Maryland law would forbid his freeing them even if he personally owned them, and his defense added for good measure the reminder that the General Conference of 1840 had passed a ruling to the effect that holding slaves was no barrier to the exercise of any office in the Church.[3]

When the four-day debate had come to an end, the appeal of Francis Harding was put to a vote and the delegates sustained the decision of the Baltimore Conference by a count of 117 to 56. That the appeal of a traveling preacher had been rejected more than two to one made clear that his case was but a rehearsal for what would happen to a bishop. It was a rehearsal in procedure as well as in drama and theory. The delegates, preachers all, acted as they had been so long accustomed—by the rote of parliamentary procedure. Straight out of the English legislative tradition, they had from the beginning accepted the authority of the majority, deciding every issue and matter by counting noses. There was among the Methodists none of the Quaker sense of consensus, of aiming at or moving toward agreement. Rather the whole principle of action was to create division, to draw sharp lines, ask that men declare themselves for or against. It was related to the either-or method the preachers used in addressing sinners, and it was also related to and imitative of the fight principle used in the British House of Commons, where parties arrayed themselves against each other and where a roll call on an issue was called a division.

It was this contentious secular method that the delegates, fully convinced of their divine appointment to rule the Church, used at the General Conference of 1844. Consensus, from its derivation, means "to feel together." Conference means that all bring or carry something with them as they come together. The preachers brought their problems and emotions and convictions and regional prejudices with them when they came together to consider the infinitely complex and delicate problems of the hour. The idea that Christian procedures as well as men could be Christian was lacking. At the most trying hour of their history the Methodist preachers in conference assembled used the tactics of conflict and the methods of the state.

When it became plain after the Harding case that the tactics of conflict would not work, and that some means of conciliation must be found, the Conference named a committee of six to confer with the bishops and report within two days "as to the possibility of adopting some plan, and what, for the permanent pacification of the church."[4] Slavery was now out in the open. The resolution calling for the committee had stated clearly that the task at hand was to deal with "the relative position of our brethren North and South on this perplexing question." The two men who had drawn up the resolution were respected leaders of the two sections now at loggerheads.

Stephen Olin represented the North. He had been born in Vermont but he had been converted in South Carolina and had entered the ministry there. He had also been a professor of English literature at the University of Georgia for seven years and president of Randolph Macon College in Virginia before becoming president of Wesleyan University at Middletown, Connecticut. Olin knew the mood of the South as few Northerners did.

Joining him in the hope that a committee might work a miracle was William Capers, an elder statesman of Methodism in the South, a leader of the South Carolina Conference, kindness incarnate. He was also respectably descended, being originally of Huguenot family, and his father had served in the Revolutionary War. His range of acquaintance and friendship was wide and through his close associations he was thought to reflect and understand the mind of southern preachers better than anyone else.

These two gentle men understood each other well enough to see that there could be no understanding on the open and hidden issues at stake. Olin summed it up: "It appears to me that we stand committed on this question and views of policy, and neither of us dare move from our position. I do not see how northern men can yield their ground, or southern men give up theirs." He pointed out with a perception few abolitionists displayed that if the southern brethren should "concede what the northern brethren wish—if they concede that holding slaves is incompatible with holding their ministry—they may as well go to the Rocky Mountains as to their own sunny plains. The people would not bear it. They feel shut up in their principles on this point." Preachers of both sections were caught in the toils of their own principles and no committee would be able to disengage them. As Olin went on to say, "If we push our principles so far to break up the connection, this may be the last time we meet. I fear it! I fear it! I see no way of escape."[5]

There was none. The distraught committee on the pacification of the Church had to give up. It had spent four heartbreaking days looking for an out, asked for more time, held separate caucuses of delegations from the North and the South. And then it was forced to report that it was "unable to agree upon any plan of compromise to reconcile the views of the northern and southern Conferences."

And now the stage was set and darkened for the case of Bishop Andrew of Georgia. Andrew was a man of irreproachable character and conduct. No one denied that or that he was lovable; or that he was a good preacher and had been a worthy and diligent bishop since his election twelve years earlier. Every detail of his life conformed to the approved pattern of the circuit riders. He

223

was the son of a Methodist preacher. He was licensed to preach when he was eighteen and had been received into the South Carolina Conference immediately afterward. He was a good pastor and became a presiding elder and in general proved to be a credit to the Church.

But shortly before coming to the General Conference he had married what was referred to as an estimable lady in Georgia. It was his second marriage. The estimable lady owned slaves, so the report ran. Everybody had talked about the matter but the General Conference and that august body now took it up, referring it politely first to the Committee on the Episcopacy, which was instructed to ascertain the facts—facts which, with a few minor distortions, the assembled preachers knew already. The committee reported the next morning and included with the report a statement by the impugned bishop.

It was confirmed that Andrew owned a mulatto girl bequeathed to him in trust and a Negro boy left to him from the estate of his first wife. He had tried to persuade the Negro girl to go to Liberia or to a free state, but in vain. The boy was not old enough to support himself. Georgia law forbade the bishop's manumitting his slaves and there was nothing that he could humanely do but to hold on to them. It was true also that his second wife was the owner of slaves inherited from her first husband. Andrew pointed out that he had no part in the ownership of these slaves and that he had taken pains to divest himself of any claim to the property of his wife. He also stressed the fact that he had never himself bought or sold a slave and that his wife could not emancipate the slaves she owned even if she desired to do so.[6]

Immediately a resolution was put before the Conference, "affectionately" requesting that Andrew resign his office as bishop. This move he had considered as he came toward the Conference, foreseeing the storm his case would stir up. But the southern delegation got word of his intention and in a body and in writing had asked him not to resign, saying that his resignation "would inflict an incurable wound on the whole South and inevitably lead to division in the Church." Bishop Andrew was not about to resign and the debate over his case and kindred matters began.

The debate went mercilessly on for six days. At the end of this period one moderating note was injected. Two delegates from Ohio offered a substitute resolution calling on Bishop Andrew to cease and desist from the exercise of his office as long as he remained a slaveowner. Outright rejection was tentatively withdrawn and the offender given a chance to mend his ways. The move did little to still the seething caldron of tempers. Debate on the substitute resolution took up another six days. An attempt was then made to end the debate but it failed to get the necessary two-thirds majority.[7]

Throughout the whole course of the highly organized combat, only two speakers made direct reference to slavery or to the position the Church ought to take on abolition. Slavery had provoked the contest but it had somehow disappeared as the main concern, like some indirect and unrecognized cause of war. The preachers addressed themselves to a single issue: Who controls the Church: the General Conference or the bishops? Where should ultimate authority repose? If it lay in the General Conference, then that body had a right to discipline or depose a bishop. If the bishops had rights only as officers of the Conference, they had no real say in the government of the Church. But if they had mystical power by virtue of the nature of their position and consecration, if they constituted an Office and were not merely officers, the General Conference had no right to turn them—specifically James O. Andrew—out. Through the tradition of the apostolic succession, though broken by the Methodists, bishops represented the mystical component, the permanent link, the continuity of religious experience. They were, in this view and by the transforming spiritual power of their office, equal with or superior to a self-constituted and self-perpetuating body of voting preachers.

It was plainly argued by the defenders of the bishop that he had broken no law of the Church, that his action was approved by the action of the previous General Conference, which had ruled that slaveholding did not disqualify a man for office. It was contended, too, with some force and much fervor, that there was nothing in the constitution of the Church which gave the General Conference power summarily to ask a bishop to resign. On this point Joshua Soule was most emphatic in a written message protesting that the Conference could not depose Bishop Andrew without trial, saying that in so doing it would give him less right than it accorded an ordinary preacher. Soule felt that the constitution of the Church would be radically changed, perhaps destroyed, if the delegates did not reject the resolution against Bishop Andrew.

Speeches were long-winded and florid, influenced more by homiletics than hermeneutics, combining the features of a sermon and a plea to the jury. There was a curious, lofty, detached quality in the debate, an abstract and legalistic tone, as if people had become principles and there were no people present. Those who supported the disciplinary resolution made no attack on the placid but stubborn Bishop Andrew. Rather they addressed themselves stoutly to the defense and praise of the legal system under which they operated, and spoke of bishops as if they were flies annoying the brethren or at least a kind of subspecies to be endured.

One of the most fervid exponents of suspension, Leonidas L. Hamline, had been a lawyer before he became a preacher, and he remained a lawyer on the floor. Only the legal aspects of the situation held his interest and it was a good time to get these legal aspects straight. What did a bishop really amount to? Hamline told the delegates: "In clerical orders every man on this floor is his equal, but in legislative functions, his superior." The General Conference was not only the "ecclesiastical legislature and high court—curia maxima—of the Methodist Episcopal Church." It was also "the *fountain* of all official executive authority."[8] James P. Durbin of Philadelphia spoke like an eloquent echo when he asked rhetorically from whence the episcopacy derived its power and answered oratorically: "Solely, sir, from the suffrages of the General Conference. There, and there only, is the source of episcopal power in our Church. And the same power that conferred the authority can remove it, if they see necessary."[9]

Those who rose in defense of Andrew held no brief for the General Conference as the supreme being of the Church—"the sun of our system," as Hamline called it. They could see as the debate wore on and wore out the delegates that the General Conference was the real enemy in the woodpile. Under the handcuff rule of government by majority they were outnumbered and would be outvoted and put to rout, no matter what course they advocated. The result of decision by division had been a foregone conclusion from the opening gun of the Conference. If there were any hope it lay in a miracle, in the intervention of some invisible factor that might pacify the Church. Protracted debate, even if speeches were meaningless when they were not repetitious, at least passed the time and postponed the inevitable. If the inevitable could be postponed, there was just that much more opportunity for a miracle.

The intervention of peace almost came on the thirtieth day of the Conference. In fact, it did come, but it was snatched away before the eyes of the delegates by forces (invisible but human) pulling strings behind the scenes. Bishop Elijah Hedding, a New Englander, requested that there be no afternoon session on Thursday, May 30, in order that the bishops might consult and come up with some solution. Permission was granted, and the next day the bishops recommended unanimously that further action on the Andrew case be postponed until the next General Conference and that during the next four years ahead Bishop Andrew be allowed to continue to serve in sections of the country "where his services would be welcome and cordial."

The delegates hardly had time to breathe a sigh of hope when J. A. Collins, a busybody from the Baltimore Conference, jumped to his feet and moved that the recommendation of the bishops be printed and circulated for discussion before the Conference acted on it. His motion carried. The ensuing delay made possible a caucus of the New England Conference. The results of this caucus were also unanimous. The delegates agreed that if Andrew were allowed to stay in office, even on the temporary basis the bishops recommended, the churches of New England would be broken up and could be repaired only if the New England Conference seceded and invited Hedding to be its presiding bishop.

Hedding had already signed the recommendation of the bishops when he heard the results of the New England caucus. He went immediately and withdrew his name, saying that facts had come to his attention to show that postponement would not lead to peace but only prolong the debate. Without Hedding's name to make it unanimous, the Conference voted to table the recommendation of the bishops, but the vote was by no means as lopsided as it had been on other questions. It was 95 to 84, and John N. Norwood, author of *Schism in the M. E. Church*, the standard account of the 1844 General Conference, believes that the wishes of the bishops would have prevailed if Hedding had not been persuaded to withdraw his name.[10]

Years later James Porter, one of the New England delegates, revealed a ruse he had worked out with the delegation from the Baltimore Conference, which, though southern in location, was strongly abolitionist. The day before the General Conference opened the two delegations privately agreed on objectives: the decision against Harding must be sustained and Bishop Andrew must purge himself of slavery or vacate the episcopal office. The two delegations fashioned a covert device by which they could work toward their goals. There would be prejudice in the Conference against abolitionists and the measures agreed on might be defeated if they were prominently urged by New England delegates. It would therefore be well for the New Englanders to remain quiet, let the conservatives from the Baltimore Conference, as Porter explained it, "take the laboring oar in their own hands, leave us to vote, and otherwise aid the desired result as we might be able. By a private understanding this method was informally accepted and carried out to a successful issue in every particular."[11] Preachers trained through long years in secular procedures had become past masters at intrigue. The General Conference of 1844 had been rigged before it opened and the plan and results written into a script.

The denouement came at noon on June 1 when "amid the most profound stillness" the roll was called in the case of Bishop James Osgood Andrew. By a tally of 110 to 68 the Conference adopted the substitute resolution asking him to cease his functions as a bishop as long as he remained a slaveowner.

Lovick Pierce of Georgia rose to say that a "manly, ministerial, and proper protest" would be lodged against the action at the earliest possible moment. It was. And it was answered, continuing the debate on paper. Not despairing, even after the blow had fallen, old Brother William Capers of South Carolina laid before the itinerants a plan whereby the Church would simply be divided into two administrative areas, each having its own General Conference and bishops but abiding by the same constitution. The plan was referred to a committee which reported that it could not agree on any recommendation. Then A. B. Longstreet of the Georgia Conference came forward with a plain declaration that the suspension of Bishop Andrew had made "the jurisdiction of this General Conference inconsistent with the success of the ministry in the slaveholding states."

It was a point the implacable foes of slavery had not been able to reckon with, much less grasp, on any basis of experience. The delegates from the slave states were also Methodists, heart and soul, as much as Asbury had been and Orange Scott was. They wanted above all things to keep the Church alive and intact as an agency of good. What they asked was the right of access to slaves and slaveholders. Only a body of preachers pledged to the salvation of the individual, free of the politics of the North and empowered to discharge duties in states where politicians defended slavery and resented outside interference, could continue the functions of Methodism. If a church belonging to America as a whole and seeking to serve all kinds and classes of people was to make abolition its primary concern, why, then, its preachers could not operate in the South.

229

Stephen Olin, a Northerner with experience in the slave states, had stated the point informally. Now Longstreet had put it in the record. His declaration was referred to a Committee of Nine with instructions that they draw up a constitutional plan, if they could think of no way out of the difficulties over slavery, "for the mutual and friendly division of the church." Two days later the Committee of Nine brought in a Plan of Separation. It provided that members of churches on the division line between North and South could decide by majority vote which connection they would abide with; and offered arrangements whereby the property, not inconsiderable, of the Methodist Book Concern should be divided.

Having disposed of the subject of slavery after a fashion and having cut the Church asunder in the process, the General Conference moved on in its ponderous businesslike way to other items on the open agenda. Methodism, for all its troubles, was still growing. Five new Annual Conferences were formed—three in the North and two in the South. New bishops were elected, including Leonidas L. Hamline. The Conference decided that a superintendent of missions to the colored people in the South should be appointed. The bishops warned the preachers and churches to stay with the requirements and build plain, cheap houses of worship and decried the increasing practice of building costly edifices that had to be financed by mortgage and long-term loans. The final act was one of brotherly love. A collection was taken for two delegates who had been robbed of their money in the city of New York.[12]

XIX God and the Most Battalions

The largest and most successful church in the United States of America, national in scope and membership, numbering half of all Protestants, had shown that it could not handle amicably in its own counsels the problem that confronted the nation. It had officially forsaken the path of brotherhood to follow sectional sentiments.

The failure was noted far and wide. There were already twelve hundred newspapers in the country. Many were small and the areas they served limited, but each quoted from others, so that in the aggregate they spread words all over the land. The secular press had covered the division closely. Two of the four columns of news on the front page of the Philadelphia *Public Ledger* of Monday, May 27, 1844, a day when the Democratic national convention was in session and by way of choosing its slate, were devoted to the debate on Bishop Andrew.[1] (The other three columns were given over to advertising, including the announcement of a new book, *How To Be Your Own Cattle Doctor*.)

Hardly a newspaper in the growing nation could ignore the breaking up of the Methodists. Attention focused on a convention of delegates from the Annual Conferences of the slavehold-

ing states held at Louisville, Kentucky, during May 1845. Press
and onlookers were present in force, including prominent Methodists from the North who had opposed the bewildering withdrawal of the southern delegates. (Among the visitors who
watched from the balcony was Matthew Simpson.) It was at
this Louisville convention that there was created what the delegates called a distinct ecclesiastical connection "to be known
by the style and title of the Methodist Episcopal Church,
South."

Many saw in the separation a rehearsal. Religion being the
full moon of politics, there might be a portent of what lay not
too far ahead. For the debate over Bishop Andrew in a church
gathering had not concerned itself with any of the basic tenets
of the Christian faith. Rather it had addressed itself to questions
of rights and authority and procedures and regulations. It was
the question of who had the right to handle slavery that troubled men in government, and it was this question that had troubled the souls of the Methodist preachers. John C. Calhoun,
archdefender of the territorial prerogatives of the South, would
cite the breakup of the Methodists and draw dire lessons from
it on the floor of the United States Senate.[2]

Moreover, a time of growing antagonisms was also a time of
ever more rapid means by which these antagonisms could be
repeated and presented as news, providing the nation with something of the immediacy and intimacy of gossip. On May 1, the
day the 1844 General Conference opened in New York, Henry
Clay was nominated for the presidency by the Whigs meeting
in Baltimore, and the news of his nomination was ticked to
Washington on a new contraption known as the telegraph, reaching the capital an hour before word of the action arrived by
train. Three weeks later, when the Democrats met in Baltimore,
the proceedings of a political convention were for the first time
reported by wire. Things were moving that fast. What a man
thought today could be read—and probably said—by millions
on the morrow.

The fast distribution of news helped to accelerate events

and brought word of happenings thick and fast, condensing actions to flashes, multiplying impressions out of hand. The General Conference of 1844 did not end with the benediction. It went on in public, with heavy artillery exchanges on each side and with the whole spectacle plain for the world to see. There was no secrecy in Methodism, no discreet attempt to hush problems or hide them in closets. Everything was open and aboveboard and fully threshed out in the religious and secular press.

Legal action over the division of property drew prolonged publicity. The General Conference of The Methodist Episcopal Church in 1848 declared null and void the Separation Agreement of 1844, which had provided that the Methodist Book Concern would be divided equitably. The Methodist Episcopal Church, South, brought three suits for the recovery of a share in the property.[3] One case went all the way to the United States Supreme Court and was decided unanimously in favor of the southern Church, giving it needed funds and a boost in morale by being recognized as a legal entity with rights independent of those granted by the sufferance of a former association with what some called "the old mother church" but that Southerners insisted was a sister church.

The years of quarrelsome separation of the Methodists north and south preceding Secession saw a contest over issues that were political, yet they were treated as if they were religious. The resounding recriminations in what one historian calls the paper war set a wretched example for the people of a country distraught by difficulties revolving, one and all, around questions of territory and ownership. The people could have used restraint and profited by counsels of moderation. They could not get, nor could they expect, any gentling influence from the Methodists, who were Americans, heart and soul, north and south. Methodism had grown up with the country and had become the country, being now the biggest and hence best of the churches, brash and confident, and even powerful enough to divide and remain strong. These were people who belonged to geography as well as a period of history. Much of what they did and said was absurd, but so were the Rocky Mountains and the Great Plains and the Mississippi and the rich delta lands. How could such a stupendous country come into being save through the unbelievable and how could men be rational when they were children of good fortune? Boasting was natural, reasoning was not. And the Methodists were the best evidence of good fortune. A small and recusant English sect, unwanted and unwelcome, had grown on these shores and on this soil into a religious giant in seven-league boots, towering over other sects and all sinners.

It was almost impossible for such a conquering tribe, having possessed the land, not to ascribe its blessings to a smiling Providence as well as to the soundness and virtue of its own beliefs. Methodism and America had grown up together and they had grown together. Their problems were identical. So were their weaknesses and their hopes, their bewilderments and the extravagance of their faith in the ultimate, their touching certainty that there would in God's good time be achieved on these plains and along these rivers and against these mountains a perfect country. The sign was a long way off, but the sign was never absent, never fully obliterated.

In the period of separation and secession the Methodists, by temperament akin, behaved as other Americans did, only with greater intensity. Religion speeded up their reactions. Religion played a role at once inscrutable and inevitable in this time of national trauma. There had been from the beginning of the country an official, generalized sense of the God idea. The Great Seal of the United States, adopted by the Continental Congress shortly after Yorktown and by the federal union in 1789, showed an aureole of light through which an eye, symbolic of the eternal eye of God, was visible. Under the eye was printed in Latin the words meaning "He has smiled at our undertaking."[4]

Much had gone on since the seal was adopted to bring God down out of the skies and make Him available. The enthusiasm of lonely people had put Him to work. He had wandered with them in the wilderness. And always He had been tied in naturally with daily doings. He had accompanied the circuit riders, joining in a mood of conquest and stressing an awareness of territory. Religion had begun to affect secular activities, causing men to turn against the solid business institution of slavery and call it into court and to talk about making it illegal. It had given the politician a sublime and mystical faith in his own ideas, such as Manifest Destiny.

Against this backdrop the Methodists rehearsed their roles in the drama of the Irrepressible Conflict. The roles were not welcome, but they were acted heartily just the same and with such élan and vigor that deep traces were left in the minds of those who watched. On the practical level to which they descended, there was much of tragedy. Making organized religion a party to politics prepared the way for making God a party to killing. The vehement piety of Americans in times of war, the practice of blessing political action with divine sanction, arose in this period and became embedded in the national consciousness, where it could be conjured up at any time.

It was the merging of the organized religious with the erstwhile secular that lent the saddest significance to the break in 1844. The aim of The Methodist Episcopal Church had avowedly been the reform of the continent and the spreading of scriptural holiness. It had set itself conspicuously above the secular. Now, through circumstances peculiar to the land of its adoption, Methodism had come to a frightful period in which it found itself not only unable to rise above the world but had actually fallen so low that it aped the political behavior of the culture of which it was a part.

The professional and habitual emotionalism of the preachers, intensified by the inner feelings about slavery and by the national temper and the telegraph, put Methodism in a position where it could hardly do more than carry out the logic of its mistakes. Each side could do no right. Any gesture of conciliation was misconstrued or misinterpreted.

In 1848 The Methodist Episcopal Church, South, sent a fraternal delegate in the person of Dr. Lovick Pierce to the General Conference of the northern church, meeting in Pittsburgh. Dr. Pierce was one of the kindest and most agreeable of men in his personal dealings, and it is interesting to see that in the account of the visit given by the *Cyclopedia of Methodism*, compiled in the 1880's, the name Lovick Pierce, by benign typographical error, appeared as Loving Pierce.[5] Loving he may have been but, after a day of deliberation and debate, The Methodist Episcopal Church adopted unanimously a resolution saying that "while we tender to the Rev. Dr. Pierce all personal courtesies and invite him to attend our sessions, this General Conference does not consider it proper, at present, to enter into fraternal relations with the Methodist E. Church, South."

So the Northerners wouldn't even speak! And this four years after they had drawn amicably a Separation Agreement, which they now rescinded! The indignation of the southern Methodists was off like a skyrocket, sputtering as it went and showering sparks as it burst. It did little good to explain calmly that Dr. Pierce's letter was tactlessly phrased, that it went beyond the commission under which he had been sent as a visiting delegate, and that, with all its drawbacks and shortcomings, it arrived before his credentials. The northern brethren were perplexed, spent a whole day trying to decide what to do. When Dr. Pierce read the journal of their deliberations, he withdrew his offer of friendship in a letter, which registered his disappointment, and said only on his own authority that the General Conference could regard "this communication as final on the part of the Methodist Episcopal Church, South."[6]

Historians could wrestle for a century with events of the times and render only judgments packed in caution. At the time the events took place, however, there was only truth or error, fact or falsehood, right or wrong, and those who heard what had taken place put their own private construction on whatever they read or heard.

The preachers were not lacking in a knowledge of how language could be used to arouse emotion, and they set themselves now to the attack on new devils that dwelt within the household of faith. A man celebrated as one of the most popular pulpit orators in the United States, Henry B. Bascom, president of Transylvania University, turned to pamphleteering. Soon after the General Conference in the North adjourned in 1848 he brought out *A Brief Appeal to Public Opinion*.

Bascom charged The Methodist Episcopal Church with "perjury and subornation of perjury, want of reverence for the word of God, bad faith and deception utterly irreconcilable with any virtue belonging to the Christian character." The northern church was "so mixed up with the whole machinery of abolition and antislavery agitation that its own chosen colors will not allow us any longer to distinguish it from the common enemy. It has become a pander to political agitation." Dr. Bascom went on to talk about the members of the northern church as persons of "no fixed principles or settled views. They are victims of a mania, constantly involving them in contradiction and inconsistency."[7]

The bombast bursting in air was all the more deplorable because the din was joined by the Baptists within a year after the southern delegates walked away from the General Conference in New York. Formation of the Southern Baptist Convention in 1845 was attended by fewer spectacular circumstances than the split of the Methodists. There was no long, grim, deadly debate to precede and advertise the impending division. But it was clear after a separate southern body had been set up that the real background cause of division was the sectional views held on slavery.

Both sections of Methodists, not to mention the Baptists, leaped earnestly to the fray after the southern states had withdrawn from the national government and formed one of their own. The preachers of both regions, whether making rousing speeches at rallies or penning their exhortations in the religious and secular press, supported the cause of the state without equivocation.

How well they did it in the North may be judged by the

statements of political leaders after the war was over. Chief Justice Salmon P. Chase, who had been Secretary of the Treasury during Lincoln's administration, exclaimed, "I have thanked God that the Methodist Church knew only one sentiment—that of devotion to our country. How we have leaned upon your bishops, your ministers, and your great people."[8] Lincoln himself is reported to have told Methodist interviewers late in the war that "we never would have gotten through this crusade without the influence of the Methodist Episcopal Church."

When the General Conference met at Philadelphia in 1864 the first order of business, after ordering the national flag raised over the edifice where the preachers assembled and appointing a day of prayer for the country's deliverance, was to name a delegation to call on the President and assure him of the unfaltering support of the Methodists. An appropriate address was drawn up and the delegation took train to present it in person. One member secured privately a copy of the address and, through his connections, called on Lincoln at his residence, explaining the urgency of the matter and presenting him with the greetings he was to receive the next day. By this arrangement the President had time in which to frame his response.

It was a replay of the carefully planned interview the Methodists had staged with President Washington, but it worked out even better. This time there was certainly no inkling of doubt about the loyalty of the visitors. Also Lincoln was not as grave as General Washington had been. Lincoln let it be known, with a twinkle and an amused smile at the organization men, that he had already read the paper they formally delivered. Then he gave the response he had had the opportunity to compose. A copy was made for the President's files, while the Methodist officials remained chatting, and the churchmen carried away with them for their own files and for posterity a classic statement of the President's confidence.

The reply acknowledged the valued support of all the churches. Lincoln noted that he would not want, of course, to say anything that might in the least appear invidious, but he went on to add that The Methodist Episcopal Church was "by virtue of its greater numbers the most important of all. It is no fault in the others that the Methodist Church sends more soldiers to the field, more nurses to the hospitals, and more prayers to heaven than any. . . ."[9]

Methodist leaders shared the generous view of northern political leaders, fancying themselves to be "the agency of the nation's deliverance." The act of being identified with right lent freedom and latitude to irresponsible comment. Zeal turned to vitriol under the spell of war. The preachers felt justified not only in expressing confidence and certainty in the righteousness of the northern cause but also in excoriating their opponents. One in Illinois called "for confiscation, subjugation and extermination . . . for employing Negroes, mules, brickbats, small arms, large arms, and bayonets to kill rebels and crush the rebellion."[10] Another reminded his listeners, "While those at the front kill rattlesnakes, we at home must kill copperheads." Of course war was grim and horrible, but in this instance there was a healthy and spiritual purpose to be served, for "the worm in the bud of the nation's existence could be killed only by bloodletting."[11]

The informal order of service, following the evangelistic tradition and leaving the sequence up to the spontaneity of the leader, lent itself splendidly to patriotic ends. Shouts and loud amens were not inappropriate. A familiar hymn could be parodied and sung to celebrate some accomplishment of arms. Tremendous effect was achieved by earsplitting renditions of the doxology, all present singing at the top of their lungs and voices "Praise God from whom all blessings flow" upon receiving the news of a Union military victory or of an election the results of which could be interpreted as providential. The American flag was carried into the church and became a common sight, especially at Annual Conferences. Occasionally it was hoisted with ceremony, resolutions were read, and patriotic songs lifted before the Conference got down to business.

The flag was the special plaything of one Dr. Charles Elliott, who edited the *Central Christian Advocate* from 1860 to

1864. Dr. Elliott's primary concern in the ecclesiastical world was the Church of Rome and the errors of its ways. He wrote learnedly on the necessary reformation of Rome and even offered to go to Rome as a missionary. He was able to spare some time for the Civil War, however, and he appeared at various gatherings and conferences wrapped in a silk flag which, as he explained, had been made for him "by five Union, Christian, Methodist ladies in St. Louis."

The tone struck by religious leaders in the South was milder than it was in the North, especially after the sobering influence of actual warfare befell the region. At the outset, while the forces of conflict were still engaged in elaborate preparations and almost everyone thought that the contest at arms would be hardly more than a glorified skirmish, southern Methodists felt little need to pin the name and claim of God on the standards of their battalions. There was joy and satisfaction that the South was "shut of the leeching influence of the North and free to go its own way to develop the superior civilization for which it had the ingredients." In 1861 William M. Wightman, an acknowledged leader among southern churchmen, spoke of the Confederacy as a new nationality. It was "strong enough to stand against the world. Its domain is the most productive on earth." Its resources, intelligence, and religion all pointed to an illustrious destiny. The millions in money that had gone to build up northern cities would now be used "to build up our own commerce, manufactures, literature. The sceptre has already fallen from the hands of New York. Grass will ere long grow in her streets, and solitude reign in her palaces and avenues. The grand, historic hour has struck . . . and a new order of things begins."[12]

Three weeks after Dr. Wightman's sanguine address the rout of Union forces at the Battle of Bull Run and the floundering retreat of those forces, leaving the Union capital virtually undefended, lent force to his predictions. But by 1863 the expected skirmish had turned into mass slaughter on a scale not hitherto witnessed, and the glow in the South turned to gloom as it became apparent that the Confederacy was not going to be allowed to go her way unmolested.

The mood of churchmen in the South changed with the fortunes of war, so fully were the churchmen committed to a successful outcome of military operations and so fully were their hopes for mankind conditioned on victory.

The difference with which each of the two sections of Methodism identified the cause of the state with its own ideals lay largely in the height of hyperbole. The membership in the North was much bigger and made more noise. The emphasis in the gatherings the northern Methodists held during the war years fell on loyalty. The Wisconsin Conference in 1861 declared, "At such a time as this, neutrality is treason, silence crime, and inaction unpardonable." The Genesee Conference in 1863 said that it would not accept into membership anyone whose patriotism could justly be called into question. It was not unusual for an entire Annual Conference to have the oath of allegiance administered by a federal officer.[13]

A reason for the effectiveness of the Methodist Church (North) in the support of the Union was the leadership and oratorical prestige of its bishops. A man's ability to preach had a good deal to do with his selection for the episcopacy. In that period he was elected by the General Conference and he had to be an able if not a powerful speaker to attract attention at all.

Chief among the warlords in the episcopacy was Matthew Simpson, said to be a friend and confidant of President Lincoln and to be a line of communication between the President and the Secretary of War, Edwin M. Stanton. Simpson came early under the touch of Methodism. He was born at Cadiz, Ohio, in 1811, and while he was yet an infant the saintly Asbury, traveling in the neighborhood, was entertained kindly by the Simpsons. The bishop baptized the baby and christened him Matthew, after the apostle who sat at the seat of customs.

As a young man Matthew showed a determined yearning for education. After getting the best schooling in his home town he set out on foot, with a few books and his clothes tied in a bundle and slung across his shoulder and with $11.25 in his pockets, to walk ninety miles to Uniontown, Pennsylvania, where he enrolled in Madison College. The next year he was a tutor in the college and he spent the next decade of his life teaching. He also studied medicine and began its practice in 1833. At that time, however, he felt an urge to enter the Methodist ministry. He was licensed to preach and received on trial in the Pittsburgh Conference. A speaker of great force, he was elected a bishop in 1852 with a chance to visit all the Conferences in the North, preaching at their sessions. He was a man who commanded attention by whatever he did and he became by degrees a kind of spokesman for The Methodist Episcopal Church, being sent abroad to represent the body at two meetings in Europe and gaining further prestige by traveling widely through Turkey, the Holy Land, Egypt, and Greece.

Bishop Simpson was back in the United States only long enough to become president of Garrett Biblical Institute at Evanston, Illinois, when war broke upon the land. By his own admission he spent little time handling the affairs of Garrett. The Union needed a man of his connections and travels to unite and organize the enthusiasm of preachers in a transcendent interpretation of the war. For this task Bishop Simpson was ideally suited and he entered upon it with a zest that did not abate but enhanced as the war wore on.

His main vehicle was a lecture which he delivered over and over again in all parts of the North, entitled "Our Country" and occasionally announced more appropriately as his War Message. The effect of his platform performance was telling and often tumultuous. The bishop knew the tricks of the experienced lecturer and adapted his message to the setting of his hearers. In New York he paid tearful tribute to the "war-torn, shot-riddled" flag of the 55th Regiment and brought five thousand listeners to their feet in a rousing three cheers for the flag. In Pittsburgh he spoke of a regiment much closer to home and, by reports, he laid his hand on "the torn and ball-riddled colors of the 73rd Ohio and spoke of the battlefields where these colors had been baptized in blood." He would describe their beauty as "some patch of azure, filled with stars that an angel had snatched from the heavenly canopy to set the stripes in blood. . . ." When Simpson spoke "men clenched their fists, shouted, stamped, stood on their feet in the seats, saluted, clapped, and wept, leaving the hall laughing in a tumult of wild patriotic excitement."[14]

The bishop placed symbols above humanity, hypostatizing these symbols by apostrophe, making the Union cause always bigger than any suffering its attainment might cost. The process belonged to the Methodist heritage, wherein the church as an institution was elevated as a thing beyond human kind, more important than the persons who composed it. Simpson substituted the United States of America for The Methodist Episcopal Church. He would not have been able to make this transfer if the Methodists had not so long and intemperately regarded their church as a cherished instrumentality of God to be preserved at all costs.

On the eve of the presidential election of 1864 Bishop Simpson imputed to his America a dignity and importance which belonged to God's view of the world as a whole. He believed it to be the "design of Providence that the Union would come out of its ordeal purer, stronger, more glorious than ever before." He cited the various virtues in the history of the United States that appealed to the rest of the world and ended up with the remarkable theological conclusion: "I would say it with all reverence, God cannot do without America."[15]

The experience of having one of their fraternity frequently visiting the White House and running to the War Department from the White House afforded the Methodist preachers a good deal of satisfaction. Methodists, whatever else they were noted for, were not noted for class. They were a religious body still fairly far down in the social scale. Their humble origins among the rejected and their early appeals primarily to the outcasts could not be forgotten. In later addresses Simpson took great pride in pointing out how far the Methodists had come in membership and property and how some of their men of wealth had given great sums to the Church. It was not without some significance that the distinguished publishing firm of Harper & Brothers, known throughout the world, was made up of four staunch and devoted Methodists, the oldest having been a class leader and all being active in New York congregations and taking no pains to conceal their connection.

Through Bishop Simpson's all-out war work, Methodism became respectable on a wider scale than ever before, being associated both subtly and in headlines with the very welfare of the Union. Simpson's name continued to be linked with Lincoln's and with the acts of the high and mighty.

What mattered supremely to Simpson, according to one of his biographers, were the interests of The Methodist Episcopal Church, and he regarded himself first and last as a servant of that institution. Any influence he exercised with officials was aimed at assuring the hegemony of the Church and in using military victories and military facilities in enlarging the territory of the northern body. It was here that his friendship with Secretary of War Stanton counted. Stanton's mother was a Methodist and the Secretary apparently understood the soundness of the Church's expansion impulses.

Agitation for the reform of the heretical southern Methodists began as early as 1861 but it mounted as Union armies occupied some of the states of the Confederacy. By the fall of 1863 the bishops felt that the time had come to yield to entreaties and send missionaries into occupied territory. They decided at least to explore the opportunities which, as they noted, Providence had opened up before them. What could be more natural than to call on Simpson's good friend Stanton to implement and facilitate the exploration through the War Department?

The move paid off. The Secretary issued appropriate orders to the northern generals commanding departments of the army in Missouri, Tennessee, and along the Mississippi and the Gulf to place at the disposal of Bishop Edward Raymond Ames "all houses of worship belonging to the Methodist Episcopal Church, South, in which a loyal minister, who has been appointed by a loyal Bishop of said Church does not officiate." The generals in the areas named were directed not only to support Bishop Ames in the "execution of his important mission" but also to provide him with transportation and subsistence. Orders followed soon for Bishop Simpson and for Bishop Edward Storer Janes to be accepted in other areas of the South.[16]

Ames was a natural-born missionary. He had been born in Ohio and had joined the connection after a few years of teaching. His work as an itinerant was done mostly in Indiana, where he served both as preacher and presiding elder. But in 1840 he had been elected missionary secretary of the Church and this had added immense scope to his wanderings. He had a good sense of conquest and traveled widely through the West, visiting Indian missions and establishing Indian schools along the Lakes and on the western frontier.

Ames set out down the broad expanse of the Mississippi early in 1864, and before he had done he had taken over Methodist churches in Memphis, Little Rock, Pine Bluff, Vicksburg, Jackson, Natchez, Baton Rouge, and New Orleans, ousting the southern pastors from their congregations. It was rescue work that would have to be extended, but it might as well be started where the Union forces held sway. The bishops followed through by naming an assistant from New York to be the preacher in New Orleans, who began his labors by explaining to the congregation on Carondelet Street that The Methodist Episcopal Church was not a sectional church because the world was its parish.[17]

The practice of naming resident assistants was followed by Simpson in Tennessee, where with his usual good eye to winning the favor of authority higher up, he chose one in the person of Michael J. Cramer, brother-in-law of General Grant. By the end of the war there were twenty-one ordained preachers of the northern church appointed to missionary work in the South. The General Conference in 1864 approved the exploratory work officially and even created a new order of missionary. Up to that time there had been foreign and home missionaries. The new order was to operate only in the South.

There was outrage at this collusion between The Methodist Episcopal Church and the Union army. Some of the generals disliked the order. If not used for worship, churches could still serve as hospitals, barracks, or stables. Southern preachers rendered their protest at a meeting in Louisville. Congressmen from the border states sought legislation to prevent the enforcement of the order. Loyal Methodists in Missouri joined the protest. Word finally reached Lincoln and he was aghast. He wrote his commanding general at St. Louis to say that "the United States government must not, as by this order, undertake to run the churches. . . . I have never interfered, nor thought of interfering as to who or who shall not preach in any church, nor have I knowingly or believingly allowed any one else to so interfere by my authority."[18]

Stanton modified his earlier order, but the imperial program to take over the southern Methodists and bring them back into the fold on terms which the northern Methodists deemed proper was fully begun. By the time Lee surrendered at Appomattox in the spring of 1865 the program was in full swing. Any defense The Methodist Episcopal Church, South, might have had on legal grounds collapsed with the Confederacy, and The Methodist Episcopal Church, with special funds appropriated for the purpose, was ready to launch an evangelistic invasion of such dimensions and manners as the world had not seen before.

The invasion was all the more painful because it was peculiarly a Methodist phenomenon. Bishop Ames had tried to induce other denominations to take over property in the South. His suggestion was turned down with contempt by Bishop Whittingham of the Protestant Episcopal Church. Dutch Reformed ministers in New Orleans were urged to seize a Presbyterian Church, but they refused indignantly. Presbyterians and Baptists engaged in no practice remotely comparable to the Methodists. In the dire days of Reconstruction the Protestant Episcopal Church in the North "gave generously to rebuild a devastated section without trying to thrust themselves on a sullen people. Their largesse, which included appropriations for Negro schooling, was distributed through the southern clergy and in accordance with the wishes of native whites.[19]

It was not what the missionaries of The Methodist Episcopal Church did that offended indelibly their brethren in the South. It was the arrogance with which they were sent and the verbal assaults that kept up in the North. These assaults carried a stern punitive tone which, even without the harshness of their language, would have been unbecoming to any who had ever heard of Christian charity. Many were indistinguishable from the diatribes of Thaddeus Stevens and other radical Republicans who bore uncompromising malice toward the late Confederacy.

The northern Methodist who hurled his jactitations with wildest abandon and most persistence was Daniel Curry, editor of *The Christian Advocate*. This gently named publication was issued under the authority of the General Conference. Curry was elected for three successive terms, beginning in 1864, and while his philippics could not be taken as official pronouncements, importance attached to what he had to say because of his position. He took very seriously his job of instructing readers in the ways they should think, and he began by telling them that the task before the northern body was "not less than for us to institute a new civilization within all the territory redeemed from rebellion."

Right after the war Curry warned readers against a soft peace: "We apprehend that there is more danger of excessive clemency than of too much severity." He was aware of the implications of his own philosophy. "It is quite evident," he wrote, "that our Church must spread its institutions all over the Southern States, and in doing so it will be compelled to sharply define its antagonism to the spurious local Methodism of the Country." *Spurious* was a mild word for Curry. On other occasions he referred to "the treason-tainted Methodism of the South" and to "this degenerate, bastard Methodism."[20]

A conference of northern clergymen, inspired and aided by

Curry's pen, declared that southern Methodism "had been so completely leagued with detestable sin that its apostate church should be exterminated."[21] In the same spirit the New England Conference adopted a lengthy report on the Reconstruction of the South. It saw the vision clearly. The Methodist Episcopal Church was called upon by "the Providence of God" to re-enter the South and plant there true principles in government, in morals, and in religion. The leaders of the southern church were "unworthy of renewing the land in righteousness which they have so long made less tolerable than Sodom and Gomorrah."[22]

When the North moved preachers and presiding elders into the South the purpose of the move was explained to the South as a plan "to give a few well-trained men from the North the positions of leadership and let them rally around them the illiterate but warm-hearted brethren."[23] Doubt was expressed over the possibility of ever reforming the Southerners because a good many of their deficiencies were said to be innate. The *Methodist Advocate* warned members in the North that they must not leave "the poor down-trodden people of the South" under the influence of "the pro-slavery, man-stealing, Negro-whipping, whiskey-drinking, Ku Klux Churches to which so many of them belong."[24]

What was said in the North was heard, often amplified, in the South. Southern papers picked up news and comment from those up north. In May of 1867 the *Southern Christian Advocate* printed an item from the *Central Christian Advocate*, which spoke of the whimpering of chagrined rebels "who have been suppressed but not taught."

The New York Conference adopted in 1866 a report which declared that "it is our calm and settled conviction, uninfluenced by passion, strife, or sectional prejudice, that expediency, constitutional law, justice, and the Bible all unite in demanding that at least some of the leaders of the rebellion be punished with death."[25] Threat of further subjugation, of doing the military job once more, occurred in not a few of the editorial decrees. When the South still showed some signs of cussedness toward northern dominance as late as 1879, the editor of the *Northwestern Christian Advocate* wrote: "If rebels persist, the people will not fail to speak on the subject. We have a notion that the world has never seen such wrath as will be shown by a patient North in case it resumes original jurisdiction. Appomattox will be a love feast in comparison."[26]

Not content with animadversions against the depravity of southern Methodists, the vast majority of brethren in the North placed themselves solidly on the side of opposing any move the government made to ameliorate the severity of the occupation of the South. Lincoln had reinstated some of the property of the southern church before his assassination and his successor, the hapless Andrew Johnson, completed the job, much to the disgust of bishops, especially Ames, who had been responsible for the conquest. And when Johnson tried to institute measures which would modify radical policies in what was called Reconstruction, who came out vociferously against him? The Methodists. The *Northwestern Christian Advocate,* at the height of the controversy which led to the attempted impeachment of the President, declared: "The whole Methodist Press is now, we believe, on one side of the national controversy. It is thoroughly radical for the . . . rebuke and legal punishment of treason . . . and the stern repression of every remnant of rebellion."[27]

Proposals for the impeachment of Johnson began to infiltrate Methodist journals more than a year before the radicals undertook proceeding which would depose him. When he vetoed legislation designed to tighten the screws of Reconstruction, the northern Methodists, led by Curry, of course, turned on him furiously. "Shall we stand with God or with the President?" they asked. There was not much choice because the President was described as "an execrable libertine, drunkard, and tyrant."[28]

There is some modest consolation the modern devotee can take from the fact that we know the worst things that Methodist preachers and editors said during the time of dissension and civil war. Extreme statements made up the record but they may not make up the truth. Records are written and kept by scribes, who tend to quote officials and persons of stature. We do not know that the screamers and spellbinders and windjammers represented the sentiments of ordinary folks who went to church Sunday after Sunday, possibly in shame at the ranting of the preacher. We do not know how many God-fearing people, troubled in their breasts by the reality of slaughter, found the florid patriotic statements they heard or read as silly as posterity would.

Just as no man is likely to get into the headlines by going through a day or a week or a lifetime of decent and moderate living, we cannot expect to find the record of a time of bloody strife replete with understatements, pleasantries, and genial summations. What survives in records of such periods is apt to be the egregious, the item that assailed the eye or ear of the scribe. Making a record of such items leaves the impression that only the ridiculous was spoken. It's a kind of Gresham's law of writing that bad words drive out good.

At any rate, we know that more than vituperation went on, that the surface record, all bad, is not complete. There were curative forces at work in both sections of the country, impulses and ideas that had not yet found voice or had not been given full expression.

XX Can These Bones Live?

It was fitting for William Tecumseh Sherman, in an address before the veterans of his march to the sea, to give the most graphic general picture of the devastation that lay like a pall over the region which had once formed the Confederate States of America. In retrospect he could see, better than in the heat of it, what war, being hell, had done to the people. "Look to the South," he told his hearers, "and you who went with me through that land can best say if they have not been too fearfully punished." The effects were no longer obscured by the smoke of battle: "Mourning in every household, desolation written in broad characters across the whole face of their country, cities in ashes and fields laid waste, their commerce gone, their system of labor annihilated and destroyed. Ruin, poverty, and distress everywhere, and now pestilence adding to the very cap sheaf of their stack of misery. . . ."[1]

Any observer could fill in the grim details and detect back of every statistic the specter of the Four Horsemen. There were no men. Nine out of ten of fighting age had gone to the field, reckoning only enlistments. Half-grown boys and men grown old had been included in the muster toward the end. Of those who went, 300,000—more than one-fourth of all fit for the field—did not return. War had taken over words as well as men and resources. The field meant the field of battle, and many of those who straggled back after Appomattox were not fit for any field where food might be grown. Hostilities had ended not so much in surrender as in exhaustion. There was nothing for the soldiers in gray to eat at the time of formal capitulation, and federal rations had to be handed out to them. They were humanely allowed to keep their horses but many of the horses were worn to the bones. The men did not return to their homes in time for spring plowing and the farm crops in 1865 were pitifully poor, bringing a threat of wholesale starvation and pestilence.[2]

In the remains of the population were not so many as half a million Methodists, subject to the same deprivation and humiliation as all Southerners but humiliated even more by the plight of the institution they had fashioned with pride in their principles. Now the shell of it was near outward collapse. Hundreds of church buildings had been destroyed, casualties of cannon fire. Others had been dismantled for war use. Some remained in the hands of the military or of northern ministers, and some were simply abandoned, standing gaunt and idle, tombstones marking the futility of religion in the dread reality of war. Most Methodist schools and colleges had been closed, their endowments dissipated, their properties in disrepair, their students and teachers scattered.

The structure and machinery of The Methodist Episcopal Church, South, the essence of its organization and the means of its functioning, had suffered grievously. There had not been a session of the General Conference in eight years. At the time of the scheduled meeting in 1862, New Orleans, the place appointed for it to assemble, was in the hands of northern soldiers and preachers. Church papers had suspended publication, leaving Methodists stranded throughout the eleven states of the Confederacy without ways of thinking and writing about their common problems. The building of the publishing house at Nashville had fallen into the hands of northern armies. Its stock had been confiscated, its machinery damaged, and what was left had been used for federal government printing.

Membership had shrunk under the emaciation of war from a stout 750,000 to 458,000. Only half the number of preachers were admitted on trial in 1866 as had been admitted six years before.[3] Few young men showed any signs of wanting to be either local or traveling preachers. The spirit of the Church had departed. Some of the best preachers had gone to the front as chaplains and their exhortations had led to stirring revivals in the camps, but there had not been any enthusiasm to pit themselves against the callous indifference and preoccupation with the severities of daily living on the home front as the war grew grimmer and grimmer. Men had not turned to God, as they were supposed to in times of dark crisis. The Methodists had done nothing to prevent or forestall the war. They might well have encouraged it by the example of their secession and the model of a separate and independent unit of government they had set up. They did nothing in the midst of the war itself to still its fury of hate. What could men expect of them and what could they expect of themselves in the future? Certainly their church would prove before long to be among the casualties. Meanwhile a kind of dull boredom, induced and increased by the narcotic of despair, would ease the pain and make the terminal reckoning more endurable.

Surely Ezekiel did not encounter a more bleached or depressing valley of dry bones than did the minor prophets of the southern Methodist Church after the stillness at Appomattox. For, lo, the bones were very dry, as Ezekiel had seen. And when the Lord said unto southern leaders, as He had to Ezekiel, "Can these bones live?" they could only answer, as Ezekiel had, "O Lord God, thou knowest."

The first faint tremor indicating that there might be new life in the Church South came out of Missouri, a turbulent border state which, during the war, had naturally been a scene of ecclesiastical confusion as well. Both Methodist branches had churches there, competing at close range for members and distinction. One of the veterans of the southern church in Missouri was Andrew Monroe. In 1854 the Kansas-Nebraska Act provided that popular sovereignty would determine whether the region would be slave or free. People from both the free and the slave-holding states rushed wildly into Kansas, each determined to build up a majority. To serve those who had gone to Kansas, the Church South created the Kansas Mission District and sent Monroe there to superintend it. The district comprised eight circuits and several Indian missions. Monroe had done well. Before long he had a white membership of 619, almost as large as that of the Church North, which numbered 631.[4] Throughout the war Monroe stayed with the cause of the Church South in the midst of rugged circumstances and he earned the respect of his fellows. They listened and responded when he called a meeting of twenty-four preachers in full connection to meet June 22, 1865, at the town of Palmyra, in northeastern Missouri, not far from Hannibal and on the banks of the Mississippi.

The purpose of the meeting was to consider the status and future of The Methodist Episcopal Church, South. Should it keep its identity or allow its members freedom of choice to coquet with the Episcopalians or the Methodist Protestants or flock back to The Methodist Episcopal Church under terms laid down by that body? Was there any real purpose the Church South could serve in the postwar period or had it run its course?

The Palmyra consortium was informal and unofficial and free to explore and discuss. At the same time it represented a cross section in a crucial area. In addition to the preachers there were present what accounts refer to as "about a dozen laymen." Attending many of the sessions was a bishop—Hubbard H. Kavanaugh. He had chosen to go with the Church South at the time of the division and he had been elected bishop in 1854. He had spent most of his ministerial life in the troubled area between the two sections of the country that were at odds and then at war. He was a rousing preacher of a school already beginning to fade, "beginning his sermons in Eden and ending them in heaven." His feet remained firmly planted on solid earth, however. All his life he had faced choices. In his youth he was apprenticed to a Presbyterian elder to learn the printer's trade, but he underwent the Methodist experience of conversion and joined the itinerancy, serving during his early years in the Kentucky mountains. Throughout the Civil War he lived at Versailles, in northern Kentucky, being the only bishop of the Church South to spend much time outside Confederate lines. He was arrested once as a Confederate spy, but military authorities released him. He stuck to religion and the health of men's souls when it came to subject matter, eschewed politics, and moved freely between the territories occupied by the Rebs and the Yanks.[5]

The time now had come for another decision, and the experience of both Kavanaugh and Monroe helped to make it and give it direction. Out of the sessions attended by laymen, preachers, and a bishop, making a conference of a new sort in miniature, came a document known as the Palmyra Manifesto. Its pronouncements disavowed the slave issue as the only question separating the two Methodisms, asserted the integrity of The Methodist Episcopal Church, South, and urged that this integrity be preserved. For members to go into any other church at this moment of crisis would be to admit that association with slavery, now defeated, was the main characteristic of the southern church. Even with slavery eliminated and no longer an issue, there were features of the southern fellowship and claims to recognition that had to be respected. The manifesto ended by declaring that The Methodist Episcopal Church, South, ardently desired to cultivate fraternal relations with "all evangelical churches."[6] The Church North might be included on that broad screen, but as one among many. The salient point was that the Church South, regardless of attacks made upon it and attempts to absorb it, was an honorable and dignified body and would remain so. It was not up for auction and its members would not be treated as penitents or traitors.

The tone of the manifesto sent a shiver along the southern spine. It struck a note Methodists had been waiting to hear, resolved a chord, phrased what was felt. Methodists were Americans, and as Americans they could still be southern and still be Methodists.

The reviving press of the South reprinted the manifesto widely. In Virginia and the Carolinas men said the message was "like life from the dead." Young preachers heard in it the news of hope and aging bishops saw the depth and fitness of it for parlous times. Joshua Soule, who had sided with the Church South and had become its senior bishop, was eighty-four. John Early was eighty. Andrew was seventy-two. The youngest, George Foster Pierce, was fifty-four. The bishops managed, however, age and condition permitting, to get together at Columbus, Georgia, in the summer of 1865. There they decided to take the Palmyra Manifesto as a point of departure and issue an episcopal address that would assert the will of the Church South to live and, following words with acts, to call a General Conference to meet in New Orleans the next year, urging the Annual Conferences to choose carefully their best and most farsighted men.

There was a sense of newness and youth at the Columbus meeting. The bishops called on a younger man skilled in words to write the address. Chosen was Holland Nimmons McTyeire, who had demonstrated his worth as a writing editor. His early background was atypical for an itinerant. Born of wealthy parents in South Carolina, he had gone at the age of twelve to a small Methodist school in that state. There he joined the Church. There is no report of a stringent conversion. Rather there seems to have been an orderly alignment. He was no part of the controversy that wracked the General Conference in 1844. At that time he was a student in Randolph Macon College, then in Mecklenburg County, Virginia.

Immediately after college McTyeire began to preach. He endeared himself to the congregations he served by his fidelity under affliction and by sharing with them the ordeal of pestilence that smote the South before the war. His predecessor in New Orleans died of yellow fever and McTyeire was stricken soon after he arrived. His own death was regarded as inevitable, but a physician "who came to assuage his suffering brought him back to life, as by a miracle." He remained in New Orleans through a succession of outbreaks of yellow fever during which as many as three hundred a day died. He was one of the few pastors who stayed with their flocks over a period that claimed eight thousand lives.[7]

It was McTyeire's ability to think and write, however, that brought him to the attention of his brethren. His gift of summary, combined with a style that moved the eye along, led to his being made editor of the *New Orleans Christian Advocate* before he was thirty, and four years later he was promoted to the editor of the chief organ of the Church, the *Nashville Christian Advocate*. This post was a nerve center as long as it lasted and it kept the young man in touch with the main currents of southern feeling while giving him a chance to hone his talent. Never aloof, he was Methodist to the center, being able to organize even his thoughts, so that much of what in his statements passed for good writing was in fact clear reasoning.

Whipped into stirring prose by the editor, the address by the bishops sounded a trumpet call to action. It was seen to mean that "neither disintegration nor absorption was to be thought of, all rumors to the contrary notwithstanding; whatever banner had fallen, that of Southern Methodism was still unfurled; whatever cause was lost, that of Southern Methodism still survived."[8] Questions raised in the division of 1844 had not been settled by the war, and thoughts of a casual reunion with the Church North, which had imposed "conditions of discipleship that Christ did not impose," were to be dismissed. There was more to life than strife and, while the address counseled tolerance of former foes, it was most emphatic in its invitation to southern Methodists to be southern Methodists and proud of it.

Response to the address and the talk that went along with it created an atmosphere of expectancy and heightened hope as the General Conference of 1866 approached. Almost a year to the day after the surrender at Appomattox, 153 preachers who had been chosen as delegates assembled in New Orleans. Change was in the air, easily detected by any who watched the vane of popular opinion. Robert E. Lee had said that the South must be "built up on a new basis." The building could begin with The Methodist Episcopal Church, South. So many proposals for altering the actual structure of the Church were brought in by the delegates that the old system of committees could not cope with them and it was necessary to create a new and unprecedented committee on Changes of Economy to consider each measure and recommend action.

The first change to be voted out of committee and on to the floor had been set forth by Holland Nimmons McTyeire. He made a proposal for all present to hear and people throughout the land to read: "*Resolved,* That it is the sense of this General Conference that Lay Representation be introduced into the Annual and General Conferences." Here was a matter moot to Methodism. The General Conference of The Methodist Episcopal Church in 1828 had held that a divinely instituted ministry could not permit its functions to be controlled by "others." Two years later the advocates of lay representation had broken away with those who formed The Methodist Protestant Church. In the years that followed scant attention had been paid to the subject, the General Conference of 1840 dismissing lay representation as "not expedient."[9] It had not come up again after that. The Church South had worked out a compromise plan in 1850, allowing laymen to speak in Annual Conferences on financial and business matters.

Now in uncompromising form and for the first time, came the proposal that laymen be permitted a part in the legislative body of the Church. Immediately it was offered, the McTyeire resolution sailed through. True, the majority was less than the two-thirds required to start a constitutional change. But the vote was big enough to put the handwriting of a trend on the wall and the delegates saw it. As McTyeire noted, "The principle once admitted, even by a numerical majority, everything was gained." He marshalled his forces and on the next ballot those who had voted casually at first swung with the tide and the

153 preachers voted to authorize laymen to sit with them in the governing of The Methodist Episcopal Church, South.

The Conference was in a mood to assess and alter practices that had been considered fundamental, part of the nature as well as the structure of the system. From the days of Asbury preachers had been kept on the move, transferred from one charge to another, often every year. There were some gallant exceptions, as in New Orleans, where it was felt that two years were needed to build up an immunity to yellow fever. In the main, however, the old system of frequent changes prevailed—until 1866. Then the General Conference of The Methodist Episcopal Church, South, proposed and overwhelmingly favored a change. The bishop would continue to make appointments annually but, as far as the rules were concerned, a preacher could stay in one pastorate the rest of his life.

Shades of Asbury! The spirit of the Prophet of the Long Road was still present, too. There had to be a limit to reform. Some of the members of the Conference drew the line on removing the limits of the pastoral term. Led by Bishop Pierce, they threatened to resign if the rule went into effect. The delegates, being of a mind to compromise and placate as well as legislate, changed the rule the next day so that a preacher could stay in one post four consecutive years.[10] But transience was no longer held up as a shining ideal. The making of a settled ministry was in process, as some leaders thought it should be, and the pastor could be identified and allied with the factors contributing to growth within his community.

Accommodation to new circumstances marked the spirit as well as the proceedings of the Conference. The three oldest bishops were relieved of their burdens and young men and minds were elected. McTyeire, closely identified with both reform and renewal, was one of the bishops chosen. His office gave him license to carry the good news of change to the Church at large. He and his confreres in the episcopacy set out to do some itinerating on their own. They traveled when travel was hard, turning up not only, as expected, to preach and preside at the

Annual Conferences, but also visiting most of the district conferences, consulting with presiding elders and pastors, putting their feet under the table with members of local churches.

These personal appearances by the chief dignitaries of the connection helped to animate and invigorate a body of believers that had not been dead but sleeping. The visits helped to send back to the communities from which it came some of the vigor of the General Conference—a vigor greatly increased because it had been made vocal and officially approved. Recovery set in with remarkable speed. In the fifteen years that followed the desolate year of 1866, when the number of adherents was at an all-time low and all looked hopeless, membership doubled. In time the membership advanced at a faster rate than the population. By 1890 Methodists as a whole made up 22 percent of the numbers in all American churches. But in the South they constituted 34 percent and in North Carolina and Alabama the number ranged between 40 and 50 percent.[11]

With growth and success came acceptance and respectability. A prominent Baptist minister and editor wrote: "In former years it was not a rare thing for rich Methodist families to go over to the Episcopalians; and not infrequently, too, their talented and inspiring young preachers were restless until they found more congenial surroundings in the old Mother church. But it is different now. The Methodists excel us all in wealth and numbers in nine-tenths of the larger cities and towns of the South, and no preachers are more loyal to their Church than they are."[12]

Loyalty grew in part out of pride. If you omitted all references to divine mission, as the secular world did, you could see that The Methodist Episcopal Church, South, had succeeded where the Confederacy had failed. It had started off in 1845 with no loss of motion after separation. It had gained speed and grown sturdily. Its numbers had increased from 450,000 in 1846 to 750,000 when war broke out. Then, having suffered the trauma of political conflict and being nearly annihilated, it had been resurrected and was stronger than ever. Part of the pride was sectional but part of it also came from the fact that the Church South had attained selfhood. Nobody was telling it what to do. It could consider itself more important than government because it had survived the fall of a government.

The recovery of the Church South brought with it the beginnings of a new mood and attitude toward the rest of the country and toward the Church North. Amazement continued among Southerners that their brethren in the faith should be so much more vindictive and vituperative than members of other denominations, but by degrees church papers made allowances and indicated that the worst attacks were not representative. The papers of the South were unwilling to believe that better-minded Methodists "could endorse the bitter utterances of their ministers and journals."[13] They knew that Methodists were never likely to be unanimous.

It transpired that there had been vigorous protest in high places of The Methodist Episcopal Church against the policy of invading the South. One bishop, Calvin Kingsley, who had had no part in the move, cried out at the folly of trying to "establish religion at the point of a bayonet."[14] Some of the missionaries who had gone south had second thoughts and wrote with regret and chagrin of what they had been a party to. A statement by one of the missionaries appeared in 1870:

"No other denomination did just as we did in that matter. Temporary occupancy of pulpits, in some instances, occurred with others; but our ministers stood in the attitude of conquerors. They differed little in appearances . . . from invaders. It did not appear so to them. It did so appear to the Church South. They may stigmatize it with unwonted severity, we may think; but their ox is gored by our bull, and we do not feel the pain. We should remember that."[15]

Bits and fragments of information from the other section were fitted together by Southerners to form a picture in perspective, and the picture suggested that the Church North was not as savage as it had seemed. Only a few of its preachers had had compelling enough interest in redeeming the rebels to volunteer for service. Many, in fact, had resisted appointments and had with one accord made excuses—that they could not be away from their books, that they had too many children for the move, that they were afraid of yellow fever, and, as one preacher put it, "My present church cannot dispense with my services."[16] There had been a hitch in the get-along of the itinerancy. Preachers of the Wesleyan persuasion might still be willing to go where the Lord wanted them to go but they were not by any means sure that He wanted them to go South.

Gradually, but even before the dreadful days of compulsory Reconstruction ended, there grew up among southern Methodists an appreciation of missionaries who had come among them for the specific purpose of teaching ex-slaves the rudiments of learning. Two-thirds of these missionaries were young women, and the hardships and ostracism they endured, staying faithfully at their thankless tasks year after year, could not fail to impress any person with even a vestige of compassion.

The schools started by the Freedmen's Aid Society were hastily improvised. By 1869 there was a system of elementary schools with 250 teachers and 250,000 pupils enrolled.[17] Two-thirds of the teachers were women. Moved by idealism, they had little else to live on. Salaries were not more than fifteen dollars a month and the teachers were to pay board and keep if they could find a place to stay. Their classes were held wherever they could assemble pupils—under trees, in warehouses, barns, or shanties. They suffered ostracism, ridicule, and violence at the hands of those who resented their presence.[18] Still they settled in and stuck to their appointed stations year after year until men of enlightened good will recognized the nobility and practicality of their achievements.

Notable among these men was Atticus Greene Haygood, a Georgian of irreproachable background, a solid citizen who spoke out in behalf of unpopular causes and yet couldn't be laughed off as an irregular. He had been converted in childhood, as became the Wesleyan pattern, and he had been licensed to preach at an early age. At the sound of guns he had volunteered as a chaplain in the Confederate army and had remained in the service until 1867. On returning to civilian life he served as presiding elder until in 1870 he was elected by the General Conference to build up the Sunday schools as agencies of education. What little elementary school system the South possessed was in chaos after the war and it was clear that many children would get what education they got through the medium of the Sunday school.

Haygood tackled his task with imagination, called a Sunday-school convention to meet in Nashville, urged that the Sunday schools be mortised directly into the structure of the Church, and in other ways validated himself to the membership throughout the connection. In 1875 he went on to become president of Emory College at Oxford, Georgia, a position that added prestige to his already wide influence in the field of education.

When Haygood spoke, then, he had an audience that would attend and meditate on what he had to say, and he reminded Southerners that "we think better of ourselves than the facts of our history and our present state of progress justify." He had his say first in a sermon, which was widely distributed, and then he put his views in a closely reasoned and sympathetic book, *Our Brother in Black,* acknowledging the imperative responsibility of the Southerner to provide opportunities of education, higher as well as elementary, for those who had been their slaves.[19]

Naturally, the book made a hit in the North, but many said that it would end the career of Atticus Haygood in the South. Not at all. He was elected a bishop, but he refused to accept the honor, believing that his real work lay in the field of education. He resigned his college presidency and became an agent of the John F. Slater Fund, set up by a wealthy Yankee. From 1882 to 1891 Haygood distributed the Fund and worked for the cause of education in the South. He encouraged the teachers from the North and told his fellow churchmen, "In God's name we ought to help them." His name was "inextricably linked with his work in behalf of Negro education, voting, and ownership of property." And his brothers in white showed the acceptance of his work when at the General Conference of 1890 Haygood was elected on the first ballot a bishop for the second time. Nearly two-thirds of the delegates voted for him, although he was not present at the Conference and there had been no campaign to put his name forward.[20]

Other men of station rose to defend the work of the teachers and to see the vital importance of it. David C. Kelley, a former Confederate officer distinguished for gallantry, expressed sympathy in Nashville for the work being done by The Methodist Episcopal Church to elevate the freedmen. Another preacher, Morgan Calloway, descendant of a distinguished Georgia family, a former slaveholder and officer in the Confederate army, felt a special call to the work of Negro education while he was vice-president of Emory. His name and connection with the college lent force to his labors and marked another barometric reading to forecast change in the dank atmosphere. It was an acknowledgment, too, of the work the missionaries of the North had commenced.

By the mid-1870's the Church South had established its self-hood sufficiently that its leaders could admit the value of some of the work done by northern missionaries. The sense of autonomy continued. It was integral. Out of it had come a measure of tolerance and in time might come a feeling of brotherhood based on equality. Now on the same footing and level with other church bodies, it was in a position to deal fraternally with all engaged in good works, including the Church North.

XXI The Second Blessing

Holy Roller is a term that came into use during the 1890's to describe a person who expressed a religious experience in a spectacular, even convulsive, way. He might have been a member of any of a score of fast-growing American sects whose adherents believed intensely and preached earnestly that a person could be perfect, above sin and incapable of doing wrong. The sudden discovery of this truth transported the believer to a level of ecstasy in which he might shout jubilantly or fall down and roll over and over or unaccountably speak in languages he had never studied or heard.

The energetic sects of the Gay Nineties have become populous churches, designated as holiness if their joys are confined to feeling perfect love and pentecostal if they claim also the gift of glossolalia. Together the groupings claim a world membership of more than fifteen million and their numbers are growing apace.[1]

Progenitors of both the holiness bodies and pentecostal sects were Methodist, and believers in the rapturous experience known as the Second Blessing (a bestowal of a sense of perfect love) remained in the bosom of Methodism until their enthusiasm created a serious administrative problem and they were asked to leave. Methodism provided the incunabula and the kindergarten from which the Holy Rollers emerged and it supplied also the basic tenet of their faith and practice.

This tenet is the belief that man can escape not only the ravages of sin but also the molestation of temptation and live in freedom with himself, not forever preoccupied with his baser nature. Such an idea was propounded in theological form and terms by John Wesley and accepted by his followers in both England and America. And it was propounded and accepted in a way that gave it universality. Perfection was for everyman. This was the distinct feature of the Wesleyan emphasis.

According to modern scholars, Mr. Wesley was indebted to Puritan writers for his central idea of holiness, but he gave it a fillip that took it out of the realm of the past and made it available for daily use. The Puritans conceived that a man could attain holiness only at death.[2] Mr. Wesley insisted that it could be attained in the midst of life. It was "a practical way of life available to and necessary for every regenerate Christian. The idea of perfection as an esoteric privilege available only to an endowed few was repugnant to him. Moreover, there was little of the speculative in his presentation of the doctrine. Recognizing its claims, he began an intensive search, seeking to recover in his own soul the 'image of God,' never quite able—or willing—to profess its attainment. Meanwhile he undertook to provide a medium by which others might be assisted in a similar search and through which holiness might find methodical and social expression."[3]

This approach posited a completely new view of God, a view not in opposition to, but at variance with and different from, other teachings in Protestantism. God was to be seen not as a harsh judge to whose rulings man must in duty conform but rather as an enabling Spirit through whose good offices every man Jack might receive the benediction of holiness. The Wesleyan doctrine carried with it also a new view of men. It "recognized that depravity, however dark, and evil circumstances, however real, do not necessarily confine man to hopeless defeat."[4]

Holiness as a possibility was firmly fixed in early Methodist doctrine—sufficiently so that the purpose the preachers avowed at the Christmas Conference for setting up The Methodist Episcopal Church was "to reform the continent and spread Scriptural holiness over the land." Holiness was not a wispy abstraction. It was as real as the rocks and rills and templed hills and a state as definite as the condition of sinful, selfish, quarrelsome, thieving, drunken men. It pitted one reality against another.

The Wesleyan doctrine was accepted by the preachers, but making it effective among a restless people in an unsettled land had not been feasible. The wilderness, with its torrents and savages and strange cries and daily toil, was no place for metaphysics. All but the most elementary means of grace were lacking in the vast parish of the itinerants, and while perfection held on as an avowed ideal, American Methodism had little experience with it.

Oddly, the subject had been kept before the public and burned into the national conscience by Charles Grandison Finney, who was no Methodist at all but a Presbyterian turned Congregationalist. Finney did not come by his belief casually. Born at Warren, Connecticut, in 1792, he was brought up in western New York while it was still frontier. He was engaged in the practice of law when in 1818 he underwent a dramatic and stringent conversion. Thereafter he received "a retainer from the Lord Jesus Christ to plead his cause."[5] He turned from law to theology and was ordained a Presbyterian minister in 1824. Aflame with a zeal that was tempted rather than dampened by his reflections, he held a series of revival meetings in central and western New York and, by his example, set others off on the same course. In 1832 he became pastor of the Chatham Street Chapel, New York City, where he commenced earnestly to search the Scriptures. In the process he became convinced that many Christians were living only in the doldrums of faith and that "an altogether higher and more stable form of Christian life was attainable, and was the privilege of all Christians."

Later Wesley's *Plain Account of Christian Perfection* fell into Finney's hands, and in a series of twenty-five lectures published shortly thereafter he devoted the last nine to the doctrine of sanctification.[6] He did not profess to have had the experience but he made it clear that all Christians might have it. His approach, although fervid, was balanced, and his sermons and lectures lent an aura of intellectual respectability to the notion that the Christian life might reach metaphysical heights. It was the period of the Transcendentalists, who brought both meditation and aspiration to experiences not generally thought of as religious, thus enlarging the scope of faith beyond prescribed and regulated forms of behavior.

There was obviously something astir. A questing and inquiring spirit quickened men's minds, and it was in this atmosphere and circumstance that Finney, through his eloquence and stature, gave the Methodist idea of perfection a new and general dignity. He withdrew conscientiously from Presbyterianism, with its unvarying attention to predestination. He did not become a Methodist but he did go over to Congregationalism, where he had latitude, being responsible only to a local church body. From 1835 to 1872 he was pastor of the First Congregational Church of Oberlin, Ohio, and during the fifteen years following 1851 he was president of Oberlin College. There his views touched both students and professors and found their way into journals sponsored by a respected seat of learning.

The view Finney and his associates expressed came to be designated as the Oberlin Theology and it caused consternation and misgivings among many theologians and preachers. But it also advertised far and wide, and especially to those in any way sensitive to trends and movements, a fresh and invigorating view of the human species. Man could be made whole. There were no trammels to hold back his soul. It was generally understood that this remarkable vision of man was Wesleyan, and its proclamation by a Congregational minister of national distinction, and a college president to boot, made it all the plainer that a sound Methodist doctrine had been so much ignored that it had fallen into the hands of persons of another denomination. This was both a compliment and an accusation.

The doctrine of Christian perfection had fallen into other alien hands as well, at once showing its tremendous appeal, the ease with which it could be perverted, and the disturbance it could create. It had been used by a young man named John Humphrey Noyes as the basis of a cult that practiced free love, that set out, as Noyes put it, to reconcile the sexes.

A graduate of Dartmouth in 1830 and later a student at Yale, Noyes had been converted in one of the revivals set off by the preaching of Finney. He was licensed as a Congregational minister, but the role was too tame for him. He was much swayed by what he had heard of Christian perfection and in his own credo Noyes worked out a philosophy which placed a person above and beyond the law and the restrictions of the mores. The spirit could triumph over the flesh and men and women could do as they pleased as long as they kept the faith.

Noyes was by no means alone in his brand of belief, although he stated the postulates of it most palatably. There had grown up around New Haven and in New York colonies of men and women who went to bed together to demonstrate either that they could bundle intimately without sin or that they could go through the experience of total sex involvement and still remain unperturbed and undefiled. It was an inviting form of perfection for the initiates but this kind of proof of purity made no favorable impression in the neighborhoods where it was demonstrated. Those caught up in the seventh heaven of a ritual new to New England were not bothered by existing marital bonds or by lingering monogamy. At New Haven and elsewhere there were shocking exposures and a contagion of spiritual mating, with letters exchanged to describe the details of the ecstasies induced by what proper people called sanctified debauchery.[7]

Early in 1834 Noyes announced that he had attained moral perfection. He lost his license as a Congregational minister, but he seems to have taken this loss as only another sign of a mis-understanding world that could not comprehend the mystery of the inner man under divine guidance. He systematically went about asserting his liberation from legal bondage. "I drank ardent spirits," he reported, "that I might reprove the spirit of legality which still hovered about me, and that I might practically transfer the keeping of my soul from the temperance pledge to the Spirit of God." He confessed that in sexual matters his reputation suffered "with those who saw only externals." He was "loosed from the moorings of ordinary prudence, and set adrift once more with no pilot but God."

The writings of Noyes in a monthly magazine, *The Perfectionist,* did much to unify the spirit of antinomianism in New England and to attract to his standard a band of ardent spirits. The first society he established was at Putney, Vermont. He escaped the old moral law but he ran afoul of civil law, being arrested on a charge of adultery. He jumped his bail and fled to New York. There his followers in due course joined him and grouped themselves around him to form the Oneida Community. In this community Noyes organized his beliefs and his votaries. There was no marriage or giving in marriage. Love without lust was the ideal. No man had an exclusive right to any woman, nor any woman to any man. As Noyes saw sex, "If a man cannot love a woman and be happy in seeing her loved by others, he is a selfish man, and his place is with the potsherds of the earth."[8]

The noise Noyes made reverberated throughout the land. The consistent and philosophical defiance of morality Noyes had carried out in the name of Christianity. The origins of his ideas were not foreign or heathen. They came straight from his own interpretation of the Wesleyan doctrine of perfectionism. His behavior had given perfection a dreadful reputation among the devout but in a strange way it had kept the subject sizzling.

The restoration of the holiness idea to the rubric of American Methodism was largely the work of women. The agency that prepared the way was a series of ladies' prayer meetings. In 1835 two separate prayer meetings were meeting in two New York churches. A woman with the organizing skill so admired in Methodism took the groups of the two churches and combined them to form the Tuesday Meeting for the Promotion of Holiness. The woman's name was Mrs. Sarah A. Lankford. It was not a name widely known in Methodist circles, but Mrs. Lankford had a brilliant and remarkably coherent sister, Phoebe, who was married to a young New York physician, Walter C. Palmer.

Phoebe Palmer had become one of the earliest women class leaders at the Allen Street Methodist Church. She was clear of mind and fluent of tongue and she took the subject of holiness out of the vapor of theory and brought it down to the plane where the Methodists lived. She experienced sanctification at one of the Tuesday Meetings, being delivered of the old perils of the flesh and achieving a state of perfect love. Soon she became the acknowledged leader of the Tuesday Meetings for the Promotion of Holiness, and attendance increased so rapidly that the gatherings had to be held in larger and larger homes to accommodate seekers.[9]

There was precedent for religious meetings held at home and led by a powerful woman, but it was not a precedent to comfort church officials. Two hundred years before, in the Massachusetts Bay Colony, another fluent female, Mrs. Anne Hutchinson, had drawn after her a following by the simple process of inviting people into her home to hear her interpretations of belief. At first indulged, she had been found to be a disturber of the theological peace, and she was accused of antinomianism. Certainly she proclaimed a doctrine of love that was beyond the severe rubric of the Puritan faith of the Boston church she attended, and in 1637 she had been expelled from the church and banished from the colony. The elders realized that a woman could make herself the center of a new theophany.[10]

Precedent called for caution. There were, however, many factors that lent distinction to the position of Phoebe Palmer—all indications of marked change in the church climate of North America. Mrs. Hutchinson spoke on her own recognizance and stated her own evolving views. Since the day of Mrs. Hutchinson a man, John Wesley, had phrased the idea of perfect love and established it with authority in minds of a large body of believers. While they had abandoned the belief in practice, they held on to it in tradition. Mrs. Palmer in her efforts had back of her the support of the founder of her faith. She also had back of her the support of her husband. Dr. Walter Palmer not only encouraged his wife's advocacy of holiness; he also joined her in promoting it, took trips with her as the scope of her activities widened, appeared with her at every step they made. Man and wife worked in harness. In 1862 Dr. and Mrs. Palmer bought an established paper, *The Guide to Holiness*, and edited it with such success that it reached a circulation of thirty thousand, had extensive influence within Methodism, and became the prototype for scores of later holiness periodicals.[11]

Phoebe Palmer could write as well as speak. She produced a clear account of her own sanctification, *The Way to Holiness*, and it went through thirty-six editions.[12] Other books followed, the most popular and far-reaching being *Faith and Its Effects*. Yet, with becoming feminine modesty, she omitted her name from the title page of most of her books and let the message speak for itself.

At first the Tuesday Meeting for the Promotion of Holiness was attended only by women, but in September of 1839 Mrs. Palmer and her sister Sarah Lankford had tea with the husband of a friend. The husband was Thomas C. Upham, a professor at Bowdoin College, a man engaged in writing philosophical treatises of scholarly appeal. Upham was captivated by the evangelical transcendentalism the sisters propounded and he abandoned his staid labors and set out to write a series of books on his views of Wesleyan perfectionism. His recognition of holiness and his attendance upon the Tuesday Meeting broadened its appeal, and men as well as women, clergymen as well as laymen, sat in on the sessions and carried away their impressions to distribute among those they met.[13]

Mrs. Palmer numbered among her friends and followers four bishops of The Methodist Episcopal Church. She attracted hundreds of preachers of all denominations. No small part of her appeal lay in offering Americans what was known as the shorter way to holiness. By placing all on the altar, one could be instantly sanctified. Anyone willing to receive the baptism of the Holy Ghost could achieve it in short order.

By degrees, then, and healthily, holiness regained standing in Methodist circles. And it retained Methodist standards. It was the Second Blessing that made it peculiarly Methodist. Sanctification might come gradually or suddenly, but it was a separate exhilarating experience. It came to individuals but it could descend on whole congregations, as it had at Pentecost. In fact, it must come to the whole body of believers, its advocates said in the late 1850's, if there was to be any way of avoiding a divided church and diverting a nation from its headlong plunge toward civil war. Methodist holiness was no cult of pietism or quietism. It was something that would renew and strengthen the churches, endue them with such power from on high that they might cope with the specter of dire events. Supertransformed men and women offered the best if not the only means by which the national crisis could be met.

It was a point generally acknowledged and bishops and officials showed an increasing willingness in the 1850's to lend sanction to sanctification. The need was evident in the anguished cries of a bruised and distraught people professing religion in a land shattered by hate. To some religious groups Armageddon was at hand. There would be an overthrow of the forces of evil and Christ would return and reign a thousand years. Millennial expectations, however, were no part of the Methodist temperament, which called for action. There could be a colossal awakening, an outpouring of the Holy Spirit, so that God could intervene through consecrated lives. To multiply these lives rapidly was the aim. If the aim were achieved, men and women would be lifted above the hates and hassles of a nation divided. The spread of scriptural holiness could still reform the continent.

There was a moment when it looked as if the Methodists would make it. There was a stupendous holiness revival in 1858, starting in New York City and sweeping most of the Northeast. It was the last cry of the spirit before war engulfed the land: ". . . business workers turned out *en masse* to sing hymns, while stevedores knelt on the docks to pray. Telegraph companies allowed messages to be sent to 'sinners' free of cost at certain times of the day. Soon a 'thousand mile prayer meeting' was inaugurated that struck one city after another."[14]

For all their fervor, believers in the Second Blessing found that they could not turn the tide of fratricide. Holiness proved to be no more than St. Elmo's fire, a luminous discharge from the towering masts of the ship of state as it moved through troubled waters toward the inevitable storm. The fire was at times spectacular and it was a sign that there was some force at work beyond the mere operation of the elements. But the force could not be captured and channeled. It was nothing to count on in the face of disaster.

For one thing, holiness was unpredictable. The idea of perfection did strange things to people who possessed it or claimed to possess it. It sharpened and deepened their sense of right and wrong. Officials were to find that men who professed perfect love were inclined to extend their sense of love to human beings enslaved and to want these human beings set free. Also, holiness people were not obedient to authority but believed rather in acting on their own convictions. Many who got the Second Blessing became critical of what they called the episcopal hierarchy and of ministers stationed in well-to-do churches, proclaiming that these preachers ought to renounce the world and its wiles and return to simple dress and self-abnegating conduct.

By the late 1850's the divisiveness caused by holiness enthusiasm reached a point where it could no longer be overlooked by the Church in the North. The scene was central New York, where the heresies and excesses of Noyes had culminated and where the Finney revivals had stirred the people to newness of life. The preachers of the region, organized in the Genesee Conference, stood arrayed in separate camps over subjects that became issues through the agitation of the sanctificationists.

Each camp had chosen an epithet as a name for the other. The holiness advocates were called Nazarites and the preachers who wanted to keep the churches respectable, orderly, and prosperous were designated as the Regency. Lines were drawn between rural and urban areas as sharply as they had been in the days of the prophets and the Pharisees. Buffalo, with its big churches, pew rents, and paid choirs was the seat of the Regency —and of the sins that were besetting the Church.

The Nazarites depicted the Regency preachers as "clerical professors in Odd-Fellow regalia, shawled to the nose and bearded to the eyes. . . ." The Regency in turn derided the Nazarites as spurious reformers, who went forth before the world, "putting on strange and uncouth airs." Among them, "a long face and sanctimonious airs answer for inward purity and goodness of heart." The clothes of the Nazarites, following the early traditions of Methodism, came in for comment: "With them, a broad-brimmed, well-crowned hat is equivalent to the helmet of salvation, and a shad-bellied coat to the robe of righteousness."[15]

The Regency formed the majority and controlled the Genesee Conference. It was thus able to determine appointments and to show favor by giving those who agreed with respectability the better churches and to discipline the fanatics by placing them in lesser charges. The system did not always work according to plan. Two presiding elders who were sent to districts for the express purpose of stamping out fanaticism both became seekers after holiness.

It was all very upsetting, but there was nothing for the Regency to do but to hold the fort. In 1856 the General Conference replaced William Hosmer, who as editor of the *Northern Christian Advocate* had been hospitable to holiness, with a moderate editor inclined to compromise. Friends joined and raised enough money for Hosmer to set up a paper of his own, the *Northern Independent*. He opened its pages to the protestations of the Nazarites. In 1857 there appeared an article that set off the fireworks. It was written by a young and aggressive preacher, Benjamin Titus Roberts, who had been converted to holiness under the instruction of Phoebe Palmer. College-trained, eloquent, and mannerly, Roberts had been for the most part successful in the pulpit up to that time. He wrote, however, from his own experience, and he knew that the Nazarites were right about Buffalo. He had been able to hold revivals in the towns where he had served as pastor, but he had found Buffalo cold and unyielding, strongly under the paralyzing grip of worldly influence.

The Roberts article appeared just before the annual meeting of the Genesee Conference. It said little more than had been said before but it put it all down well and in one place, noting that what he styled the New School Methodists auctioned pews to the highest bidder and conducted "parties of pleasure, oyster suppers, fairs, grab-bags, festivals and lotteries." At the next session of the Conference Roberts was sentenced to be reproved by the bishop "for immoral and unchristian conduct." By way of indirect discipline, he was assigned to a miserable and remote circuit. He took the job with good grace, did a rousing evangelistic job, and proved that he could restore some of the old-time religion to Methodism.

At the 1858 meeting of the Genesee Conference, however, he faced a new and far more serious charge—that of disobedience to discipline. A local preacher reissued the Roberts article and added to it a libelous account of the way in which the case had been handled by the Conference. He charged that the Regency had "an annual sacrifice of a human victim" and added for good measure: "No man is safe who dares even whisper a word against this secret Inquisition in our midst." It was alleged that Roberts had helped to prepare and distribute the scurrilous document prepared by the local preacher. Evidence was by no means conclusive but Roberts was expelled from the Conference and the Church.

The expulsion struck a tocsin that brought together a Gideon's band of Nazarites, remarkable in constitution because it was made up of laymen. Some two hundred of these laymen, having no rights in the procedures of the Conference, gathered in defense of Roberts and another preacher expelled at the same time, Joseph McCreery. The laymen let it be known that they considered the charges against the men groundless, agreed to support them financially, and encouraged them to make the rounds on their own responsibility and preach the true gospel. It was the first time laymen had banded together against the episcopal hierarchy and it came about as a result of the holiness agitation.[16]

At the next session of the Annual Conference the holiness people put up a tent seating three thousand persons within sight and almost within sound of the church where the Conference sessions were held. The meetings held nightly were revivalistic and they served to flaunt the power of holiness and taunt the authority of the episcopacy. They had no effect, however, on the deliberations of the governing body. Four other preachers were dismissed as unchristian. And at the General Conference of 1860, meeting at Buffalo, the decisions taken by the Annual Conference were upheld.

Holiness was one thing but disturbance was another. Disobedience to discipline, as one writer put it, is the cardinal sin in Methodism. By now disobedience had reached the dimensions of schism. A host of preachers withdrew and, flocking around Roberts, formed the Free Methodist Church. In it salvation was to be free and so were pews. So many itinerants went with the new church that membership in the Genesee Conference declined by almost a third during the next six years.[17]

Once the fanatics were disposed of, the emphasis on holiness resumed. Even the cold blood of the Civil War had not chilled the fervent. Right after the war there was evidence that, among many, faith in love had returned. It was an improbable time. The enormity of the most destructive war in history could be seen if not grasped. Cities lay in rubble and there were pictures to prove it. The maimed walked the streets. Hatred and recrimination were rife. Yet at the moment when the horror of war was ready to continue in the agony of peace, there arose an effulgence of belief, bringing with it a mystical approach to human conduct, so that there was admitted into the churches of the two sections something bigger than polity. You might say that the Methodists got religion, right when they needed it most. They wanted again to follow out the implications of their deepest conviction. Man might attain perfect love.

Soon after Appomattox, Dr. and Mrs. Palmer took to the hustings again, holding their most successful meetings at a dozen different points throughout the northern part of the stricken land. In 1866 The Methodist Episcopal Church held centenary services to mark the growth and work of believers since Philip Embury stood up in his New York cottage and, timorous, preached what was officially reckoned to be the first Wesleyan sermon on American shores. In charge of the centennial celebration was a prominent preacher, John C. McClintock, who chose to proclaim in his own New York pulpit, that of a prosperous church, that the Methodist ministry must hold to "the central idea of the whole book of God, from beginning to end—the holiness of the human heart, mind, soul, and will." It was a daring declaration at a time of victory, defeat, and sorrow.

In 1867 another New York pastor, John Swannell Inskip, helped to persuade some of his confreres to sponsor a camp meeting at Vineland, New Jersey. It would not be an ordinary camp meeting; it would bring people together to receive the Second Blessing. People from all over the northeastern seaboard responded. The new railroads, with their powerful locomotives and their rattling cars, aided the cause and brought the devout from far and near. Many got the blessed experience for which they had come, and at the end of the assembly the leaders formed a National Camp Meeting Association for the Promotion of Holiness and immediately plans were laid to have another great gathering the next year at Manheim, Pennsylvania.

The meeting at Manheim lived up to the lofty expectations of the devout. It carried the holiness cause into new territory and attracted to the banners of the movement two powerful Methodist forces who were separated from The Methodist Episcopal Church only because they spoke German. One group was the United Brethren in Christ, spiritual descendants of Philip Otterbein, who had aided in the ceremony consecrating Francis Asbury. Originally a German Reformed preacher, Otterbein had been deeply influenced by the Methodists and, after Asbury had made the decision to stick to English in The Methodist Episcopal Church, he began to evangelize among the Germans, together with Martin Boehm, a preacher who had had a deeply emotional conversion. By 1800 the converts made by the efforts of the two men were organized as the United Brethren in Christ, with Otterbein and Boehm as bishops. The work of developing the organization fell later to a man who bore the wonderfully appropriate name of Christian Newcomer. He spread the Word and the organization beyond Pennsylvania into Ohio, Indiana, and Kentucky.

The United Brethren had held steadfastly and naturally to the Wesleyan belief in holiness. Another German group with even stronger Methodist leanings had been organized in Pennsylvania in 1803. The leader was Jacob Albright, a Lutheran layman who had joined a Methodist church after his conversion. Overtures had been made to form a German-speaking branch of Methodism but Asbury did not relent in his view, and Albright's followers grouped themselves into the Evangelical Association. Save for the difference in language, the Evangelical Association was thoroughly Methodist, producing its own great body of itinerants who in the vigor and extent of their work followed the pattern of the English-speaking church. One of their leaders, John Seybert, covered 175,000 miles by horseback from 1820 to 1860, preaching 9850 sermons and making 46,000 pastoral visits in that time.[18]

At Manheim the Methodists who spoke English and those who spoke German found a common cause in the doctrine of holiness —one more bond that might draw them together. The Evangelicals were particularly perfectionist, having preached the importance of the experience from the first. By 1855 they considered those who were not sanctified, who were merely regenerated, to be sinners or lost souls. And now it appeared that the emphasis on holiness, so energetically kept alive among the Germans, was beginning to find its place again among the Methodists who spoke American. There had been found in holiness, as in music, a language of agreement.

Gathering after great gathering followed. One at Troy, New York, in 1869 brought together 150 preachers. The first Sunday saw an attendance of twenty thousand, although trains were not allowed on the grounds and men and women from a distance had to walk the last mile. During the Love Feast at the final session at Troy no fewer than four hundred persons testified that they had received the "consciousness of sanctifying grace." Again the scope of the cause was broadened. The meeting was attended by persons from every state save Texas, Louisiana, and Florida. Seven bishops of the northern and southern Methodist Churches were present. One preacher from Virginia said that the Methodists there "were reconstructing the Old Dominion upon the basis of holiness."[19]

Thus there had begun a modicum of fellowship between Methodists north and south. It was not official and it was not substantial, but it indicated a common faith in faith. It afforded a conspicuous area of agreement. An idea that belonged to both sections had caught hold, and a belief that belonged to the heritage of both had become current. The bishops of The Methodist Episcopal Church, South, asserted in 1870 that their church and section needed more than anything else "a general and powerful revival of scriptural holiness."

For more than two decades following the close of the Civil War the need and possibility of Christian perfection continued to be an accepted postulate in the Methodist household of faith. Moreover, the vision of holiness entranced an increasing number of believers in all parts of the country, giving them convictions that went beyond the bounds of the routine and directed them inwardly toward independent action. Preachers and members alike joined the ranks of the shouting Methodists. At the height of the movement 200 out of the 240 preachers composing the North Georgia Conference testified that they had received the Second Blessing. The National Holiness Association in 1891 listed 304 holiness evangelists who toured the land preaching sanctification. In the same year there were 354 weekday meetings for the promotion of holiness patterned after those started by Phoebe Palmer.[20] With holiness as a focus, the small group returned for a while to Methodism.

The idea of the Second Blessing had mainly mass appeal, however, and any presentation of it would draw throngs. In one five-year period there were twenty-eight big holiness camp meetings, spreading from Tennessee to Maine, touching Iowa and Nebraska, and enlivening Baltimore and Washington, all attracting visitors, it was said, from the country as a whole.[21]

Elaborate facilities arose to house the crowds and accommodate the seekers. In 1870 the New Jersey Legislature granted a charter to the Ocean Grove Camp Meeting Association of The Methodist Episcopal Church. A vigorous and enterprising preacher, William M. Osborn, "with hair and beard to rival David," had bought a tract of rare beauty along the Jersey shore near Long Branch. During the next decade Osborn and the Association busied themselves building a holiness city, with streets three hundred feet wide as they approached the sea, with cottages, both small and imposing, as well as numerous hotels and boardinghouses, covering the grounds. Evangelistic services were held throughout the year but there was an annual camp meeting also, addressed by the Palmers, and more than six hundred temporary tents were needed to accommodate the seekers.[22]

In time the same severity that characterized the Nazarites of the Genesee Conference marked the holiness craze throughout the country, creating strictures and dividing structures. The perfectionists were troublemakers, insisting on the old-time religion and upright conduct with the same vehemence that the early circuit riders showed, recalling to Methodists the days of their austerity. Distaste grew for the insistence of the perfectionists in arrogating to themselves the role of the only true believers. They had a way of taking over churches almost before you knew what was happening. Harold Vinson Synan, a close student of the scene in the late nineteenth century, describes the way the Methodists had to deal with the problem in local situations. The North Georgia Conference, repenting somewhat of its earlier zeal, assigned most of the holiness preachers to the Gainsville District, "thereby hoping to localize the contagion." But before the year was out a letter to the Georgia *Wesleyan Advocate* told what had happened: "They have changed the name of our meetings, substituting Holiness for Methodist. They preach a different doctrine . . . they sing different songs; they patronize and circulate a different literature; they have adopted radically different words of worship. . . ."[23]

A spirit highly critical of the Church itself possessed some of the holiness advocates, adding to official exasperation. The advocates urged true believers to leave the Church, to forsake it as a corrupt and unredeemable body. Based on the Pauline injunction to the early Christians, "Wherefore come ye out from among them and be ye separate," agitators started an exodus known as Come-Outism, posing the threat of another schism. Moreover, the National Holiness Association had developed into an independent interdenominational body with its own management, budget, and staff, and with its own songbooks and publications. While it continued to use Methodist prestige and facilities, it had passed beyond the point where it could be directed, much less controlled, by the Methodists north or south. Traveling evangelists even carried and sold their own songbooks, competing with regular Methodist hymnals, and urged the use of special songs to replace old stand-bys.

It became apparent that Methodism would have to come to grips administratively with problems raised by the holiness movement. It did. The break came at the General Conference of The Methodist Episcopal Church, South, in 1894. The South had been the scene of particularly aggressive activity among the perfectionists, who not only almost took over control but also needled their opponents unconscionably about their imperfections, especially the deplorable habit of smoking. That they could not stop smoking was a favorite charge against the old-line preachers. One holiness advocate noted that he had not himself been able to stop until he got the Second Blessing and went so far as to suggest that some of the preachers might not even have the *first* blessing.[24]

Raillery and accusation did not improve the disposition of the preachers who failed to swing along with the new emphasis. Atticus Greene Haygood deplored the ceaseless agitation and the critical outlook of what was called the New Puritanism. He lampooned the extremists, called the traveling evangelists tramps, and in his last book, *The Monk and the Prince,* portrayed Savonarola in the role of a Georgia Methodist holiness preacher four centuries later.[25] As a bishop and hence an administrator he deplored the commotion caused even more than he did the sniping conduct, and the statement made at the General Conference of 1894 followed a line familiar to those who were well acquainted with Haygood's writings. It recognized the earnestness and the godly example of many of the holiness preachers, but added: ". . . we deplore their teaching and methods in so far as they claim a monopoly of the experience, practice, and advocacy of holiness, and separate themselves from the body of ministers and disciples."[26]

The statement was taken by the holiness people as an open rejection and disavowal and it was followed by a quick flocking to other standards. Never before in the history of the nation, Synan says, had so many churches been founded in so short a time. The seven years before 1900 saw twenty-three holiness or pentecostal denominations come into being. The new bodies grew as fast as children and it was not many years before they were populating vast regions with new enthusiasts, moving toward a world count that, if figures from some countries are reliable, puts their membership up with, if not ahead of, the aggregate Methodists.

Methodism survived once more and on a national scale another crisis created by its own doctrine and practice. It had avoided a schism. Only 100,000 out of approximately four million members went off after the rapidly multiplying sects. Structure and polity were not disturbed, and the Church went its stately way along the road of broad interpretation. It would not make one doctrine seem to be the all of faith.

A strange silence shrouded the subject of holiness. There was an embarrassment over all the excitement, the tremendous excitement, that the idea of perfect love had caused. There were still tributes to holiness, but they were paid with less and less fervor and finally turned to memories. Today in Methodist circles you are not likely to hear reminiscences of, or even references to, the Second Blessing.

Yet both in terms of events and of volumes written and spoken, the doctrine bulks large in the story and thought of the American Wesleyans. Theological students still study it along with other articles of faith. Theologians analyze it and trace its origins. Among them there is now and then some suggestion of a feeling of curiosity, a wistful notion that perhaps the subject might well be taken up again and considered anew in a day when the old ferocities have somewhat subsided.

Reaffirmation, following rediscovery, turns up in unexpected places. Lately Herbert W. Richardson, associate professor of theology at St. Michael's College, University of Toronto, writing on "The Holy Spirit and Protestantism" in *Commonweal*, a Catholic weekly, suggested that the real Reformation took place under John Wesley.[27] The early reforms instituted by Luther dealt merely with the seat of authority and, as was evidenced by the ruthless suppression of the Peasants' Revolt, left the aspirations of the masses untouched. Wesley in his stress on holiness shifted the attention of religion from the state to the soul and thereby gave the common people a sense of their potential. If man can be perfect, does it not follow that he can create a society marked by perfect love?

Whatever the answer, it is plain from the record that in the days before, during, and after the darkest hour of the Republic, when hatred and animosity ruled, Methodism asserted and kept alive the audacious idea that man can be perfect. Alone among other large denominations or religious groupings, Methodists

THE SECOND BLESSING

preached infinitude through faith. They stretched the aspirations of quite ordinary men and women to indefinite heights. The very existence of the idea of perfection touched the imagination, and the insistence that perfection was attainable exalted the will. The idea might not be practical, it might fade. Even so, it was made part of the human situation, firmly planted in the conscience and consciousness of the people called Methodists and through them into the querulous but recurrent idealism of the people called Americans.

XXII The Rocky Road to Reunion

At the time the American Methodists celebrated their second centennial there was produced a remarkable music-dance-drama that compressed two hundred years of history into fifty minutes. In the highly accelerated action the time devoted to the separation and reunion of the two branches north and south occupied only ten minutes, yet the adroit use of ballet summed up the events brilliantly.

The struggle between the two sections was represented quite appropriately by a tug of war, with divided forces on the opposite ends of a long rope. When the struggle was over, both sides fell prostrate, thus proclaiming dramatically that nobody had won.

There followed a scene acted out by four young women dancers. These young dancers represented the Church. Whenever the four came together, you had the Church in symbol form, accentuated and strengthened by a leitmotif of certain clearly defined chords from an accompanying orchestra.

After the tug of war was over, the dancers drew apart, two in blue capes and two in gray. Soon they made tentative moves toward each other but quickly drew back. The steps were repeated, forward and back, again and again. Each time the dancers withdrew they conferred. And each time they moved toward each other, they came closer. At last the hands of each pair of dancers touched the others timidly. Then each pair withdrew again. At the end of what by skillful suspense in the dance was made to seem an age, the dancers came together, swiftly reversed their capes so that they were all one golden color, embraced, and in a superbly executed acrobatic maneuver, formed a human pyramid of triumph.[1]

Action condensed to drama and set to music gives insight after the fact, but it is not effective unless the action has been charged with emotion. The ballet of separation and reunion was powerful and poignant because it caught and stressed in perspective a sweep of events of which those who took part were barely aware. They were too busy with the job at hand and what emotion they had was attenuated by tedium. Compression brings out what happenings cannot.

In real life it lacked a month of being ninety-five years from the time of separation until The Methodist Episcopal Church and The Methodist Episcopal Church, South, got officially back together again. The final sixty-three years of that time were attended by painstaking negotiations, by attempts to find a meeting ground on which to pitch the tents of agreement. There was hardly a day, or a night, during those years when some commission was not in session or when some official was not cogitating on compromises that might make it possible to put the pieces together into a unit once more. When in 1939 the two sections did unite and were joined by The Methodist Protestant Church, which had departed the fold in 1830, the achievement was a tribute not only to American engineering genius but also to the inveterate love Methodists bear for conferences and the joy they take in setting sentiments tidily down on paper, so that all things may be done decently and in order.

The whole prodigious undertaking of joining the Churches together and truing up the structure was voluntary. The efforts could have been abandoned at any moment, and there were moments when some of the negotiators were heartily willing to let the whole thing go. Union was not necessary.

The Baptists and the Presbyterians remained divided and were doing very well. Making the three branches of Methodism into a single body could only increase work and probably cause dislocations that would decrease the efficiency of each division. Yet it had to be done and it was done, and the endless years, weeks, and days that bishops and preachers and laymen gave to the evolution and formation of the union tell more about the inherent character of Methodism than does the accomplishment itself.

Not that the business was all grim. Methodists are jovial. They find talking with others natural and there is nothing they like better than meetings relieved by a flash of wit. Preacher stories enliven any gathering and are to be expected as part of the proceedings. Along with humor, there is a practical and pragmatic quality about the breed, best summed up in the classic statement of Bishop Gerald Kennedy that Methodism is simply sanctified common sense.[2]

The union of the Churches came about as a result of many factors, including a love of polity, but one that must not be overlooked is a turn of mind that led to the negotiations and that was developed as the negotiations went on. The very word *negotiate* means "to do business." Its aim is to seek agreement and consent and results based on agreement and consent. Throughout the epic of joining the Churches, those who took part sought accommodation, convinced that some way could be found out of or around the repeated difficulties that seemed at times to mock the efforts of the best will in the world. The Methodists united their Churches partly because they made uniting a habit of mind. When they decided to found a family magazine the title they chose was *Together.*

One who wants to follow the story, including heartaches, from the beginning will find it cogently told in *The Long Road to Methodist Union* by John M. Moore, a bishop of The Methodist Episcopal Church, South, who sat through the last twenty years of the joint meetings and lived to preside over the final glorious scene. Moore kept copious notes of dates, persons, events, and ideas. No man could have been better acquainted both with the actors or with the forces moving behind the scenes. The fact that he wrote first and last from the point of view of the South, even in his most judicial moments, makes his chronicle all the more revealing, for it was the Church South in its insistence on certain postulates of polity that delayed the proceedings interminably and that at last determined the structure of the united church.

Four years after the Civil War ended, the Church North made a move to bring the southern brethren back into communion. Bishops Janes and Simpson, messengers appointed by their fellow bishops, called on the southern Methodist bishops holding a meeting in St. Louis. The northern bishops spoke of the good that would come of the reunion of the two bodies. They went on to say: "As the main cause of separation has been removed, so has the chief obstacle to the restoration."

To this observation the southern bishops, in a statement prepared by Bishop Holland McTyeire in cooperation with Bishop Robert Paine, made reply, pointing out that slavery was not, in any proper sense, the cause but only the occasion of the separation. The statement continued: "That which you are pleased to call—no doubt sincerely thinking it so—'the great cause' of separation, existed in the Church from its organization, and yet for sixty years there was no separation. But when those theories incidentally involved in connection with it began to be put into practice, then separation came." The statement sounded a declaration of principle and position:

Allow us in all kindness, brethren, to remind you and to keep the important fact of history prominent that we separated from you in no sense in which you did not separate from us. The separation was by compact and mutual, and nearer approaches to each other can be conducted with hope of successful issue only on this basis.[3]

The first diffident steps in the Methodist minuet were taken in 1872 when The Methodist Episcopal Church instructed the bishops to send fraternal messengers to the session of General Conference of the southern church to meet at Louisville in 1874. The messengers were received gallantly but reminded by a committee of the Conference that the causes that led to the separation in 1844 had not disappeared, chief among them being the difference in conception of the powers of the General Conference. The committee said quite frankly that as long as the causes of division remained, each church could do its work "and fulfill its mission most effectively by maintaining a separate organization." Organic union was not to be considered, but the General Conference did authorize the appointment of messengers to attend the General Conference of the Church North in 1876. More remarkable, it also authorized the appointment of a commission to meet with a commission from the Church North "to remove all obstacles to formal fraternity between the two Churches."

That The Methodist Episcopal Church, South, was still in essence if not in polity a part of The Methodist Episcopal Church was a point to which the southern ecclesiastical mind returned repeatedly. It was coequal if not the same size. And it was this point that was recognized officially in the next move toward union. In 1876 the Church North in its General Conference, now comprised of lay as well as ministerial delegates, named a commission to meet with the commission the Church South had authorized for the purpose of removing all obstacles to fraternity.

Those appointed met in Cape May, New Jersey, August 16, 1876. The commissioners from the North met the southern insistence more than halfway and worked out what Bishop Moore called a magnanimous formula. It asserted: "Each of said Churches is a legitimate branch of Episcopal Methodism in the United States, having a common origin in the Methodist Episcopal Church organized in 1784."

The declaration went on to say that The Methodist Episcopal Church, South, had been brought into being by the voluntary exercise of the right of its Annual Conferences and that its "ministers and members, with those of the Methodist Episcopal Church, have constituted one Methodist family, though in distinct ecclesiastical connections."[4] Both General Conferences approved the declaration in their next sessions, and when in the Church North some question about the Camp May statement was raised at the General Conference of 1880, a resolution was put forward, and promptly passed, to say that the statement of the commission on fraternal relations was to be regarded as final.[5]

The idea of union, once started, acquired momentum. Most of the deliberations were carried out in public, and the findings and the semi-actions of joint commissions got attention in the church press of both sections and, seeing that the denomination involved was the largest, coverage in the news. The Methodists are good copy because their churches are probably the best ventilated in the world of the fourth estate. Whether they are dealing with a scandal or an aspiration, they are quick to let the press know.

In the case of overtures toward uniting North and South, accumulated talk had its effect. It encouraged further action. The work of church bodies puts things into the air, pollutants possibly but clarifiers often, setting off currents that have unconscious influence. Other Methodist bodies in the 1870's thought and talked of union, and the way in which The Methodist Protestant Church met and carried out its plan of union may well have had an inspiring effect on the Episcopal Methodists, even down to the ceremonies with which the consummation of the union was celebrated. Nothing good is lost in history.

The Methodist Protestants had split over a question of polity connected with slavery in 1858. The original constitution of the parent body had limited the right of suffrage and of holding office to white males—for all the provisions it made in the direction of democratic church government, such as lay representations. The limitation on color caused no little agitation with the increase of abolitionist sentiment in the North and West, and in 1857 a convention was held in Cincinnati to prepare memorials

THE ROCKY ROAD TO REUNION

for the next session of the Methodist Protestant governing body, petitioning the omission of the word *white* from the constitution and asking that slaveholding and slave trading be made barriers to membership.

When The Methodist Protestant Church declined to act on the memorials, leaders of northern and western conferences withdrew, taking with them about half of the membership and setting up an organization named The Methodist Church. Shortly after the Civil War there was talk of getting the two bodies back together again. In 1871 commissions began to confer. Negotiations, inevitably but pleasantly, went on for five years and ended with the joint call of a uniting convention to be held in May 1877. The place was Baltimore. Separate conventions in different churches met at first, each hammering out difficulties for a week until a plan of union was drawn.

Then the stage was set for the act of union, and it was consummated with a Methodist love of the visible and the symbolic. Members of the two conventions marched single file along Lombard Street, one from the East, the other from the West, to the intersection of Fremont Street, where they met. Here the members of one group joined arm in arm with those in the other group coming from the opposite direction and two by two marched to the Starr Methodist Church, where the ceremonies would be completed. The presidents of the two uniting churches, arm in arm, took the lead, followed by all the delegates paired in the same manner. The process of mingling and consolidation attracted much attention and it was deeply touching to those who took part. A delegate tells of his encounter at the intersection where the two bodies joined. He found himself linked with a man from North Carolina who had voted against the union and every measure connected with it. But the two joined arms and the act itself seemed to bring a sudden sense of agreement and fellowship. The delegate suddenly asked himself, "How could we two walk together unless we are agreed?"[6]

Inside Starr Church there were handclasps, embraces, smiles, tears, prayers, and, of course, speeches. These went on far into the night. At last the union was formally announced and the delegates, hoarse by now, stood and sang in throaty unison, "Praise God from Whom All Blessing Flow."

Next day, the parade and fanfare over, the delegates reassembled and settled down to true up the *Disciplines* of the two Churches and to attend to organizational matters. It was a perfect balance, a model of Methodist procedure, this mingling of the theatrical and the practical.

The union helped to set mood, to mark a trend, to indicate direction, to foreshadow, especially because the Methodist Protestants, united after sectional division, began to make overtures toward union with the larger Methodist bodies. These overtures were received genially but the idea of such a union had to be held in abeyance for years. The problem of joining the Episcopal Methodists was gnarled and complicated and it would have to be worked out before a union with other Methodists could be seriously taken up.

The Cape May declaration of 1876 established beyond cavil the two largest Methodist bodies as of equal stature and integrity at the bargaining table. That is all. It proclaimed a principle without which further negotiations would have been doomed to fruitlessness. But the declaration left an agenda a mile long that ran in and out of thickets that hid practically every problem of human government, in the church and out. In 1876 the views of the two sections appeared to be as irreconcilable as they were irrepressible and no one had the faintest idea how they could ever be conciliated into anything remotely resembling a united church. The Southerners made it clear, as Bishop John M. Moore phrased it, that they would never again "go under, or stay under, a supreme General Conference, a centralized power, that even passed on the constitutionality of its own acts, and that was independent in action, of the ministry and membership of the church. Henceforth they wanted a government of distributed power with checks and balances, and only a union on that basis would ever be acceptable."[7]

Obviously such a union as the South might accept would

THE ROCKY ROAD TO REUNION

alter the very structure of what the North deemed to be the true and inherited Methodist Episcopal Church set up at the Christmas Conference. When, after forty years of talks across glass-topped tables in scores of meeting places, the South did come up with a tentative plan it would possibly accept, a northern bishop said:

> The South in this plan will not trust the North. It con-
> solidates itself but cuts up the rest. No section is to trust the
> other to make laws, rules, and regulations for the other.
> Each shall make its own laws. In this plan the Supreme
> General Conference at bottom is nothing more than a clear-
> ing house for the Boards. . . . It is union by disruption.
> Instead of a Union of Methodism, we have a disruption of
> Methodism. . . . The Methodist Episcopal Church is invited
> to commit suicide. It is to carve itself, under the guise of
> reorganization, into segments, fragments, divisions, each seg-
> ment to think itself a unit, in itself independent and yet
> dependent, with about as much unity in a collective whole
> as there is in a scrap heap.[8]

The plan of union which so exercised the northern bishop, R. J. Cooke, evolved at the meeting of the General Conference of The Methodist Episcopal Church, South, at Oklahoma City in 1914. The essence of the tentative plan was a series of sectional conferences, each conference to have the right to draw the laws and rules germane to the region it governed. The General Conference would remain, but it would not constitute the only lawmaking body.

It was the first time the proposal for sectional (later called jurisdictional) conferences had been made. The action got down on record and in concrete form what the southern leaders had had on their minds all along. Union would have to be on grounds that had been established in the southern mind after the delegates had been outvoted by a northern majority at the General Conference of 1844. What is remarkable enough to be a mystery is the spirit of accommodation shown by the Church North to the type of insistence with which its representatives had constantly to deal. This accommodation may have been in some of its aspects the result of attrition—hearing possibly the same ideas repeated so often that they began to sound less outrageous than they had at first. Also entering in was the pleasure of maneuvering and give-and-take, which for Methodists north and south, was a thing of beauty and a joy forever. At any rate and for whatever reason, northern negotiators proved themselves capable of resipiscence. Many changed their minds on important points as a result of conference and reflection. They had convictions as strong as those of their southern brothers, but it was necessary for them to make concessions if union was to be achieved, and they made these concessions in a way that called for charity of mind and enlightened perception.

In time one of the northern leaders, Dr. Edgar Blake, saw, accepted, and stated the southern position to the satisfaction of the Church South and the consternation of some in the Church North. Blake was secretary of the Sunday School Board of his branch. He had the respect of his peers. He was on the way to becoming a bishop and great importance was attached to his act when he came out for one lawmaking General Conference and a series of what he called Synodical Conferences in various parts of the country. These bodies would supervise and promote the work of the Church in their own territories and they, rather than the General Conference, would have the power to elect bishops.[9]

The statement by Dr. Blake had shock value. More than a concession, it was an advocacy of the southern viewpoint. Force was added to it by the fact that it was not made at a meeting of any of the negotiating bodies but at a working conference of church leaders called together at Evanston, Illinois, in February 1916. The working conference assembled under the auspices of the John Richard Lindgren Foundation for the Promotion of International Peace and Christian Unity. The object was to draw together carefully selected representatives of all points of view and give them a chance to think objectively together without having to feel that their opinions were commitments. There would be no resolutions but merely a series of scholarly papers designed to show where the whole question of unification stood.

The Evanston unofficial gathering, as it turned out, provided one of the most important occasions for appraising the mind of the northern and southern branches. It came at a time when negotiations were at more or less of a standstill anyway, or when possibly there was the start of a new stirring. For the Church South in its 1914 declaration had come up with the phrase "unification by reorganization." It took a while for the term to gain currency and a while longer for its subliminal appeal to become fully felt. But it proved in the long run to be prophetic. If there was anything on earth more appealing than organization, it was reorganization, taking an established structure and rearranging it to suit new needs.

Here was new motivation—strong enough to sustain another twenty years of commissions and fill volumes with proceedings, reports, exhortations, and counter-arguments. The two main bodies of Methodism continued to meet, now and then touching hands and retreating into hesitancy and sometimes into confusion, but always turning toward each other again. The retreat over some problems was greater and deeper than it was over others, for the commissions systematically and methodically dealt with one problem at a time.

The problem of the status and place of the Negro in any united church that might be formed was no greater, technically, than the ways and means of fashioning proper checks and balances. In their negotiations Methodists chose to treat the matter publicly and in the way they had treated it in the past: administratively. Each section was inclined to respect what it considered the prejudices of the other. The problem at hand was the union of the Churches, not the handling of the race problem growing out of an era of organized slavery.

The truth is that there was no antipodal difference between

Methodists north and south on the status of the Negro in Methodism. The two sections agreed by deed that Negro Methodists should be separate and distinct from white Methodists. The Methodist Episcopal Church before the Civil War had set up separate conferences for Negro members. The Church South had done the same after the war and, then, for good measure, had helped to organize the freedmen into what proved to be an autonomous religious order. During the war what was known as the colored membership in the Church South had fallen from 207,703 to 48,702. Many had joined one of the two African Methodist bodies. Others had united with the Church North, active in many southern sections. By 1869 colored membership had dropped to 19,986. In 1870 the southern General Conference arranged for a self-governing body which, it was assumed, would be called The Colored Methodist Episcopal Church, South. The colored delegates who convened to organize, however, omitted the word "South" from the title. The Colored Methodist Episcopal Church began at once to assert its independence and to maintain it. Leaders comported themselves in the presence of prejudice and violence and the burning of church property with a spirit of charity that more than poetically justified the change of name, after almost a century of progress, to The Christian Methodist Episcopal Church.[10]

But there were many of dark skin who, over the years, as at the outset, chose to remain affiliated with one of the white branches of Methodism. Segregated, as in civil life, they still held on to their membership instead of joining strong independent bodies organized on the basis of race. They were Methodists first and colored second. These loyal and devoted members must be accommodated in a new church formed out of the old ones. The Church South wanted all the Negro Methodists north and south organized—into a separate church with warm fraternal relations maintained between white and colored conferences. The Methodists North wanted the Negroes in a separate conference but being a part of the corporate body of Methodism and with rights to be represented in the new General Conference and on boards that conducted various church activities.[11]

What did trouble the dreams of the elders was that the shadow of their brother in black fell across every conference table, the uninvited guest ever present, whether he was there or not. He had not been present in person at the Conference that divided the Church, but concern with his status and the difference in views Methodists held of him had been the unspoken and unacknowledged cause of separation. He played an increasing role as negotiations wore on and he seemed to hold the balance of power right when the delicate business of union showed some promise of becoming a reality.

Old divisions deepened in 1920, a year of racial tension and violence, when the bishops of the Church North sounded a stern and prophetic note of warning on race: "Much of the talk today about race consciousness is an unconscious recrudescence of the spirit which Jesus came to destroy, and leads straight to new hostilities." With a side glance at Calvinism in contrast to good Methodist doctrine, the bishops went on: "We have repudiated election as applied to individuals and largely retained it as applied to races. But our church must this day cry out in Christ's name that in Christ there is neither Jew nor Greek, barbarian, Scythian, bond or free; that no men and no races are at the mercy of their environment or their heredity."[12]

In the same year the General Conference of the Church North elected a black bishop in the person of Robert E. Jones. He had shown himself to be an able administrator on several boards of his Church and had been editor of the *Southeast Christian Advocate*. He had also been a member of various commissions dealing with unification. Jones was elected on merit but his election was an act of theater as well as recognition, and the General Conference ceremoniously made the most of it. The moment his election was announced two white bishops went immediately to him and, each taking an arm, escorted him to the platform. Members of the Conference rose to their feet and broke into thunderous applause that shook the rafters of prejudice. Then they sang the Doxology and "The Battle Hymn of the Republic."[13]

The office of bishop was more honored as an office in the South than it was in the North, and the action of the Church North had a chilling effect in the South, as if it were a pointed act. By other actions also the Church North made it clear that it would follow an enlightened conscience on race. In 1928 its General Conference voted to hold its meetings thereafter only in cities where Negro delegates would be entertained upon the same basis as white delegates. One of the bishops of the Church South, Edwin D. Mouzon, a man who had been prominent in the work of every commission on unification since 1916, gave out an interview in which he said that this action had postponed the cause of union indefinitely.[14]

Still negotiations did not stop. There were men in both sections who were determined that nothing would stand in the way of agreement, that every stone would be rolled away. One was Bishop Moore, who looked upon the 1928 action philosophically. The position taken might keep the General Conference from meeting in the South for many years, but that was all. Besides, the matter could be settled when the time came. If the Churches united, the resolution, to be valid and binding, would have to be passed again by the governing body of the united church.

In the end patience and polity won. By sticking to the one goal of uniting the Churches the Methodists got around all hazards and over all hurdles in the obstacle race to ecclesiastical brotherhood. By 1935 they had in hand a feasible plan that might be accepted by the three main bodies. The Methodist Protestants, favoring union all along, had stood sympathetically by while the others sweated it out. Their commissioners, however, were in on and agreed to the master plan. Its provisions were several but the chief feature lay in a series of Jurisdictional Conferences, designed to be balancing bodies against the power of the General Conference, each having the right to conduct its own affairs and to elect bishops, not only for itself but for the entire Church. The General Conference remained, with its powers clearly defined. Atop it, however, was to be a Judicial Council, a tribunal with final authority to decide on questions involving the constitutionality of legislative acts.

Would the Church North accept an arrangement that turned the whole organization topsy-turvy, introduced new and untried bodies created for the diffusion of authority and for the satisfaction of the South? Yes. The General Conference of The Methodist Episcopal Church met in May of 1936 and voted 470 to 83 in favor of the Plan of Union. When referred to the Annual Conferences, the majority favoring the Plan was overwhelming, with a total of 17,239 for and 1862 against. The vote of the General Conference and of the Annual Conferences of The Methodist Protestant Church was equally impressive.

In the Church South the Annual Conferences did not wait for the General Conference to meet but petitioned the bishops to let them vote first during the conference year of 1937. The vote of their members was 7650 for and 1247 against the plan.[15]

It was all over but the singing, and the singing was important to the Methodists. It might be loud enough to drown out some of the strident objections that had been raised in debate over the provisions while the plan was being considered. In the South opponents cried out against the tremendous power still left to the General Conference through the numerical majority of the northern Methodists and its ability to control all legislation, policies, and properties. These opponents were in the main suspicious of any concentrated authority and went so far as to claim that the matter of union should have been submitted to plebiscite in local churches. Such a thing had not been heard of in Methodism and had no legal footing there, yet the fact that the objection was raised showed that there were new as well as familiar forces afoot and that the demand for more democracy might in time have to be reckoned with.

Opposition in the North turned chiefly on the Central Jurisdiction, one set aside for the Negro Annual Conferences. The other five Jurisdictional Conferences were geographical but the

Central, while called Central, in reality covered all the scattered Negro bodies and put them into an artificial and segregated unit. Opponents of the plan said the Negro Annual Conferences ought to be part of the Jurisdictional Conference in which or near which they were located.

But the opposition was stilled if not silenced as the stupendous and widespread acceptance of union expressed itself through the official votes. The unsatisfied were wise enough to know that Methodists did not accept any act as final, and that if a constitution could be drawn it could be amended.

The uniting conference of the three Churches met at Kansas City, Missouri, April 26, 1939. The name had been agreed upon. It would be The Methodist Church. Every detail of the gigantic uniting ceremony had been planned weeks and months in advance, the joint commission in its far-sighted labors having foreseen triumph and having set up such administrative units as the Committee on Program, Public Meetings and Addresses.

Fifty bishops and nine hundred delegates attended. Before going to the first session on the morning of the first day, bishops and delegates went to the Cathedral of the Protestant Episcopal Church and there celebrated Communion. Then the Methodists, having come a long and lordly way from the little band John Wesley had gathered around him, marched in stately procession along the city streets to the auditorium big enough to accommodate the crowds who wanted to watch this unprecedented meeting.

After days of business came the final act of the Conference, the one event toward which the creation of the commissions had moved for years. It was the adoption of the Declaration of Union. The first draft of it had been prepared nine months before by a lawyer. It had been written out and revised by John M. Moore. Then it had been turned over to a Nashville judge, a former member of the Supreme Court of Tennessee. Both he and a former member of the Supreme Court of Mississippi scrutinized it carefully, and made suggestions and revisions in the interest of legal accuracy. To make sure that there was no slip, still other lawyers were consulted.

At last it was ready—and worthy of the attention given it by the lawyers and of the jubilant but carefully planned adoption given it by the delegates. The ritual by which it would be adopted had been written out almost a year earlier by Bishop Moore, but he had kept the script to himself and had revealed it to the proper committee on arrangements at the time the program for the closing session was drawn up. The very fact that he had kept the procedure hidden until exactly the right moment showed a sense of high drama. Mild in manner, small of stature, quiet in pulpit style, the South's leading bishop proved to be nonetheless a maestro, director, and actor rolled into one. With a sense of mission formed by conviction and refined in the crucible of negotiation, it was fitting that he should hold the center of the stage.

The setting could not have been better. The auditorium was packed with fourteen thousand people. There was a mammoth organ and a massed choir of three hundred voices. The delegates came in quietly and modestly and took their appointed seats on the conference floor. The bishops marched in, led by the three chairmen of the joint commission. They marched straight up to the platform, above the audience but in the presence and sight of all, signifying some of the majesty that had been associated with prelates through the centuries, and on display again tonight. You couldn't help but feel that the sainted Asbury, his piercing blue-gray eyes missing no detail, was there.

It might have startled him to see a Negro bishop announce the hymn, but it would have thrilled him to hear what it was: "O for a thousand tongues to sing/ My great Redeemer's praise!/ The glories of my God and King/ The triumphs of His grace." The past was present again. Charles Wesley had written that hymn on the first anniversary of his conversion. And he had based it on words spoken by Peter Bohler, the Moravian missionary, "If I had a thousand tongues, I'd praise Christ with all of them." How far back in time a hymn could carry one!

And how far into infinity! The vast auditorium was converted into a cathedral, as had been the forests in the days of the camp meetings. The Methodists were united in the only way they would ever be really united: in song. Each of the thousands there that night wished for a thousand tongues to sing, as so many had before. Asbury had said that there were many who could outpreach him but none who could outsing him.

The address of the evening was delivered by a bishop of the Church North, Edwin Holt Hughes, who used as a refrain the line "The Methodists Are One People." And now the time had come for the Declaration of Union. The audience stood. A bishop of The Methodist Protestant Church read the Preamble, a bishop of The Methodist Episcopal Church read the Affirmation. Bishop Moore read the five Declarations, and after each Declaration the nine hundred members of the Conference and the fifty bishops, standing, lifted their right hands and said in a stupendous chorus, "We do so declare." The sixth Declaration was read in unison, chanted like a litany, by all the bishops and delegates.

Following the Declaration came an antiphonal prayer with a bishop and all the assembled multitude taking part. But the end was not yet. To come was a display of parliamentary legality combined with a high sense of symbolism, the mark of a true Methodist gathering, large or small. The chair (Bishop Moore) recognized Judge H. H. White, of Louisiana, who said, "I consider it a high privilege and honor to move that the Declaration of Union, which has been adopted section by section, be now adopted as a whole." The motion was no sooner made than it was seconded by a delegate from The Methodist Episcopal Church and, just to make it all-round, by one from The Methodist Protestant Church.

The chairman then asked all those who favored the adoption as a whole to stand with uplifted right hand. The delegates stood en masse. When they were seated again the chair then asked those who opposed to stand. Not a muscle moved.

The chair then declared: "No one stands in opposition. . . . The Declaration has been adopted. The Methodist Church now is! Long live The Methodist Church!"[16]

XXIII Every Man His Own College

Chautauqua.

The term has become generic. It wears several faces, conjures up varied images. To those in the know it describes an institution housed on an old Methodist camp-meeting ground along the shores of Lake Chautauqua in western New York, where each summer for almost a century thousands of persons, most of them in families, have assembled to listen and learn while enjoying the beauties of a rustic setting and the pleasures of innocent recreation.

Others who have heard or overheard the word associate it with a series of closely scheduled lectures and concerts that visited American towns for one intense week once a year. It was the poor man's lyceum, a medium that brought the benefits and blessings of talent to people in remote areas, far from the madding throngs of cities, and in some measure increased knowledge of and curiosity about the outside world. The week carried a wisp and a waft of Europe to the crossroads and the grass roots and cow chips. For two decades before the days of radio it offered small-town America its first and only contact with the performing arts.

The one thing in common between the institution still attracting summer crowds to the assembly ground in western New York and the tent shows now of blessed memory is the name Chautauqua. The traveling shows that beguiled yokel America and enlivened the doldrums of small towns once a year had no organic connection with the original Chautauqua. The entrepreneurs simply appropriated, without so much as by-your-leave, a name which, even at the beginning of the twentieth century, was already famous—a name that had enough sales appeal to draw crowds. In turn the tent shows, being highly and heavily promoted, gave the name extraordinary currency and fixed it in the language. They helped to put *chautauqua* into the dictionaries with a small *c* to become synonymous with any spot where people gather voluntarily for painless self-improvement, for learning and entertainment combined.

There is a story as well as magic in the word because it unfolds in narrative form the whole Methodist philosophy of education. Chautauqua, whether as an institution or a common noun or a recollection of the not-so-dead past, is Methodist in concept and reality. Not only was the first assembly set on a Methodist camp-meeting site and the result of Methodist planning; it was also the direct outgrowth of the conviction that every man should help himself to education. Growth through self-cultivation must go along with the duties and chores of daily life. The learner need not be separated from his work or segregated behind ivied walls or put in an ivory tower. The Methodist does not withdraw; he doubles up. He learns while doing.

The colophon of the Methodist Publishing House illustrates the attitude. It shows an old-time itinerant, in stylized costume with a broad-brimmed hat, reading as he rides. His horse, evidently used to the loose rein of the preoccupied horseman, plods along amiably and the man in the saddle holds an open book in his right hand at a proper distance from his eyes. There is not a moment for the itinerant to lose on his appointed rounds. When he reaches the next point of his circuit he will be better equipped to minister to and hearten his hearers because he has studied on the way. He is carrying out a moral responsibility to develop the mind along with the soul.

To send such a man to college would take him out of production and possibly return him to his chores with some alienating sense of superiority. At least this was the theory at the outset of the societies and during the years of Methodism's early strides. It is true that today The United Methodist Church has 143 institutions with an enrollment of 250,000 students. Nearly 50 percent of the enrollment of all Protestant-related colleges is in these institutions.[1] The number of institutions named Wesleyan tells us always of Methodist origin, if not present control, and is one sign of the widespread Methodist interest in higher learning. With all the impressive statistics and performance, however, the practice of relying on colleges and universities for learning is tangential to the paradigm of education John Wesley drew up with his unexampled precision and then energetically executed.

The aim of the Wesleyan system was to share the wealth of the world's culture with "persons of common sense and no learning." Mr. Wesley, as Louis B. Wright observes, was "scarcely more concerned over the souls than over the minds of his followers in Britain and America." How could this concern be shown save by making available to members of the societies what they might feed on to their nourishment? He wrote 233 books and pamphlets, including *The Concise History of England* and *A Survey of the Wisdom of God in the Creation or a Compendium of Natural Philosophy*. In addition to the books he wrote, he abridged many more—so many that, as one scholar whimsically remarks, "It is a wonder that Mr. Wesley did not abridge the Gospel according to St. John."[2] In one six-year period he published fifty volumes of the *Christian Library: Consisting of Extracts from, and Abridgment of, the Choicest pieces of Practical Divinity which have been published in the English Tongue.*[3]

There was no end of his efforts to make literature available in comprehensible form, for after having extracted, summarized, and annotated for years, he decided to compile a dictionary wherein readers might learn the meaning of difficult terms encountered in their reading. *The Complete English Dictionary* was published in 1753, two years before Dr. Samuel Johnson's monumental work appeared. Mr. Wesley's was one of a succession of dictionaries that had begun to appear in 1603, each trying to outdo the others in claims and pretensions. It was small in the number of entries and the title was ironic, as was the boast on the title page: "The author assures you that he thinks this is the best English Dictionary in the World." The introduction notified the reader that the book was not published to get money, that it was "not a heap of Greek and Latin words, not a scroll of barbarous law expressions, not a crowd of technical terms. . . ." It was simply a part of his attempt to make knowledge as attractive, easy, and as accessible as possible.[4]

In Mr. Wesley's mind there was no antagonism to formal learning. He was himself schooled. He was a Fellow of Lincoln College, Oxford. He mastered six languages. He was at home in the classics. For Kingswood School, which he founded, he prepared grammars in five languages and the school had standards as stiff as any. But beyond the range of the formal, what Mr. Wesley sought was the diffusion of knowledge, just as he sought the diffusion of grace. In theology he held that any man, however lowly or sinful, might be saved and might be made perfect—not merely the few salted away in abbeys from temptations and distractions. Likewise every man might learn. Not all could be given the discipline of colleges, but all might find the means through print by which they could work out their own salvation.

There was a point at which both the pragmatic and the religious motives of the founder of Methodism met. He knew that the work of furthering the work of the societies could not wait until the men needed to carry it forward had been formally schooled. Having, as Thomas Babington Macaulay noted, a genius for government not inferior to that of Richelieu, he would employ and train what was available. He could expect help only from lay brothers—artisans, merchants, workers in iron and wood. These were his preachers, and his only choice was to teach the preachers to teach themselves. They must learn to read—not casually, but religiously and habitually. On the matter of reading, Mr. Wesley said to them, "Contract a habit for it by use, or return to your trade."

That his preachers might cultivate reading habits as a part of their religious life, Mr. Wesley went into publishing. He wanted publications that were thin and cheap, so that as many as possible might be crammed into saddlebags. And through the reading of the preachers every member of the societies would get a chance to learn. He used his itinerants as distributing agents. Leland D. Case points out that every circuit rider became a book salesman, every local society a book club. Mr. Wesley bragged on his best salesmen and cited them as examples others might well follow. He cited Billy Pennington, for example, and noted pointedly that Billy had sold more books in Cornwall than had been sold for seven years before, adding significantly in a sales appeal to other preachers: "So may you, if you take the same method. Carry one sort of book with you the first time you go the round; another sort the second time; and so on. Preach on the same subject at each place; and, after preaching, encourage the congregation to buy and read the tract."[5] Stewards kept account of books sold to members and made quarterly payments to the visiting preacher, who forwarded the reports and the monies to the central Book Room in London.

There was a general and popular market for Mr. Wesley's works in America long before his first missionaries arrived. His *Primitive Physick: or An Easy and Natural Method of Curing Most Diseases* went through twenty editions by 1774 and four of these had been in America. The concern of the founder of the societies, however, was not with a popular sale outside the circle but with the influence of books among people who made up the growing membership. The transfer to the societies in America of the double emphasis on preaching and reading was naturally, you might say inevitably, made. The first step was taken out of sheer exuberance by Robert Williams, who came in 1769. An irrepressible itinerant whose trip to the Colonies had been approved in a general way, he had arrived ahead of the two appointed missionaries, James Pilmour and Richard Boardman. Williams, seeing the need, set about with a right good will to do what he had seen done in England. He printed and sold the founder's sermons far and wide.

At the end of four years Williams had done so well with the Wesley books and tracts that the preachers assembled in the first American Conference decided that the publishing business had best be organized. Mr. Wesley had announced himself as sorely displeased with the unauthorized printing of his works, and the preachers decided firmly that, while Robert Williams was allowed to sell the books he had already printed, no preacher in the future was to print any of Mr. Wesley's works "without his authority (when it can be got) and the consent of the brethren."[6]

Consent meant that the traveling preachers would control the publishing program of the Church. It prepared the way for a further decision taken by the General Conference of 1808 forbidding the preachers "to publish any book or pamphlet without the approbation of the annual conference . . . or a committee chosen by them." The manuscript committee of the same General Conference refused to approve the publication of Jesse Lee's *Short History of the Methodists in the United States,* saying that it was crude and simple.[7] What Methodists wrote and read remained for many years under the close auspices of the preachers acting ex officio as editors.

It was fitting that the publishing agency, when formally launched in 1789, should be called The Methodist Book Concern. It was the concern of all. The money would go to the welfare of the itinerants as a whole. Being a part of the family, it was all the more important that the publishing project be managed with great sagacity. Everything fitted. The preachers were both book salesmen and readers by habit. With the esprit de corps and prestige of the Church back of publishing, Methodists as Methodists could become an enormous audience.

No other denomination thought of starting its own publishing house at the outset. The Methodists had a healthy and fruitful business in prospect eleven years before The Methodist Episcopal Church was organized. The years of the Revolution saw little activity. Mr. Wesley suggested that the books on hand be hidden ("if a safe place for them in America can be found") and distributed as well as possible. But once the war was over, the bookmen were ready to go. The modest decision taken at the Conference in 1773 proved momentous.

Presiding over the Conference which made this decision was Thomas Rankin, a Scot of no geniality with his colleagues in the faith but a man who knew Mr. Wesley well enough to be called Dear Tommy. He had been named Mr. Wesley's general assistant and he had been sent as a disciplinarian to whip the colonials into better shape. And so he acted, to the annoyance of the colonials. But with all his other activities and along with them, the promotion of books and tracts was a vital part of his mission. His diary records that on Sunday, September 4, 1774, he decided to have a day of rest for the consolation of his soul. And how did he spend it? ". . . Unpacking books sent from London and also in packing five boxes to send to Virginia, Maryland, and the Jersies." Two months later he notes that he rode to Philadelphia, and adds: "The remaining part of the week, as well as Sunday, was spent in the usual labors, besides writing many letters and sending of books to the country circuits."[8]

A general book steward for the societies was appointed, with an office in Philadelphia, and a book steward was named for each circuit. Religion and reading must go together. What Case calls the partnership of press and pulpit, begun in England, was established here.

Those who had notions that learning should take place in a walled institution were early disappointed, for the first college the new Church set up in the United States failed disastrously and perhaps symbolically. It was a pretentious undertaking, anyway, and Mr. Wesley was disgusted that it was ever called a college instead of a school. He was not pleased either that it was given the name Cokesbury College—by truncating and combining the names of the two superintendents who called themselves bishops. To start the college Coke and Asbury collected the then colossal sum of forty thousand dollars in small amounts from widely scattered people, many of whom were poor and could ill afford to give, particularly to a cause so dubious.[9]

The amount raised before Cokesbury College opened its doors at Abingdon, Maryland, was impressive as a sign of the new Church's generosity, but more and more money was needed to keep it open. By 1793 it suffered undernourishment from insufficient funds. Two years later it burned down. Two years after that it was moved to Baltimore and a building purchased to house the scholars. In 1796 this building was also destroyed by fire, and the college project was abandoned. It was not until twenty years had passed that another attempt was made, this one also in Baltimore. By now, Coke as a British citizen had been politely banished from the American connection and the college was simply called Asbury. It lasted three years.

Methodism and the nomenclature of the higher learning did not seem to belong together. Efforts to build the colleges had been made with conscientious ambition and carried out with great exertion. Failure was conspicuous and repeated, as if destiny had had a hand. It looked as if an institution to offer Methodists book learning was not what God intended. All up and down the line, and in every other undertaking, the Church succeeded. Membership swelled. Horizons widened or were pushed back. There had been a resounding answer to the question posed in the first Conference where Rankin had presided: "Can we spread the books?" The press prospered. Preachers continued to learn, but from printed matter and not from professors. The groove of discipline deepened as the business of getting an education became a continuing job to be done by the individual preacher or by the layman who caught the brand of inspiration from circuit riders who made the rounds.

It thus became a fixed part of the Methodist inner way of life to improve each shining hour in the light shed by the printed word. Naturally, there were lapses during periods of dissension, debate, and schism, as in the time of O'Kelly. Not all was smooth and steady. Some preachers held out against the idea of reading at all or much, taking the position, as one did, that all one had to do was to open his mouth and the Lord would fill it—with wind, as one of the members of his congregation said privately. But the hammer of emphasis sounded repeatedly on the anvil of the book. Those preachers who read often became sterling examples. Others vied to show that they could go as far as the best had gone and that they could match the occasional preacher who had the benefits of formal schooling. By degrees the Methodist preacher was marked as a man who wanted to improve.

In this respect the reading circuit rider became more than a symbol. There was evidence and fact behind the symbol. It was fleshed out, both the horse and the rider, and the book was real. There was never a time from the landing of Robert Williams on when the value of reading was not advertised. Word went out through the ganglia of the connection that reading was for Methodists. The *Discipline* advised every preacher to "read the most useful Books, and that regularly and constantly." He was instructed to "spend all the Morning in this Employment, or at least Five Hours in four and twenty."

When Jesse Walker moved his family from Virginia to Illinois in 1808 he took four horses, one for himself, one for his wife and the youngest daughter who rode behind her, one for an older daughter. The fourth horse carried Walker's library and books he had for sale to Methodists along the way.

Being consecrated activists called to a holy cause, it is all the more remarkable that the itinerants, constantly on the move, adhered as closely as they did to the rule that they must read. Many young men reported on what they had read, making it a matter of exemplary record. William Winans was born in Pennsylvania and received into the Western Conference in 1808.

313

He volunteered to go to distant and sparsely settled parts of the country and spent most of his life in Mississippi and Louisiana. He made it his practice to read fifty pages a day and he kept up the pace for seventeen years, being rewarded with a good reputation both as a preacher and a writer.[10]

As the Church grew bigger and more complex, unevenness and irregularity in reading began to trouble officials. Reading ought not to be left to chance or promoted merely by exhortation and example. There ought to be a plan. Reading, in a word, must be organized. The General Conference of 1816, after due deliberation, made it a rule that no man could be received into full connection in any Annual Conference until he had passed a course of study required by that Conference. The course lasted two years and the content varied from place to place. Often the examination of candidates who took the course was casual, being, as one writer puts it, "little more than conversations of a general nature on the topics, not the specific subject matter, of the books." One trouble was that the examiners in many cases had not read the books on which the course was based. Even so, guided reading followed by annual conversation helped to put the preachers on their mettle and to remind them again that study and preaching must go hand in hand. By 1844 the required course of study was extended to cover a period of four years and later the four-year course was made general throughout both north and south divisions of the Church.[11]

The Methodist home study approach to education produced a preacher who, around the middle of the nineteenth century, showed some promise to denominations with trained ministries. Horace Bushnell, one of the distinguished Congregational clergymen of his day, noted improvement among the Wesleyan preachers. Himself a graduate of Yale and a student at the Yale Divinity School before entering the ministry, Bushnell remarked on the itinerants' rude demonstrations and their violent spirit of rivalry, but continued: "When they have reached the state of intelligence they are after, they are sure to become effectually, if not formally, one of us."[12]

314

The Wesleyans were the last denomination of any size to set up a seminary in which nascent preachers could be trained. When the move did come it was prompted by the need to keep converts from drifting over to other faiths. A preacher named John Dempster, serving as presiding elder in the Oneida Conference of upstate New York, saw that many converts in Methodist meetings joined another church and said frankly that it was because they wanted to listen Sunday after Sunday to a preacher who had an education. Dempster himself was a graduate of the University of Edinburgh. He thought it was time that the Methodists had a seminary where young men going into the ministry could be intentionally trained. His persistent insistence led to the founding in 1839 of the Newbury Biblical Institute at Newbury, Vermont. It got off to a fair start but fell on hard days. In 1847 it needed thirty-seven thousand dollars to keep going and the Methodists were not willing to put up the sum. Fortunately, the Congregationalists came forward with sympathetic funds to support what they deemed to be a worthy project. The Institute was moved to Concord, New Hampshire, remaining there until 1868. By then it had a life of its own and a future with promise. It moved to Boston to become Boston Theological Seminary.[13] In 1871 the Seminary became the first department of Boston University. The Methodists were at last in the intellectual business. At about the same time the Church South established Central University at Nashville, Tennessee. Shortly after the founding, Cornelius Vanderbilt gave the institution half a million dollars, later raised to a million. He directed that Bishop Holland McTyeire should be president of the board of trustees and should manage the organization and program of the new university.

Soon to be renamed Vanderbilt University for its chief benefactor, the institution exercised wide influence and set high standards in educational circles throughout the South. It established and sustained the principle that Methodists could organize the higher learning in the manner that they organized other activities related to the cultural life. And when in 1914 the

315

Church South partly lost and partly gave over control of Vanderbilt, it set about at once founding two new universities, one east
and one west of the Mississippi. Southern Methodist University,
started by Texas Methodists in 1911, opened its doors in 1915.
A gift of a million dollars in 1914 from Asa Candler, developer
of Coca-Cola and brother of Bishop Warren G. Candler, made
possible Emory University, with Emory College at Atlanta as its
liberal arts division.

Generosity was catching. James B. and Benjamin N. Duke of
tobacco fame had long supported Trinity College at Durham,
North Carolina, and in 1924 they announced a gift of forty million dollars, described as "the largest made to Christian higher
education in the United States." Duke University was the result.[14]

Interest in formal education increased, partly on the tide of
the times, but the sustained emphasis in the various branches of
Methodism continued to be on self-help, on what could be
learned in the university of print. The presses had created a
new world, and any person who really wanted to learn could
develop his own course of study.

That this belief was peculiarly if not exclusively Methodist
was to be seen in the fact that the German Methodists were
most diligent in promoting the printed word. Their program
was more catholic and permeating than that of the English-
speaking branches, and it advertised to the public what could
be done with the Wesleyan idea. Beginning in 1838, German
language presses poured out books in ever-increasing volume
and for the whole family. Some of the books and magazines had
to do with faith and ritual, but in the carefully prepared plan
under which the Germans operated there were books of inspiration also. One category presented general literature and introduced children as well as adults to the joys of reading in the
home. A series for small children grew to sixty volumes, and
another for youth reached a hundred.[15]

It was an English-speaking Methodist of German descent who
brought the Wesleyan view of education to culmination in the

United States. He was a layman and consequently gets scant reference in Methodist records. But he teamed up with a prominent preacher, and together the two established what came to be a mecca for persons, clerical and lay alike, who were bent on educating themselves outside the classroom.

The place where the first assembly of amateur learners met was Fair Point, New York. (The name was changed to Chautauqua in 1879.) The layman was Lewis Miller, an Akron, Ohio, manufacturer of farm machinery. Son of a German immigrant, he had been brought up on his father's farm near Greentown, Ohio, and had enjoyed virtually no schooling. Ingenious and inventive, though, he had made a fortune out of a succession of improvements in farm implements, the most notable being a hinge which enabled a farmer to raise the cutting bar of a mowing machine to an upright position and get the mower through gates from one field to another.[16]

Methodist to the core, Lewis Miller was one of the new emerging Americans, his German mind responding to the unprecedented conditions around him. He combined things and ideas. He foresaw the increase of leisure time. His inventions and those of others would help to deliver men from drudgery, and, if men were delivered, they would have time on their hands, time to spend on pursuits other than toil. The day of peasants and slaves was coming to an end. Upright men would have to do the world's work, and the quicker the better, for man did not live by bread alone.

Miller brought his ingenuity to bear on the physical but always in a way that turned the material into a service. As Sunday-school superintendent of the First Methodist Church at Akron in the early 1870's, he helped to fashion a new kind of church design known as the Akron Plan. Rooms for Sunday-school classes were placed in a semicircle around the outside of the auditorium. Folding doors closed off the rooms while the classes were in session. The doors were opened at the end of the class period and the whole Sunday school could move together. The plan provided for both the group and the mass.

317

It made pupils part of the church body. They were not sent off or put in cells.[17]

Constantly thinking how things could be experimented with and possibly improved, having a sense of both the outward and the inward, and being both devout and well-to-do, Miller's advice was widely and naturally solicited when problems arose. In 1874 he was asked what should be done about a camp-meeting ground seventy miles east of Buffalo, New York. The site was Fair Point, being a slight protrusion of land on a lake twenty miles long and two miles wide in most places, though it narrowed at a point about half its length. The name of the lake, Chautauqua, derived from a local Indian word meaning bag-tied-in-the-middle.

There were steamers on the lake and there was a railroad at Jamestown, twenty miles away, and at nearby Mayville. Fair Point had served well for camp meetings and it seemed to Miller that it might be put to use as a place where some of the new and emerging demands of the Church could be met. To explore possibilities he made a trip to the place with John Heyl Vincent, a preacher who had held a number of successful pastorates but was at the time of the visit to the Chautauqua property in charge of the Sunday-school work of the Church North.

Many of the teachers in the Sunday schools of The Methodist Episcopal Church, Miller and Vincent agreed, were poorly equipped to carry out the mission with which they were charged. Vincent had already made a start toward reform by instituting uniform lessons. This meant that there was some content in the lessons, but there was still need of finding ways to fit teachers better for their tasks and to give them esprit de corps. Chautauqua would be an ideal spot on which to bring together teachers from far and wide for a period of study and inspiration. The idea appealed equally to the preacher and the layman and the project needed to embody it had only to be organized. For this task the two Methodists showed themselves to be richly equipped. A date was chosen and invitations went out not

318

merely to teachers under Vincent's care but also to teachers in other denominations.

The first assembly met among the maples along the shore of the shimmering Lake Chautauqua on August 10, 1874. A capacity crowd came from the United States and Canada, with color added by visitors from Ireland, Scotland, and India. No fewer than two thousand persons crammed themselves into accommodations that were crude by any standard of comfort. There were five hundred tents. (Lewis Miller later shipped in a prefabricated house from Akron.) At least a hundred roughly constructed cottages had gone up and the sound of hammers was hardly stilled by the time the first-night ceremonies began.

A huge half-tent half-cottage affair had been hastily erected to house important visitors and lecturers, and the heavy rains that fell made appropriate the name jocularly given it: Knowers Ark. For all the inconvenience and weather, the place had an atmosphere of jubilation and mirth. It bore out the conviction that had led Miller to propose the gathering in the first place: recreation and education could be combined. The learning process did not have to be severe.

The assembly lasted two weeks. The teachers heard twenty-two lectures on Sunday-school work and seven lectures on Bible history and geography. In other sessions they met to talk among themselves about their common concerns. Also they had time for games and bathing and boating. There was hearty singing every night on the old campground.

Circumstances afforded John Heyl Vincent a remarkable stage on which to display his talents, and they were many. My friend and associate Samuel A. Schreiner, Jr., who made a study of the early days of Chautauqua, calls Vincent an ecclesiastical Barnum, and at times he seemed intent not to let Phineas T. (who had opened "The Greastest Show on Earth" only three years before) outdo him. Vincent had a gift for the graphic. On the shores of the lake, which to him represented the Mediterranean, he caused to be built a topographical map of Palestine, laid out to precise scale, complete with a water-filled and tadpole-in-

319

fested declivity called the Dead Sea. For good measure, a man named A. O. Van Lennep was engaged to walk among the hills of Palestine as "an Eastern shepherd in full Oriental costume." The teachers were to get a visual as well as an oral education.

Vincent's efforts to achieve dramatic effects were by no means confined to the assembly grounds. At the time of the second assembly, the first having been a huge success, he engineered a performance that gave Chautauqua a national name. He persuaded the President of the United States to pay a visit of state to the grounds. The President was Ulysses Simpson Grant. During the days when Grant was a hardware merchant in Galena, Illinois, he had occasionally attended the church of which Vincent was pastor. Presuming upon an old and slight acquaintance, Vincent managed to get to the President with an invitation. The President accepted, moved, some said, by a desire to be seen in such pious surroundings when his administration was under fire and there were whispers and signs of corruption.

On Saturday, August 25, 1875, the presidential party arrived by train at nearby Jamestown. There the President boarded a side-wheeler, the *Josie Belle,* for the trip up Lake Chautauqua. The vessel was so bedecked with red, white, and blue that one reporter described it as "something out of fairyland." President Grant sat grandly in the bow and in full view of thousands who followed in "lesser but equally gaudy craft."

Ulysses S. Grant was doubtless the least talkative fellow ever to appear on the Chautauqua platform. In fact, he never said a mumblin' word when Vincent presented him with an embossed Bible as a souvenir of the visit, but it was construed that his heart was simply too full for utterance. Vincent's ready eloquence covered for the silent President and the scene of the presentation ended with a flourish of good will and in the sight of the assembled multitude.[18]

The President of the United States had let himself be seen at Chautauqua, a place few persons other than the faithful had ever heard of up to that time, and the event of his visit of state went by word and pictures all over the world. The General's mother had been a Methodist but the son had not been active, to say the least. Yet these points made his visit to Chautauqua all the more significant. They made the place something besides an assembly ground for Methodists. Chautauqua was bigger now, a meeting place and focal point for those who wanted to rub shoulders with the great. Chautauqua was Methodist, but it was more. The other denominations had members present from the first. Separate chapels were built for separate worship services, but all joined the Methodists in the learning process and in activities which might be considered cultural.

A thing perfectly timed had been set off. The proliferation of imitation Chautauquas across the land paid the idea high tribute. By the 1890's there were some two hundred of them—none tied in with the first one but all with the aim to lay a table for new learners, for those who wanted to drink, if only a little, at the Pierian spring. Soon after the turn of the century, lecture bureaus and booking agents had caught on to the eagerness of Americans to enjoy the benefits and by-products of culture. The result was the string of educational variety shows tying the country vaguely together through the experience of learning while being entertained. There was no license or copyright attached to the Methodist plan of self-improvement. The traveling shows were under canvas, the big tent embodying both the recollections of the circus and of revivals. They were complete with brass bands, choruses, Swiss bell ringers, crayon artists, but, one and all, they featured as their hallmark the inspirational lecturer. His message was the high-water mark of Chautauqua Week, reminding people constantly of their better selves in a wild and growing and restless land.[19]

Traveling Chautauquas with talent of every description are said to have played to more than thirty-five million people between 1904 and 1920. So great was the lure of the term that some managers of vaudeville artists and road shows, bewildered by the craze, billed their offerings as Carnival Chautauquas. In small cities and big towns Chautauqua Week was the event of the year. One ticket sold in advance covered all performances, morning, afternoon, and evening. Business houses often closed their doors for the big fanfare. So too did some churches. There was nothing the rest of the year that called for so much concentrated attention on the nonmaterial. The shows continued to be the national highlight of American entertainment until radio brought a substitute for personal appearances.

Possibly the unlicensed and unceasing use of the word *Chautauqua* may have contributed a mite to the growth of the institution at Fair Point. Whatever the reason, Chautauqua flourished. The original was a kind of bureau of standards. People came to the old site in greater and greater numbers. Houses replaced tents. The season was lengthened. Other Presidents—seven in all—honored the platform. The atmosphere continued to be devout but it was also hospitable, as it had been to Grant. John Dewey spent a week on the grounds and was responsible for establishing a Vacation School. A woman, Frances E. Willard, who would not be allowed to speak before the General Conference of The Methodist Episcopal Church, was invited to address the assembly. In a word, the Chautauqua program at Chautauqua grew steadily more varied, aiming at supplying those without a college education some of the satisfaction usually reserved for those within academic walls. Curriculum for the casuals in time included science and philosophy and a new subject called psychology, with popular lectures by the distinguished Harvard don, William James.

Even a widening range of subjects, however, did not satisfy John Heyl Vincent and the ambitions he felt for the program. In August 1878, after a dramatic series of hints to show that something momentous was about to take place, he announced that Chautauqua would offer a course of study by which anybody, anywhere, at any time, could get a college education without going to college. Those who wanted a degree could get it by mail!

Vincent created a subdivision of the regular program and designated it the Chautauqua Literary and Scientific Circle, with texts at the college level covering the whole spectrum of classical and scientific learning standard at the time. It was the kind of curriculum and experience Vincent wished he could have enjoyed. Virtually forced by his father into the itinerant life at the age of seventeen, he had done the best he could to educate himself, but always there had been that nagging embarrassment of not having a degree and the beckoning of those vast fields of learning he had not glimpsed, much less traversed. No one need any longer be deprived as he had been deprived.

Within a week after the announcement of the college course a thousand persons had signed up for it. Within seven years after the Chautauqua Literary and Scientific Circle was formed it had on its rolls the names of 100,000 men and women and its branches ranged from Tokyo to London to Capetown. There were ninety-four members of the Russian Chautauqua circle. Ever the showman, Vincent made use of every analogy to stress the values of college achievement. He fashioned a Recognition Day at the end of the first four years for those who had finished the correspondence course. Those who had cleared the hurdles marched through a Golden Gate and under pine-covered arches to the Greek-style Hall of Philosophy, situated in a grove suggesting Academe, while bands played and children flung flowers at their feet.[20]

It was not merely the ceremonies and the trappings that lent Vincent's scheme of education by mail an authentic ring. Chautauqua was chartered as a university. Vincent assembled a faculty of irreproachable standing, including William Rainey Harper, who held his doctorate in Hebrew from Yale. Harper gave a summer course at Chautauqua and also headed the college of liberal arts there. He was keen about the possibilities of teaching through correspondence; when, in 1892, the University of Chicago was established and Harper was offered the post of president, he made one of his conditions of acceptance the agreement that there would be an extension division of the new university and that a correspondence department be a part of its work.

Other colleges and universities followed suit and by 1941 nearly a hundred institutions of higher learning were giving courses to hundreds of thousands of students. The Chautauqua academic program was put under the auspices of Syracuse University, one of the institutions of higher learning the Methodists founded. In 1969 it became part of the State University of New York at Fredonia.

The response to the college career offered ordinary Americans through the Chautauqua Literary and Scientific Circle marked the successful beginning of that distinctly American phenomenon known as the correspondence school. More significant is the fact that John Heyl Vincent both detected and encouraged a new attitude toward education in America, spreading a general and enormous interest in what came to be known as adult or continuing education. There had been mechanics institutes earlier, but they were instructional units modeled on English efforts to suit rural workers to industrial requirements. The institutes had specific vocational aims and they faded and passed away at the time of the Civil War.

Vincent's appeal was to Everyman. It was an invitation to learning, having some of the hearty American spirit of the logging camp and the chuck wagon: come and get it. Before Chautauqua, education in this land was pretty much confined to the educated. It was a school affair. You either had it or you didn't. True, prodigious efforts had been made to open colleges to the neglected. Women, for example, were gradually admitted to institutions of higher learning. The Justin Morrill Land Grant Act of 1862 had even gone so far as to set up a group of colleges for the sons of artisans and farmers. But even the A and M colleges sought to draw students into halls behind walls, to separate them from farms and shops. What Chautauqua did was to establish a demonstration station where anyone could find out how to get an education if he wanted one. Learning was to be an ever-continuing process tied up with daily life, needing only periods of refreshment and inspiration.

Miller and Vincent continued to work in tandem until Miller's death in 1889. Their functions remained distinct. Miller looked after the details of an increasingly complex and costly enterprise. He did it shrewdly and quietly, without the pretensions of largesse. Vincent planned, ran, and extended the educational program until the Methodists bestowed upon him what they considered their highest accolade. They made him a bishop and his son, George, took over.

Chautauqua no longer abides under Methodist auspices. Yet it is still there. There are now more than five hundred cottages, houses, and dumpy hotels, many of them built in the days of Miller and Vincent, sitting cheek by jowl in a wooded area of 395 acres bordering on the dazzling lake.

On these grounds any day during July and August you may find as many as thirteen thousand persons from every part of the United States and Canada, bent on betterment. Thus one of the chief characteristics of the old camp meeting survives. The early meetings built around evangelism brought together periodically and in small space persons from far away who had been living long distances apart, who rarely saw or had neighbors. On campgrounds neighbors were as close as they were in towns; closer. So it is at Chautauqua. There is proximity. There is still preaching on the grounds every day, and although outside artists such as Ella Fitzgerald and Skitch Henderson are invited in, the atmosphere is in a strange way still essentially religious. It is quiet. There is reverence, whether it be for the Lord or for learning. In either case it is a part of the Methodist tradition.

XXIV Woman at the Door

The neglect of women's talents—a neglect characteristic of American society—had prevailed also in official circles of Methodism. The mingling of gallantry and condescension that marks the attitude of men in business and education and politics, the assumption that men alone should run the show, is to be seen over and over again in the actions of the Church. These actions beat time to the prejudices of the secular world. But at least there is a prospect of enlightened change.

A study of happenings within this enormous religious order brings to light points that are bound to have some bearing on the changing status of woman from creature to citizen. The story indicates factors that may point toward an ultimate ideal in the man-woman management of vast enterprises, even the Republic. For Methodist women have made good and the churchmen admit it. In all branches, and measured by official standards, women have displayed an amazing competence. Men have never been able to escape the evidence of this competence. It's in the minutes and in the till. Precise and impressive records confront managers at every turn. The records afford at the minimum a sidewalk superintendent's peephole through which officials see the women at work and note what they have done.

Impressive too is the fact that women have carried on their operations in all sorts of circumstances and under varying sets of directives. They have shown in some branches of the denomination an amicable ability to cooperate as a subordinate group. In other branches they have demonstrated their capacity to run affairs efficiently in complete independence of men. Whether subordinate or autonomous, they have performed their tasks on a national scale and as part of an organization as complicated and diverse and as thick with details as any corporation.

Methodist women have been in big business for almost a century. They have proved in a way plain for all to see that American women have business and managerial ability and a remarkable aptitude for working with men. Where else has this combination been so clearly demonstrated? Women's clubs and leagues and movements have their appeal and have given women calisthenics as executives, but these activities deal with a variety of purposes and their records of achievement are scattered and not directly related to the male world. Within such a highly complex society as the Methodist churches represent, the achievements of women are at every point connected with a program in which men and women have a common concern. Their activities belong to the operations of a continuing society not dissimilar to American society as a whole.

With a record to prove their worth, women within the Church have developed quite naturally a faith in themselves. They have also educated themselves both in the lessons of history and in a knowledge of procedures. They are wise to the world's ways and to the shortcomings of a religion that does not make full use of women. They have been saying politely for a long time what outraged militants of their sex say vehemently, namely, that there ought to be more recognition of women. But Methodist women have the discipline of patience and hope, which leads to a degree of detachment and sophistication.

Speaking at a national seminar of Methodist women in 1963, Elizabeth Palmer, general secretary of the world Y.W.C.A., noted "the almost complete absence of women in places where the decisions, which so greatly affect all our lives, are being made—decisions of war and peace, the use of nuclear power, the planning of industry and commerce. . . ." She cited the fact that there were only 20 women present among the 1140 delegates at one annual Labor Organization conference in Geneva the year before, yet this conference was directly involved with the working conditions of women the world over. Miss Palmer noted that in religion, perhaps more than in any other field, "the decision as to women's role seems to be in the hands of the men." Then she added: "I can only say that in this realm too we find women struggling with a man-made world, with male concepts and ways of thinking and doing."[1]

In Methodism male concepts are writ large and their roots run deep. The emotions formed and institutionalized in early American Methodism grew out of an environment which daily called for hardy and manly turns of mind and muscle. The men who laid the physical foundations of the faith had to hew logs, haul or carry water, ford streams, scout new territory, build houses and churches, subdue ruffians. There was little need in the onsweep of the circuit riders for women's ideas or advice. What the Church took pride in was its male leadership, and success justified the pride.

The formative years of American Methodism also saw the society of which it was a part turn increasingly toward the subordination of women. During most of the colonial period women were not deliberately excluded from the deliberations of government bodies. Some had the right to vote. None of the constitutions of the thirteen states explicitly restricted suffrage to men. In 1778, however, New York inserted the word "male" among its qualifications for voting. The other states followed suit.[2] Stress was formally placed on male rights as well as concepts and values.

The Methodist Episcopal Church, governed by men, entered lustily into the environment of the new nation. Its preachers proved in time to be particularly zealous because the loyalty of the early itinerants had been generally open to question. Some, including Freeborn Garrettson and Jesse Lee, had actually refused to bear arms in the Revolution. The unwarlike behavior of all had been suspect. It must not be suspect again. Church leaders found themselves in hand-to-hand agreement with leaders of the state on the dominant doctrines of the hour. A cardinal principle of statecraft was the use of organized violence in behalf of a cause which the state deemed to be good. Approval of the state's approval of this violence became a primary test of patriotism—devotion to the fatherland.

The Methodists embraced the principle and passed the test. They entered into wars that followed the formation of the Union and into the Indian fighting entailed in western expansion. By accepting the orders of the political system they endorsed and carried out aggressive and punitive policies that were not only repugnant to women but that in execution worked immense hardship on women and on the children whose care was woman's chief responsibility.

There was nothing remotely resembling pacifist sentiment in the broad reaches of American Methodism after the success of the Revolution. Once the state was established, even if through revolutionary action, its right to demand obedience at arms was not only not denied but in the main heartily accepted. Methodists did not think for or against military procedure; they acted. The right to fight in a cause that the state deemed vital was respected in a matter-of-fact way—along with other rights that were dearly won and sacred.

How naturally, almost jovially, the military view of events prevailed in Methodist circles was illustrated by the celebrated case of John M. Chivington, who was sent in 1860 to be presiding elder of a new district in Colorado. Two missionaries had been dispatched to the Territory the year before to stake out a claim for The Methodist Episcopal Church lest The Methodist Episcopal Church, South, move in. A membership of forty-five had been rounded up. Under Chivington's aggressive leadership the numbers grew to 348 in the course of a year.[3]

The Methodist Episcopal Church, South, did not move in but the Confederate army did. Part of the hope of the South under Jefferson Davis lay in annexing the whole stretch of land between Texas and California and in then persuading California to join the Confederacy, bringing along with it vast resources.

Anticipating an attack through Texas, and troubled by the secessionist sentiment in Denver during 1861, the territorial governor of Colorado announced the formation of a regiment of volunteers to fight for the North. Chivington immediately offered his services. He was proffered a chaplaincy but declined and requested "a fighting commission instead." In a sermon earlier he had made clear his attitude: "I am a man of lawful age and full size, and was an American citizen before I became a minister." He was made a major, became active in recruiting and, when the Confederate attack came, led a few chosen militiamen in a wild clamber over the mountains, circumventing the front, to reach and destroy the Confederate supply train of eighty wagons at the invaders' rear.[4]

The coup was a surprise to the Confederates and it astonished the Yankees who caught the full import of it. It ended the battle of Glorieta Pass and the Confederate threat to the Southwest. The Union commander, upon a petition signed by his officers, raised Chivington to the rank of colonel in the nationalized militia, subject to the governor's approval.[5]

The governor approved, and it was Colonel J. M. Chivington who in 1864 led the militia in another surprise attack—this one on an Indian encampment at Sand Creek, part of a loosely defined reservation thirty miles from Fort Lyon, Colorado. Nine hundred militia struck at dawn and without warning, leaving more than five hundred Indians dead—among them, by some accounts, many squaws and children. Whether squaws and children were slain or fled the scene, whether the Indians were peaceably assembled under a promised truce or were in fact plotting further depredations on the whites and further disruption of forces defending the Union cause became subjects of bitter controversy and of congressional investigation. Chivington and his defenders called the attack a battle in a punitive campaign. The Commissioner of Indian Affairs described the attack as a massacre in which Indians were "butchered in cold blood by troops in the service of the United States."[6]

331

The man who became known as the Fighting Parson did not go back into pastoral work, but two years after the war he was appointed an agent of the Church Extension Society in the Nebraska Conference. Later he did editorial work for various papers and was for a time on the staff of the *Christian Advocate* in St. Louis. There was no sign of remorse in his writings or actions. At the time death approached in 1894 a preacher asked him if the presence of Jesus was precious to him, and Chivington answered, "His presence dwells within. It's all around me. It fills the room."[7]

Chivington's warlike behavior was but an egregious instance of the collusion between conviction and violence that followed the standards of an age. The collusion continued beyond sectional strife and Indian fighting and formed again at the time of the Spanish-American War. With only a small part of the populace involved in actual combat, violence then became vicarious and verbal, perhaps revealing all the more the ease with which the emotions of the day, at stark variance with the Christian idea, could be championed and promoted in a fervid religious order.

The circumstances were set like a stage at the *fin de siècle* for the church of Chivington to display again its pious aggressiveness. Theodore Roosevelt esteemed the Church as the most representative in the country and said he would rather address a Methodist audience than any other audience in America. Its main branches made up the largest Protestant denomination. It was the church of the middle class. Membership included one out of every eighteen in the population.[8] It also included the President of the United States, William McKinley.

Well before the outbreak of the Spanish-American War in April 1898 the President as commander of the armed forces was assured also that he could command the support of his fellow churchmen. One Syracuse preacher publicly reminded the authorities that Methodism would offer its men, its means, and its prayers on the altar of its country; every Methodist preacher would be a recruiting officer; the male membership would serve at the front and the women would hasten to serve as nurses in the hospitals.[9]

When war was declared it was declared by one preacher to be "a holy war for humanity," although he added by way of afterthought, "Of course we should obtain a coaling station . . . or two or three. . . ." The welkin rang with such sounds as: "The sword had often carved the way for the cross." "This war is the Kingdom of God coming."[10] A particularly ferocious preacher said that he regarded sending his son into the army as an act of evangelizing the heathen, and he displayed his sentiments for all to see. When the lad left home he wore on his shirt the motto of the Epworth League, the young people's society of his Church. To his father's mind he was fully equipped: "With Christ in his heart, the New Testament in his pocket, Look up and Lift up on his shirt, and forty rounds of ammunition in his belt, we have sent out the first missionary of the family. If he should fail, I should simply inscribe his name on the long and noble list of Christ-martyrs for the world's salvation. . . ."[11]

A sense of mission and expansion and Manifest Destiny now reached beyond the borders of the U.S.A., and it was unrelenting. When Emilio Aguinaldo, who had led a revolt of the Filipinos against Spain, dared stir an insurrection against American authority, it was taken as a high sign that it was high time to press for even firmer action against Aguinaldo than had been undertaken against Spain. The flag must advance from outpost to outpost, it was said. "The shriek of the shell is a stern invitation to become civilized—the only one that has never failed of a hearing."[12]

The question of what to do about the Philippines was much on President McKinley's mind and the way he resolved the matter reinforced the assumption that Methodists were a part of Manifest Destiny and that a religious undertaking could be carried out by political and military means. To a group of his fellow Methodists he later spoke with feeling about his quandary:

I walked the floor of the White House, night after night, and I am not shamed to tell you, gentlemen, that I went down on my knees and prayed to Almighty God for light

333

and guidance more than one night. And one night late
it came to me. . . . There was nothing left for us to do
but to take them all, and to educate the Filipinos, and
uplift and civilize and Christianize them. . . .[13]

There were, of course, strong protests from Methodists against
the Spanish-American War and the policies that followed it.
But whether there was agreement or disagreement on policies,
the ideas that were accepted and acted upon in Methodist
circles during the century of expansion and growth were traditional and conventional. Thanks to industrialization and weap-
onry, the environment was even more physical than it had been
earlier, and there was little disposition on the part of those
charged with the responsibilities of such a huge enterprise as
the Church to show any but a polite interest in the gender
that could not meet the requirements of the strenuous life.
Women were gratefully accepted as housekeepers in the exact-
ing work of keeping things in decency and order, but their
counsel was not welcome on major matters.

Nor was their presence welcome in places where men ruled.
When, almost a hundred years after the founding of The Methodist Episcopal Church, a bid was made by a woman simply
to bring greetings from a woman's organization to the official
body of the Church, it met with something less than cordiality.
Allowing even one woman an audience, it appeared, would
signify the thin edge of the wedge.

The woman in the case was Frances E. Willard, a Methodist
born and bred, president of the Woman's Christian Temperance
Union. It was in her capacity as president that she wished to
bring the greetings of the Union to the General Conference of
The Methodist Episcopal Church meeting at Cincinnati in 1880.
The cause of temperance was at the time beginning to be
dear to the heart of Methodism. Hence the greetings would
be logical and might also help to advertise a cause in which
men and women both had a deep concern. It seemed but natural, nay obligatory, to salute the Methodists and solicit their
continued cooperation.

Knowing her wishes, a delegate and a friend offered a resolution asking permission for the president of the W.C.T.U. to have ten minutes of Conference time. Hardly had the resolution been put before the house when another delegate, James M. Buckley, a New Englander who had served pastorates in various parts of the North, rose to his feet and spoke in opposition. His remarks touched off a debate that lasted two hours. At the end of it two-thirds of the delegates voted to hear President Willard, but the implacable Buckley then announced that, in spite of the vote, he would exhaust all parliamentary resources to prevent a woman's speaking before the General Conference. His statement and the tone of the opposition in the debate were so inhospitable that friends advised Frances Willard to withdraw her request for an audience. She did, sending a note to her Honored Brethren, thanking them for the final vote but explaining that she had not been at a General Conference before and had no idea of the strong objection that would be raised. She concluded by saying, "I decline to use the hard-earned ten minutes allotted me," and signed her missive as "Your sister in Christian work."[14]

Eight years later five women were elected by Annual Conferences to sit as delegates in the sessions of the General Conference of the Church North. Miss Willard was one. She was overjoyed by the change in atmosphere. A companion with her at the time she received the news records that she was so moved that she could hardly speak for tears. She reached New York, where the 1888 General Conference was to meet, several days before the sessions were scheduled to begin. She was informed soon after her arrival that Buckley had been busy as a mole, undermining the roots of courtesy. There would be a floor fight over eligibility.

Sessions were held in the Metropolitan Opera House, which was packed to the chandeliers. There was not a vacant seat in the boxes or the galleries. Ladies occupied most of the grandstand, watching the dignified antics of the delegates below. True to prediction, the committee on eligibility, by a vote of eleven to six, brought in a report saying that the original provision for allowing laymen to sit as delegates to the General Conference contemplated that men only were to be admitted.

The report set off a noisy controversy. The Met reverberated with arias pro and con for almost a week. The libretto provided for a casuistical consideration of one simple question: Were laymen men only—or both men and women? The delegates debated this tremendous technicality as if there were no other subject before the human mind. There was no frontal attention on the question of whether women should be accepted as delegates.

Buckley, in supporting the stand of the committee on eligibility, could only rest his case on rhetoric, choosing words as weapons. Laymen meant men. One delegate, G. W. Hughey, took him on his own terms and cited instances from the Bible wherein man was used as a generic phrase. In the case of "except a man be born again . . ." did this mean only lay men and not women? Hughey noted that the *Discipline* used masculine personal pronouns throughout in referring to members and asked if this meant that women could not be disciplined under the rules of the Church.[15]

Many delegates spoke eloquently in behalf of putting a broad interpretation on the word *layman,* so that it could mean, as one wag put it, man embracing woman. It was the score that counted, however, and when the vote came the report of the committee was accepted by a margin of thirty-nine votes. The women could go back to their homes, where they belonged. With a sheepish mien and with a meticulous sense of detail, the delegates did vote to pay them for their travel expenses. The motion to reimburse was put forward gallantly and appropriately by James M. Buckley, who explained as he presented it that the Annual Conferences at least thought they were acting legally when they chose women as lay delegates.[16]

XXV Service Entrance

Bids for acceptance by official church bodies make up only a part—and the only frustrating part—of the story of women in American Methodism. The greater and better part of the story is filled with feats of organizing skill, of using consummate tact and resourcefulness in doing decent deeds. The women began their good works before the middle of the nineteenth century, moving out from church buildings into communities, especially those where physical needs were direst, ministering to people cut off from standard religious services. It was a part of what later came to be known as the larger housekeeping. The women were determined, as the old wheeze had it, to make themselves useful as well as ornamental.

The first important result of this new kind of collective labor was an exhibit that attracted national interest and long served as a model for all churches working in slum areas. It was called Five Points Mission and it came about through the sustained efforts of the Ladies' Home Missionary Society, a city-wide organization of Methodist women who in the 1850's refused to accept New York as irremediable.

The work commenced modestly. The Society picked a derelict area in a rum-soaked section of the city and, like the earliest

Methodists in New York, rented a room for religious services. They announced a meeting. The turnout, which filled the room, was a spectacle. Children encased in filth and rags poured from garrets, alleys, and cellars of the neighborhood. One lady described the gamins as a more vivid representation of hell than she had ever imagined. Even so, the children yielded to treatment and a Sunday school with an initial enrollment of seventy was organized. The need for a day school was soon apparent and one was added. The rented room was crowded and in steady use.

Up to this point the Ladies' Home Missionary Society had done the work alone. The ladies had not asked for aid from any other church group. They had, however, secured an advisory committee of businessmen at the outset of their operation and had laid before this committee their ultimate plans and hopes for a mission house. The advisory committee had agreed to watch developments, and when the program outgrew the rented room the men, convinced, pledged money to purchase a proper site for a mission in the disreputable section known as Five Points, named for a place in lower Manhattan where five streets converged to form a park.

On the site chosen stood a gaunt building known as the Old Brewery. It was made for a religious fairy tale. For forty years the Old Brewery had been a place where spirits evil for men round-about were brewed. For the past twenty years it had been abandoned and had become what the ladies described as a pesthouse of sin. It was "the haunt of murderers and robbers, who within the shades of its dark and winding passages concealed their stolen goods and forever hid from sight their victims." This bastion of degradation the ladies proposed to transform "into a school of virtue." And they had something psychic in their favor. The Old Brewery was situated on Paradise Square.[1]

The land was purchased and the building razed in December 1852. The cause of the ladies had been presented at two public meetings, one addressed by Henry Ward Beecher, and the necessary thousands of dollars raised. Weeks after the Old

Brewery went down the cornerstone was laid for Five Points Mission. There arose a new brick building on Paradise Square, five stories high, with a chapel that seated five hundred persons. The upper floors were for occupancy by poor families, while the ground floor was given over to offices and schoolrooms.

Additions ensued, both in premises and program. The day school expanded, poor children were sent to the country for rest spells, food and clothing distributed to the neediest cases. Next door Lewis Morris Pease, the preacher the New York Conference had appointed to the mission, organized the Five Points House of Industry, soliciting piecework from a shirt manufacturer so that the hall could serve as a gospel center at night and a garment shop by day. The Five Points Mission and the Five Points House of Industry were soon established in the life of the city, affording visitors from far and wide a demonstration center where they could see how that new thing known as an institutional church worked.[2]

As problems of American society grew more urgent under the stresses of industrialism and the cruelties and horrors of the Civil War, there was more and more of a place for the work of those who could help bind up the nation's wounds, who could take ameliorating action in the grievous circumstances of a society turned sick. Persons who combined tenderness and efficiency, sympathy and leadership, emerged. Charity moved toward becoming an art.

One who exemplified the new spirit in the churches was Mrs. Annie Wittenmeyer. Born in Ohio, brought up in Kentucky, and a resident of Iowa at the outbreak of the Civil War, she was a faithful member of her church and worked through it in various eleemosynary endeavors, learning as she went along. At the beginning of the war she had enough stature to be appointed by the Iowa legislature as agent of the United States Sanitary Commission, a voluntary organization working throughout the North to get supplementary supplies of food and medicine to soldiers at the front. Later Mrs. Wittenmeyer resigned her position and entered the service of the United States Christian

Commission, a body in which all evangelical church bodies joined. Its aim originally had been to distribute tracts to the soldiers and carry on religious services. It shifted to being an agency that brought the touches of home to the casualties of war. Special dishes and delicacies were prepared and the wounded and the sick got luxuries military routine could not supply.

In her work with the Christian Commission Mrs. Wittenmeyer worked out a plan of special diet kitchens. The first was opened at Nashville after its capture by Federal troops, and there she supervised the work of two hundred women in preparing and serving food for eighteen hundred sick and wounded soldiers. Throughout the war her labors drew the commendation of General Grant and she worked in close cooperation with the Surgeon General.

Such a woman, tireless and gathering experience and momentum, could not stop or waste in idleness. At the close of the war she not only established a home for soldiers' orphans in Iowa but also took over the barracks at Davenport for the purpose, getting the approval of Congress for the transaction and having the government throw in the medical supplies left in the barracks. The home accommodated five hundred children.

Mrs. Wittenmeyer was a Methodist first and last, however, and what she wanted was a scheme of activity that could be carried on through her church. Her restlessness in well-doing represented the old and early itinerancy in changed conditions. It was prompted by the same compulsions: be on the wing and do all the good you can while you are at it. She moved to Philadelphia, where she established the Ladies' and Pastors' Union. The aim was to get women out of the pew and out of the church and away from church teas and suppers and let them work among those who had no normal contact with formal religion. Visitations were organized and systematic. Records showed visits to fifty thousand families in the year 1876.[3]

It was logical that the visitation program should encourage

the image and office of deaconess into The Methodist Episcopal Church. The idea was rather startling. It came from European sources and its adoption indicated a willingness both to draw on outside sources for means of widening the scope of the work of the Church and to make increasing use of distaff resources. There was an element of distinction, if not status, involved. The deaconess wore a uniform, if not a habit. She was set apart for service. The word *deacon* derived from the Greek word for servant. Deacon was the name given the lower order of Methodist ministry and a deaconess had a certain dignity by subtle association. She had at least semi-status.

The founder of the Ladies' and Pastors' Union began promoting a deaconess program with the encouragement of Bishop Matthew Simpson, who knew the precedents provided by the Church of Rome and the Greek Orthodox Church. He had also made trips to Germany and had observed women active and useful in church labors there. Mrs. Wittenmeyer made a trip to Germany in 1870. Inspired, she established on her return *The Christian Woman* and through this periodical and widespread lecturing drummed up recruits for the deaconess corps.

In 1872 the Ladies' and Pastors' Union was sanctioned by the General Conference of The Methodist Episcopal Church and put under the direction of a board of managers comprising "thirteen ministers and twelve Christian ladies." During the next four years growth was rapid. It was noted that "thousands of women who were at ease in Zion, and indifferent to the claims of the perishing multitudes around them, have been aroused and have consecrated themselves to the work. . . ." In 1876 the board reported forty Conference auxiliaries, with almost four hundred local societies having a membership of 9375.[4]

The Union marked the beginning of a women's movement that was church-wide. As such it lit up the imagination, but the Union faded as fast as it grew, and by the end of the 1870's it had disappeared and left only memories. The memories it left, however, were rich. From effective local efforts made by such bodies as the Ladies' Home Missionary Society in New

York and other cities, the women had progressed to efforts that could spread in an organized way throughout the connection. Each success taught the women that they could work with each other, together, as fellow sisters in worthy enterprises. Only the dimensions needed to be increased, and this increase was natural as women appeared who showed, as Mrs. Wittenmeyer did, that they could extend a local undertaking into a national project.

One woman who showed this ability to a dumfounding degree was Jennie Culver Hartzell. She was the wife of a young preacher, Joseph C. Hartzell, who was transferred in 1870 by The Methodist Episcopal Church from a pastorate at Pekin, Illinois, to a church in New Orleans. In that southern city Mrs. Hartzell realized firsthand the plight of Negro women when she was called upon to visit a young Negro dying in a house of prostitution. Concern with the misery of dislocated Negro families came next, New Orleans being at the time a refugee center for eight thousand Negroes in flight from the persecutions of the Ku Klux Klan.[5]

Discovery of one need led to the uncovering of others as Jennie Hartzell visited families from door to door, doing what she could to render personal services. After several years she managed to get a school started. She raised what funds she could and took full responsibility for the school. Friends from the North helped, including Mrs. R. S. Rust and her husband, secretary of the Freedman's Aid Society. Once on a visit to Cincinnati Mrs. Hartzell collected seven hundred dollars from white friends and, upon her return south, set up eight schools, enrolling five hundred girls in sewing and other domestic arts.

Exactions of the job in time took their toll of Jennie Hartzell's health and she faced the prospect that she would have to abandon her post. In 1880 she went with her husband, who was a delegate, to the General Conference meeting at Cincinnati, hoping that the Church might accept responsibility for the New Orleans work. Alas, though, the agenda was so long and crowded that she did not get a hearing.

There was a stirring, however, within the Church—almost a vortex of Christian sentiment—as the 1880's opened. The call was not only for women who could do women's work among the prostitutes and other victims of greed. There were other problems "which centered around illiteracy, low standards of living, disease, poverty, and social ills." The needs were at the door, not in distant lands, and there was no agency of the Church prepared or pledged to deal with grim areas the women recognized. A way must be found to organize and direct remedial programs and there must be groups to support the work and raise money for it.

The attempt was made to persuade the Woman's Foreign Missionary Society, which had been organized in 1869, to drop the word *Foreign* from its title and broaden its gauge, but the attempt came to naught. The women who saw the need for action on the home front next thought of working through the Freedman's Aid Society, engaged in educational work among the liberated slaves. In 1875 a petition was put forward asking that women be elected to the board of managers. The decision on the petition was foregone and automatic. The act of incorporation of the Freedman's Aid Society provided that only males were eligible as members.[6]

Thwarted in this design, the women recommended a woman's auxiliary under the direction of a lady (with the wonderful name of Mrs. Jennie F. Willing) who would serve as an assistant corresponding secretary. The Freedman's Aid Society was kind but firm, explaining that a lady as an assistant corresponding secretary simply could not be. The Society did offer to let Mrs. Willing serve as an agent under the direction of the regular corresponding secretary. She would be permitted in this position "to present the cause, collect funds, and organize auxiliary societies." Mrs. Willing was not *that* willing. Besides, she and a determined group around her felt that their position in a noble and neglected cause should not be subordinate to any existing organization, that they "could and should conduct and control an independent society."

When the General Conference failed to hear Mrs. Hartzell's plea in 1880 it seemed to Mrs. Willing and others that the time for an independent society had come. Certain men agreed and came to the ladies' aid—not as officials but as gentlemen. General Conference delegates might not act with alacrity on what the women considered an urgent need, but there were individual preachers who took initiative and showed hospitality to the hopes of the women. The presiding elder of the Cincinnati district, A. B. Leonard, heard of Mrs. Hartzell's disappointment. Through one of the pastors in his district Leonard invited the women to a meeting of their own at Trinity Church on June 8, 1880. Fifty responded. They heard Jennie Hartzell plead the need. They applauded her by forming then and there the Woman's Home Missionary Society.

There was need of a president whose stature was commensurate with the importance of the new enterprise, a prominent name that would attract national attention to the Woman's Home Missionary Society. It was a man who came to the aid of the ladies and thought of the proper name. In the middle of the night before the day that the nominating committee was due to make its report Dr. Rust woke his wife. "Elizabeth, I have found your president," he said. "It is Mrs. Rutherford B. Hayes."[7]

Lucy Webb Hayes, reportedly the first lady to be called the First Lady of the Land when she moved into the White House, was widely known and genially regarded as a gracious person with strong convictions. Members of the press dubbed her Lemonade Lucy because she would not serve alcoholic beverages, even at dinners of state. She was a practicing Methodist and her fidelity to her local church in Fremont, Ohio, was such that the nominating committee thought best to break the news of her selection to her through her pastor. Mrs. Hayes hesitated a long time, but she finally accepted and the new organization had a feather in its cap. That the wife of the President should become president of a church society devoted to working out current problems called further attention to the fact that there were women of talent and prestige in the land and that they were on the move. Methodist officials were impressed with Mrs. Hayes and the force of the new body. When the General Conference convened again in 1884 it made the Women's Home Missionary Society part of The Methodist Episcopal Church.

The experience with mass organization in the Church South was vast and varied and showed an uncanny ability to maneuver as well as to get a job done. Getting a job done, as usual, came first with women. It was a commonplace in Methodist circles of every branch and section that you could count on letting the women do the work. It might be a task taken on through the initiative of one strong and convinced daughter of the faith, as in the case of Mrs. Hartzell, or it might be a task assigned.

Among southern Methodists it was the response to an urgent appeal for help from officials that led to the formation of a church-wide society devoted to treating problems on the home front. In the early 1880's a revived and vigorous Methodist Episcopal Church, South, was expanding so fast that there were not enough parsonages for the preachers and their families to live in and many churches could not be supplied. The board in charge of church extension turned to the women and asked a devout and earnest church woman, Lucinda B. Helm, if she could draw up a plan. She drew up a plan in the form of a constitution for a new action agency. The board had in mind a woman's adjunct which would work under its direction and raise money for the needed parsonages. Miss Helm, however, quickly saw and seized the opportunity to set up a body pledged to carry out the building program but one that was much broader in purpose and that had identity if not independence.

Opposition arose at the very thought, but Lucinda B. Helm was a woman who saw clearly: The parsonages had to be built. The women could raise the funds and oversee the work. Who else could? Miss Helm persuaded the Board of Church Extension, which had to have the help of the women, to become the advocate of her plan at the General Conference in 1886. The

345

Conference approved and the Woman's Parsonage and Home Mission Society came into business. It had a measure of status and before long it had a superb reputation. It discharged its duties so rapidly and well that within eight years it had built or helped to build 550 parsonages. Officials acknowledged that "many of these have been the means of establishing our church where otherwise it would have had no existence, or at best a feeble existence. . . ."[8]

With a society in which talent could be discovered and put to work, women had a chance to develop public skills. New leaders came out of the wings, leaders who combined charm and dignity and were increasingly restive in subsidiary positions. One was Miss Belle Harris Bennett, who was elected president of the Woman's Parsonage and Home Mission Society in 1894. A woman of spirit as well as talent, a speaker and organizer, Miss Bennett had pride in what members of her sex had done in the South and found distasteful the fact that, with all of their achievements, they still had to file out of their own meetings and report to the Board of Church Extension and be referred to patronizingly as "the good women" and "the elect ladies."[9] The women conducted their business efficiently and yet they were not allowed to feel equal or responsible.

Out of righteous resentment and backed by a remarkable record, the southern women in 1898 made strong representations for a change in status. They got what they wanted. It was understood and agreed that they would still help the Church Extension Board in the parsonage building program, but the name was condensed to the Woman's Home Missionary Society. It became a separate corporation, managed by its own board made up of officers from the Annual Conference societies. It was no longer tied to church extension but was responsible only to the General Conference. The board of the Society was granted the right to own property and to make such changes as it wished from time to time in its own organization.

Southern Methodist women now had substance as well as status. Autonomy did not last, but it was sweet while it did, and it added to the sum total of women's experience in corporate management. A complete reorganization, announced without warning by the bishops at the General Conference of 1906 and effected four years later, left the women stunned for a while. In due course, however, they showed that they had the capacity to accept change and get on with their job. The work of foreign missions and home missions was combined in a single unit called the Woman's Missionary Council. Miss Helm was so disappointed that she resigned but fortunately Belle Bennett took the helm. She traveled throughout the connection, exhorting, encouraging, praising, and, most important, helping to institute programs by which workers could be trained and qualified, whatever their choice of field. Taking no fee or salary, Miss Bennett helped to set up Wesley Community Houses and Bethlehem Centers far and wide.[10]

As they grew strong through organization, Southern Methodist women were alert to attitudes that lay back of actions and of pretenses invoked to cover some of the most hideous crimes. In the two decades following World War I there were 528 lynchings in the United States. To get at the roots of prejudice traditionally associated with womanhood in the South, they helped provide leadership for and cooperated with a remarkable organization formed at Atlanta in 1930: the Association of Southern Women for the Prevention of Lynching. It was an action group working at the local level, with members primed to bring immediate pressure on officers of the law at any sign or threat of mob action.[11]

The General Conference of The Methodist Episcopal Church, South, had approved a deaconess program in 1902 and the emphasis in both sections fell more and more upon teaching women something besides generalized and vaporized good will. There had come into being "an organized force trained in those ministering functions that have their root in woman's nature."

A renewed urging of the deaconess idea had been begun in the Church North as early as 1886 when Bishop J. M. Thoburn put before the Central Ohio Conference a suggested plan. Two

347

years later the General Conference accepted the plan and announced that women wishing to engage in this work were to abandon other pursuits and "to devote themselves in a general way to such forms of Christian labor as may be suited to their abilities." No vows were to be exacted of those who joined but the order was to be set apart with a uniform and it was free to draw up rules and regulations and lay out a program of ministering to those in sore bodily need.

With each new program emerged the talent necessary to put it across. In the North the person who came to full stature under the demands of organizing deaconesses was Miss Jane M. Bancroft. Born in 1847, the daughter of a Methodist preacher, she had nonetheless enjoyed all the advantages of college in her day, holding a doctorate from Syracuse University. For seven years she had been a dean at Northwestern and had studied at the University of Zurich and at the University of Paris. While abroad she had observed deaconesses at work both on the Continent and in London. She returned to the United States the year the office of deaconess was authorized by The Methodist Episcopal Church and brought firsthand reports to the Woman's Home Missionary Society. Immediately after hearing her the executive board of the Society created a deaconess committee and put her in charge.[12] The next year, as the work expanded, the committee became a bureau, with Miss Bancroft still in charge, and in the next fifteen years she helped to establish thirty deaconess homes in as many cities.[13]

These homes were training centers for women who wanted to do good well and were not content to remain charity ladies. The work involved education at every turn. The women wanted to learn. They had a study program which attracted the attention of the whole Church and, through the Chautauqua Literary and Scientific Circle, a three-year correspondence and study course was set up in local churches, so that women of the Methodist persuasion were led to contemplate the whole social problem and to assess what remedial work was being done and what more was needed.

348

City missions set up for the training of deaconesses in time came to be demonstration centers for work among the urban poor. The model center was in Ohio. It was located in Cincinnati and was called the Glenn Home. Opening in 1890, it carried on its work with a corps of resident workers, pastoral assistants, and teachers. It had a kindergarten and a school of domestic science. Glenn Home was singular but not unique, for there were similar homes in Chicago, New York, Boston, and Philadelphia. By 1900 the Methodists had seventy-three deaconess homes—as many as those of other denominations combined "Compared with the Methodists," one objective writer says, "the contributions of the other American denominations were insignificant."[14]

By the time of the unification in 1939 of the standard brands of Methodism, the women of the several churches had built an amazing distributing system for ideas and good will. They had met every test of Christian action and, above all, had shown sheer genius in the new and emerging art of cooperation. There was no doubt that their work must be given continuity in the new denomination called The Methodist Church, although Mrs. Francis J. McConnell, wife of a leading bishop of the former Methodist Episcopal Church, noted that not one woman had been asked to serve on official commissions that had brought the union to pass. John R. Mott, distinguished layman and leader of the world Y.M.C.A., later understated, "There is a tendency on the part of men to neglect women in the set-up and conduct of organizations." The combined membership of the many committees to work out the details of the new denomination was 172; of these 9 were women.[15]

Even so, there was a woman's section of the Ad Interim Committee. The purpose of this section was to determine how the women's societies of the former churches could be fitted into the working arrangements of the new body. Lines were drawn and, understandably enough, on the basis of gender and the rights of women. The societies of The Methodist Protestant Church and of The Methodist Episcopal Church, South, had

349

enjoyed autonomy for a season and had reluctantly given it up. The loss of independence had not been all bad, however. Mrs. C. W. Turpin of the Southern Methodists stated with some feeling the values of a board made up of both men and women: "For 34 years we Southern women have sat side by side with men. . . . It's been a harmonious plan. . . . If the three branches of the church are to be united, it's a silly idea to segregate women's work. . . ." On the other hand, Mrs. W. H. C. Goode of the Church North noted that the women did not want to toss over all they had done by joining a board that would be dominated by men. "We have accomplished too much to relinquish our leadership to men," she said. "We've demonstrated that we know our business, can handle money, and statistics prove that we've been successful."[16]

Independence won. The new body was called the Woman's Division of Christian Service and it had from The Methodist Church authority "to regulate its own proceedings; to select fields of labor; to accept, train, commission and maintain workers; to sue and be sued; to secure and administer funds for all work under its charge."

Certain changes beyond prerogatives were also introduced. Old terms, belonging to a dead day, were dropped. There would no longer be foreign and home missionary societies and certainly no ladies' aid societies. Accepting the term *Christian service*, the women enlarged their view of missions "from geographical areas to include 'any area of life untouched by the spirit of Christ.'" They wanted an organization "free to swing into harmony with the needs of the age in which the work is to be done," and they interpreted progress as "the ability to see old familiar things in new relationships."

With its enlarged view of missions and of the function of religion in a complex world, the Woman's Division anticipated needs that were deep before they became visible and reached headline proportions. Putting from the first a strong emphasis on problems of race, it set up a Department of Christian Social

350

Relations in 1940—a dozen years before The Methodist Church created its Board of Christian Social Concerns.

On the organizational chart the Woman's Division could be seen as a box tied by lines to the Board of Missions. Yet partly by the indulgence of the board and partly out of the assertiveness of the women, Division statements took on a tone that was loud and clear and, considering the auspices, could be taken by many as official pronouncements. Some preachers admitted privately that the Woman's Division was the conscience of the Church, constantly calling Methodist men to the memory of their social mission.

The women met once a year at the same time the Board of Missions met. The deliberations of Division leaders (about seventy in all—most of them women) extended over a week and they covered social and political issues facing the country. They drew up provocative resolutions on each issue they considered major or a must. The resolutions were not only submitted to the Board of Missions but they were also transmitted to women's societies in local churches with recommendations for study to be followed by action. Some resolutions were sent to government officials when public policy was involved, and not a few of the plain-spoken ones were released to the secular press through the information office of the Church.

Over the years the scope of the resolutions showed the range of women's interests and their fields of inquiry. Before our deep involvement through purely executive decisions in Vietnam the board strongly asked that Congress take a more active part in determining foreign policy. At the same time the women asked that full consideration be given to the problem of admitting mainland China into the United Nations. They deplored preparations for chemical and bacteriological warfare and called on the government to transform such facilities as those at Fort Detrick into centers for world health research.

In another resolution the Woman's Division noted with deep regret that the Congress had authorized a five-year commemora-

351

tion and observance of the hundredth anniversary of the Civil War. From their Methodist background the women prophetically saw no good that could come of the observance, and that it might "well provide the means of stimulating divisive elements, stirring up slumbering sectionalism and generating strife that can result in untold damage."[17]

In The United Methodist Church the nomenclature and some of the administrative procedures have been changed. Woman has given way to women. The body operates under the supervision of The Women's Division of the Board of Missions. But the vigor remains undiminished and the recommendations and resolutions are as up-to-date as tomorrow's headlines. Within a year after the new Church came into being, the Women's Division voted to sell 5414 shares of Dow Chemical Company stock for $400,000 and turn half the proceeds over to the Black Methodists for Church Renewal, a caucus of ministers and laymen within the denomination. With an eye ever to the practical and the down-to-earth, the women voted to deposit $15,000 each in savings accounts in two black banks in two sections of the country and, for good measure, use a Harlem firm headed by a black broker to handle its security transactions. The Division works through 36,500 local Women's Societies of Christian Service and Wesleyan Service Guilds (for employed women) with a membership of 1,700,000, and each of the local units was urged to give support to black banks everywhere by opening checking accounts.[18]

Considering that The United Methodist Church, with more than eleven million members, embraces every shade of political and social opinion, many actions taken by the Women's Division cannot but be construed as radical if not wild. Yet the confidence of the Church in its women is attested by the fact that in a day when contributions to charitable and worthy causes are on the decline, those to the Women's Societies of the Church are on the rise.[19]

It surprises many that Methodist women, with their verve and drive as well as their devotion, have not been included by the Church in high official circles. They are still represented only nominally in governing agencies. Not until 1909 in The Methodist Episcopal Church and 1922 in The Methodist Episcopal Church, South, were they admitted as delegates to the General Conference. Of the 893 delegates to the Uniting Conference that formed The Methodist Church in 1939, 76 were women. At the Uniting Conference in 1968 there were seated only 97 women delegates out of a total of 1270. The right of women to be traveling preachers with full clergy rights was granted by The Methodist Church in 1956, well ahead of some denominations but in arrears of The African Methodist Episcopal Zion Church, which as early as 1868 deleted the word "male" from its requirements for ordination.

Even with all the sexual lag in majority Methodism, there are encouraging signs to be seen by the sanguine. The 1968 General Conference made the unprecedented move of naming a woman, Mrs. Dwight P. Grove of Philadelphia, to the Judicial Council—the supreme court of the Church that passes on the constitutionality of the acts of the General Conference. And in 1970 the established Fondren Lectures at Southern Methodist University in Dallas were delivered for the first time by a woman. The series, which in the course of the previous fifty years had numbered among its lecturers some of the ablest preachers and professors of various denominations, was given by Miss Theressa Hoover, a black and an associate general secretary of The United Methodist Church Board of Missions.

It was a red-letter day when a black woman lectured southern Methodist preachers on the demands of social justice. That a woman up from Methodism should be accorded the deference usually reserved for a seasoned dignitary is not without significance. Something was honored that had not been honored before and the occasion might adumbrate change. Or it might be only another token recognition. For all their background and performance in matters of mind, there is not a much greater proportional representation of women in the government of Methodism than there is in the government of the United

States. There is among Methodist women, however, a solid pride and self-sufficiency. Possibly one reason they are not better represented in official posts may be that they are no longer willing to bang on doors and seek admittance. Through a display of their abilities in every phase of a highly complicated social structure they have gained selfhood.

The attainment of selfhood is the lesson of their history for our history. There can no longer be any doubt in any mind about the corporate competence of women. The only question now is whether there can be found some way by which this competence can be further drawn into the management of the Church at large. If a way can be found, in a day of declining membership and confused outlook, officials will tap a luxuriant source of ideas. Full acceptance of women by Methodism would set a model for other bodies—in education and business and government—to study.

XXVI The Demon Rum

Prohibition was Methodist. Temperance, which was at first essentially educational in tone and reach and aim, was sharpened by Methodist crusaders into Prohibition, which was legal and harsh and compulsory.

The temperance movement was identified with the Woman's Christian Temperance Union, which was identified with Frances E. Willard who, as one preacher put it, was the incarnation of modern Methodism. Prohibition was the work of the Anti-Saloon League which was founded by a Methodist, largely staffed by Methodist men, and had the vociferous and energetic support of officialdom in the Churches North and South.[1]

Both the cause of temperance and the enactment of laws making liquor illegal marked a turnabout in the philosophy and program of American Methodism. From the lenient stance of early days when circuit riders peddled liquor and Methodist merchants kept barrels of whiskey and rum in their stores to attract customers, the Church moved to a position where it forbade not only its own members but all Americans to drink.

For the first time the two cultures of Methodism and Americanism became inimical to each other. A church body generally agreeable to the decrees and blandishments of politicians in such matters as Indian removal and the shedding of blood called war took on the whole political kit and caboodle and pitted itself against vast vested interests in the bargain. It had taken on another gigantic and legitimate business approved by government when it opposed slavery, but the opposition had led to a split in the Church. The two main branches which had divided over slavery joined forces in the attack on liquor. They had a program that called for action by activists against entrenched business. There was a difference at last between Methodism and unregulated pioneer social life.

An even more remarkable reversal arose from the fact that a church that had preached and stressed individual responsibility for conduct, putting the emphasis almost exclusively on the salvation of individual souls, now concerned itself with the nature of the social order. The reversal was a confession that individual uprightness was not enough. It had been known that drunkenness led to poverty, but, as Frances E. Willard discovered and said, poverty might lead to drunkenness.

When The Methodist Episcopal Church was formed in 1784, drinking was not a serious national problem. It became one. In England, an emerging industrial order with extremes of callous wealth and degrading poverty, alcohol was a culprit from the beginning of the Methodist societies. John Wesley and William Hogarth, contemporaries in an age of cruelty, knew and depicted the effects of drink. Both the transformed Anglican priest and the great pictorial satirist saw the horrors of the gin mill and of the uncontrolled appetite of the addict. Members of the Wesleyan Methodist societies were forbidden to imbibe, manufacture, sell, or distribute alcoholic beverages.

The severe Wesleyan restrictions were brought to America and incorporated in the constitution of the new Church here. However, times and circumstances were found to be radically different in a nation of scattered people constantly on the move or engaged in steady physical exertions. The manufacture and sale of alcohol seemed to belong to the very nature of the economy. Making liquor was the cheapest and best way to get grain to market. It meant shipping the concentrate rather than the bulk—a blessed advantage in a day of limited transportation facilities. Often in remote areas distilled grain was the only product that could be transported at a cost low enough to bring in a cash return.[2]

Dram drinking also enlivened diet in an era of dull food. In colder regions it provided supplementary sugar content when sugar was scarce and hard to come by. In the English tradition punch and beer belonged to social occasions. The wassail bowl gave a touch of ceremony to weddings and buryings. Hard liquor in the form of rum and whiskey afforded a natural accompaniment to, or reward for, hard work in the great outdoors. Brewing beverages of alcohol and malt and distributing the products tied in at every point with merchandising routines.

The loosening of prohibitions in the American Methodist societies followed the trends of the times. Early regulations were watered down fast. In 1780 those who distilled spirits were excluded from the societies. In 1783 they were not, although the selling and drinking of liquor were still forbidden. By 1789 the buying or selling or drinking of distilled liquors was forbidden, even in cases of necessity. Two years later drinking in cases of necessity was allowed, whereas the provision against buying and selling was dropped. The General Conference of 1796 provided that if there was abuse of liquor and disorder resulted, the offenders should be proceeded against as in any other instance of immorality.[3] The Methodists had begun to deal with effects and were confining their discipline to those who could not carry their liquor. The Church had accepted the world, even if it still urged men to wrestle with the flesh and the devil.

There being no rules against traffic in liquor, it fell out that some of the preachers were not averse to taking spirits of the earthly sort with them on their rounds. The itinerancy was made to order for the purpose. No one could begrudge the little the circuit riders were able to add to their scrawny incomes from the sales, and there was every occasion for gratitude among those who could buy the brews, because they could always serve a medicinal purpose if there were scruples against drinking for pleasure.

It was this arrant and vagrant peddling of liquor that started the return of restrictions on alcohol in The Methodist Episcopal Church. Not a few of the itinerants deplored the practice, especially as corn became more and more plentiful and liquor cheaper. In Kentucky a preacher named James Axley, a converted hunter, saw the woe brought to his region by corn liquor and set about to get its sale dissociated from the itinerants. The campaign took him years, partly because he was known among his fellows as earnest and devoted but a man of little culture and many eccentricities.

Axley was a good friend of the equally rough and ready but more experienced Peter Cartwright, who knew his worth and validated him to many. Once he took Axley to dine in the home of Edward Tiffin, first governor of Ohio. Axley had not before been in a room with rugs on the floor or paper on the walls. Chicken was served and when he ate, he simply gnawed the bones and tossed them on the floor. Later Peter Cartwright remonstrated with Axley and the big woodsman was crushed and broke out in tears, asking Cartwright why he had not told him the proper way to behave.

It was this fellow, uncouth even by early frontier standards, who set about to change the attitude of the mighty Methodist Church toward liquor. On May 9 at the General Conference of 1812 Axley moved a resolution, as recorded in the minutes, that "no stationed or local preacher shall retail spirituous or malt liquors without forfeiting his ministerial character among us." The motion tabled. It came up again a week later. It again specified "spirituous or malt liquors" but a prohibition against distilling was added. Consideration was postponed until the following Wednesday, when it was laid over until the next day. The next day it came to a vote and the minutes bear the simple notation: Lost.[4]

Four years later the General Conference did pass the Axley resolution, but not with spirit, and the Church was by no means

out of the liquor business. A complaint among temperance crusaders was that in many Methodist stores more wet goods than
dry goods were sold. In the General Conference of 1820 an
attempt to make the distilling of liquor a cause for the forfeiture
of church membership failed. In 1848 the General Conference
of The Methodist Episcopal Church did restore to its *Discipline*
the original Wesley rule against buying or selling or drinking
liquor. The Methodist Episcopal Church, South, however, did
not. Hunter Dickinson Farish in his study of the social history
of southern Methodism reports that during 1867 three different
firms were allowed to advertise whiskey in the columns of a
southern Methodist paper.[5]

Only by degrees, and under the pressure of events, did mighty
Methodism harden its face toward liquor. Influences outside
the connection, north and south, were at work. These influences
led to the creeping consciousness that the American people
were intemperate not only in fervor and speech but also in the
consumption of alcohol.

Scattered statistics came to light slowly to show that Uncle
Sam was drinking more and more—in a convivial way, for
the most part, but with an intake of the sort that turns a drinker
into a drunk. It was brought out that when Massachusetts had
only 150,000 people it had distilled fifteen thousand hogsheads
of rum a year, and a very large part of it had been consumed
by Massachusetts citizens.[6]

After the middle of the nineteenth century there was every
prospect, and then sign, of a stupendous increase in guzzling.
The Congress of the United States of America in 1862 passed
an Internal Revenue Act to collect from those who made and
sold alcoholic beverages.[7] The approval of complete legality was
thus placed on a business operation which many Methodists considered quite as bad as legal slavery had been. Traffic in liquor,
sanctioned by tax laws at the very time of a great inpouring of
immigrants who brought their appetites and dram habits with
them, rose from peanuts to big business. Sales increased in the
years between 1860 and 1880 from $29,000,000 to $190,000,000.

The outlook for brewers was rosy and they rubbed their hands in anticipation of the day when the "enormous influx of immigration" would "overreach the Puritanical element in every state in the union."[8]

Still another element entered into the compound of religious opinion as the sale of liquor increased. This was the conviction that the effects of alcohol went far beyond the deterioration of the person who drank to excess. Effects were to be found in every nook and cranny of the common life. Drinking was no longer a morals problem but a moral problem, a public issue, because it struck at the roots of the home. Those who drank were often cruel to, and not uncommonly negligent of, those who did not drink. As reformers saw it, drinking took bread out of the mouths of children both because alcohol used grain that should be used for bread and because sots would see their children starve before they would forgo a dram. The problem was so big that it could not be dealt with save on a wide and uncompassing scale and by a program aimed at changing the mind of a nation.

Through children and threatened homes the emotions of women were affected, and women were the first to take to the streets and demonstrate. There had been lectures and clubs and pledges and abstinence societies and pleas before, but the first pageant that paraded in colorful fashion the emotions of victims was put on the day before Christmas, 1873 in the town of Hillsboro, Ohio, a town of some three thousand persons, "noted for quietude, culture, and refinement." It had been settled by Virginians. The men were habitual drinkers, who had resisted all efforts of the temperance movement.

Dioclesian Lewis, a temperance lecturer and health expert, founder of the Boston Institute of Physical Education, had addressed an audience of women in the town the day before. He had proposed that the women could halt the sale of liquor by prayer and visitations to places where it was sold. Seventy women assembled the next morning at the Presbyterian Church and, led by Mrs. Eliza J. Thompson, daughter of a former governor of Ohio, a lady of culture, filed out of the church, singing "Give to the Winds thy Fears." They visited saloons, druggists, hotels.[9]

It was the beginning of the Women's Crusade. Nothing quite like it had been seen or fancied before. The women in Hillsboro did not get immediate results among the liquor dealers, but they got the immediate attention of women in nearby towns. Two days after the Hillsboro demonstration forty-four women met at The Methodist Episcopal Church in Washington Courthouse and, after an hour of prayer, marched to the first drugstore on their list, the tolling of the church bell "keeping time to the solemn march of the women." At the drugstore, as in every other place, "they entered singing, every woman taking up the sacred strain as she crossed the threshold." According to Mrs. Annie Wittenmeyer's account, the singing was followed by the reading of an appeal the women had drafted. Then came prayer and an earnest verbal plea to the proprietor to desist from his soul-destroying traffic and sign the dealer's pledge.

Next day the women found the doors locked but they went back to the church and had a union mass meeting and on the day following their number grew to one hundred. That day "a liquor dealer surrendered his stock in answer to their prayers and poured it into the streets while nearly a thousand watched; bells were ringing, men and boys shouting and women singing and praying to God." Within eight days every liquor dealer had given up the ghost and his supplies.[10]

Word of the prayer fests spread fast. Within a few weeks the marching and singing and praying was going on in a dozen states. The women varied their tactics from time to time and place to place. In some cases they entered saloons and knelt on sawdust floors. Sometimes they stood outside for hours at a time and watched the customers come and go.

Contagion was catching. What was called the praying infection reached town after town day after day for six months, and only gradually subsided. Results were impressive if not lasting. It was reported that saloons were closed in more than two hundred towns during the first two months of 1874 and that, all told, three thousand saloons were shut down before the furor ended. Tax revenues fell markedly in districts where the women had demonstrated. But the main effect was on those who had taken no part in what was soon termed the Women's Crusade. Wire services distributed the news nationwide. Writers, among them Mark Twain, were assigned to do special features. The great humorist turned serious in treating the spectacle, pointing out that the women engaged in the marches were the finest people in their communities and yet were "voiceless in the making of laws."[11] The Women's Crusade gave the voiceless a chance to speak, or at least to whisper. Even the silent had power.

What impressed everyone as much as it did Mark Twain was the patent fact that the marchers were ordinary women, aroused, straight out of homes and churches—women who, as Mary Earhart observes in her biography of Frances Willard, had been shocked by the suffrage movement. They were not agitators. They paraded a problem rather than a set of prejudices. The crusade was not so much a planned campaign as "an emotional outburst against old customs, old restrictions, old laws."

As an outburst it would have left no more than the memory of a brilliant flash, but, thanks to the strength and managerial ability of Frances Willard and her sisters in the temperance movement, the Women's Crusade marked the crossroads in the history of American women. It was a display of women's rights and wrongs. The combination was new and powerful and the zeal it generated was not to be allowed to evaporate. It was to seal the zeal in containers that might be tapped again that caused the good women gathered at Chautauqua in the summer of 1874 to issue their call for a national convention of women interested in the cause of temperance.

Elation greeted the call. From seventeen states two hundred women representing churches and temperance societies flocked to Cleveland. They were in session only three days but the momentum was so great and the purpose so clear that those

assembled managed to found and put into operation the Woman's
Christian Temperance Union.

Woman's. Not Women's. Women were one thing. Woman was
another. Women could be ladies or sluts or battle-axes or merely
females. Woman was the singular and woman was also singular, an entity, a totality, an abstraction full of mystery, who
might be blamed for a man's ills but not for the world's ills.
And when the word *Woman* was linked with *Christian* the
concept of Woman as ideal was invoked, and it was invoked
for *Temperance*, for conservation and preservation, for moderation. *Union* expressed strength, for in union, there is strength.
Women had been told that by the men. Now they would find
out for themselves.

The woman whose spirit brooded over and permeated the first
national organization of American women was only thirty-five
at the time. She nonetheless enjoyed distinction as a college
president and dean, as a lecturer, and as one who had traveled
in Europe, Asia, and Africa. In the long and varied strands of
circumstance and heritage that produced Frances Willard, there
had been many men connected with education and some who
held enlightened views of women. One ancestor appealed to her
in particular because he was both an educator and kind—Samuel
Willard, pastor of Old South Church in Boston and vice-president of Harvard College during the witchcraft trials at Salem,
Massachusetts, in 1692. Samuel Willard, singular among his
fellow clergymen, had refused to have any part in the craze
that brought accusations against many women and some men.
From his pulpit and position he had courageously and soberly
spoken out against the trials at a time when they were popular,
and he had used his influence to bring them to an end. Of him
Frances wrote, "I am glad that he was a gentle Willard, this
Samuel."

There was much in the childhood and upbringing of Frances
Willard to make her as complex as the problems faced by the
new Union of which she became corresponding secretary. Not
all Willards were gentle. Her father's first name was Josiah but

his middle name was Flint, and he brought his children up by rules hard as nails. His severity prompted in Frances, his second child and first daughter, a rebellious spirit by which she could often outwit her father. He forbade her as a young girl to ride horseback, so she trained a heifer to the saddle, accepting his rule and transcending it rather than breaking it. At fifteen she was allowed to ride horseback.[12]

A redhead and a tomboy, strenuously trying to escape the boredom of a remote Wisconsin farm to which her father had moved the family for his health, Frances Elizabeth Caroline Willard was known to herself, her older brother, and younger sister as Frank. To friends she was Frank all her life. The girl who took and kept a boy's name grew into a gawky young woman, inept at dress, self-consciously unattractive, reminded of the advantages of feminine appeal by the beauty of her sister Mary, envious of the advantages of being a man, with all the privileges appertaining thereto, by her smooth and successful brother. There were certain things you got, Frank realized, because of gender and there were certain other things—such as education and voting—denied you if you were of the wrong gender.

Her brother Oliver went to college quite naturally and as a matter of course. Frank and her sister would not have made it at all if it had not been for the persistence of her mother. When the two did finally arrive at college they found mostly females of class whose parents had sent them there to finish them. The other students accepted Mary immediately but rejected Frank and made fun of her clothes until she knocked one of them down.[13] Very soon, however, she found that there were girls of mind on the campus who recognized and accepted her for her mind. Within a week after she arrived she was editor of the college paper. Her new friends referred to her as fascinating and her teachers as brilliant.

Youth and college formed a forecast for Frank. There were certain fixed patterns and conventions and yet there was flexibility. There were ways in which conventions could be tested and circumvented. The world was willing to recognize a mind that rose resourcefully above patterns. Men held the whip hand but they had out of sentiment to recognize that the hand of woman held gifts. While the record shows many of her encounters with men—in college administration as well as General Conferences—you do not detect in the writings of Frances Willard a note of acerbity or bitterness or sardonic resentment. The more she met with the male mind the more resourceful her own mind became. She did not imitate male posturing. She relied on contrast rather than conflict.

Both in the Declaration of Principles, which Frances Willard wrote, and in suggestions she made for the conduct of the members, she set the tone of the W.C.T.U. Society was seen as a whole and reform was not to be fanatically narrow. The Declaration declared its belief in equal rights and responsibilities for men and women, a living wage, an eight-hour day, courts of conciliation and arbitration, justice as opposed to greed. The two primary purposes were announced as educating the young and forming a better public sentiment. A resolution put forward by Miss Willard anticipated the difficulties sure to arise and suggested the spirit with which these difficulties should be met:

> Recognizing that our cause will be combated by mighty, determined and relentless forces, we will, trusting in him who is the Prince of Peace, meet argument with argument, misjudgment with patience, denunciation with kindness, and all our difficulties and dangers with prayer.[14]

If the women planned on conciliation and persuasion as their keynotes, they planned also to take advantage of all they could learn from Methodist men and women both about organization. The Union was conceived on a national scale with state bodies federated in a general structure but reaching down into every local community. Within a year after it was established the seventeen states which had sent representatives to the first convention were solidly in business, complete with standing committees. The term was appropriated from male nomenclature and was hardly apt. Running committees would have been better, seeing that the women were swiftly moving about on errands of education. There were clear-cut divisions of labor and responsibility as shown in the names of the six major departments: preventive, evangelistic, special legal, educational and, yes, organizational.

Growth was rapid. By 1880 the convention at Boston seated 177 delegates from twenty-five states. Seven years later there were 341 delegates from forty-one states, and in 1900 the Woman's Christian Temperance Union encompassed the whole of the Federal Union and its territories.

Women in action were news and the women were not averse to aiding the cause of temperance by discreetly making news at every opportunity. Miss Willard publicly praised Mrs. Rutherford B. Hayes for removing wine from the White House table. To call attention to the extent to which alcohol had seeped into holy places, the W.C.T.U. executive urged all churches to follow the practice of the stricter denominations and use "unfermented wine" in communion services. She asked the convention in 1883 to ask physicians to use nonalcoholic medicines and keep their patients from swilling for ostensibly therapeutic purposes.

Wiles and stratagems were employed to focus attention, to bring into the open problems and attitudes commonly ignored, and to do it through those most affected, the women. The aim was awareness—awareness being the first step toward education. Salient in all the multifarious activities was the idea of teaching, of nurturing curiosity and doubt about alcohol. If there was hope of change in customs, it lay with the young. One of Miss Willard's first acts when she succeeded Mrs. Annie Wittenmeyer as president in 1879 was to enlist the National Education Association as an ally in a program of getting schools to adopt courses on the nature and effects of alcohol. Vermont was the first state to put the policy in force. The year was 1882. New Hampshire followed the next year, and the year after that ten other states came along. Thanks to perseverance and organization and peppery insistence, every one of the United States had temperance courses in their schools shortly after the turn of the century.[15]

The Anti-Saloon League of America came into being in 1895 and was able to take advantage of almost twenty years of alcohol-consciousness promoted by the W.C.T.U. Actually, the League had been in being if not in form since the General Conference of The Methodist Episcopal Church in 1872 expressed its conviction of "the absolute need of total legal prohibition" in handling the liquor problem. By this declaration it announced the intention of the Church to achieve moral reform through the agency of the state. Calling itself the Church in Action Against the Saloon, the League was a lobby to carry out the task.

Once the Church in Action Against the Saloon chose to settle the liquor question in the arena of politics, it let the politicians choose both the weapons and the rules. Victory alone mattered. The air was filled with fight symbols and negatives, and the language itself was distorted beyond recognition. Prohibition itself was a negative word, even though those who championed the cause were known as pros and sounded positive. Those opposed to prohibition were antis because they were antiprohibitionists and they sounded awful and unclean.

The pros won, hands-down and to a fare-thee-well, which made them sound all the more pro. They outfoxed and outmaneuvered the experienced antis and, through fast footwork, changed the Constitution of the United States of America. The Eighteenth Amendment was a fluke and a surprise and more than the pros had bargained or hoped for, but they could and did claim credit for it.

News of much of the action was lost in the headlines of the day because it took place shortly after the United States had entered the world war in April 1917, but the broad outlines were there and clear, and they illustrate the extraordinary speed and skill with which Methodist-trained lobbyists operated.

There had been agitation before and after America's entry into the war for a prohibition law which would forbid the manufacture and sale of beverages of malt or alcohol during the period of the war and for a year afterward. Good arguments could be brought up in behalf of the proposal. The grain used in beer alone destroyed potentially eleven million loaves of bread a day. Sober soldiers made the fiercest fighters. Only clear-eyed young men could sight their rifles with deadly accuracy. The arguments sounded plausible and, by all reckonings, they commanded wide support—enough, certainly, to make the brewers oppose the idea mightily and craftily.

One of the advocates of wartime prohibition, Irving Fisher, professor of economics at Yale, was appointed to a high government agency, the Council of National Defense, and asked to call a conference on what to do about the soldiers and alcohol. Wartime prohibition was recommended by the conference and the recommendation was supposed to be passed along to the Council of National Defense. But, according to Professor Fisher, the brewers touched the key people on the Council and blocked consideration of it.

Now the Anti-Saloon League stepped in. Although wartime prohibition had been snubbed by an advisory agency of the government, the League saw to it that it was offered to the House of Representatives in the form of a rider to the Lever bill, which provided for the proper allocation of foodstuffs for war use. The Lever bill, which was essential to the war effort, passed the House with flying colors and carried the wartime prohibition measure with it. It was headed for fast passage in the Senate too, much to the dismay of the brewers.[16]

The best the antiprohibitionists could do was to muster a filibuster and threaten to keep it up all summer. By late June matters had reached an impasse and it was apparent that the food bill, the passage of which President Wilson considered imperative, might be held up indefinitely. Accordingly he called on the Democratic floor leader of the Senate to see if he could persuade the Anti-Saloon League to withdraw the prohibition provisions from the bill. Senator Martin of Virginia, the floor leader, summoned the legislative committee to his office and made the request. It was not well received but the committee did say that they would consider what could be done if the President would put his wishes in writing.

The President was reluctant, naturally. It was odd for a severe Presbyterian to have to write a Methodist lobby to get the acceptance of national legislation needed for fighting a war. But so powerful was the position of the League that the Chief Executive had no choice and he wrote the letter. Members of the legislative committee were editors as well as politicians, however, and they did not like the letter. Only when the President rewrote it to their liking did the League withdraw the objectionable provisions and allow the Lever bill to become the Lever Act.[17]

Wartime prohibition seemed safely dead. But immediately the League followed up with a stronger thrust to take advantage of the force it had displayed in Congress. A resolution to make the manufacture and sale of liquor unconstitutional was put forward and passed by the House and Senate. The antis raised no great obstacles. It was not a decision measure. National prohibition achieved in this way would require an amendment to the Constitution, and an amendment would have to be ratified by three-fourths of the states. This cumbersome process would take a long time. Besides, there was scant chance of ratification.

Forty-six of the forty-eight states ratified the proposed Eighteenth Amendment in a year's time, and constitutional prohibition, to the astonishment of pros and antis alike, was a fact—to become effective a year after ratification. Meanwhile the Anti-Saloon League, just for good measure, had also put through wartime prohibition. As originally intended, it was to last for the duration of the war and for a year thereafter. The war was virtually over when President Wilson signed wartime prohibition into law, and the act would have been meaningless if it had not carried the extra year's provision. This was the year that the brewers had hoped to use as the year in which to get rid of their stocks before the Eighteenth Amendment went into effect. Now it was the year that wasn't.

Suddenly, almost without warning, the country was dry.

Methodists and their cohorts had changed the Constitution, and they were now in a position to change the habits of the people. It had been a magnificent venture, this taking on of the minions of darkness. They had made one of their moral convictions the law of the land. The church was the state. It was an intoxicating experience.

Yet for all their heroic efforts to change the culture of which they were a part, the Methodists had ended up by being more closely identified than ever with the nation. They had used national tactics of violence and combat to achieve their end. As Professor Robert Moats Miller says, the vocabulary of the prohibition movement was militaristic. "The wet 'monsters of iniquity' would be 'crushed' by the dry 'soldiers of righteousness,'" There was need for "a new national preparedness," "a Pentecost of divine mobilization," men "armed with breach loading opinions" and "white bayonets of peace and goodwill."[18]

Forgotten in the elation of victory was the fact that the victories won by the prohibitionists, both in the state and the nation during the first two decades of the twentieth century, may be traced, as a modern standard reference book puts it, "to voters educated as children concerning the evil effects of alcohol." It was the Willard generation come to voting age.

Forgotten also was the study of alcohol. Education stopped with victory. Courses in the schools were allowed to lapse, and they were not restored to the curriculum in the rebound of repeal. Work so widely and earnestly begun under the influence of women—the study of the problem of alcohol—was abandoned, and it was not to return until a decade or so after repeal. By that time the word *alcohol* had changed to *alcoholism*.

XXVII Into the Pit

"What sophistry to brand prohibition as sumptuary legislation or an invasion of personal liberty! Could not the same indictment be made of civil-rights legislation or traffic regulations or minimum-wage laws or safety and sanitary codes? Methodists believed that man was freer and life was sweeter when the state banned liquor, just as when the state banned slavery and dueling and narcotics."[1]

This comment, made by a historian of Methodism from the perspective of thirty years after repeal, brings to light a point lost to sight during the turbulent days when the Volstead Act was in force, namely, that making liquor illegal was not the only societal interest of the Methodist Churches. It simply aroused the most attention. Critics found it easy to make fun of the Methodists for the failure of enforcement and the collapse of prohibition. The Methodists were presented to the world as strait-laced and Pecksniffian reformers bent on supervising morals.

It was an irony growing out of ignorance. Nothing in temperament, background, or doctrine prepared them to be a part of a theocracy or made them deserve the image of the Puritan in which they were cast. From John Wesley on, the tradition of personal freedom and live-and-let-live and think-and-let-think had run deep under all their beliefs. If there was to be restraint, it was to be exercised by the Church on its own members or by the individual on himself. It was not to be imposed by outside authority. Yet, with the coming of prohibition achieved through the law of the land, the Church was suddenly thrust into the position of taking on the character of a state and of requiring obedience from all men, regardless of their religious convictions or lack of any. To obtain such obedience was an impossible task and by its very nature doomed.

What did suit the temperament of Methodism was the extension of its zeal beyond the range of the earlier evangelism designed to save souls, either retail or wholesale. The movement resulting in prohibition was only one prong of this extension, so that whereas enforcement was a farce, the concern that brought prohibition about was not, and this concern was bound to express itself in other ways.

At the time the Methodists were working toward the abolition of liquor, and could be presented as narrow-minded fanatics, they were also working toward reasonable hours and wages in industry and the right of men to bargain collectively for the improvement of their lot. And at about the time when they played a dramatic part in the enactment of prohibition, some of their most distinguished leaders were investigating—by means of personal interviews with the workers and executives involved—the conditions in the mills of the United States Steel Corporation that led to the ruinous strike of 1919.

Wesleyans were caught in the implications of their own faith. The profligate growth of industrialism meant that the individual could no longer, as in pioneer and agrarian days, be thought of as the sole arbiter of his destiny. Destiny in earlier times was an abstract concept advanced by theologians of other faiths. The new destiny was made by politicians and men of power. It was real. Perhaps in time it also could be transcended but not without corporate effort.

Meanwhile, with that practicality for which they were famous,

372

the Methodists could suit their doctrines to the unprecedented task at hand. The individual remained supreme in their thinking. They could still believe in the infinite worth of every man. They merely raised their sights and pushed back their horizons and applied their basic principle to a wider circle, a circle as wide as the world. By this wider application every man was of infinite worth—even if he wasn't a Methodist or even a prospect. He must have circumstances under which he could grow. To provide these circumstances was the function of the churches.

For helping to discharge this function the Methodists had been ill equipped by experience when the industrial age made its advent in America. Their habitat was the prairies and the canebrakes. They had been brought up on creek bottoms, in hollows, and amid tall timbers. The mind of the Methodists was rural and neighborly, given to finding out what was beyond the horizon. In their organized bodies, church extension—which meant expansion, exploring, taking over, building where nothing had been built before—was earnestly cherished. The log cabin, the sod house, and in prosperous times the modest dwelling on a shaded street—these seemed to provide the proper home. It was not the tenement. Slums were not places where middle-class people lived.

Hence members of the Wesleyan persuasion had scant chance for any daily contact with the new Americans flooding into the country to work on railroads, in mines, in factories, at spindles. The prosperity of the Methodists in a growing and expanding economy tended to isolate them in sentiment from those who were not of the same frame of faith. Preoccupation with the individual soul and with the good life that good conduct brought about kept the great white body of Methodists inured against the corrosions of society until, toward the end of the nineteenth century, conflicts, riots, marches, strikes, and civil commotion explosively confronted them with the fact that the world was not all Methodist.

There were some warning tremors of the wrath to come—a new kind of wrath from which men could not flee—as early as the

1870's. Labor became a commodity. Corporations arose, icy and impersonal, with powers hidden in the woodwork of front offices and upstairs where strangers schemed. Men told how you couldn't talk to the boss any more. He didn't talk to you, or, if he did, it was casually and paternally, not about business. He issued orders after talking with other men, men with money in big banks, probably on Wall Street. And after the orders were issued you were laid off. What happened to you and the kids he didn't see. You weren't a person; you were a hand. If you didn't like it, you could lump it. Or you could make trouble, agitate, stir up your fellow hands. Some did. But there were spies in the plant and they had your number and the boss stopped your pay and you got mad and quit. Then you were on a general Son-of-a-Bitch List that passed from plant to plant and they turned you down when you tried to get another job. Nobody wanted troublemakers.

But there were signs that workingmen, now called laborers, were getting sullen. They were organizing among themselves—the railroad workers, in particular. And when, in 1877, the managers and owners of railroads reduced wages and simply said so and without so much as by-your-leave, laborers stopped laboring—on the Baltimore & Ohio first, then the Pennsylvania, then the New York Central, then many western lines. You couldn't believe the headlines. This was America, yet here were men striking and fighting. In one riot at Martinsburg, West Virginia, nine persons were killed. President Rutherford B. Hayes sent troops. The act of sending troops set off rioting in the big cities. Pittsburgh was the worst, by far. Bystanders sided with the strikers, actually joined in the fight with the gendarmes. It was known that the militia stationed in Pittsburgh would not attack fellow citizens just because they were striking, so the militia was brought in from Philadelphia. Outsiders invading. The strikers won. They forced the Phillies into a roundhouse, then they ran amuck, setting fire to machine shops and destroying the Union Depot. In all, five million dollars went down the

374

destruction drain. Twenty-six persons were killed before a citizen posse and federal troops stilled the rioters.[2]

The sweeping and unexpected railroad strikes of 1877 were nationwide but not nationally organized. They sprang up through local grievances. They spread by imitative violence. About two-thirds of the country's total rail mileage was in the strike-affected area. Where the strikers struck there were shootings, burnings, or depredations. The governor of Maryland informed the President of the United States that rioters had taken over the B. & O. depot in Baltimore, set fire to it and driven off the firemen who sought to extinguish the blaze. He added that it was impossible to disperse the rioters. In Chicago police attempted to clear the streets. Rioters resisted. Police and militia charged the crowd. The melee left nineteen dead and more than a hundred injured.[3]

It was a man-made world of twisted steel and fire and brimstone middle-class Methodists faced as the nineteenth century moved toward its close. It was not a place for circuit riders or a time when exhortation would suffice. The response of the Protestant press was one of shock and outrage, as became champions of decency and law and order. One church paper compared events with those of the French Revolution and the leaders to those who had brought on the worst days of Paris: "Very likely scores, if not hundreds of those reckless desperadoes to whom the most fiendish excesses of the days of the Commune in Paris were due, may now be here, fervid apostles of the same redhanded and blazing license." Another cried: "Bring on then the troops—the armed police—in overwhelming numbers. Bring out the Gatling guns. Let there be no fooling with blank cartridges. But let the mob know, everywhere, that for it to stand one moment after it has been ordered by proper authorities to disperse, will be to be shot down in its tracks. . . . A little of the vigor of the first Napoleon is the thing we need now."[4]

Most if not all of the violence of the period was spontaneous and unrehearsed, arising out of the natural proclivities of men in groups, intensified by fury against unseen enemies. Enough evidence was at hand, however, to suggest that there might be premeditated violence in the offing. Anarchists were out in the open: men who believed in direct action, assassination for the common good. An anarchist conference in Berne, Switzerland, had promulgated as early as 1876 the principle of "propaganda by the deed," which had been interpreted to mean terroristic acts against individuals, and it lay back of the activities of an organization known as the People's Will, culminating in the assassination of Czar Alexander II of Russia in 1881. Organizations accepting the principle of propaganda by the deed existed in Chicago during the 1880's, their members regularly drilling with arms, learning to fashion homemade bombs, and saying openly that the overthrow of capitalism by force would be necessary before any important social change could be brought about.[5]

Background fear of such groups had a bearing on the Haymarket Riot in Chicago and on the hysterical comments that followed. When 160 Chicago police ordered a crowd gathered in the Haymarket on May Day 1886 to disperse, someone threw a bomb and seven policemen were killed; many others were injured. In a trial where the atmosphere crackled with tension, eight anarchists were convicted of conspiracy; four were hanged.

Sympathy of much of the religious press lay with the authorities and it was expressed with such emphasis as to reveal abysmal bewilderment over the way things were going. One church paper declared, "A mob should be crushed by knocking down or shooting down the men engaged in it; and the more promptly this is done the better." *The Christian Advocate* was stern: "To talk about pity, sympathy or delay in connection with such demons, is to encourage their kind; to speak of their offense as political, is to hide their character and engender the sentiment that breeds them."[6]

Wretched as conditions were in the 1880's, there was worse to come: another strike against virtually all the railroads simultaneously, affecting the vitals of the American system of business. Also sorely affected was the convenience and comfort of the traveling public, and the fact that the strike arose out of the sleeping-car industry showed just how complicated comfort had become. A New Yorker living in Chicago, George Mortimer Pullman, finally perfected with a partner the device for folding away the upper berth of a railroad coach on which passengers could go to bed. By 1867 the Pullman Palace Car Company was in business and the energy and get-up-and-go Pullman put into the business made it the greatest car-building organization in the world.

Meanwhile at a town he named for himself in Illinois, site of his plant, Pullman set up rows of cottages, all very neat and orderly, in which his workers were said to live contentedly at a modest rent. Shopping was convenient in the company store. Religious leaders cited Pullman, Illinois, as a new phase of industrial development. There the employer had the interest of the workers at heart. In 1894, however, the Pullman Company reduced wages about 25 percent, having been smitten by heavy losses as a result of the panic of 1893. At the same time the company did not reduce rents workers had to pay in the company town or prices workers had to pay in the company store.

There was no union but the workers sent a committee of protest to call upon Pullman. He did not yield but rather dismissed from his employ some of the members of the committee. About four thousand Pullman employees then joined the new American Railway Union, headed by Eugene V. Debs. The union had won a strike the month before against the Great Northern, and with 150,000 members, was ready to go places. But Pullman was not willing to negotiate with the American Railway Union. In the face of this refusal, and against the advice of Debs, the Union ordered its members not to handle Pullman cars, which were everywhere cut out of trains. By June thirty railroads throughout the country were tied up by the strike. The mails being affected, federal judges issued an injunction against the union's interference with interstate commerce. The union defied the injunction, Debs was arrested, and President Cleveland sent federal troops to Chicago. This move in turn provoked rioting and widespread destruction of property as far away as California. By early July troops were riding the trains and by the middle of that month the strike was broken.

Church opinion was again on the side of settlement by force, approving the injunction and the use of federal troops. But this time there was a change. One voice was raised in defense of the strike and the strikers. It was the voice of the Methodist preacher at Pullman—William H. Carwardine. He described the atmosphere surrounding the workers as poisoned by espionage and petty tyranny. He denounced as lies press stories of high wages and contributions to relief. The town, he said, "is a civilized relic of European serfdom. We all enjoy living here because there is an equality of interest, and we have a common enemy, the Company, but our daily prayer is, 'Lord keep us from dying here.'"

Carwardine put his views in a sermon preached in Chicago. It was published in the Chicago *Herald* and later embraced in a book. He spoke up out of experience and he told firsthand of the tyranny of the company and pictured the "dangerous inequalities and class gulfs" that existed in the company and its town, thus bringing his contemporaries a view of what the world beyond the ends of their noses was getting to be like. He argued for compulsory arbitration and, if the management refused, suggested that the plants ought to be seized and operated in the public interest. He saw no wisdom in using the force of the government solely on the side of the company.[7]

By degrees, but more precisely by experience, Methodist preachers began to have some of the same acquaintance with the industrial world that they had once had with pioneer and rural society. They found out what was going on and, when they did, many rapidly adapted themselves and their message to the times. Not given much to theorizing, they were good at practice and then evolving theories based on practice. The man, for example, who became Methodism's most ardent advocate of social change, Harry F. Ward, got his start and many of his views by taking over in 1895 a run-down and virtually abandoned church on Wabash Avenue in Chicago and transforming it into a center where the kind of people often ignored by Methodists found a home and a center of education as well as religion.

At the beginning of the twentieth century, disorders arising out of the conflict between capital and labor were no longer spectacular. They were commonplace, permeating the consciousness all the more and bringing the problems of industrial society home to people in widespread areas. During the thirty-month period following January 1902, no fewer than 180 union men were killed, 1651 injured, and over 5000 arrested. A spirited Methodist writer of a later day described the situation in general but vivid terms: "Labor faced mammoth corporate empires; tough captains of industry; a hostile Congress and state legislatures and courts; armies of scabs, spies, and hired thugs; and, above all, almost unbroken enmity of the middle-class white-collar and farming America and its allies—the schools, the press, indeed the churches."[8]

In these circumstances certain lay and clerical leaders of The Methodist Episcopal Church drew together for a two-day discussion in Washington, D.C. The aim was to form an agency to stimulate study by the Church of neglected social problems. The men who initiated the Washington meeting were men of balance, not flighty. One was Herbert Welch, president of Ohio Wesleyan University. Welch was described by an associate as "a man of profound scholarship and ripe wisdom, of infinite tact and inexhaustible patience."[9] He represented the Wesleyan conscience at its most perceptive, and his moderation and temperance carried him on to the remarkable age of 106 and gave him a chance to sum up change in a book entitled *As I Recall My Past Century.*

Such men lent the agency a thoughtful mien, one showing the desire to widen awareness rather than to leap at once into any single program of reform. The name chosen was The Methodist Federation for Social Service. Its status was ideal for its purpose. It would operate within the Church and be allowed to call itself Methodist but it would not be a part of the corporate structure. Thus freedom of inquiry and outspokenness was assured. The Federation could explore and recommend but it did not commit. Many advantages besides range and latitude came from the arrangement. One was that it invited minds to concentrate on the problems of society. It was a hall where men could be heard and, knowing that there would be some attention paid, they were encouraged to speak and write in a definite direction, being no longer left to general comment or occasional sermons. Those active in the writing and thinking of the Federation had also the hope that their statements and recommendations would be considered on merit by the General Conference.

The setup was according to structure and it worked out according to plan. In 1908 the General Conference of The Methodist Episcopal Church recognized the Federation, accepted memorials it presented, and asked the new body to do some research into such specific matters as how the curricula of theological seminaries and courses of study for young preachers within the Church could be changed or modified better to "prepare our preachers for efficiency in social reform."[10]

The Federation was also asked to discover and recommend the ways in which The Methodist Episcopal Church could best cooperate with other denominations in stressing the social gospel. For Methodists it was a day of awakening and back to the spirit of the camp meetings when they had worked with other groups toward a common objective. The objective was still common but it was much more difficult to attain. Now help was needed from any human source as well as from on high. They got an abundance of it from a Baptist. In 1907 appeared *Christianity and the Social Crisis* by Walter Rauschenbusch, a book of such cogency and spirit that it was accepted as the classic statement of faith for all who thought that society must be changed fundamentally through religious motives. Salvation could no longer be limited to the regeneration of individuals.

It was a point Methodists had begun to act on, but Rauschenbusch rounded out the argument and put it so unforgettably that those who were familiar with it seemed to see it for the first time.

One reason for the effectiveness of the book was that Rauschenbusch came by his views through the knowledge of experience. He served for eleven years as the pastor of the Second German Baptist Church in New York City. Here he found what was at the bottom of the barrel in a region genially known as Hell's Kitchen. Some mischief was always cooking. Those who tried to live upright lives were often pushed into evil ways. He saw "men out of work, out of shoes, out of hope." When times were bad, as they often were, men and women and children were casualties of circumstance. They were castoffs. Boys turned to gangsters, little girls to harlots, and the aged and destitute suffered indescribable misery for which neither church nor society offered more than temporary relief.

It was in this desolate area in the city of dreadful nights that Rauschenbusch got into his blood the ideas he later got into his books. He still believed in conversion. He had undergone a deep religious experience himself, but he now saw that salvation must be social. It was one thing, as a Methodist bishop later phrased it, to have a nation of converted individuals and quite another to have a converted nation. Bishop F. Gerald Ensley later interpreted the views of Rauschenbusch to mean: "Salvation always begins with a change in the individual, *but it must change him completely*—in his business attitude, his political allegiance, his behavior toward race and class, as well as in his face-to-face relationships."[11]

In the year after the publication of *Christianity and the Social Crisis* the General Conference of The Methodist Episcopal Church adopted the Methodist Social Creed, calling for elementary reforms such as ending the atrocity of child labor and the regulation of conditions of labor for women—three years ahead of the Triangle Waist Company fire in New York that took 147 lives. The statement of needed reforms was taken over and, with slight alterations, became the Social Creed of the Churches in the newly formed Federal Council of the Churches of Christ in America, the first organized cooperative body of Protestant churchmen. The main Methodist bodies, black and white, were among the founding members of the Council. A bishop of the Church South, E. R. Hendrix, was made its first president, and, as a part of the opening convention, Hendrix and a vice-president of the American Federation of Labor addressed a special meeting on church and labor, said by one labor official to have been the largest gathering of laboring men he had ever seen in Philadelphia.

The Methodists had come down out of the clouds. They began to mingle with men of like mind, regardless of affiliation, and often those who were trying to think in terms of applying Christian principles to the conduct of institutions found that they had more in common with men and women of other denominations than they did with some members of their own. The term *Methodism* broadened. It had to. In radically changed circumstances and in the presence of new beliefs publicly declared, there were many shades of meaning to the term. Yet it not only remained in force but actually provided a cohesiveness strong enough to accommodate variety—even variance, in fact.

Several Methodists were prominent in the program proposed by the Interchurch World Movement, an agency formed right after the world war with plans as ambitious (some said grandiose) as its name. The aim was in part to enlist the interest of the general public, including the unchurched, in considering social issues and the part religion might play in helping the world recover—start over, in fact—after a period of war, strife, and disenchantment.

Chairman of the executive committee of the Interchurch World Movement was a highly vocal Methodist layman, John R. Mott, a friend or acquaintance of many of the noted political leaders of various countries around the globe and as much of a declaimer as any preacher. Head of the industrial department was Frederick Bohn Fisher, one of the esteemed preachers of the

Church North, a rational and philosophical advocate in the cause of prohibition and a staunch defender of the enforcement program. Also on the executive committee was a bishop of The Methodist Episcopal Church, South, James Cannon, Jr., a fiery and warlike zealot who had the nose of his interest in many enterprises, including and in particular, enforcement.

From Fisher came the suggestion that the Interchurch World Movement investigate the steel strike, and the man chosen to be chairman of the specially appointed commission to do the work was Francis J. McConnell, a bishop of The Methodist Episcopal Church. To round out the picture of Methodist diversity in the period and to show the extremes involved in any approach to the problems of the hour, the chairman of the board of the United States Steel Corporation was Elbert Henry Gary, a devout Methodist layman, firm in his faith and fervent in his convictions.

Gary completed the cast of leading characters in the drama of social change played out under a broad Methodist canvas at the onset of the twenties. Seventy-four at the time the strike began, Gary was a kindly man, immensely successful. Having been a corporation lawyer, he bore the honorary title of Judge, and it bespoke his smooth manner and suggested his dignity. He took pride in the great concern U. S. Steel had shown in its mills for the safety of the worker under highly hazardous conditions. He and his managers felt that their wages were fair and the Judge had plans for increased benefits and for the sharing of stock. He was precise and scrupulous in his business dealings and fancied himself altogether fair in his dealings with his 191,000 employes. He occasionally walked through some of the mills.[12]

As Judge Gary testified later before a U. S. Senate investigating committee, he gave positive orders that his men be treated well at all times. These orders were issued repeatedly and put in writing to the presidents of the subsidiary companies that made up U. S. Steel. He had the innocence of the eminently successful businessman, underscored by the philosophy of the old-time Methodism: I made good—why can't others?

Both the general kindness Gary displayed and the ability in management he demonstrated in his vast enterprise followed a Methodist upbringing. A highly energetic lad, he had worked and grubbed endless hours on a farm in his boyhood, and he never forgot it. He went to a Methodist college and entered actively into the work of his church at Wheaton, Illinois, when he was getting a start in his profession. He taught a young ladies' Sunday-school class and developed a habit of homily, discoursing to the end of his days on the Bible as a full and sufficient guide for living. When he came into wealth he made large donations to the Wheaton Church in memory of his mother and his father. His ability at organization was attested by the fact that in 1903 J. P. Morgan chose him to put together the complex of the United States Steel Corporation and entrusted him with its management.

Bishop McConnell had also been brought up on a farm and he had gone to a Methodist college. But he had gone to a theological seminary, too, and had entered the ministry. His background was much more professionally religious. His father was a Methodist preacher and his mother had taken as direct a part in politics as a woman of the 1890's was allowed to. She would go out in her buggy before elections and talk with people about issues, often commenting when she returned on "soft heads"—her name for people who didn't believe that religion had anything to do with political and social issues.

Frank McConnell had himself shown a full measure of competence, having been elected a bishop in 1912 at the age of forty-one. Before that age he had been pastor of five Methodist churches and president of DePauw University. There he had shown that he was not lacking in organizing ability or a way with money, having put on a financial campaign that doubled the university's endowment.[13]

The decision of the churchmen to investigate the background of the steel strike was not taken until a week and a half after it began on September 22, 1919. A hundred ministers meeting in New York at the invitation of the Interchurch World Movement discussed the strike and the public ignorance of its causes and the methods by which it was being handled. Nothing but statistics had got into the papers and these statistics were so dazzling that they almost crowded out any occasion for curiosity. The strike, involving a total of 365,000 workers, counting some who struck in sympathy, was by far the largest strike in history. Not since 1892, when the Carnegie Steel Company, aided by the state militia, had broken up a strike staged at Homestead, Pennsylvania, had there been any attempt to unionize the growing steel industry.

Beginning in 1918, organizers from the American Federation of Labor had been busy in the plants of U. S. Steel. By June 1919 the A.F. of L. claimed 100,000 members. Samuel Gompers, president of the union, felt he could lead from strength and he addressed a letter to the head of U. S. Steel and suggested that he and his associates might have a talk with representatives of the labor force about working arrangements. Judge Gary did not answer the letter.

Organization of the workers went on apace. In August union officials took a ballot of members and got an astonishing 98 percent vote in support of a strike. Again Judge Gary was approached. This time the chairman of the board answered courteously but firmly, saying that the corporation would not discuss with representatives of a labor union "any matter relating to employees." The strike call then went out. Two hundred thousand copies were printed in seven languages. The call was issued to laborers in the entire steel industry.[14] It was clear from the number of languages in which the call was printed that the preponderance of strikers involved were foreigners, unable to speak or comprehend English. They were called hunkeys and polacks and said to be under Bolshevik influence.

To get back of the black headlines and to get at the members of the human species engaged in the strike, was the aim of the commission headed by McConnell. It set out to raise two questions with the workers: Why did you strike? (Or refuse to strike.) What do you want? The third question affected management chiefly: What means of *conference* exist in the steel mills?[15]

Those who carried on the investigation found the answer to the last question first. Both labor and management agreed that the occasion of the strike was Gary's denial of a conference requested by organized labor. If the investigators needed any further firsthand confirmation of the lack of a conference atmosphere, they got it when they sought a hearing with Gary. He let McConnell cool his heels for two hours in his office waiting room. S. Parkes Cadman, a distinguished preacher of the day who started out as a Methodist, said that to keep McConnell waiting was the worst mistake of Gary's life.[16] It showed a complete failure to understand both the importance of the inquiry and the nature of the man charged with the chief responsibility for carrying it out. McConnell had been a distance runner as a boy. Once two men wagered five dollars on whether the preacher's kid could catch a wayward calf. The boy agreed to try, but he did not sprint or put on a burst of speed, as the men expected. He simply jogged along after the calf all afternoon until the animal, bewildered and exhausted, gave in.[17]

The boy grown to bishop used the same tactics in dealing with the uncommunicative men who held responsible positions in the plants that made up the United States Steel Corporation. At first these officials were indifferent and disdainful of preachers who thought they had the savvy to grasp the intricacies of big business. Later they showed an admixture of amusement and scorn. In the case of McConnell they overlooked the fact that the Methodists chose their bishops for administrative ability, not theological erudition. They were executives with a businesslike approach to practical problems, and McConnell, with all his humanitarian zeal, was a money-raiser and a man conscious of dollars and cents.

In a Pennsylvania city the president of a steel company asked to see the bishop and, when he came, told him politely that it was a mistake for him to get mixed up in a situation that touched on facts and figures. The president cited the wage scale in one of his departments. McConnell told him, "I want to give you full credit for your wage scale. In fact, the hourly wage scale in that department is ten cents higher than you have said." The president replied, "I have the wage scale right here, and I'll show you." An assistant handed him a sheet and the two men consulted it. McConnell's recollection had been right.[18]

Members of the commission, including Daniel A. Poling, editor of *The Christian Herald,* vice-chairman of the commission, and a representative of the United Evangelical Church, talked with steelworkers and their families in homes and on the streets of the mill towns. They examined some five hundred statements from strikers and nonstrikers. Talks with man after man revealed feelings that could not get into company reports but that had entered into the incentive to strike.

The preachers were trying to discover what steel work did to human values. One man told McConnell how he had the Sunday before buried his daughter, twelve years of age, "and as I stood by her grave, I thought, 'I have never had a chance to know this child. I was too tired when I got home from work, or she was already in bed, and I am burying my own flesh and blood, and yet a stranger to me.'" A Pole made his first public speech in English at a strikers' meeting: "Just like horse and wagon. Put horse in wagon, work all day. Take horse out of wagon—put in stable. Take horse out of stable, put in wagon. Same way like mills. Work all day. Come home—go sleep. Get up, go work in mills, come home. . . ."[19]

The statistical data, when put together and made precise, proved to be as sad as the stories told by some of the men and their families. It was found that more than half of all workers were subjected to the twelve-hour day. One-half of these were forced to work seven days a week. A worker could not elect to lay off at the end of eight hours. He could not bargain over his job hours. The average time of work for all employees was 68.7 hours per week, or over 11.4 hours per day on a six-day mathematical average. And this was in a day when the rest of industry was giving in to the eight-hour day. The British steel industry had abolished the twelve-hour day in 1915. In the United States, a hundred years before, the hours per day had been reduced to ten for workers on government projects.

The commission's report stated that it was the twelve-hour day that drove steelworkers to despair and had driven them into the strike. Critics of the inquiry charged that McConnell was a Bolshevik and claimed that the workers were striking for a classless state. But the commission found no ideology had any influence on the workers. "Of the hundreds of strikers and non-strikers interviewed . . . few could put together two sentences on 'soviets' but almost all discoursed on, or more accurately, cursed 'long hours.' "[20]

The inquiry, being honest and of wide range, turned up attitudes sobering and instructive to churchmen. Steelworkers had little or no interest in religion of any kind. McConnell said that "a fair and comprehensive history of the strike would not require mention of either the Protestant Church or the Catholic Church." The minds of the men were on daily bread, and when the strike ended they were not looking forward to what the church could do for them but to the next strike. The next one might succeed and it might somehow improve their lot. The church was regarded as hand-in-glove with industry. As one old laborer put it, "The preacher points your eyes to heaven, and then the boss picks your pocket."[21]

The strike was broken January 8, 1920, and the workers straggled back to their jobs. It had gained the men nothing, not one solitary concession, after having cost them $112,000,000 in lost wages. In the violence of it twenty had been killed and hundreds injured.

The investigation did not end with the strike because it continued to seek causes. The churchmen kept on the job for another six weeks, and by the time the field work was done and the report prepared for the commission that had authorized it seven months had elapsed. It was July 27, 1920, before a copy of the full report was laid on the desk of the President of the United States, stating that only the authority of the federal government would make further inquiry possible and remedies feasible.

At first blush the report accomplished no more than the strike. Nothing could be directly traced to its publication a year after the strike was over—nothing you could hang your hat on. Yet certain conditions which had been hidden or obscure were now plain. Even the steel men, who had relied on hired informers, began to know what was going on in their plants. So did the public. All that can be said is that after the investigation the twelve-hour day and the seven-day week were by degrees eliminated. As early as April 18, 1920, the chairman of U. S. Steel announced that the majority of its executives were in favor of abolishing the twelve-hour day. He referred to public sentiment as a factor in arriving at this judgment and said that he hoped for a decrease in working hours "in the comparatively near future."

When the "long turn at the shifts" was formally ended in July 1923, management showed some satisfaction in the improvement that had come about. One official said, "It didn't cost us any more to be human. Production went up and absenteeism declined."[22] The twelve-hour day had gone the way of the lash. Another item in man's inhumanity had been crossed off the list. Some writers said jubilantly that the steel industry had yielded to the religious forces of America. The claim would have been hard to substantiate, and it was not necessary to do so. It was enough that the churches felt the strength of their new ethic. The Methodist press responded favorably when the *Report of the Steel Strike of 1919* was finally published late in 1920. *Zion's Herald* defended the right of the Church to investigate, accepted and stressed the evidence that conditions in the industry were bad, and urged a wide reading of the report. The steel strike and its ramifications must be made part of the Methodist educational experience.

There was enough in the response to show that those closely

identified with the inquiry were not regarded as odd creatures working in isolation but messengers of a trend. What heartened McConnell was the attitude of the Pittsburgh Annual Conference, of which he was the episcopal head at the time of the investigation. The natural supposition, as he pointed out, was that the Conference, in the center of a group of industrial leaders, would be tied hand and foot to the steel industry. Also the bishop had been widely attacked and brought some measure of public reproach on the Church. There was no reason why the preachers and laymen assembled should not keep silence. Not at all. The body approved the report and supported the plan for its publication.

XXVIII To Serve the Present Age

Far back of what appeared to be a sudden flood of Methodist interest in society lay headwaters of many and varied sources long in the making.

In the teaching and enlightened labors of John Wesley in his own day there was abundant precedent for the religious person to do what he could in practical ways to ameliorate the lot of the unfortunate. The founder of the Societies had proclaimed, "The Gospel of Christ knows no religion but social; no holiness but social holiness." To turn Christianity into "a solitary religion," he had said, "is indeed to destroy it." In 1740 Mr. Wesley started an employment bureau. "In 1746 he promoted a loan fund to stake men in the development of small business. He conducted a charity school, organized a free dispensary, ran an orphan's home, establishing a home for poor widows, and supported a Stranger's Friend Society for the indigent. Wesley himself begged and collected for the poor to the end of his life. . . . He advised that all resources above one's necessities be devoted to the welfare of society."[1]

A strong reminder of the Wesleyan emphasis on welfare as a part of genuine religion came in 1880 when a commissioner and seven women workers of the Salvation Army from Great

Britain established a branch in Pennsylvania. The origin and activities of the Army recapitulated and re-enacted some of Mr. Wesley's own experience with the established Church of his day. The founders of the Army, William Booth and his wife Catherine, had left British Methodism because, as Booth's biographer put it, the Conference "wanted the machine to run smoothly." The young preacher had insisted upon going out and talking in the fields and tents and theaters and warehouses to the rag, tag, and bobtail, the riffraff of England, the very dregs of society. The Conference had insisted that the young preacher desist from his practices. When hailed before a session of the Conference and confronted with a choice of leaving or obeying the orders of the elders, Booth had had the decision taken out of his hands. His wife, devoted both to the importance of the work and to her husband, arose from a seat in the balcony, exclaiming, "Never!" Booth bowed to the chair and walked off the floor to the accompaniment of cries of "Order! Order!"[2]

The Booths had continued their preaching work with great success under variously named societies until the Salvation Army was chosen as a title in 1878. Arriving in the United States at a time when the Methodists were beginning to wake up to the concealed but ubiquitous poverty and degradation of the cities, the Army brought home a discarded aspect of the Wesleyan milieu. It not only addressed its message to the hapless and the derelict but it also added soup to the offer of salvation and approached the whole man, treating him as a person to be helped. Although urgently evangelistic, Army workers were not content with exhortation but labored to meet whatever needs they found, going so far as to try to get men and women temporary jobs to aid their rehabilitation so that, once renewed in faith or saved, they might take a responsible part in society.

The Army's combination of evangelistic zeal and practical care, of calling on sinners to be born again and of helping them to their feet for a new start, brought to memory also an earlier soul and social concern in American Methodism—that fostered by the holiness movement. In *Revivalism and Social Reform* Timothy L. Smith has examined and documented the generally overlooked connection between the experience of sanctification and the desire to move out and be of immediate service to one's fellows. It was as natural as cause and effect, and there were many instances in which the connection was demonstrated. Mrs. Phoebe Palmer, inspired by the idea of perfect love as the crowning obligation of the Christian life, had shown a genius for good works, identifying herself with many uplift programs that promised to improve the lot of the unfortunate in the cities, including the New York Female Assistance Society for the Relief and Religious Instruction of the Sick Poor. Relief came first.

It was Mrs. Palmer who in the 1850's provided the moving spirit in the prophetic project that led to Five Points Mission in New York—a model long followed by Protestant churches working in the slums. It was the prototype of the institutional church, an entity ideally suited to the Methodist frame of mind and, after the Civil War, when men turned again to the way of kindness, it multiplied throughout urban centers in the North. The institutional church afforded diversity in activities aimed at human improvement, rewarded managerial efficiency, and fitted aptly into the jigsaw of structure. It allowed local workers and pastors range and imagination and at the same time backed their efforts with the resources of the Church at large. It also lent itself to the purpose of adapting city churches to rapidly and visibly shifting circumstances.

In Cincinnati, for example, the oldest Methodist house of worship, Wesley Chapel, found itself stranded as a downtown church when its regular constituents moved to better parts of the city. Under a new and stylized program Wesley Chapel set out to offer "all-round salvation." It was "honeycombed with educational, musical and industrial appliances, doing their work along with the sermon, the Sunday school and the prayer meeting. . . ." By 1895, Wesley Chapel had a kindergarten, a day nursery, "a bureau of justice in which four lawyers gave their services to the poor, a building association in which people were taught to save toward a home."[3]

In New York the Central Methodist Church at Seventh Avenue and Fourteenth Street was transformed, after it had served its middle-class function, into the Metropolitan Temple, under the direction of S. Parkes Cadman, recently arrived from England and at that time a Methodist. Other Methodist churches in the neighborhood disbanded and threw in their equipment, personnel, and membership. The consolidation enabled the Temple, by the use of both lay and clerical help, to hold fifty services a week, breaking with the tradition of two at fixed hours. "Every 'legitimate method of reaching men' was pressed into service." Activities and enterprises included choral societies, a reading room, an employment bureau, an athletic association, young people's organizations, a sewing school and millinery and dressmaking classes. There was not only a kindergarten but also a normal institute to train kindergarten teachers along the lines laid down by Friedrich Froebel.[4]

The consolidated beehive at the Metropolitan Temple showed a pattern by which the Methodists would cut their program to reach people they had in their exuberance neglected. They would merge churches. And then they would form societies to back the merged churches and organize all the merged churches into a union so that each could gain from the experience of the others.

During the last two decades of the century the Methodists founded nearly fifty of what they called church extension societies and then federated them to boot. It was all carefully directed and fully approved by the bishops, made alert to the new problems of the cities by the labors of men who took part in mission work. The bishops endorsed the church extension societies in 1888 and, approving the work done eight years later, put into the journal of the General Conference this declaration: "Methodism in our cities should be slow to abandon what are called downtown populations because of change from native to foreign, rich to poor. The greater the change the more need of remaining. Combine the plants, if need be; adapt the services to the new surroundings but remain and save the people."⁵

It was all very businesslike and according to the Methodist Hoyle and faithfully recorded. By the end of the century the Methodists knew that in New York alone they had expended over two and a half million dollars and set up forty-five separate enterprises to help new churches in the city and to shore up those that had been weakened by shifts in population. Missions became part of the approved activity of the Church at large in the North. They had sanction. And not a few. Methodist laymen of wealth caught the vision in the muck and gave generously to the cause of putting the Church back in touch with the people. Some saw mud and some saw stars.

Horace Benton, a drug manufacturer of Cleveland, Ohio, put together a set of ganglia called the National City Evangelization Union of The Methodist Episcopal Church. No one but a Methodist could have thought it up. The Union was a highly and skillfully organized body that brought together ministers and laymen of the churches "for the prosecution of movements necessitating concurrent action." There were church extension societies that provided and often raised money to keep Methodists in touch with the poor. And, in addition, there was a band of preachers and laymen getting together locally and in national conventions just to make sure that the attack on poverty and its results got full attention from the total membership of the church. It was freely stated that "if you wish to prevent the perpetuation of slum life, you may well understand that it will not be done altogether by direct evangelization."⁶

All over the North, where the urban glut was greatest, the Methodists had their well-rounded missions that looked to the welfare of the needy and to the trends of change. Allen Street Memorial Church in New York, for example, was once a flourishing family church on the Lower East Side. Then the Jews invaded the neighborhood in great numbers and there was no circumstance for continuing a Methodist family church. Allen

Street Memorial was re-established a few blocks away on Rivington Street, with facilities for serving all comers.

Methodism, priding itself on being connectional, with a system of nerves that joined the head and the heels, had good internal communications. A job well done in one place was likely to be known in other places and, before long, even at headquarters. In 1900 the General Conference of the Church North realized that the General Missionary Society had been neglecting the city churches in favor of frontier churches and missions in foreign fields. The General Conference told the General Missionary Society to cooperate with and back up the city mission societies and then it took a stand without precedent in the system of the itinerancy. It told the presiding elders of the districts in cities to consider social service first of all and to abolish the time limit on urban pastorates.[7] A Methodist preacher was now to stay put—if he was doing a good job and if he had going a program that required continuity for completion.

Methodism had returned from the West. The revivalism which was part of the camp meetings and that continued in the holiness movement had invigorated its ethic and brought a vitality not to be despised. But this vitality was less surprising than the adaptability the Church showed in meeting the unpredicted. Its first genius had been displayed by itinerants on the frontier. It was a church body highly mobile and always in search of new territory, in the van of migrations and emotions. Now it had begun in its own organized way to find the means of affecting beneficently a new society which people of its own temper had helped to create, a society by no means ideal and in sore need of help.

By the end of the nineteenth century the Church was wide enough in geographical spread to embrace and feel the influence of forces from all directions. In it East and West met while North and South worked toward getting together and influenced each other in the process. The East included migratory ideas from Britain and Europe. The East was in broad terms likely to be theoretical and the West energetically practical. But the main point is that Methodism brought together influences of all sorts from all directions and gave them a theater in which to operate, especially at a time of emerging social interest.

Harry Frederick Ward was English, a Londoner educated in the Midwest. He had arrived in 1891 and had enrolled in Northwestern, working his way through. In time he became a student pastor of the ramshackle and rundown Wabash Avenue Methodist Church in Chicago. It was in a tough neighborhood inhabited by persons of many nationalities and many creeds and none, but with common physical needs. Ward socialized the Church, working through ministers who knew the tongues of those they taught. Back of him in his program to meet the daily practical demands of seekers after faith and bread made was the City Extension Society of Chicago and the National City Evangelization Union of The Methodist Episcopal Church. The ardent spirit of the young preacher had the support of the giant organization of which he was a part.

Four years after Harry Ward had undertaken the work on Wabash Avenue he was ordained. Like Walter Rauschenbusch, he was affected intellectually as well as emotionally by what he encountered in industrialized America. He became pastor of a respectable church in a Chicago suburb, but already he had begun to write provocative interpretations of the Christian message and to challenge his fellow Methodists to look at the current scene in the light of social ethics. He went on to teach in Boston Theological Seminary, became chairman of the American Civil Liberties Union and professor of Christian ethics at Union Theological Seminary in New York. There, as well as in his travels and lectures, Ward inseminated young minds with ideas. He was a thinker, a searcher, a teacher, and a prophet of old—Amos with statistics.

At a time when Ward was talking in gifted and animated generalities about such matters as the rapprochement between organized labor and organized religion there were an estimated 500,000 homeless, shiftless, unproductive vagrants in the United States. It was said that their annual cost to the public was $100,-

000,000 and that the railroads lost $25,000,000 as a result of their depredations.[8]

Another preacher, Edgar James Helms, was at the same time dealing firsthand, directly, personally, and yet in a thoroughly organized way with men made vagrants by what Ward considered unjust and inequitable features of the economic order. The intellectual dealt with causes, the missioner with effects. Helms in his efforts to redeem individuals caught in the maw of impersonal industry was more traditionally Methodist and more representative of the social awakening taking place within the Church than was Ward. Yet Helms also was affected by new emphases and he dealt with men in the light of their circumstances as he moved toward a cooperative and intricate work program that took advantage both of the nature of society and the Methodist talent for fitting people and functions into structure.

There is no sign in any of the writings of Helms that he wanted to reconstitute the social order on Christian grounds or form a society that did not have victims. He did not cry out against malefactors of great wealth or exhort the Church to become Christian. Rather in the worst slums of Boston during the far-from-gay nineties and in the depression-ridden days of the 1900's he dealt on a day-to-day basis with men and families out of work and without the simplest necessities. He established and tested the principle of making men out of rubbish, of lending self-respect through work to those degraded by poverty. He brought from the West and communicated to the foreign-born living in an eastern city some of the self-reliance and resourcefulness that belonged to the region of his upbringing.

The parents of Edgar Helms were God-fearing Methodist people, strict and simple in their faith. They were also American. One of the boy's grandfathers had been the youngest soldier in George Washington's forces, a fifer, no less, who was allowed to roam with the army because he had such a cheerful and stirring effect on the men.[9]

Two years after Edgar was born near Malone in northern

New York in 1863, the family headed west in a covered wagon with all household belongings. They were destined for Iowa, where the father had a brother who assured him that there would be a church there and that they would soon feel at home. In Iowa the lad was brought up. He early learned from his father some of the lessons of resourcefulness and ingenuity that he was to apply later.

The first lesson came with a plague of locusts as bad as any that ever befell Pharaoh. The first crop on the new farm was far enough along to hold the buds of promise when the swarms filled the sky—silently at the outset, then with a buzz, and then a roar. They descended on the hapless countryside, laid it waste, left nothing standing, not even the scrawny and solitary geranium Edgar's sister, Alzina, had growing in the yard. It was as if a giant hand had mauled the earth, mashing everything flat. Corn and forage were gone. Seed for next year's crops now were only a thought that had perished in the attack, along with every growing thing.

Young Ed went out with his father to study the land and guess the toll. There was not much to do but to stare. He heard his mother's lament as he left. "What are we going to do?" she asked her husband. And he heard his father answer, "I don't know," and then add firmly, "but *something*."[10]

In the course of the day Ed's father rigged up a trough on wheels with a sail at the back of it. To this contraption he hitched a team and drove around the lakeside near the house. What grasshoppers were left, swarmed against the sail, were stunned and dropped into the trough. When it was filled father and son dumped the catch into barrels. "I'll feed the turkeys and hogs with them," Ed's father explained.

Turkeys and hogs fared well enough to sell for cash enough to buy seeds for the next crop and grain for the horses.

The Helms family eked by, but the swarm was only the first of four that came year after year. The boy became acquainted with the destitution that befalls people, the misery that comes from being without food or work even when people have the best of intentions and lead good lives. And he watched his father cope, one way or another, and even help pay the preacher, the Reverend William Preston. His sympathies quickened by the experience of those around him, but he also came to the conclusion, much to his father's disappointment, that farming was no way to make a living. It did not suit him. He wanted the world of words. Young Helms impressed the local editor who offered him a job as a printer's devil in the county newspaper office. By the time Helms was eighteen he owned two small-town newspapers and was ready for a fling at politics. The fling was not successful but the papers were. He ran them while he attended Cornell College at Mount Vernon, Iowa, two hundred miles away from the towns where his papers were.

The papers prospered. Helms knew that he could become well-to-do if not actually rich by staying in the newspaper business. But he had an urge to religion that would not down. He had little interest in the theories of religion and, in conversations with his mother, discounted what people believed, laying stress constantly on the importance of Christian behavior. He had gone forward and given his hand in a Methodist revival meeting, seeking later some assurance that he had enjoyed conversion through the act.

Such a conversion was far from the norm, however, and Helms was never satisfied with it. When he finally made his decision it was by logic and determination. Yielding to the long and subtle influence of his mother, he decided, after wrestling all one night in prayer, that he would go into the ministry, train himself thoroughly and then ask for the hardest assignment anywhere anyone could find. The decision made, he announced it, asked his fiancée, Jean Preston, daughter of the Methodist preacher of his childhood, if she would go with him into the ministry, then set about in a businesslike way selling his newspaper properties. The sale netted enough to get him through his final year at Cornell and to see him on his way to the Boston Theological Seminary.

Later in Boston he plunged into mission work while he did his theological training. Jean followed him a year later and began training as a deaconess. Meanwhile Helms had his ey on India and he made representations to the mission authorities to send him and Jean to that difficult field. However, funds were short and those who took the India assignment would have to agree to go for five years without marrying. Helms was sorely disappointed and it looked for a while as if he would have to accept some assignment at home.

He and Jean married and applied to the Methodist Missionary and Church Extension Society of Boston, run by a board which had a sense of the needs of the various areas of the city.

The proposal Helms put before the Society was that he and his wife and friends from the seminary be allowed to set up a settlement house along the lines of Toynbee Hall in London and Hull House, which Jane Addams had started in Chicago. The essential of a settlement was that the workers would settle in and identify themselves with unfortunate persons in a run-down section of a city and make the settlement house the focus of a new community which it would attempt to create. Workers settled. They put down stakes, as settlers had in the West. They did not preach and run, go down to do good and go home. They lived where they worked. Necessary to the scheme was a program that offered a fare beyond worship or evangelistic services, one that would experiment with ways to round out the lives of people with limited resources. The idea was new enough to appeal to the young man from the West.

The City Missionary Society owned the former home of Lyman Beecher on Charter Street in Boston's North End and it was here that the Helms and their friends were asked to start their settlement. The work there was intended to help Italian immigrants who were homesick, disillusioned with America and, Helms soon found, horribly exploited and cheated by Italian padrones and Yankee contractors. Immigrants were charged preposterous prices for rent, exorbitant fees for being put to work, and then, when they were paid they put their money in what they thought were banks to send to the folks back home. It never got there.

Here was a cause ideally suited to the energy and ethics of Edgar Helms. You didn't need to be a theologian to see the outrage in this kind of fleecing. The young preacher went first to the swindlers and told them to stop. They told him to mind his own business. Helms told them he would and left the men to remember his dark and piercing eyes. One was deeper in hue than the other and it gave his look a haunting and disturbing quality. Helms went to the public with the news about the treatment of the Italians and before long the whole city was talking. The swindlers threatened the young preacher but they did not silence him.

When threats didn't work, the padrones bought the only Italian newspaper in the colony and used it to abuse and lie about Helms and his staff and the settlement. Helms used to be a newspaperman himself and he bought a printing press and started a newspaper of his own and printed it in Italian, telling the immigrants what was being done to them. Next the preacher called a mass protest meeting at Faneuil Hall. The turnout was excellent and it identified some of the best citizens of Boston with the cause, among them Edward Everett Hale, at that time chaplain of the U. S. Senate, and Julia Ward Howe. The dignitaries helped Helms start a legitimate Italian bank where the immigrants could safely deposit their money and have a part of it sent back to Italy.

The next assignment that fell to the lot of Edgar and Jean Helms was in the worst slum area of Boston. The place was called Morgan Chapel and it was located at 85 Shawmut Avenue. Surrounding it were lice- and rat-infested tenements housing foreign-born waifs of the industrial era. Jean had occasionally helped in the rescue work there and Edgar had preached in the chapel to an assembly of wretched men who were lured there on Sunday mornings by the promise of a free breakfast. The chapel was Methodist and yet it wasn't. The man for whom the chapel was named, Henry Morgan, had been an evangelist who had stirred Boston with his fervor, but he had come to no good end and had left only a ruin as a monument to mark the great work he had done before his death in 1884.

Morgan had been an earnest Methodist in every respect save one. He insisted that those who joined his church must be immersed. The *Discipline* offered every convert his choice of the way to be baptized. Morgan did not. He had installed a baptistry at the foot of the pulpit and there he soused those who wanted to become members of his body of believers. This insistence on immersion did not please the authorities of the New England Conference and they repeatedly refused to ordain Henry Morgan. Moreover, the property of Morgan Chapel was his, the result of a generous gift. If Morgan joined the Conference he would have to deed his property to the great commune of the Church, for all Methodist property is owned by all Methodists. Morgan finally set up an independent Methodist Church, and in his will he left the chapel to the Unitarian Missionary Society but with the strict provision that its pulpit should always be filled by a Methodist preacher who was a member of the New England Conference.

That provision and the toughness of the neighborhood and the task accounted for the fact that the Helmses took over. They set about organizing the place. The first decision Helms made was to dispense with the free breakfast, reducing his Sunday morning congregation from 300 to 40 or thereabouts. He lit in with volunteers and cleaned the chapel from top to bottom. He used the big baptistry at the foot of the pulpit as a basin to hold water for showers he had installed in the basement.[11] Then the Helmses started a day nursery to care for the children of mothers who had to work.

In his first pastoral letter Helms announced the opening of a night school, with classes in printing, shoe repair, tailoring and carpentry, adding that if there were sufficient demand he would open classes in sign painting, dressmaking, and sewing. There followed a music school with lessons in violin, mandolin, and voice, all courses taught by volunteers Helms had rounded up. In every case there was a small charge—at the outset one dollar for thirty lessons—and if the slum dweller couldn't pay anything he could attend a free class in penmanship.

It was in these circumstances that Helms moved forward toward his great mutual self-help enterprise. It grew out of Methodism and of the man. Even under the peculiar arrangements bequeathed by Henry Morgan, of Morgan Memorial Chapel, Helms had the support of and connection with The Methodist Episcopal Church. He followed the practices that other members of the preacher fraternity of his persuasion were using all over the land when they faced the plight of the poor in cities. He was identified with his people and their lives and he knew their needs as well as their aspirations.

This sense of identification deepened his sympathies and stirred his imagination as the depression years of 1902–1905 brought unemployment and plunged proud people into desperation. First there was no work to be had, then no clothes to be found to replace rags that wore out. Helms, being of good reputation, was able to beg money from wealthy homes. In time, though, even the well-to-do stopped giving money. They still had clothes and Helms took a bag and went to Back Bay houses and gathered up castoffs for the poor. After a few expeditions he laid the clothes out in the church and invited his members to come and take what they needed.

The result shocked him beyond belief. The people stormed into the church, grabbing things right and left. They fought over the garments before he was able to take command of the situation, and only the respect in which they had long held him enabled him to quiet the throng. He saw in a flash that he had treated them as beggars. Later he set up a small shop in the church and allowed people to have clothes for whatever pittance they might possibly pay.

The shop restored the dignity of the congregation but it left much yet to be done. People cried for work. They needed wages. Helms had opened an employment office in the church and here the demand for work, some kind of work, any kind of work, grew more and more urgent as the gloom of the depression years deepened.

One day a group of the jobless called on Helms. There was no work to be had through the employment office and the men had tramped the streets and answered ads in vain. They had a strange faith that, with all their helplessness and with conditions impossible, the preacher could somehow help. Those who could speak English spoke for all, because their lot was a sadly common one. They reeled off their troubles and then almost demanded of Helms to know what he was going to do. He thought back to the days of the grasshoppers and then said in a commanding voice, "Something! I'm going to do something to help you people." He then went on to outline his scheme. He would scrounge Boston for old clothes and furniture. These would be repaired and refurbished and then sold. Those who worked on the job of repairing the goods brought in would receive small wages from the coffers of the church. They would thus be at least modestly employed while they waited for jobs with better pay to open up in regular business plants or shops. Meanwhile the cast-off clothing and furniture, skillfully cleaned and repaired, could be put on display in the church and sold at low prices to people in the impoverished neighborhood. They could have the satisfaction of buying at bargain prices rather than grabbing the items or having goods doled out to them.

The scheme Helms spontaneously proposed to his visitors made an immediate hit and it was quickly organized and it worked like a trick. It had in it all the elements needed for the success of a vast charitable enterprise. The public responded to the common sense involved. Assistants were drafted to help with the collections. Later a wagon was engaged, then a fleet of wagons, then a fleet of trucks. All sorts of goods came in: hats and ties as well as raiment of every description, clocks, umbrellas, books, bed linen, bedsteads, and other furniture. Forty years after the first faint start, the charity that runs like a business had a six-story factory in Boston, paying a thousand dollars a day in wages to persons processing rummage from 191,000 contributors.[12]

Before his death in 1942 Helms saw his idea established throughout the United States and in many countries abroad. Adaptable from the first, the program has changed to keep pace with circumstances. As wars and accidents increased the number of physically disabled, and as government took responsibility for the relief of the unemployed, emphasis fell more and more on help for the handicapped. What was later named Goodwill Industries, Inc., grew into the largest and most experienced rehabilitation agency of the modern day, with a record, as *Time* notes, equaled by no other organization in the world.[13] It developed into an independent operation beyond Methodism, yet it cannot be divorced from its religious origin. It must be seen as a part of the great awakening of Methodism to its world. This awakening had in it a remarkable balance between a strong organization and freedom of individual initiative, and it was marked in a number of ways by the conviction that men and women are more important than institutions, whether the institutions be corporations or churches.

XXIX Forever Beginning

At Kansas City in 1939 the Wesleyans formed and proclaimed a new religious entity and, at the height of the ceremonies, heard the words ring out: The Methodist Church now is! Long live The Methodist Church! It was a case, however, of "The king is dead! Long live the king!" For at Dallas in 1968 The Methodist Church ceased to be and in its place appeared another body, requiring new stationery and calling cards and bulletin boards, as well as alterations in the setup and nomenclature of governing agencies and commissions. What had been The Methodist Church became The United Methodist Church, and while the altered name suggested little difference to the public, the changes up and down the line were numerous and significant, and before the Uniting Conference ended its sessions the Methodists behaved in a way that suggested that they had never had a church before but were certainly in business now. The spirit and the tone were different. There was a firmer confidence and a fresh and forthright approach to problems that deviled the world and the age of which the Church was a part.

The Uniting Conference solemnized what was surely the most unnecessary union of church bodies in the history of denominationalism. Yet no pains had been spared to make the event possible and important. For eight committee-laden years representatives of The Methodist Church, which itself had been formed by a union of three segments of the connection originally established in Baltimore, had been meeting with delegates of the Evangelical United Brethren Church, which had been formed in 1946 by joining the United Brethren Church and the Evangelical Church. The minute details of a joint constitution for an organic embodiment of a new church had by degrees been worked out, down to the last jot and tittle.

In 1966 this constitution had been submitted to sessions of the General Conference of both The Methodist Church and the Evangelical United Brethren Church. Both official groups had met separately but simultaneously in two ballrooms of a Chicago hotel and there, after four days of deliberation, they had approved a new constitution for a new church by the necessary overriding majorities. The constitution and the arrangements for union had then in turn been duly referred to the Annual Conferences of both The Methodist Church and the Evangelical United Brethren Church. Action taken by the main legislative bodies had been ratified, with varying degrees of enthusiasm and not without some protest and dissent, by the summer of 1967, and a new church with a new name was a part of the religious firmament.

Force of habit had played its part in bringing about the new creation—habit based on the practice of putting things together instead of tearing them apart. There was no compelling reason why the Evangelical United Brethren Church and The Methodist Church should, at no small cost in money and much cost in time and travel, be mortised into one organization. Not a few members of both communions had grave doubts about the wisdom of the merging—certainly about the urgency of it. Why bother? A few of the churches here and there might be combined to meet the problems thrust forward by urbanization, but this could be done at the local level. There was no point in working out the thousand and one details required to make an organic union.

But it was done—dramatically and with a flair that gave the Uniting Conference an air of profound importance to the future of Christendom. Obviously something more than a mere business merger was at stake. The German and American Methodists, with temperaments and memories in common, did not belong apart. It was a matter of adhesives as well as adherents. Besides, a long period of overture and negotiation had set up momentum. The hopeful intent to link, to join, and to bond puts on the conference table elements of cooperation, making a kind of practical and sustained sacrament of fellowship. A desire to unite extends Christian experience more and more into the realm of corporate life. It becomes a process of finding and codifying means by which persons can work together. Negotiation gets to be a way of life.

It was in the light of this background that members of the Uniting Conference assembled in Dallas. The first order of business was to act out the act of union. This was done with ceremonies and symbols, both fitting and dramatic, in the presence of ten thousand witnesses who crowded the Dallas Municipal Auditorium and in the light of television cameras carrying the scene and advertising the union to the electronic world round about. Once the ceremonies were past, the Uniting Conference became the first General Conference of The United Methodist Church and it settled down to grim business, with an agenda as long as history and with so many exhausting sessions that one woman delegate said toward the end that she was so worn out and used up that nothing held her together but her hair spray.

On the surface the union brought together unequal yoke fellows, the Methodists sporting 10,300,000 members and the Evangelical United Brethren claiming only 750,000. Yet, even on a statistical basis, the smaller unit showed a far better record of per capita giving to church causes.[1] And the smaller unit had obviously kept its character and distinction and had been able to stay closer to its ethic as a sect. It had never had to deal with the question of slavery or the status of those who once were slaves and it had not written into its laws and regulations any rules of pious discrimination. The E.U.B.'s were a different, a peculiar, people possessed of a purity and intensity of belief encouraged by the cohesion of small numbers.

Methodism, on the other hand, had been handicapped by its size and success and its attempt to be a national church. Treading the broad road of accommodation, it had become a strong church haunted by the ethic of a sect. Brought in touch with a new source of vitality, the conscience of Methodism reappeared. The official body of The United Methodist Church spoke with joint authority and one voice, and many of the measures adopted were at variance with views that had been expressed, or pointedly left unexpressed, by Methodist bodies in the past. They showed a troubled concern for the part the new church should take by way of setting Christian standards in a day when many political decisions are still based on the use of force.

Views differed, of course, among the 1270 delegates, coming from every state and territory in the United States and representing many nuances of opinion. But the judgments rendered by the delegates told of a church convinced that the standards of a religious body ought always to be higher and firmer by far than the postulates by which politicians habitually act. There was a glimpse of principle above and beyond the rim of the routine. If man be of infinite worth and capable of becoming perfect in love, something besides force and discrimination ought to be set as an ideal.

Issues usually ignored were posed, debated, and declared upon. A church that had justified and sanctified wars in the past and hence approved war as an instrument of politics heard delegates debate at the very beginning the question of the war in Vietnam, adjourn the matter for further deliberation, then later put forth a resolution commending the President for his recent move to enter into negotiations with North Vietnam and calling upon "the government of the United States to fulfill its repeatedly expressed offer to send a representative anywhere, any time to make such talks possible."

There was a spirited debate over the words "anywhere, any

time." An amendment to eliminate the words from the resolution was defeated by the narrow margin of 604 to 557, but once the amendment was defeated the resolution passed overwhelmingly, a show of hands being sufficient to establish the hearty acceptance.[2] Some delegates could have wished the declaration more full-throated, but the point to note is that what The United Methodist Church said was no echo of the past but a very far cry from those stentorian calls for victorious military action which had often rung out to the rafters in official Methodist gatherings.

The mold had changed since the days of Matthew Simpson. Not that all eleven million members of the new church found themselves in happy unanimity. In fact, a public opinion survey made shortly before the action revealed that church and non-church members registered about the same opinions on issues before the American people.[3] But members of The United Methodist Church, elected as delegates to the General Conference and vested with authority to speak in the only gathering entitled to represent the Church, had their say and put themselves on record. Whatever individual Methodists might think, the Uniting Conference had raised a standard that had to be seen and thought about.

Before the end of the sessions the standard raised had been made even more visible. The Church declared that all groups in South Vietnam should take part in political negotiations and that all Vietnamese should share in the future political life of the nation. A resolution urged the people to recognize that "national power, even of super powers like the United States, has its limitations and cannot solve the problems of developing nations nor shape their destinies." The statement invoked primary principles, saying that "this General Conference . . . emphasizes that the first allegiance of Christians is to God, under whose judgment the policies and actions of all nations must pass." Then the principles were applied. The responsibility of the Church under God, the resolution continued, "leads us to express a growing concern over the course and consequences of United States foreign policy, especially in Southeast Asia."[4]

411

Isaiah had come to Dallas, and a religious body with all its size and encumbrances and shades of opinion and vested interests had taken a prophetic role. It had said that the world was not to be placidly accepted but was to be seen again from the point of view of the whole Judaeo-Christian ethic. It bore out and illustrated the statement of the American church historian Sidney Mead: "The chief social purpose of religion is to remind the State that it is not God."

The Conference came to and stated conclusions that were not ruled by precedent. Methodists had shaken off the deterring hand of the past. The Conference invited Roman Catholic Archbishop John H. Carberry of St. Louis to address the delegates and visitors, who listened while the archbishop reminded them of the concerns Catholics and Methodists had in common and while he reminded them also that if Wesleyanism had grown up in the Catholic tradition, it might well have been a religious order comparable to the Franciscans.[5]

Later the Conference supported a request to the Theological Study Commission on Doctrine and Doctrinal Practices to remove from the Articles of Religion of The United Methodist Church "any derogatory references to the Roman Catholic Church."

Represented by the delegates at Dallas was a changed church, one full of new intentions, confident enough to be willing to edit the past, to examine some of the anachronisms of its own sacred literature and bring its documents into harmony with the present age. The very act of the union of the larger body with the smaller body having different views and practices signaled newness. The Methodist Church in its overtures and negotiations could not possibly have asked that a union of the two churches include that peculiar institution known as the Central Jurisdiction, embracing ten Annual Conferences made up of nonwhites. It had been a foregone conclusion at the outset that a new constitution would do away with segregated conferences. The provision of the old constitution creating this Jurisdiction would be dropped and official segregation would be legally ended. It might not be done away with at once but it would be taken care of automatically, almost without being mentioned.

It was for this reason that infinite care and pains had been taken with the construction of the constitution under which The United Methodist Church acted. Most of the work had been done by commissions but the full discussion and acceptance of the uniting document by the official bodies of both Churches had taken place at the special sessions of the two General Conferences in November 1966. Here each provision of the proposed new constitution was taken up line by line by each deliberative body, acting as the committee of the whole, discussed, debated, approved or discarded or amended then and there.

No discussion of Christian ethics or theory ventilated the proceedings of the General Conference of The Methodist Church at Chicago in 1966. There was a job to be done. It was to draw up to submit a constitution which would unite. There was an atmosphere of almost soulless detachment, leaving the impression that the Priest and the Levite were in charge and passing by. But behind every administrative problem was a moral consideration, and it was sure to intrude upon a gathering of religious men and women. Present as delegates were men from the Central Jurisdiction, representing not only their conferences but their race—men who had first been called African, then Negro, and were calling themselves Black.

These delegates had been duly elected. They had the same rights as delegates of privileged color. They were members of The Methodist Church, not of autonomous black groupings who wanted no part of standard white Methodism. A dignified and gracious representative of one of these bodies, which had quadrupled its size since its founding, was on hand to present the fraternal greetings of what had originally been The Colored Methodist Episcopal Church and was now The Christian Methodist Episcopal Church. These greetings were part of the order of the day, but the delegates who spoke their pieces on race issues were members of a body that had come down from the Christmas Conference. They might be kept in segregated churches back home but they held seats and voting and speaking rights in the General Conference. They were black persons who, on the basis of Christian principles, wanted prejudice acknowledged and wiped out in a religious body of high pretensions that had always been, and still was, preponderantly white. The setting provided these delegates and those who sympathized with them a golden, made-to-order opportunity to address themselves to the subject of discrimination—and to register their views and their cause in the minutes.

The opportunity came with the report of a commission on race appointed by the 1964 General Conference. It recommended ending all forms of segregation within the Church by 1972. This was declared to be a target date. Black delegates from the South urged that the 1972 date be mandatory and that the special session of the General Conference so affirm. The arguments of the delegates were cogently and fluently presented. One of the most clear-cut and penetrating statements on the plight of the minority race within the Church was voiced by J. E. Lowery of the Central Alabama Conference.

"Is there something wrong with us?" Lowery pleaded. "If we are discriminated against because we are unclean, we wash. If we are discriminated against because we are ignorant, we seek to learn. If we are discriminated against because we are loud and boisterous, we seek to be refined and intelligent. But, if we are rejected on the basis of our color, we are helpless, because God made us black, and there is nothing we can do about it. . . . We ask you to settle an issue that has already been settled on the actor's stage, on the athlete's field, in the dancer's pavilion. It's been settled in the beer-drinker's saloon, but it has not been settled at the altar beneath the Cross of Jesus, where it was settled long ago."[6]

The sentiment expressed brought forth an eloquent statement by a delegate from India, who pointed out how much official Methodist discrimination hurt the cause of Christianity in the East. There was a special motion made and carried that the Lowery utterance be printed and circulated among the delegates.

But when the vote finally came to make the 1972 date mandatory instead of merely one to shoot for, the motion was overwhelmingly voted down.

Hardly had the decision been taken when black delegates arose from their places and, accompanied by a few other delegates, walked to the front of the assembly and knelt before an obscure altar. The altar was there. The minutes said so. But to those who could not see the altar the delegates simply knelt before the dais on which were seated some sixty bishops, white and black. The bishops had no right to vote in the Conference, no power to rule or overrule. They simply occupied an elevated position in the seating arrangements. They did, however, represent officialdom, and to the casual observer it looked for all the world as if the petitioning delegates were bowed once more in supplication to their fellow man for justice.

No one who saw the scene will ever forget it or cease to reflect on it. For a few moments the most intimate intimations of the Christian idea of the equality of men before God had interrupted the proceedings of a church legislative body, bringing first a chill and then warmth and then suffusing a hotel ballroom with radiance reminiscent of the reports of Pentecost. But it passed. Shortly the delegates returned to their official seats. Meanwhile business as usual had continued on the Conference floor, attention being given to the proposed constitution—page twelve, paragraph twenty-eight, sub-paragraph five, line two. But there were glazed eyes here and there and a kind of preoccupation with something else hung over the assembly. The Rev. Ray Ragsdale of the Southern California–Arizona Annual Conference got the attention of the presiding bishop in the chair, whose name was Lord.

"I move," said Mr. Ragsdale, "that we adjourn and retire to our rooms for prayer."[7] The motion was duly seconded and put to a vote. It did not carry. The conference went on. The constitution was the thing. It was the Ark of the Covenant. Not race relations, not minority rights, not remedial justice mattered to the Methodists as much as the creation of a new church along lines that might be accepted by the combined membership and the Almighty. And it was created and accepted, at least by the membership, both by those of German and of English-American background. Its very being eliminated the legal sanction given to segregation in the Central Jurisdiction of the former Methodist Church.

It did not eliminate segregation. A further effort made at the Uniting Conference in Dallas to make 1972 a date when all Conferences of the Central Jurisdiction must be integrated in membership and worship and administration with white churches was again defeated.[8] The United Methodist Church left outside its bounds three strong autonomous African bodies which resisted all overtures to be included. It was united in name only. But at least it was legal. The marriage of the Evangelical United Brethren Church and The Methodist Church had taken place. With it came a full and constitutional declaration of intent. The United Methodist Church was constitutionally inclusive and it would move forward as rapidly as possible to become inclusive in truth.

In a word, the whole awkward, creaking, ponderous polity process had produced results, if not a harvest. And if it seemed in general and at crucial moments backward and obsolete, it had moved the Church forward. The same process which in 1844 had led to division led in 1968 to union.

Realists can point out that Dallas was a show window, with the best goods of the Church on display, all ceremony and all glow. In spite of the glad-hand atmosphere and oratorical good will, big conference gatherings leave literally a thousand and one details to be sorted out. Church unions are in fact business mergers, with the grief and displacements that inevitably attend the joining of corporations. Many facilities must be discarded, sold, or jettisoned. Faithful workers have to be retired or fired. Endless committee meetings are needed to treat difficulties that could not be seen ahead of time, as well as those that could.

Worse, as the critics say, mergers called unions tend to lead Methodists into an even deeper morass of preoccupation with polity, so that concern with process becomes all-consuming, conscience takes a holiday, and the mission of the Church is lost to sight. One bishop noted privately that many of the practical and property problems that had come about with the 1939 Methodist merger had not been settled by the time of the union of The Methodist Church and the United Brethren. When a friend asked if possibly Methodists enjoyed uniting simply because they loved the consequent straightening out of details and documents, the bishop said, "Oh, of course. And this new merger is good for at least fifty years."

To the outside observer, however, not charged with administrative responsibility, the Methodist yen for union has exhilarating effects.

The religious elements in Methodism are to be looked for in the motives that move men to corporate action for the common good. The steps taken in this corporate action may be slow, but they are educative. The very act of deliberating over ethical problems pragmatically and continually keeps the mind on the relevance of religious ideas to social life. And it calls for a high standard of conduct, especially seeing that the workaday outside world, for all its criticism of, and indifference to, religious influence, continues to expect a church body to be ahead of a golf club in social insights.

If you want to know whether Methodism in our day has religion as its source or is merely given over to the worship of the golden calf of institutionalism, you reason back from its acts and find in that way the beliefs that sustain and support it. The Wesleyan belief that God can transform human life remains firm. Today primary attention is shifted from the individual to the social order, but the certainty that a divine force can bring about profound change is as sublime and naive as ever.

One result is a kind of characteristic patience and indiscourageability. The human prospect is not altogether hopeless. Methodists know what they face: approaching famine that will wipe out millions, politicians pushing mankind to the brink by their continued addiction to force as a means of settling disputes, racial conflict based on old postulates of inequality, the likelihood that part if not all of the earth will be burned to a cinder in nuclear war. These are matters the Methodists are willing to contemplate openly and have commissions to study. But there persists unabashed the conviction that if the love that belongs to religious faith can be put into effect, earth may yet become a place of peace.

Listen to a good Methodist sermon. In no lay critique of the social order will you find a more down-to-earth portrayal of what the current world is like or what it is moving toward or how gnarled it is with impossibilities and contradictions. But although the depiction in the first part of the sermon may be stark and depressing, the exhortation at the end, usually quite brief in comparison with the length of the sermon as a whole, confronts the congregation with the contention that God and man working in tandem can avert disaster and that nothing would please God more.

For the past 250 years the Wesleyan emphasis in Great Britain and in the United States has fallen solidly on the immediacy of God and His eagerness to work with man. In the aggregate of this belief lies the glacial strength of Methodist faith. During the centuries at least 200,000,000 persons have held the conviction that the universe is good and that God loves the world. Of these more than forty million here and abroad are still alive. Among the others, those dead may be more powerful than those who live, for by their example and writing and preaching they have transmitted a conviction that is cumulative in effect, compounding interest as it goes along.

A common basic belief provides continuity in the experience of so great a body of believers. From this steady background some men and women dramatically exemplify the spirit of belief. Others state the belief. Both underline it. In the great procession there are practitioners and there are theorists—Methodists by temperament and Methodists by reflection.

Let two characters emerge from the past to act out the essential component of the Wesleyan faith.

They have the same name: McCabe.

Not that there is a case of mistaken identity or that one is the double of the other. Although they were contemporaries in the nineteenth century, there were sharp and telling differences between them. Both proclaimed, one mainly by deeds and the other chiefly in words, the infinite possibilities of the common man—and they did it as exuberantly as any circuit rider ever did.

First comes the irrepressible Charles Cardwell McCabe, known as the Singing Chaplain, the man who gave "The Battle Hymn of the Republic" its big send-off, to the satisfaction of Julia Ward Howe and to the enthusiasm of Abraham Lincoln who, when he first heard McCabe roll out the notes, cried, "Sing it again!"

McCabe was an Ohio preacher who in 1862 volunteered as a chaplain of the 102nd Ohio Regiment. He was a young man but a soldier of the old school, of the sword as well as the cross, an admirer of the preaching and patriotism of Bishop Matthew Simpson. There is not the slightest indication in any of his observations—and they were many—that he had any misgivings about war as an instrument of politics. Rather his concern was with the rescue of men's souls. At bringing men to terms with themselves he was a master.

When he first joined his regiment it was not engaged in active fighting, so he got the soldiers to build a brush arbor church and he commenced a protracted meeting—preaching every day and night. One day the colonel went out after the bugle had sounded for a three o'clock parade. Only a few soldiers responded and the colonel stood almost alone. He shouted to the adjutant, "Where are the men?" To which the adjutant replied, "The chaplain has them all in that church, and he declares that the meeting is so good that he won't let them come."[9]

The colonel sent a message ordering McCabe to dismiss the meeting. McCabe sent word back that he could not obey because the meeting was going on with such power that he did not feel it would be right, whereupon the colonel sent a guard and arrested the chaplain and brought him to headquarters. There he was dressed down for interfering with military discipline. The colonel and the chaplain were out of sorts for several days until the chaplain apologized and said he would obey orders in the future.

He did not obey orders, however, that seemed to him as a chaplain contrary to the good of his men. At the battle of Winchester in 1863 he refused to retreat and leave the wounded and the dying, among them many whose souls were in need of succor. He was captured by the Confederates and taken before General Jubal Early. Up to this time captured chaplains and surgeons had been released, but General Early said to McCabe, "You are a preacher, are you?" When McCabe said he was, the general went on, "Well, you preachers have done more to bring on this war than anybody and I'm going to send you to Richmond. . . . They tell me you've been shouting 'On to Richmond' for a long time, and to Richmond you shall go."

In Richmond McCabe was incarcerated in an old warehouse formerly occupied by Libby & Sons, Ship Chandlers and Grocers, from which business came the name of Libby Prison. A three-story brick structure with eight rooms, 103 by 42 feet, with a stove in each room, on which rations could be cooked, it was a prison for commissioned officers. Although it was a prison and a grim one, beginning to be overcrowded, McCabe saw at once that the place had possibilities and he set about to improve it, making the best of the worst. He made a survey of resources and he found that among the officers were doctors, teachers, editors, merchants, and forty lawyers.

Such talent ought to be organized. The men could teach each other. Courses of study were arranged and the result called the University of Libby Prison. Language classes were the order of the day because of the varied background of the inmates. There were classes in German, French, Spanish, and Italian, all taught by those to whom these tongues were native. French was McCabe's special interest, and at his table, where he served what he had cooked for twenty men, it was a rule that no one could have anything to eat, even the watered-down soup, unless he could ask for it in French.

"My college is prospering," wrote the chaplain later in one of his many ebullient letters to his wife, telling her in the same letter not to send him any clothes or eatables, that he can get along well without them. It is education and what the men are doing together that excites him. Courses were added in Greek and Latin, in rhetoric and grammar, arithmetic, algebra, geometry, and natural philosophy. A singing society was organized and it gave rousing concerts in which there were solos, duets, trios, and a grand chorus. During one of the concerts a guard shouted, "Lights out up there!" The lights went out but the singing went on—with only one candle "so dim that it served only to make the darkness visible."

McCabe's voice was deep, rich, and beautiful, and there was a kind of doxology in whatever he sang. There were times when guards and passersby would group themselves in Cary Street outside the prison just to hear the singing. The voice of the chaplain rang out night and day, and time and time again, especially after the news of the battle of Gettysburg, he would sing "The Battle Hymn of the Republic." He had memorized the words during 1862 when they were published in *Atlantic Monthly*, not knowing at the time that they could be fitted to "John Brown's Body." He heard the hymn sung to this tune at a great rally in Zanesville, Ohio, and took it with him to the front. In Libby Prison he had it ready when the news of Gettysburg penetrated the walls there. Everybody knew the chorus by then but he knew the hymn by heart and he would sing it through without a break, the men joining in on the chorus at the top of their voices, swaying as they sang.

Typhoid fever silenced the voice of the Singing Chaplain while he was in Libby Prison. The doctors thought the fever would still it forever, but they didn't know McCabe or about the communion of the saints. The day the doctors thought would be his last an officer of the prison who had become a close friend, visited McCabe, cut his hair and trimmed his beard with pocket scissors, made him as comfortable as possible, and then read him a letter from a member of his own Conference. There had just been a session of the Conference and when McCabe's name was called, someone had said, "He's in Libby Prison." The bishop presiding spoke of the time Paul and Barnabas were prayed out of prison and suggested that the brethren pray for McCabe.

The news in the letter deeply affected the stricken man:

Two hundred and fifty Methodist preachers got down on their knees and asked for my relief. I was used to suffering; I could endure loneliness without tears, but I was not used to tenderness and that tender letter broke me down. The tears rolled down my cheeks like rain. As soon as I could control myself I began to sing. I broke out into a profuse perspiration and the tide was turned. In the evening the doctor came in and felt my pulse and started back in surprise. "Why," said he, "there's a big change in you. That last medicine has helped you wonderfully," and he rolled up a big blue-mass pill and gave it to me with a drink of water; but I got well all the same![10]

Twelve days later the Singing Chaplain was released—and with what a story to tell! He went to rejoin his regiment but he was captured by the Christian Commission and sent around to stir up public support of that agency. Everybody wanted to hear McCabe tell his story and sing his bit, and so great was his appeal that audiences would contribute to any cause he espoused. He would "let them in free and charge them to get out." He was, as he put it with jocular bitterness, doomed to raise money. First for the Christian Commission and then for the Church Extension Society of The Methodist Episcopal Church he toured the land, proving himself to be one of the great money raisers for charitable purposes of all time. And what was the topic of the talk that raked in the shekels? "The Bright Side of Life in Libby Prison." If he had kept the money the lecture brought in it would have made him a fortune for his day—a quarter of a million dollars.

The Methodist Episcopal Church acknowledged and rewarded McCabe's great powers by making him a bishop. As a bishop he remained a chaplain. He was not used to, schooled in, or patient with the protocol of parliamentary procedure. Occasionally it would be his turn to preside over the complications of the General Conference. The legend has it that in his confusion he might allow as many as a dozen motions to get put before the house, none of which he had any right to entertain. An uproar from the floor would follow and McCabe would call out, "The brethren are getting restless. Let's sing a little."[11] Whether out of confusion or joy in singing, the bishop would often break into the opening lines of "Sweet Bye and Bye," a song the preachers all knew and none could resist, resent, or keep from singing: "There is a land that is fairer than day/ And by faith we can see it afar. . . ."

To Methodists the line that mattered most was, "And by faith we can see it afar." In McCabe's day it was heaven, but it was as real as the rent just the same, and even then it was coming to mean a better land in the U.S.A. Before McCabe's death in 1906 the land faith could see from afar was a new world that could be created in the here and now or in the not-too-distant future. Both the old heaven and the new earth were outgrowths of Methodist imagination, which was expanding.

Such enthusiasm (literally *en theos*) as the Singing Chaplain displayed up and down the land and all over the lot, is likely to leave the impression that Methodists are optimists. They are not. They are meliorists. They eschew the gloom of the philosophy of pessimism, which sees the world as a place of suffering and pointless pain, but they do not embrace the premises of optimism as propounded by Leibniz and satirized by Voltaire. This is not the best of all possible worlds, but it has the makings. The confident expectancy one finds in Methodist preaching wells up out of belief and the belief has deep springs in thought about the nature of God.

To think about the nature of God was the function of such men as the other McCabe, whose parents had named him for Lorenzo Dow, the mad waif of the itinerancy. Lorenzo Dow McCabe was also an Ohio preacher. After filling various appointments in the pastorate he was appointed professor of philosophy at Ohio Wesleyan University at Delaware, Ohio. He had been in on the founding of the university and had served as its president for a while. He was a preacher-administrator, not a theologian, but as a teacher of philosophy in touch with generations of ephebic preachers, he had immense influence on those who sat in his classes and enjoyed his companionship. He was a close friend, although not always in agreement with, Borden P. Bowne, who taught philosophy in Boston University from 1876 until his death in 1910 and is credited with reaching the minds of more professing Christians than any other philosopher of religion in the United States.

Both Bowne and L. D. McCabe thought hard about the nature of God. McCabe was profoundly concerned with the bearing of the idea of God on human conduct, especially its bearing on the freedom of the individual to make choices. Predestination troubled him sorely, not merely because it was alien to the whole Methodist concept but also because it posited a God who must have foreknowledge. If God was all-wise, He knew what was going to happen. But L. D. McCabe worked out a theory that foreknowledge did not necessarily mean foreordination. The resulting doctrine he named Divine Nescience— a form of restricted knowing. God might have a knowledge of contingencies but not of individual acts. In this view, as interpreted by one of his admirers, God "would limit his own knowledge to foreknowledge of all possibilities of human choices without foreknowledge of what any particular choice would be. This would be self-limitation by the Divine; but in as much as it would be *self*-limitation, it is hard to see how it could do harm to the dignity of the Divine." It was a view that stood in sharp contrast to those theologians "who proclaim so extreme a doctrine of the transcendence of God that they make him of no earthly use."[12]

In his determination to keep God useful L. D. McCabe showed just as much enthusiasm among students and intimates as C. C. McCabe did before the masses. To a visitor who called on him shortly before his death in 1897 McCabe said, "The doctors tell me I am near the end. Do you know what I am going to do as soon as I get to the other world? First I shall salute my blessed Lord, then I shall hunt up the apostle Paul and tell him what I think of those predestination passages in his epistles."

Predestination continues to plague the Methodists. Its staying power is to be seen in the fact that, while the doctrine as a tenet of theology has little general currency, the widespread recrudescence of interest in astrology shows how people want to believe that an outside force rules their lives and delivers them of full responsibility. In a strange way, too, although the Methodists deny the doctrine of predestination for the individual, they accept the idea of destiny when it comes to the ultimate reign of peace and good will. It is in the cards. But it will come to pass only through human choice and effort.

Not casually or by accident but to express their sense of renewal and ongoing did the Methodists choose as the slogan for the celebration of their second contennial in America the words *Forever Beginning.* The words describe with inspired accuracy Wesleyan faith and practice. Earlier they fitted the personal experience of conversion and of growing in grace, and they have come of late to fit with equal aptness the actions of the corporate body, revealing a spirit of resourcefulness and renewal, a willingness to start over and remedy the failings of the past, a disposition to adapt to circumstances that are without precedent.

This disposition was evident in the views that prevailed at the Uniting Conference. It was even more apparent in the structural repairs approved at that Conference, and it was made manifest in the actions taken by the special session of the General Conference of the new Church in the spring of 1970. New attitudes have become definite enough to be written into the rules. Measures embracing new attitudes stand out as mileposts of progress and they bring to mind Sir Norman Angell's dictum that a trend is more important than a fact because a trend indicates change.

Conspicuous among the laws denoting change are those that accord woman and youth increasing recognition. It is now provided that women and young people must be present on boards that administer the program of the Church. A board, differing from a commission, is a corporation. It has legal authority. And the Church declares that women and young people in specified numbers be members of boards.

In some cases it is written that women must outnumber men. This provision was enacted by the General Conference of 1964 of the former Methodist Church and continued in the new United body. On the board of managers of the Board of Missions, for example, each Jurisdictional Conference has three lay members for each 600,000 of the Church population; two of the three must be women. No Jurisdictional Conference is to have fewer than six lay members on the Board, and four of these must be women. The preachers and bishops remain in command posts, but women, once ignored at the national level, are officially invited to have some part in the management.

Willingness to live in a new age symbolized at the 1970 General Conference by the introduction of a computer to count in a minute's time the votes of the delegates. One of the measures on which the new machine tallied far more than the necessary two-thirds majority eliminated the old requirement that delegates to the Annual Conferences must be at least twenty-one years of age.[18] The constitutional change, which had to be referred to the Annual Conferences for ratification, looked to ending the segregation of youth, recognizing that age does not in itself qualify a person for government.

The computer was not needed to count ballots in a proposal that young people be seated as delegates to the General Conference for the first time. The vote was unanimous. Five youths, male and female, were seated—as non-voting delegates, to be sure, but they were not non-talking. At one point, when a ministerial delegate, Jameson Jones, put forward a motion to postpone for two years a bid by youth to control the Youth Service Fund of the Church, a member of the youth delegation asked permission to have a member of the audience speak to the motion. It was granted, and a lad of fifteen cogently presented the case for allowing youth to determine what the youth agency of a religious body should be and do. And he contended that it should be given this chance at once while youth was "still willing to work through the system." He added that "paternalism is what youth is fighting against."

The argument was given all the more force because the fifteen-year-old, Scott Jones, was the son of the ministerial delegate who asked postponement. The Conference voted overwhelmingly against deferring action and in favor of letting a board of twenty youths and ten adults administer a fund that may amount to $600,000 annually.[14]

Methodism is still organizing to beat the devil. The mien of the devil has changed from that of a tempter luring men to frivolity and debauchery to that of a grinning demon promoting old prejudices and urging men to divisiveness. He is more diabolically clever than he once was, having taken up his abode in respectable circumstances, even in rooms where boards meet. But if he is there, men of conscience know it and know what to do about it. Preoccupation with organization, besides helping to establish the priceless principle that means are more important than the end, may prove to be a prophetic form of efficiency suited to a complex and conglomerate society. As shown by recent changes, Methodism has the tested methods by which it can alter its procedures and refine its processes.

One agency carried over into the new United Methodist Church was the Commission on the Structure of Methodism Overseas: COSMOS. The name of the agency was later changed, but the acronym, repeatedly used, long served as a reminder that the Wesleyan faith regards itself as related to the universe.

This faith considers itself to belong to something beyond its present setting. Early in 1960 Bishop G. Bromley Oxnam, addressing a session of the General Conference, served notice that when life is discovered on another planet, the Methodists will be ready with their rocket riders.[15] God and man can work together out there if man is properly organized.

Notes

I. HIDDEN HISTORY

1. Max Weber, *The Protestant Ethic and the Spirit of Capitalism* (New York, 1930), pp. 139–143. Weber describes the characteristics of the Methodist societies later instituted by John Wesley: "The emotional act of conversion was methodically induced. And after it was attained there did not follow a pious enjoyment of community with God, after the manner of the emotional Pietism of Zinzendorf, but the emotion, once awakened, was directed into a rational struggle for perfection."

II. HAIL TO THE CHIEF

1. Richard M. Cameron, "The New Church Takes Root," *The History of American Methodism,* edited by Emory Stevens Bucke (Nashville, 1964), Vol. I, p. 250.
2. Jacob S. Payton, "Methodism's Spread in America," *Methodism,* edited by William K. Anderson (Nashville, 1947), p. 68.
3. Coen G. Pierson, "Methodism and the Revolution," *The History of American Methodism,* Vol. I, p. 163.
4. *Cyclopedia of Methodism, Embracing Sketches of Its Rise, Progress and Present Condition,* edited by Matthew Simpson (Philadelphia, 1881), p. 501.
5. James Penn Pilkington, *The Methodist Publishing House: A History* (Nashville, 1968), Vol. I, p. 57.
6. *The Journal and Letters of Francis Asbury,* edited by Elmer T. Clark (Nashville, 1958), Vol. I, p. 181. March 19, 1776.
7. Samuel Drew, *The Life of the Rev. Thomas Coke, LL.D.: His Various Travels and Extraordinary Missionary Exertions, Etc.* (New York, 1818), pp. 137–138.
8. "1789–1959 History Repeats," *Together,* March 1959, pp. 35, 37.
9. *Ibid.,* p. 14.

III. AUTONOMY ABOVE ALL

1. Samuel A. Seaman, *Annals of New York Methodism, Being a History of the Methodist Episcopal Church in the City of New York from A.D. 1766 to 1892* (New York, 1892), pp. 102–103.
2. *Concise Dictionary of American History,* edited by Wayne Andrews (New York, 1961), p. 634.
3. Norman W. Spellman, "The Formation of the Methodist Episcopal Church," *The History of American Methodism,* edited by Emory Stevens Bucke (Nashville, 1964), Vol. I, p. 212.
4. Ezra Squier Tipple, *Freeborn Garrettson* (New York, 1910), p. 39.
5. *Extracts of the Journals of the Rev. T. Coke's Five Visits to America* (London, 1790), p. 13.
6. John Lednum, *A History of the Rise of Methodism in America, etc.* (Philadelphia, 1859), p. 265.
7. *Ibid.,* p. 410.
8. Quoted, Spellman, *op. cit.,* p. 199.
9. Quoted, *Together,* March 1959, p. 34.
10. Nathan Bangs, *The Life of the Rev. Freeborn Garrettson, Compiled from His Printed and Manuscript Journals and Other Authentic Documents* (New York and Cincinnati, 1832), p. 134.
11. Tipple, *op. cit.,* p. 95.

IV. CONFERENCE IS KING

1. John Lednum, *A History of the Rise of Methodism in America, etc.* (Philadelphia, 1859), p. 91. The site of the original Lovely Lane Chapel is now marked by a bronze tablet on the face of the Merchant's Club at 206 East Redwood Street. *Official Souvenir Book American Methodist Bicentennial* (Baltimore, 1966), p. 64.
2. Quoted by Charles A. Johnson, *The Frontier Camp Meeting* (Dallas, 1955), p. 46.
3. Quoted by Ezra Squier Tipple, *Francis Asbury, Prophet of the Long Road* (New York and Cincinnati, 1916), p. 145.
4. *Cyclopedia of Methodism,* edited by Matthew Simpson (Philadelphia, 1881), p. 415.
5. Hartzell Spence, "How Methodism Grew Up," *Together,* March 1959, p. 49.
6. Norman W. Spellman, "The Formation of the Methodist Episcopal Church," *The History of American Methodism,* edited by Emory Stevens Bucke (Nashville, 1964), pp. 155–157, 213–214.
7. Quoted, Tipple, *op. cit.,* p. 152.
8. Coen G. Pierson, "Methodism and the Revolution," *The History of American Methodism,* Vol. I, pp. 178–179.
9. *American Methodist Bicentennial 1766–1966* (Baltimore, 1966), p. 59. Picture, p. 18.
10. Quoted, William Warren Sweet, "Methodism's Debt to the Church of England," *Methodism,* edited by William K. Anderson (Nashville, 1947), p. 48. From a letter to Bishop William White of Pennsylvania in 1791, proposing a reunion between the American Methodists and the Episcopalians.

11. Spellman, *op. cit.*, p. 205.

12. Gerald F. Moede, *The Office of Bishop in Methodism: Its History and Development* (Zurich and Nashville, 1964), p. 57.

13. *Ibid.*, p. 58.

14. Sidney Benjamin Bradley, *The Life of Bishop Richard Whatcoat* (Louisville, 1936), p. 89.

V. WHEN THE WEST BEGAN

1. *The Story of America as Reported by Its Newspapers 1690–1965*, edited by Edwin Emery (New York, 1965), p. 21.

2. Sidney Benjamin Bradley, *The Life of Bishop Richard Whatcoat* (Louisville, 1936), pp. 72, 63.

3. *Concise Dictionary of American History*, edited by Wayne Andrews (New York, 1962), pp. 364–365.

4. *The Journal and Letters of Francis Asbury*, edited by Elmer T. Clark (London and Nashville, 1958), p. 445. November 2, 1804.

5. William Warren Sweet, *The Story of Religions in America* (revised edition, New York, 1950), p. 207.

6. Dale Van Every, *Ark of Empire: The American Frontier 1784–1803* (New York, 1963), Foreword and p. 13. Thomas D. Clark, *Frontier America: The Story of the Westward Movement* (New York, 1959), pp. 155–156.

7. Van Every, *op. cit.*, p. 22.

8. Harriette Simpson Arnow, *Seedtime on the Cumberland* (New York, 1960), p. 223.

9. *Ibid.*, pp. 353, 360.

10. Clark, *op. cit.*, p. 210.

11. *Ibid.*, pp. 222–223.

12. Arnow, *op. cit.*, p. 304.

13. *Autobiography of James B. Finley*, edited by W. P. Strickland (Cincinnati, 1856), p. 38.

14. *Ibid.*, p. 34.

15. Clark, *op. cit.*, p. 201.

16. *Ibid.*, p. 145.

17. Quoted, van Every, *op. cit.*, p. 8.

VI. VOW OF OBEDIENCE

1. Jacob S. Payton, "Methodism's Spread in America," *Methodism*, edited by William K. Anderson (Nashville, 1947), p. 79.

2. James B. Finley, *Sketches of Western Methodism*, edited by W. P. Strickland (Cincinnati, 1855), pp. 202 ff.

3. Payton, *op. cit.*, p. 73.

4. Stuart C. Henry, editor, *A Miscellany of American Christianity: Essays in Honor of H. Shelton Smith* (Durham, N.C., 1963), p. 83.

5. John Lednum, *A History of the Rise of Methodism in America, etc.* (Philadelphia, 1859), pp. 414–415.

6. Halford E. Luccock and Paul Hutchinson, *The Story of Methodism* (New York and Cincinnati, 1926), p. 235.

7. *The Journal and Letters of Francis Asbury,* edited by Elmer T. Clark (London and Nashville, 1958), Vol. I, p. 18. January 23, 1772.

8. Edward J. Drinkhouse, *History of Methodist Reform* (Baltimore and Pittsburgh, 1899), Vol I, p. 185.

9. *Cyclopedia of Methodism,* edited by Matthew Simpson (Philadelphia, 1881), p. 58.

10. *Journal and Letters,* Vol. I, p. 7. October 27, 1771.

11. Quoted, Lednum, *op. cit.,* p. 108.

12. Quoted, Richard M. Cameron, *Methodism and Society in Historical Perspective* (New York, 1961), p. 90.

13. *Journal and Letters,* Vol. I, pp. 263–264.

14. Lednum, *op. cit.,* p. 226.

15. *Ibid.,* p. 15.

16. Elmer T. Clark, *An Album of Methodist History* (Nashville, 1952), pp. 143 ff.

17. Drinkhouse, *op. cit.,* pp. 177–178.

18. *Journal and Letters,* Vol. III, p. 356. October 7, 1806.

19. Quoted in various places, including Drinkhouse, *op. cit.,* p. 336. It comes from a letter written October 31, 1789, by Wesley, reporting a remark Asbury is said to have made to George Shadford.

VII. WHERE A FEW WERE GATHERED TOGETHER

1. Wade Crawford Barclay, *Early American Methodism 1769–1844* (New York, 1950), Vol. II, pp. 345–346.

2. Halford E. Luccock and Paul Hutchinson, *The Story of Methodism* (New York and Cincinnati, 1926), pp. 169–172.

3. Stephen R. Beggs, *Pages from the Early History of the West and North-West, etc.* (Cincinnati, 1868), p. 18.

4. Elizabeth K. Nottingham, *Methodism and the Frontier: Indiana Proving Ground* (New York, 1941), p. 111.

5. *Cyclopedia of Methodism,* edited by Matthew Simpson (Philadelphia, 1881), p. 228.

6. *Ibid.,* pp. 84–85.

7. Barclay, *op. cit.,* p. 342.

VIII. THE CIRCUIT RIDERS: WHAT MANNER OF MEN?

1. Richard M. Cameron, *Methodism and Society in Historical Perspective,* edited by the Board of Social and Economic Relations of the Methodist Church. Volume I of *Methodism and Society* (Nashville, 1961), p. 326.

2. Frederic Logan Paxson, *The Last American Frontier* (New York, 1910), p. 116.

3. Halford E. Luccock and Paul Hutchinson, *The Story of Methodism* (New York and Cincinnati, 1926), p. 146.

4. *Cyclopedia of Methodism,* edited by Matthew Simpson (Philadelphia, 1881), p. 906.

5. A. B. Hyde, *The Story of Methodism Throughout the World* (New York, 1898), p. 351.

6. James B. Finley, *Sketches of Western Methodism* (Cincinnati, 1855), p. 241.

7. John Lednum, *A History of the Rise of Methodism in America* (Philadelphia, 1859), p. 366.

8. *Autobiography of Rev. James B. Finley*, edited by W. P. Strickland (Cincinnati, 1856), pp. 237, 262.

9. Finley, *Sketches*, p. 431.

10. Stephen R. Beggs, *Pages from the Early History of the West and North-West, etc.* (Cincinnati, 1868), p. 298.

11. Finley, *Sketches*, p. 232.

12. Wade Crawford Barclay, *Early American Methodism 1769–1844* (New York, 1950), Vol. II, p. 353.

13. *Ibid.*, p. 375.

14. Quoted in Jacob S. Payton, *Our Fathers Have Told Us:* The Story of the Founding of Methodism in Western Pennsylvania (Cincinnati, 1938), p. 92.

15. Charles A. Johnson, *The Frontier Camp Meeting* (Dallas, 1955), p. 147.

16. Beggs, *op. cit.*, p. 25.

17. *Ibid.*, p. 293.

18. Robert Guy McCutchan, *Our Hymnody: A Manual of the Methodist Hymnal* (Nashville, 1937), pp. 256, 51.

19. Beggs, *op. cit.*, p. 156.

20. Umphrey Lee, *The Lord's Horseman: John Wesley the Man* (Nashville, 1928), p. 66.

21. William E. H. Lecky, *The History of England in the Eighteenth Century* (New York, 1882), Vol. II, pp. 682–699.

22. William T. Watkins, "Wesley's Message to His Own Age," *Methodism*, edited by William K. Anderson (New York and Nashville, 1947), p. 22.

IX. POVERTY LEADS TO CHASTITY

1. Wade Crawford Barclay, *Early American Methodism 1769–1844* (New York, 1950), Vol. II, p. 290.

2. Herman B. Teeter, "Mr. Wesley and the Tax Collector," *Together*, May 1963, p. 33.

3. Charles A. Johnson, *The Frontier Camp Meeting* (Dallas, 1955), p. 163.

4. Jacob Young, *Autobiography of a Pioneer* (Cincinnati, 1857), p. 152.

5. James B. Finley, *Sketches of Western Methodism* (Cincinnati, 1855), p. 53.

6. Quoted, Barclay, *op. cit.*, p. 290.

7. *Ibid.*, p. 290.

8. *The Journal and Letters of Francis Asbury*, edited by Elmer T. Clark (London and Nashville, 1958), Vol. II, p. 474. July 9, 1805.

9. A. B. Hyde, *The Story of Methodism Throughout the World* (New York, 1898), p. 478.

10. Umphrey Lee, *The Lord's Horseman: John Wesley the Man* (Nashville, 1954), pp. 129–134. For an uncaptioned but elegant picture of the woman Mr. Wesley married, see Elmer T. Clark, *An Album of Methodist History* (New York and Nashville, 1962), p. 117.

11. Finley, *Sketches*, p. 27.

12. *Ibid.*, p. 82.

13. William Warren Sweet, *Religion on the American Frontier* (revised edition, New York, 1964), p. 63.

14. Lorenzo Dow, *The Dealings of God, Man and the Devil, Etc.*, To Which is Added The Vicissitudes of Life by Peggy Dow (New York, 1856), p. 97.

15. John Lednum, *A History of the Rise of Methodism in America, etc.* (Philadelphia, 1859), p. 284.

X. THE STERN DISCIPLINE

1. *Extracts of the Journals of the Rev. T. Coke's Five Visits to America* (London, 1790), p. 18.

2. *The Journal and Letters of Francis Asbury*, edited by Elmer T. Clark (London and Nashville, 1958), Vol. I, p. 362, n.

3. A. B. Hyde, *The Story of Methodism Throughout the World* (New York, 1898), p. 409.

4. Elizabeth K. Nottingham, *Methodism and the Frontier* (New York, 1941), p. 48.

5. Abel Stevens, *History of the Methodist Episcopal Church* (New York, 1865), Vol. III, pp. 482–483.

6. Paul Neff Garber, *The Methodists Are One People* (Nashville, 1939), p. 19.

7. Wade Crawford Barclay, *Early American Methodism 1769–1844* (New York, 1950), p. 441. Citing Jesse Lee.

8. Elmer T. Clark, *An Album of Methodist History* (Nashville, 1952), p. 198.

9. Barclay, *op. cit.*, p. 355.

10. William Warren Sweet, *Religion on the American Frontier 1783–1840*, Vol. IV, *The Methodists: A Collection of Source Materials* (New York, 1964), pp. 642–643.

11. *Ibid.*, p. 644.

12. Quoted in Walter N. Vernon, Jr., *Methodism Moves Across West Texas* (Nashville, 1967), p. 35.

13. Paul H. Boase, "Moral Policemen on the Ohio Frontier," *Ohio Historical Quarterly*, January 1959, p. 41.

14. Sweet, *op. cit.*, p. 648.

15. *Ibid.*, p. 659.

16. *Ibid.*, p. 664.

17. *Ibid.*, p. 675.

18. Arthur W. Calhoun, *A Social History of the American Family* (Cleveland, 1919), Vol. I, p. 40.

19. J. Milton Yinger, *Religion in the Struggle for Power: A Study in the Sociology of Religion* (Durham, N.C., 1946), pp. 18 ff.

XI. FROLIC OF FAITH: CAMP MEETINGS

1. Umphrey Lee, *The Lord's Horseman: John Wesley the Man* (New York and Nashville, 1928), p. 74.

2. Frederick Morgan Davenport, *Primitive Traits in Religious Revivals: A Study in Mental and Social Evolution* (New York, 1905), pp. 72–73.

3. Thomas D. Clark, *Frontier America, The Story of the Westward Movement* (New York, 1959), p. 227.
4. Davenport, *op. cit.*, pp. 60, 63.
5. Catherine Cleveland, *The Great Revival in the West* (Gloucester, Mass., 1959), p. 39.
6. *Ibid.*, p. 39. See also Elmer T. Clark, *The Small Sects in America* (Nashville, 1937), p. 115.
7. Quoted in Charles A. Johnson, *The Frontier Camp Meeting* (Dallas, 1955), p. 35.
8. Cleveland, *op. cit.*, p. 77.
9. *Ibid.*, p. 32.

XII. RELEASED BY THE LORD

1. Charles A. Johnson, *The Frontier Camp Meeting* (Dallas, 1955), p. 121.
2. *Ibid.*, p. 49. Quoted from a letter to Thomas Coke.
3. *Ibid.*, p. 46.
4. *Ibid.*, p. 27.
5. *Ibid.*, p. 57.
6 *Ibid.*, pp. 65–66.
7. *Ibid.*, pp. 214–215. Quoting a writer in *The Methodist Quarterly Review*, Vol. III, pp. 600–601.
8. Catherine Cleveland, *The Great Revival in the West* (Gloucester, Mass., 1959), p. 101.
9. *Ibid.*, p. 89.
10. Elmer T. Clark, *The Small Sects in America* (Nashville, 1937), p. 116. Quoted by Tyler, *The Disciples*, American Church History Series, Vol. XI, p. 14.
11. Frederick Morgan Davenport, *Primitive Traits in Religious Revivals* (New York, 1905), p. 77, quoting McMaster, *History of the United States*, Vol. II, p. 581.
12. *Ibid.*, p. 76.
13. Cleveland, *op. cit.*, p. 95
14. Cleveland, *op. cit.*, p. 98.
15. *Ibid.*, p. 99.
16. Peter Cartwright, *The Autobiography of Peter Cartwright*, with an introduction, bibliography, and index by Charles L. Wallis (Nashville, 1956), p. 45.
17. *Autobiography of Rev. James B. Finley*, edited by W. P. Strickland (Cincinnati, 1856), pp. 166 ff.

XIII. THE MEETINGS COME TO ORDER

1. *The Journal and Letters of Francis Asbury*, edited by Elmer T. Clark (New York and Nashville, 1958), Vol. III, p. 333.
2. Edwin Scott Gaustad, *Historical Atlas of Religion in America* (New York and Evanston, 1963), p. 88.
3. James B. Finley, *Sketches of Western Methodism*, edited by W. P. Strickland (Cincinnati, 1855), p. 25.

4. George Rosen, *Madness in Society: Chapters in the Historical Sociology of Mental Illness* (Chicago, 1968), p. 216.

5. Charles A. Johnson, *The Frontier Camp Meeting* (Dallas, 1955), p. 50.

6. *Journal and Letters*, Vol. III, p. 196. January 20, 1801.

7. *Ibid.*, p. 381. December 14, 1807.

8. *Ibid.*, p. 251. December 2, 1802. p. 255. December 30, 1802.

9. Johnson, *op. cit.*, p. 215.

10 *Ibid.*, pp. 89, 90.

11. *Cyclopedia of Methodism*, edited by Matthew Simpson (Philadelphia, 1881), p. 253.

12. Johnson, *op. cit.*, p. 92.

13. *Journal and Letters*, Vol. III, p. 436. August 25, 1810.

14. Thomas L. Agnew, "Methodism on the Frontier," *The History of American Methodism*, edited by Emory Stevens Bucke (Nashville, 1964), pp. 521–522.

15. Johnson, *op. cit.*, p. 105.

16. *Ibid.*, pp. 43, 47, for diagrams of the shapes of the camps. For a vivid description of the layout of early camp-meeting grounds see Jesse Lee, *A Short History of the Methodists in the United States of America* (Baltimore, 1810), pp. 360 ff.

17. *Ibid.*, p. 219.

18. *Selected Chapters from the History of the Wyandott Mission at Upper Sandusky, Ohio* by Rev. James B. Finley. Edited by R. T. Stevenson (Cincinnati, 1916), p. 15.

XIV. THE METHODISTS TAKE OREGON

1. Walter N. Vernon, Jr., *William Stevenson, Riding Preacher* (Dallas, 1964), pp. 38–40. See also Macum Phelan, *A History of Early Methodism in Texas, 1817–1866* (Nashville, 1924), pp. 13–14.

2. Almer Pennewell, *A Voice in the Wilderness 1766–1835: Jesse Walker* (Nashville, 1959), pp. 99–101, 107–113.

3. Ray A. Billington, "Oregon Epic: A Letter That Jarred America," *The Pacific Historian*, Summer 1968, pp. 30 ff.

4. *Ibid.*, p. 34.

5. William R. Cannon, "Education, Publication, Benevolent Work, and Missions," *The History of American Methodism*, edited by Emory Stevens Bucke, Vol. I, p. 594.

6. Cornelius J. Brosnan, *Jason Lee: Prophet of the New Oregon* (New York, 1932), p. 13.

7. *Ibid.*, p. 32.

8. Oscar Osburn Winther, *The Old Oregon Country* (Stanford, 1950), p. 92.

9. *Ibid.*, p. 93.

10. Brosnan, *op. cit.*, p. 48.

11. Wade Crawford Barclay, *Early American Methodism 1769–1844* (New York, 1950), Vol. II, p. 207.

12. *The Oregon Almanac and Book of Facts 1961–1962*, edited by James E. Brooks (Portland, 1961), pp. 237–238.

13. Richard G. Montgomery, *The White-Headed Eagle: John McLoughlin* (New York, 1934), p. 201.

14. Billington, *op. cit.*, p. 31.

15. Brosnan, *op. cit.*, pp. 75–76, quoting Z. A. Mudge, *The Missionary Teacher: A Memoir of Cyrus Shepard.*

16. Brosnan, *op. cit.*, p. 78.

17. *Ibid.*, p. 73.

18. Dorothy O. Johansen and Charles M. Gates, *Empire of the Columbia: A History of the Pacific Northwest* (New York, 1957), p. 211.

19. *Ibid.*, p. 166.

20. *Ibid.*, p. 172.

21. Winther, *op. cit.*, p. 137.

22. Brosnan, *op. cit.*, p. 219.

23. Johansen and Gates, op. cit., p. 228.

24. Quoted in Brosnan, *op. cit.*, pp. 94–95.

25. Stephen R. Beggs, *Pages from the Early History of the West and North-West, etc.* (Cincinnati, 1868) p. 258.

26. Brosnan, *op. cit.*, p. 158. Johansen and Gates, *op. cit.*, p. 210.

27. Billington, *op. cit*, p. 36.

28. *Ibid.*

29. Brosnan, *op. cit.*, pp. 211–212.

30. *Ibid.*, p. 274.

XV. THE MISCHIEF BEGINS

1. Frederick E. Maser and George A. Singleton, "Further Branches of Methodism Are Founded," *The History of American Methodism*, edited by Emory Stevens Bucke (New York and Nashville, 1964), Vol. I, pp. 617–618. See also Edward J. Drinkhouse, *History of Methodist Reform* (Baltimore and Pittsburgh, 1899), pp. 388–390. The account is substantially the same, although Drinkhouse cites correspondence between Hammett and Mr. Wesley to indicate that Hammett was acting under a British connection and that Mr. Wesley approved the Hammett arrangement and the Primitive Methodists more than he did the actions taken at and after the Christmas Conference.

2. *The Journal and Letters of Francis Asbury*, edited by Elmer T. Clark (Nashville, 1958), Vol. I, p. 707. February 18, 1792.

3. Maser and Singleton, *op. cit.*, p. 619.

4. *Ibid.*, p. 620.

5. John Lednum, *A History of the Rise of Methodism in America* (Philadelphia, 1859), p. 222.

6. Frederick A. Norwood, "The Church Takes Shape," *The History of American Methodism*, Vol. I, p. 444.

7. Drinkhouse, *op. cit.*, Vol. I, p. 450.

8. *Cyclopedia of Methodism*, edited by Matthew Simpson (Philadelphia, 1881), pp. 678–679.

9. Sidney Benjamin Bradley, *The Life of Bishop Richard Whatcoat* (Louisville, 1936), p. 195.

10. *Cyclopedia of Methodism*, edited by Matthew Simpson (Philadelphia, 1881), pp. 935–936. The quotation is from Laban Clark, who as a young preacher came under the influence of Bishop Whatcoat.

11. *Journals of the General Conference of the Methodist Episcopal Church 1796–1836*, Vol. I (New York, 1836), p. 76.

12. Samuel Drew, *The Life of the Rev. Thomas Coke: His Various Travels Etc.* (New York, 1818), pp. 322. ff.

13. *Ibid.*, p. 358.

XVI. REFORM WITH A VENGEANCE

1. Wade Crawford Barclay, *Early American Methodism 1769–1844* (New York, 1950), Vol. II, p. 423.

2. *Cyclopedia of Methodism*, edited by Matthew Simpson (Philadelphia, 1881), p. 578.

3. Barclay, *op. cit.*, p. 293.

4. Stephen R. Beggs, *Pages from the Early History of the West and North-West, etc.* (Cincinnati, 1868), p. 299.

5. Barclay, *op. cit.*, p. 336.

6. Elmer T. Clark, "Asbury's Last Journey," *The Journal and Letters of Francis Asbury*, edited by Elmer T. Clark (Nashville, 1964), Vol. II, pp. 804 ff. See also Ezra Squier Tipple, *Francis Asbury, Prophet of the Long Road* (New York and Cincinnati, 1916), pp. 294 ff.

7. Robert D. Simpson, "Freeborn Garrettson, American Methodist Pioneer," unpublished dissertation (Drew University, 1954), pp. 208–12.

8. Douglas R. Chandler, "The Formation of the Methodist Protestant Church," *The History of American Methodism*, edited by Emory Stevens Bucke (Nashville, 1964), Vol. I, p. 662.

9. *Ibid.*, p. 642.

10. Edward J. Drinkhouse, *History of Methodist Reform* (Baltimore and Pittsburgh, 1899), Vol. II, p. 9.

11. Chandler, *op. cit.*, p. 648.

12. *Ibid.*, pp. 656–657.

13. *Cyclopedia of Methodism*, p. 603.

XVII. HALF SLAVE AND HALF FREE

1. Wade Crawford Barclay, *Early American Methodism 1769–1844* (New York, 1950), Vol. II, pp. 53, 54.

2. *Ibid.*, p. 71.

3. *Ibid.*, p. 72.

4. *The Journal and Letters of Francis Asbury*, edited by Elmer T. Clark (Nashville, 1964), Vol. II, p. 591. February 1, 1809.

5. Herbert Aptheker, *American Slave Revolts* (New York, 1943), p. 246.

6. *Ibid.*, p. 162.

7. *Ibid.*, p. 220.

8. *Ibid.*, p. 23.

9. *Cyclopedia of Methodism*, edited by Matthew Simpson (Philadelphia, 1881), p. 791, for an account of the life and work of Orange Scott.

10. Charles H. Wesley, *Richard Allen, Apostle of Freedom* (Washington, 1935), p. 15.

11. *Ibid.*, p. 32.
12. *Ibid.*, p. 48
13. *Ibid.*, pp. 52–53.
14. *Ibid.*, p. 72.
15. Frederick E. Maser and George A. Singleton, "Further Branches of Methodism Are Founded," *The History of American Methodism*, edited by Emory Stevens Bucke (Nashville, 1964), pp. 605–609.
16. *Ibid.*, pp. 609–614.

XVIII. A CHURCH DIVIDES A NATION

1. George R. Crooks, *The Life of Bishop Matthew Simpson* (New York, 1891), p. 229.
2. *Journal of the General Conference 1844*, p. 165.
3. John N. Norwood, *The Schism in the Methodist Episcopal Church, 1844–1846* (Alfred, N.Y., 1923), p. 51.
4. *The Life and Letters of Stephen Olin* (New York, 1853), Vol. II, p. 156.
5. *Ibid.*, p. 158.
6. Norwood, *op. cit.*, pp. 69 ff.
7. Norman W. Spellman, "The Church Divides, 1844," *The History of American Methodism*, edited by Emory Stevens Bucke (Nashville, 1964), p. 57.
8. *Ibid.*, p. 71, quoting *Report of Debates in the General Conference of the Methodist Episcopal Church, Held in the City of New York, 1844* (New York, 1844).
9. *Ibid.*, p. 76.
10. Norwood, *op. cit.*, p. 80.
11. *Ibid.*, p. 76.
12. Spellman, *op. cit.*, p. 65.

XIX. GOD AND THE MOST BATTALIONS

1. *The Story of America as Reported By Its Newspapers 1690–1965*, edited by Edwin Emery (New York, 1954), p. 51.
2. "Senator Calhoun's Proposal to Restore a Sectional Equilibrium," quoted in *The Compromise of 1850*, edited by Edwin C. Rozwenc (Boston, 1957), pp. 26 ff.
3. Arthur E. Jones, Jr., "The Years of Disagreement, 1844–1861," *The History of American Methodism*, edited by Emory Stevens Bucke (Nashville, 1964), p. 180. For an account of the Louisville Convention, see pp. 111 ff.
4. *Reader's Digest Almanac 1966* (Pleasantville, N.Y., 1965), p. 273.
5. *Cyclopedia of Methodism*, edited by Matthew Simpson (Philadelphia, 1881), p. 600.
6. Jones, *op. cit.*, p. 172.
7. *Ibid.*, p. 176.
8. Ralph E. Morrow, *Northern Methodism and Reconstruction* (East Lansing, Mich., 1956), pp. 14–15.

9. George R. Crooks, *The Life of Bishop Matthew Simpson* (New York, 1891), pp. 397–398. Reproduction of the letter Lincoln wrote in reply to the greetings from the 1864 General Conference.

10. Morrow, *op. cit.*, pp. 14–15 ff.

11. *Ibid.*, p. 17.

12. Quoted by James W. May, "The War Years," *The History of American Methodism*, Vol. II, p. 230.

13. *Ibid.*, p. 218.

14. Morrow, *op. cit.*, p. 17.

15. Crooks, *op. cit.*, p. 382.

16. Morrow, *op. cit.*, p. 33.

17. May, *op. cit.*, p. 250.

18. William Warren Sweet, *The Story of Religions in America* (New York, 1930), p. 463.

19. Morrow, *op. cit.*, p. 248.

20. Hunter Dickinson Farish, *The Circuit Rider Dismounts* (Richmond, 1938), p. 43.

21. Morrow, *op. cit.*, p. 65.

22. Farish, op. cit., p. 48.

23. Morrow, *op. cit.*, p. 49.

24. Farish, *op. cit.*, p. 110.

25. *Ibid.*, p. 123.

26. *Ibid.*, p. 122.

27. *Ibid.*, p. 117.

28. Morrow, *op. cit.*, p. 207.

XX. CAN THESE BONES LIVE?

1. Quoted in E. Merton Coulter, *The South During Reconstruction 1865–1877* (Baton Rouge, 1947), p. 2. From the *Weekly Constitutionalist* (Augusta, Ga., Nov. 27, 1867).

2. Woodrow Wilson, *A History of the American People* (New York and London, 1902), pp. 311–312. Charles T. Thrift, Jr., "Rebuilding the Southern Church," *The History of American Methodism*, edited by Emory Stevens Bucke (New York and Nashville, 1964), Vol. II, p. 258.

3. James W. May, "The War Years," *The History of American Methodism*, Vol. II, p. 246.

4. Martin Rist, "Methodism Goes West," *The History of American Methodism*, Vol. II, p. 431.

5. May, *op. cit.*, p. 247

6. Thrift, *op. cit.*, p. 268.

7. John J. Tigert IV, *Bishop Holland Nimmons McTyeire: Ecclesiastical and Educational Architect* (Nashville, Vanderbilt University Press), p. 103.

8. Quoted, Thrift, *op. cit.*, pp. 268–269.

9. *Ibid.*, p. 274.

10. *Ibid.*, p. 277.

11. Hunter Dickinson Farish, *The Circuit Rider Dismounts* (Richmond, 1938), p. 1.

12. *Ibid.*, p. 76.

13. *Ibid.*, p. 151.

14. Ralph E. Morrow, *Northern Methodism and Reconstruction* (East Lansing, Mich., 1956), p. 35.
15. Thrift, *op. cit.*, p. 265.
16. Morrow, *op. cit.*, p. 54.
17. Farish, *op. cit.*, p. 180.
18. Walter W. Benjamin, "The Methodist Episcopal Church in the Postwar Era," *The History of American Methodism*, Vol. II, pp. 369–371.
19. Farish, *op. cit.*, pp. 190 ff.
20. Harold W. Mann, *Atticus Greene Haygood, Methodist Bishop, Editor and Educator* (Athens, Ga., 1965), pp. 154, 182.

XXI. THE SECOND BLESSING

1. Estimate by Walter Hallenweger, staff specialist of the World Council of Churches. Lack of reliable records in the underdeveloped countries makes accuracy impossible. Hallenweger thinks world membership may be as high as thirty-five million.
2. Robert C. Monk, *John Wesley: His Puritan Heritage* (New York and Nashville, 1966), p. 111.
3. John Leland Peters, *Christian Perfection and American Methodism* (Nashville, 1956), pp. 182–183, 185.
4. *Ibid.*, p. 184.
5. Winthrop S. Hudson, *American Protestantism* (Chicago, 1961), p. 101.
6. Timothy L. Smith, *Revivalism and Social Reform* (Nashville, 1937), pp. 103 ff.
7. Elmer T. Clark, *The Small Sects in America* (Nashville, 1937), p. 176.
8. *Ibid.*, p. 177. Quotations from George Wallingford Noyes, *Religious Experience of John Humphrey Noyes, Founder of the Oneida Community* (New York, 1923), pp. 123, 225, 226.
9. Smith, *Revivalism*, p. 105.
10. Winifred King Rugg, *Unafraid, A Life of Anne Hutchinson* (Boston, 1930), especially pp. 185 ff. See also a more recent study by Emery Battis, *Saints and Sectaries: Anne Hutchinson and the Antinomian Controversy in Massachusetts Bay Colony* (Chapel Hill, N.C., 1962).
11. Harold Vinson Synan, "The Pentecostal Movement in the United States," unpublished dissertation (University of Georgia, 1967), p. 24.
12. Smith, *op. cit.*, p. 117.
13. *Ibid.*, p. 105.
14. Synan, *op. cit.*, p. 26.
15. Walter W. Benjamin, "The Methodist Church in the Postwar Era," *The History of American Methodism*, edited by Emory Stevens Bucke (Nashville, 1964), p. 346.
16. *Ibid.*, pp. 347 ff.
17. Smith, *op. cit.*, p. 132.
18. Edwin Scott Gausted, *Historical Atlas of Religion in America* (New York, 1962), p. 134.
19. Timothy L. Smith, "The Holiness Crusade," *The History of American Methodism*, Vol. II, p. 613.
20. Synan, *op. cit.*, p. 41.
21. Smith, "Holiness," Vol. II, p. 614.

22. John T. Cunningham, "Ocean Grove Centennial: To These Shores," *Newark News,* July 27, 1969, p. 4. For background, *Cyclopedia of Methodism,* edited by Matthew Simpson (Philadelphia, 1881), pp. 672–673.

23. Quoted by Synan, *op. cit.,* p. 52.

24. Harold W. Mann, *Atticus Greene Haygood: Methodist Bishop, Editor and Educator* (Athens, Ga., 1965), p. 162.

25. *Ibid.,* p. 167.

26. Quoted by Synan, *op. cit.,* p. 53.

27. Herbert Richardson, "Holy Spirit and Protestantism," *Commonweal,* November 8, 1868, p. 195.

XXII. THE ROCKY ROAD TO REUNION

1. "The Church Is Here!" A musical-dance-drama sketching two hundred years of Methodism in America. For the combined Texas Conferences, Wednesday, June 8, 1966. Moody Coliseum, Southern Methodist University, Dallas, Texas. Script by Kermit Hunter.

2. "Methodists: The Challenge of Fortune," *Time,* May 8, 1964, p. 74.

3. John M. Moore, *The Long Road to Methodist Union* (New York and Nashville, 1943), p. 58. The text of the letter is given in full.

4. Dow Kirkpatrick, "Early Efforts at Reunion," *The History of American Methodism,* edited by Emory Stevens Bucke (New York and Nashville, 1964), Vol, II, p. 667.

5. Moore, *op. cit.,* p. 65.

6. Douglas R. Chandler, "The Methodist Protestant Church 1865–1900," *The History of American Methodism,* Vol. II, p. 401.

7. Moore, *op. cit.,* pp. 119–120.

8. *Ibid.,* pp. 123–124.

9. *Ibid.,* p. 121.

10. On the organization and early days of The Colored Methodist Episcopal Church, see Edwin Scott Gausted, *Historical Atlas of Religion in America* (New York, 1962), p. 81; Charles T. Thrift, Jr., "Rebuilding the Southern Church," *The History of American Methodism,* Vol. II, pp. 285, 314.

11. See Dwight W. Culver, *Negro Segregation in the Methodist Church* (New Haven and London, 1953), esp. pp. 53 ff. Also see Kirkpatrick, *op. cit.,* p. 688, and Moore, *op. cit.,* pp. 136–137.

12. Robert Moats Miller, "Methodism and American Society 1900–1939," *The History of American Methodism,* Vol. III, p. 366.

13. *Ibid.,* p. 367.

14. Moore, *op. cit.,* p. 183.

15. *Ibid.,* p. 194.

16. *Ibid.,* pp. 208 ff.

XXIII. EVERY MAN HIS OWN COLLEGE

1. William P. Tolley, "Address," reported in *Daily Advocate,* April 24, 1968, p. 76.

2. Leland D. Case, "Origins of Methodist Publishing in America," paper

read before the Mississippi Valley Regional Meeting of the Bibliographical Society of America in St. Louis, June 28, 1964, p. 13.

3. De Witt T. Starnes and Gertrude E. Noyes, *The English Dictionary from Cawdrey to Johnson* (Chapel Hill, N.C., 1946), p. 175.

4. *Ibid.*, pp. 172, 173.

5. Case, *op. cit.*, p. 15.

6. James Penn Pilkington, *The Methodist Publishing House: A History* (New York and Nashville, 1968), Vol. I, p. 32.

7. *Ibid.*, quoting *Journals of the General Conferences of the Methodist Episcopal Church.* Published quadrennially. "Journal of 1808," pp. 83, 87.

8. Case, *op. cit.*, p. 23, quoting Thomas Rankin, MS. Journal, Library, Garrett Theological Seminary, Evanston, Ill.

9. Sylvanus Milne Duvall, *The Methodist Episcopal Church and Education up to 1869* (New York, 1928), pp. 31–32.

10. William R. Cannon, "Education, Publication, Benevolent Work, and Missions," *The History of American Methodism*, edited by Emory Stevens Bucke (Nashville, 1964), Vol. I, p. 568.

11. *Ibid.*, p. 567.

12. Quoted by Winthrop S. Hudson, *American Protestantism* (Chicago, 1961), p. 61.

13. Duvall, *op. cit.*, pp. 47 ff. Dempster testified that he carried on his campaign in the face of fierce opposition on the part of at least two-thirds of the entire Methodist Ministry.

14. John O. Gross, "The Field of Education," *The History of American Methodism*, Vol. III, pp. 228 ff.

15. Paul Douglas, "Bilingual Work and Language Conferences," *The History of American Methodism*, Vol. II, p. 490.

16. Ellwood Hendrick, *Lewis Miller, A Biographical Essay* (New York, 1925), pp. 68–69.

17. *Ibid.*, p. 147.

18. Samuel A. Schreiner, Jr., "A Place Called Chautauqua." Unpublished manuscript.

19. Raymond Schuessler, "There'll Always Be a Chautauqua," *Ford Times*, August 1967, p. 4.

20. Rebecca Richmond, *Chautauqua: An American Place* (New York, 1943), pp. 72 ff.

XXIV. WOMAN AT THE DOOR

1. Elizabeth Palmer, "Women in a New Age," Selected Materials from the National Seminar of the Woman's Division of Christian Service. Held at the University of Puget Sound, Tacoma, Washington, July 31–August 9, 1963, pp. 23–25.

2. Arthur W. Calhoun, *Social History of the American Family from Colonial Times to the Present* (Cleveland, 1918), Vol. I, p. 79.

3. Martin Rist, "Methodism Goes West," *The History of American Methodism*, edited by Emory Stevens Bucke (New York and Nashville, 1964), Vol. II, pp. 464–465.

4. Reginald S. Craig, *The Fighting Parson, the Biography of Colonel John M. Chivington* (Los Angeles, 1959), pp. 121 ff.

5. *Ibid.*, p. 131.

6. Frederic L. Paxson, *History of the American Frontier 1763–1893* (Boston and New York, 1924), p. 490.

7. Craig, *op. cit.*, 237.

8. Jacob S. Payton, "Methodism's Spread in America," *Methodism*, edited by William K. Anderson (Nashville, 1947), p. 68.

9. Kenneth M. Mackenzie, *The Robe and the Sword* (Washington, D.C., 1961), p. 59.

10. *Ibid.*, p. 69.

11. *Ibid.*, p. 73.

12. *Ibid.*, p. 94.

13. Quoted in Charles A. and Mary R. Beard, *The Rise of American Civilization* (revised and enlarged edition, New York, 1933), pp. 375–376.

14. Mary Earhart, *Frances Willard: From Prayers to Politics* (Chicago, 1944), pp. 298–299.

15. *Ibid.*, p. 302.

16. *Journal of the General Conference of the Methodist Episcopal Church 1888*, p. 112.

XXV. SERVICE ENTRANCE

1. Timothy L. Smith, *Revivalism and Social Reform* (New York and Nashville, 1967), pp. 170–171.

2. *Cyclopedia of Methodism*, edited by Matthew Simpson (Philadelphia, 1881), pp. 364–365.

3. *Ibid.*, pp. 960–961.

4. Ruth Esther Meeker, *1880–1940: A History of the Woman's Home Missionary Society of the Methodist Episcopal Church* (New York, 1969), p. 3.

5. Sidney Thomas Davis, "Woman's Work in the Methodist Church," unpublished dissertation (University of Pittsburgh, 1963), pp. 215–216.

6. Meeker, *op. cit.*, p. 5.

7. Davis, *op. cit.*, p. 217.

8. *Ibid.*, pp. 286–289.

9. *Ibid.*, p. 220.

10. W. Richey Hogg, "The Missions of American Methodism," *The History of American Methodism*, edited by Emory Stevens Bucke (Nashville, 1964), Vol. III, p. 71.

11. Lewis T. Nordyke, "The Ladies and the Lynchers," *The Reader's Digest*, November 1939, p. 110. Also Robert Moats Miller, "Methodism and American Society 1900–1939," *The History of American Methodism*, Vol. III, pp. 369–370.

12. Meeker, *op. cit.*, pp. 25–26.

13. Aaron Ignatius Abell, *The Urban Impact on American Protestantism 1865–1900* (Cambridge, Mass., 1943), p. 200.

14. *Ibid.*, p. 202.

15. Davis, *op. cit.*, p. 366.

16. *Ibid.*, p. 370.

17. Release from the Board of Missions of the Methodist Church, January 17, 1961.

18. Release from United Methodist Information, November 4, 1969.

19. Support had been steady and upward over a thirty-year period until a decline of $617,118 for 1969 was reported by the treasurer of the Division. Considering the trend of giving since the Division was formed, the decline may be attributed to economic conditions rather than to criticism of policy.

XXVI. THE DEMON RUM

1. Robert Moats Miller, "Methodism and American Society, 1900–1939," *The History of American Methodism*, edited by Emory Stevens Bucke (New York and Nashville, 1964), Vol. III, p. 335.

2. Richard M. Cameron, "The New Church Takes Root," *The History of American Methodism*, Vol. I, p. 256.

3. *Ibid.*, p. 257.

4. *Journals of The General Conference of the Methodist Episcopal Church*, Vol. I, 1796–1836, pp. 106 ff.

5. Hunter Dickinson Farish, *The Circuit Rider Dismounts* (Richmond, 1938), pp. 308–309.

6. Horace Bushnell, *Barbarism the First Danger* (New York, 1947), p. 15.

7. John Allen Krout, *The Origins of Prohibition* (New York, 1925), p. 99.

8. Miller, *op. cit.*, p. 326.

9. Annie Wittenmeyer, *History of the Woman's Temperance Crusade* (Boston, 1882), pp. 34–37.

10. *Ibid.*, p. 51.

11. Mary Earhart, *Frances Willard: From Prayers to Politics* (Chicago, 1944), p. 141.

12. Frances E. Willard, *Glimpses of Fifty Years: The Autobiography of an American Woman* (Chicago, 1889), p. 31.

13. Lydia Jones Trowbridge, *Frances Willard of Evanston* (Chicago, 1928), p. 32.

14. *Ibid.*, p. 93.

15. Trowbridge, *op. cit.*, pp. 201 ff.

16. Irving Fisher, *Prohibition at Its Worst* (New York, 1926), p. 10.

17. Peter H. Odegard, *Pressure Politics: The Story of the Anti-Saloon League* (New York, 1928), pp. 166–167.

18. Miller, *op. cit.*, p. 338.

XXVII. INTO THE PIT

1. Robert Moats Miller, "Methodism and American Society," *The History of American Methodism*, edited by Emory Stevens Bucke (New York and Nashville, 1964), Vol. III, p. 334.

2. *Concise Dictionary of American History*, edited by Wayne Andrews (New York, 1962), p. 525.

3. Philip Taft and Philip Ross, "American Labor Violence: Its Causes, Character, and Outcome," *Violence in America: Historical and Comparative Perspectives* by Hugh Davis Graham and Ted Robert Gurr. A Report Submitted to the

National Commission on the Causes and Prevention of Violence (New York, 1969), pp. 288–289.

4. Quoted by Henry F. May, *Protestant Churches and Industrial America* (New York, 1949), p. 93.

5. Taft and Ross, *op. cit.*, pp. 283–284.

6. Quoted by May, *op. cit.*, p. 101.

7. *Ibid.*, pp. 109–110.

8. Miller, *op. cit.*, p. 371.

9. Francis J. McConnell, *By the Way: An Autobiography* (New York and Nashville, 1952), p. 249.

10. Walter G. Muelder, *Methodism and Society in the Twentieth Century* (New York and Nashville, 1961), p. 47.

11. F. Gerald Ensley, "Walter Rauschenbusch: Prophet of the Social Gospel," *Together*, July 1963, p. 32.

12. *Report on the Steel Strike of 1919* by the Commission of Inquiry, the Interchurch World Movement (New York, 1920), pp. 23–25.

13. J. Paul Williams, *What Americans Believe and How They Worship* (New York, 1952), p. 290.

14. Walter W. Benjamin, "Bishop Francis J. McConnell and the Great Steel Strike of 1919–1920," *A Miscellany of American Christianity*, Essays in Honor of H. Shelton Smith, edited by Stuart C. Henry (Durham, N.C., 1963), pp. 26, 27.

15. *Report*, p. 10.

16. Miller, *op. cit.*, p. 385.

17. Benjamin, *op. cit.*, p. 22.

18. McConnell, *op. cit.*, p. 216.

19. Benjamin, *op. cit.*, pp. 30, 32.

20. *Report*, p. 54.

21. Benjamin, *op. cit.*, p. 43.

22. *Ibid.*, p. 43, quoting "Three Shifts in Steel," *Survey*, Vol. XLV, December 11, 1920, p. 387.

XXVIII. TO SERVE THE PRESENT AGE

1. Lycurgus M. Starkey, "Social Concern: A Methodist Tradition," *Together*, March 1964, p. 43.

2. Halford E. Luccock and Paul Hutchinson, *The Story of Methodism* (New York and Cincinnati, 1926), pp. 331–333.

3. Aaron Ignatius Abell, *The Urban Impact on American Protestantism, 1865–1900* (Cambridge, Mass., and London, 1943), p. 158.

4. *Ibid.*, p. 159.

5. *Ibid.*, p. 166.

6. *Ibid.*, pp. 168–169.

7. *Ibid.*, p. 171.

8. Walter G. Muelder, *Methodism and Society in the Twentieth Century* (New York and Nashville, 1961), p. 57.

9. Beatrice Plumb, *Edgar James Helms: The Goodwill Man* (Minneapolis, 1965), p. 9.

10. *Ibid.*, p. 26.
11. *Ibid.*, p. 109.
12. J. Frazier Vance, "Making Men Out of Rubbish," *The Reader's Digest,* December 1935, p. 22. For later details on the amazing work of Goodwill Industries, see "Salvaging Men, Things," *Worker with Youth,* May 1961, p. 937. Helms remained a member of the New England Conference. An obituary appears in Methodist Churches (U.S.) Conferences, New England Minutes, 1943, p. 937.
13. "Enterprise of the Heart," *Time,* May 5, 1952.

XXIX. FOREVER BEGINNING

1. "Profile of the United Methodist Church," *Together,* May 1968, p. 20. The per capita giving of the former E.U.B. Church was $80.18, that of the former Methodist Church was $64.61.
2. *Daily Christian Advocate,* April 30, 1968, p. 359.
3. American Institute of Public Opinion Poll, reported in *The New York Times* by Edward B. Fiske, January 19, 1967.
4. *Daily Advocate,* May 6, 1968, p. 794. The text of the resolution appears in the *Daily Advocate,* April 29, 1968, p. 325.
5. *Daily Advocate,* April 29, 1968, p. 303.
6. *Daily Advocate,* September 12, 1966, p. 911.
7. *Daily Advocate,* September 13, 1966, p. 913.
8. Frank Milton Bristol, *The Life of Chaplain McCabe* (New York and Cincinnati, 1908), p. 78.
9. *Ibid.,* pp. 132 ff.
10. *Ibid.,* p. 143.
11. Francis J. McConnell, *By the Way: An Autobiography* (New York and Nashville, 1952), pp. 233–234.
12. *Ibid.,* p. 66.
13. Release by the Communications Staff of the General Conference of The United Methodist Church, April 23, 1970.
14. *Ibid.,* April 24, 1970.
15. See Edwin Scott Gaustad, "Methodists," *Historical Atlas of Religion in America* (New York, 1962), p. 81. See also G. Bromley Oxnam, "Methodism Facing the Future," Methodist Church (U.S.) General Conference, 1960. *Journal,* pp. 1975–1983. The Gausted phrase "rocket riders" does not appear in the Oxnam address, but the address did urge Methodists to go beyond the celebrated Wesley declaration, "The world is my parish," and, in the space age, make the universe their parish.

To Give Thanks

Drafts of the manuscript of this book have been read by critics qualified to appraise and vet it from various points of view. Also parts of the manuscript were submitted to persons who know well particular phases of the subject or whose criticism might help lend it popular interest. None of those mentioned can be held responsible for inaccuracies that survive, but all deserve my abiding gratitude for making the book better than it would have been without their exertions.

Leland Davidson Case, editor of the Methodist family magazine *Together* from its inception in 1956 until 1963, gave the draft he saw such close scrutiny that his memorandum of comment ran to thirty-six pages. An ardent student of the history of the denomination, Case wanted far more English background than I provided. It was not possible to accommodate all his wishes, but every suggestion he made in reading the manuscript, and later in reading the galleys, was scrupulously studied.

Arthur West, executive secretary of United Methodist Information, an alert agency dealing with current events and actions against their background within the Church, read the manuscript for general accuracy, making changes in points of fact and of tact. Leonard M. Perryman, whose responsibilities include the handling of information about the organization of women within Methodism, supplied leads and data—often on demand. Charlotte O'Neal discussed recent conference enactments relating to women and pointed out developments I had overlooked.

Welcome attention came from the executive editor of general publications, division of curriculum resources, of the General Board of Education of The United Methodist Church, Walter N. Vernon, Jr. With a remarkable sense of detail and a keen knowledge of records, Mr. Vernon made important corrections in the manuscript as a whole and raised questions that led to revisions. Certain lacunae he noted—among them the absence of adequate reference to Sunday schools and young people's work—I was not able, both because of schedule and the limited aim of the book, to fill.

The two chapters devoted to women were reviewed by Thelma Stevens, who made pointed observations and then studied the rewrites resulting from her criticism. Miss Stevens served as an executive secretary of the Woman's Division of the Board of Missions from its formation in 1940. The revised chapters, as well as the galleys of the book as a whole, were read by Eleanor Loveland Welch, daughter of the late Bishop Herbert Welch and for twenty-five years associated with the Board of Missions.

I am grateful to the Sam Churchills of Yakima, Washington, for excellent source material on the Oregon country, for hospitality and guidance in touring the region of the Jason Lee mission, and for reading the Oregon chapter. Harold Vinson Synan of Emmanuel College critically examined the chapter on The Second Blessing as well as gave me the benefit of his thesis on the Pentecostal movement in the United States. Margaret Copeland of the Smith Library of Chautauqua Institution made available to me much unpublished detail on Chautauqua and read and corrected the chapter on education. Elizabeth Atkinson Plaisted, expert copy editor and counselor on all my writing, read the manuscript with care and perception, and offered pointers touching titles, emphasis, consistency, and taste.

Genevieve Egerton covered books basic to the study, turning over more than a thousand pages of notes. Her acquaintance with the essential literature enabled her to make excellent suggestions about both construction and revision, and her notes and bibliography served me well for checking and reference throughout the years the book was in preparation. Her wide range of reading was made possible by the cooperation of the West Chester Public Library and the Chester County Library at West Chester, Pennsylvania, and the Paoli Library at Paoli, Pennsylvania. Local libraries gave her access through interlibrary loan to the resources of the Pennsylvania State Library, the Library of the University of Pennsylvania, the Library of Pennsylvania State University, Bucknell Library at Crozer Theological Seminary, the Free Library of Philadelphia, Temple University Library, the Pennsylvania Historical Society Library, West Chester Historical Society Library, and the Library of the Presbyterian Historical Society.

For books used in verification and supplementary reading I am in debt to the patience and diligence of the staff of the Mount Kisco Public Library in my home town of Mount Kisco, New York, and to the remarkable inter-library loan service of Westchester County. Also I had access to the New York Public Library, where the collection of books is dumfoundingly catholic, calculated to meet every need and fancied need of a diverse urban area.

Books and records of special usefulness in the field of my inquiry were to be found in part at the United Mission Library, 475 Riverside Drive, New York. Material vital to clearing up obscure points and original source material reposed in the Rose Memorial Library of Drew University, Madison, New Jersey. I was much cheered at Drew by courtesies of the staff and by the guidance of Kenneth E. Rowe, Methodist librarian and editor of the new *Methodist Union Catalogue,* which will give the location throughout the nation of all material bearing on Methodism in America.

It would take a Lord Peter Wimsey to sort out the mysteries of my less obvious obligations. Friends have stood by. Caroline Rogers commented on parts of the manuscript, stimulating my phagocytes and calling for further efforts at clarity. Others sent me pertinent clippings and contributions or directed me to events indicating profound change. Ann Yeager Barnes put me in touch with the unprecedented system of lay deacons at Highland Park Methodist Church, Dallas, and the communion service wherein women are allowed to pass the elements. Both my next-door neighbor Belle Green and Ruth Morgan of San Francisco offered encouragement at crucial moments. From the sermons of my pastor, Charles D. Barton, I have gathered information and turns of phrase, and through his work I have been able to observe firsthand the wonders of Methodist polity in a local church.

All that happened helped. The celerity and zeal with which Betty Sears typed drafts of the manuscript at odd hours under pressure I took as further evidence of the good fortune that has blessed a book requiring cooperative effort at every turn.

CHARLES W. FERGUSON

Summer 1970

As the two hundredth year of Methodism in America is celebrated in 1984, it is appropriate to review some of its history and accomplishments. Few have captured the spirit of United Methodist involvement in the making of America more dramatically than Charles Ferguson in his book *Organizing to Beat the Devil*. The enthusiasm of so many who had read the book and their desire to have it available for reading and study during the Bicentennial year, encouraged the obtaining of rights for the reprinting. It is with much appreciation that we are indebted to the Eakin Press of Austin, Texas, for making this possible.

This brief "Update 1970-83" was designed to be nothing more than a reminder of some of the significant events of these past thirteen years that have had an impact upon religion in general, and United Methodism in particular. Far more exhaustive and in-depth writing on each of these subjects is readily available for serious studies.

In writing the following addendum to the original work, Methodist publications, particularly *Interpreter,* proved to be most useful. The Yearbooks of the *Encyclopaedia Britannica* were helpful in providing detailed information concerning the chronology of events.

In no way has any attempt been made to imitate Charles Ferguson's style, which has an inimitable quality all its own, but there is appreciation for the confidence that he placed in this being done by another.

Gordon D. Casad, District Superintendent
Dallas-Denton District
United Methodist Church

Dallas, Texas
June 28, 1983

AN UPDATE
1970–1983

In the twelve years since *Organizing to Beat the Devil* first appeared in print, the winds of change have furiously whipped the rigging of Methodism. Not only has it been given new sail, but new ports of call as well. The course has changed from the relatively placid waters of local concerns to the frequently raging storms of overwhelming worldwide social crises. The radical demonstrations of the sixties on the college campuses and the memories of burning cities, along with the nation's painful involvement in Vietnam, all caught the church in the crosscurrents of external and internal controversy.

If there was one event that could be said to have set the agenda of the church for the seventies, it was when James Forman, on Sunday, May 4, 1968, read the Black Manifesto from the pulpit of Riverside Church, New York City. This called for funding by ten major religious agencies and was as Forman termed the Manifesto, "a seizure of power." Based on the principle that blacks were entitled to reparations for damages from America's whites, the initial goal of five hundred million dollars was later raised to three billion. The money was to be used to secure land for black farmers, gain black control in publishing and broadcasting interests, develop research and training centers, and meet the needs that poverty had brought upon blacks.

The reaction ranged from outright rejection to pleas for understanding. Many in the National Association for the Advancement of Colored People rejected it. The United Methodist Bishops repudiated its ideology and pointed out that a twenty-million-dollar Fund for Reconciliation had already been established. It did not take long for all segments of the religious world to express their feelings about it. The ultimate effect, however, was not all negative since it did painfully point out the depths of injustice, violence, and racism that blacks experience and fired a warning that something must be done.

It was in the midst of tensions created by this and other traumatizing events of the period that a special session of an interim General Conference was held in St. Louis in 1970. This conference was convened to make certain that the machinery established in 1968 was functioning properly. As the time neared, the issues on race, campus unrest, and the war in Vietnam made it a conference no one wanted. Confronted as it was with these pressures, priorities were revised and by reducing funds to general agencies, two million dollars was designated for use by the Commission on Religion and Race. Goals for black colleges were raised to four million and one million was allocated for new black scholarships each year.

With the word "United" attached at the uniting conference in 1968, the merger between Methodist and Evangelical United Brethren churches came quickly, but it was to be six years before the last all-black annual conference would be merged.

While the conferences of 1968 and 1970 set the course of Methodism for the decade, the conference that most dramatically refitted the new riggings and changed the structure of the church was the General Conference of 1972 in Atlanta. It was here that a new statement of doctrine was formulated. The doctrinal study commission had been named at the uniting conference four years before and it was generally assumed a new creedal statement would be written. Not so. The commission sensed such a statement would fail and recommended that earlier faith statements of both Methodism and the Evangelical United Brethren should be used as source documents with scripture, tradition, reason and experience being recognized as the basis for theologizing. The doctrinal statement was approved by a vote of 925 to 17.

So thorough was the overhaul process at Atlanta that a new

statement of United Methodist Social Principles and a new Social Creed was written and adopted. It was a memorable and moving moment when Bishop James S. Thomas, head of the commission, led the conference in its first public reading.

While the church was moving to become more responsive to social problems, it was also involved in a massive restructuring plan of its national boards and agencies. This involved combining nine program agencies into four boards: Discipleship, Global Ministries. Church and Society, and Higher Education and Ministry. As nearly as possible the governing body of each of the new boards was to consist of one-third laymen, one-third laywomen, and one-third clergy, rather than the traditional half lay and half clergy. Each agency was to include representation from each major ethnic group, youth under 18, and young adults 19–30.

It was obvious the church was searching for relevancy. It addressed the problems of race, poverty, youth rebellion, and war, but there were often few evidences that those efforts were always effective or welcome. Congregations were raising more money than ever before, but in most cases it was being used locally and not going to social and missional efforts.

It was evident that more was needed to bring life, vitality, and renewal in depth to the new denomination. The missing component in the minds of many thoughtful leaders was evangelism. This was being stressed by both United Methodism and the World Methodist Council with increasing emphasis. More than 2,400 attended the United Methodist Congress on Evangelism, convened in new Orleans in January 1971. A stirring series of presentations was made by Dr. Albert Outler, and was subsequently published as *Evangelism in the Wesleyan Spirit*. At an unofficial convocation on Evangelism in Cincinnati, over 1,600 attended, and a convocation of 2,800 American Indian United Methodists gathered in Oklahoma City to strengthen their Indian heritage and their call in Christ.

Key 73, an interdenominational evangelism emphasis, became the official program of the General Board of Discipleship in 1973 and involved more than 20,000 United Methodist Congregations. In 1974 a small contingent of United Methodists joined over 3,000 Christians from around the world at the International Congress on Evangelism in Lausanne, Switzerland. The purpose was to discuss the task of evangelizing the world. It challenged Christian churches to preach the gospel, work for the liberation of the whole man, and implement the social dimensions of the Gospel. The outcome was the Lausanne Covenant which influenced many conservative denominations, but had little impact upon mainline Methodism.

The theme of evangelism continued to be sounded for Methodists. At the World Consultation and Convocation in Jerusalem in 1974, a commissioning service and communiqué from Methodists to the world went forth emphasizing the need for faith in Christ. The General Conference in Portland in 1976, made its quadrennial emphasis: Evangelism along with Ethnic Minorities and World Hunger. A stirring theme was chosen, "Committed to Christ . . . Called to Change." More recently the Mission to the Eighties, followed by the Bishops Call to the Church for Evangelism, has been made. The need is felt, but the response has not been all that the leadership could hope for. As impressive as the evangelistic efforts have been, they have not stemmed the tide of membership loss the denomination has experienced. The fact is that during the decade of the seventies there was a net loss of more than one million in membership. Now in the eighties the bottoming out of losses has not yet arrived. While many are hopeful the reversal is near, it does not yet seem to be in sight. There are indications here and there that the spark is being rekindled and evangelistic fervor once again ignited, but it remains to be seen how far it will go.

Along with the loss in membership, 2,000 churches were closed during the decade of the seventies, and although most of them were small rural churches, with a few in the inner city, it is a concern. The data is being carefully studied and programs are being developed for revitalization of rural churches and inner-city communities.

During this period over 2,000 additional ministers entered the ranks of United Methodist clergy. The church is being forced to adjust to this by helping in the development of multistaff positions, and special ministries supported by district and conference funding.

The change that has most strikingly affected the operation of the church in administration and in the setting of policy has been the emergence of a political phenomenon known as the caucus. Representing various regional, racial, and ideological groups, the caucus has provided a means through which minorities can speak and organize with more effectiveness in addressing a church still ten million strong. The caucus, in the process, has come to be an accepted operating style in United Methodism.

The first caucus to be formed was that of Methodists for Church Renewal in the sixties. This was followed by the organization of Black Methodists for Church Renewal. The Good News caucus began as the sponsor of an evangelical magazine, but it very quickly became an organization supporting evangelical concerns. Asian Americans and Hispanics saw in the example of the blacks how useful this approach was and organized their own caucuses, to be followed by caucuses organized by youth, seminarians and eventually by what has become the one most influential: the Women's Caucus, formed in 1971.

It was no secret that women had long been a moving force in the United Methodist Church, but they had rarely served on influential boards of the local church or annual conference, let alone the general boards and agencies of the denomination. There were inequities, and women saw the caucus as a means of helping to equate the differences. Leadership is increasingly being shared with women and their influence is being felt, due in part at least, to the significant work of the Commission on the Status and Role of Women in every annual conference.

An amazing pattern, noted not only in the United Methodist Church but also in many Protestant churches, is the number of young women who are being ordained for ministry. Seminaries in every geographical area of the country are registering in certain instances over 30 percent women in freshmen classes. By 1980 over 1,200 ordained women were United Methodist ministers, 6 were District Superintendents, and 1 was a Bishop. At the North Central Jurisdictional Conference in 1980, Marjorie Matthews was elected a Bishop of the United Methodist Church and assigned to the Wisconsin area, where she has proven herself in very able episcopal leadership.

The increasing number of ordained women clergy has created another type of ministry in the church, that of clergy couples, where both husband and wife are ordained. This has created situations that add to the challenge of creative appointment making, but at the same time it may very well bring an exciting dimension of ministry into the church. The excitement coming from the complementary talents and gifts each would bring into a situation.

Many District Superintendents, particularly in rural areas, are pointing to the need for United Methodism to become more intentional in providing good leadership for the small church. In spite of the industrial age and the rapidly arriving technical and information age, rural and small-town life still remains a very important part of Americana, and the small church is still very much a part of it. Over 65 percent of all United Methodist Churches have 200 members or less. This has been put an obligation upon church leadership to provide more planning and support for these churches. The General Conference of 1980, in recognition of this, clarified and simplified the organizational plan for small churches by providing an optional administrative body known as the Administrative Council. This supersedes the two bodies known as the Administrative Board and the Council on Ministries. Small churches generally develop family-like relationships, and with this simplified Administrative Council plan it is hoped they will become both more efficient and effective. To be fully implemented, however, the most vital ingredient for growth must be provided, namely well-trained and committed ministers.

It was in 1970 that the bubble burst on the Plan of Union devised by the Consultation on Church Union. The Consultation had its genesis in a sermon preached in 1960 at the Grace Episcopal Church, San Francisco, by the then stated clerk of the United Presbyterian Church USA, Eugene Carson Blake. COCU presented the long-awaited draft of the Plan of Union in March, 1970. At the convocation convened in St. Louis it was hailed as an expression of faith all could subscribe to. It affirmed the Lordship of Christ; the three historic ordinations of ministry, support of lay leadership, openness to persons regardless of age, race, sex, wealth, or culture; emphasized worship; and pledged to be in mission in the public sphere as well as the private. Yet with all it's many enthusiastic supporters, it failed to come into being. It had a vision, but fears and apprehension destroyed its possibilities. The scheme for union between British Methodists and the Anglicans was also decisively voted down during this period as well.

The United Methodist Church has always been sensitive to human need on a global scale, and with its unique organizational network it has been exceptionally efficient in responding to t hat need. Of increasing concern for Methodists has been world hunger. Through the network of districts, annual conferences, and a centralized agency, the United Methodist Committee for Overseas Relief in New York, millions of dollars and many tons of food have been provided for world hunger. When well-fed Christians in the U.S.A. were confronted with global hunger through newspaper and television reports of floods, droughts, and the effects of overpopulation in Africa and Asia particularly, great concern developed for doing something more than lip-service about world hunger. The oil crisis contributed to the problem because third-world nations, confronted with the rapid escalation of oil prices, were unable to buy the fertilizer needed to increase their production of food. The General Conference of 1976 made World Hunger a Missional Priority for the 1977-80 quadrennium and endorsed several plans to meet the emergency. It became a genuine grassroots movement as people responded with great concern. This resulted in many people modifying their life style to more conscientiously face the seriousness of the issue.

One of the overlooked and often unappreciated treasures of United Methodism has been the rich fellowship enjoyed by its many constituents of varied ethnic and cultural backgrounds. Articles in publications of official church agencies such as *New World Outlook, Interpreter, Circuit Rider, Engage/Social Action, Response, Newscope,* and *Quarterly Review,* frequently have printed dramatic articles on the contribution that ethnicity has made to the church. The unofficial but influential *United Methodist Reporter* frequently features articles on this subject as well.

The deep spirituality of the black, Asian, Latin, and native American has added a dimension of understanding and appreciation that has had an influence on United Methodism. Political and community leaders who have come under this influence often reflect it in the kind of leadership they give. Often United Methodists appreciate this uniqueness, but are still unaware of the serious problems ethnic communities have, as they confront today's world of inflation, unemployment and racism. In order to meet this need, the church has given much time and effort to bridge the gap.

Studies made prior to the 1976 General Conference recommended that the conference act in establishing the Ethnic Minority Local Church as a quadrennial emphasis along with Evangelism and World Hunger. The 1980 General Conference felt the need to be so great that it made Ethnic Minority Local Church the single quadrennial emphasis. To carry out the programming and to improve the facilities of ethnic minority churches, five million dollars was allocated each year. The United Methodist Church obviously refuses to let its minorities suffer without helping as fully as possible in community development and the strengthening of the local church in ministry to otherwise neglected communities.

The sudden ending of the Vietnam War created a problem few had anticipated, the plight of the Vietnamese refugee. When the emergency call went out, United Methodist churches, with many other denominations and groups, responded. Subsequently, when the "boat people" sought refuge from the persecutions that followed in their countries, again many United Methodists found ways to help these families in the transition. The Cubans that flooded the Miami area, particularly during the infamous "Mariel boatlift," became another challenge to the American people already numbed with the refugee problem. Meeting the illegal alien situation along our Mexican border almost defies solution, but the church stands ready to face up to this problem morally and ethically, and is prepared to be equal to the spiritual responsibilities involved.

Since 1973 when the U.S. Supreme Court struck down restrictive abortion, there has been a divided house in Protestantism that has precipitated one of the most controversial issues in America. While no Protestant church had said abortion should be approached casually, many denominations have taken liberal stands on it. Conservative and evangelical groups call abortion "morally wrong" except in cases of rape or incest or when the mother's life is threatened. There is clearly no Protestant consensus comparable to the Roman Catholic stand of adamant disapproval. It remains an unresolved issue, and will undoubtedly continue to be an issue that perennially confronts all denominations.

Another of the unresolved issues that is threatening to fracture unity is homosexuality. When the matter of ordination in United Methodism is addressed, opposing positions leave little room for compromise. Wise and patient leadership is seeking opportunities for sound intelligent discussion on the issue, in the hope that genuine compassion and understanding can develop in this highly emotional controversy. The righteousness of God and the weakness of humanity has always been the theological problem for sinful man. The issue of homosexuality provides an abundance of material for this discussion.

An issue that not only evangelicals and conservatives are concerned about, but many conscientious persons of the liberal persuasion as well, is the campaign for wholesome television programming. Donald E. Wildmon's Coalition for Better Television has claimed a few victories, but not nearly enough for caring parents concerned not only for the sexual exploitation presented, but the violence, profanity and ethical standards that fall far short of good training for children. In due time perhaps the church will muster its forces to make a difference, but at the present the difficulties are overwhelming.

The rapid growth of the charismatic movement in mainline churches became increasingly evident through the decade of the seventies. It was not long before opposition developed. In the beginning it came primarily from conservative and fundamentalist Christians, while moderates and liberals were more sympathetic. As the charismatic movements progressed, however, it seemed to develop inherent dangers. Neo-charismatic groups often wittingly or unwittingly fostered an attitude that the mainline church was not needed, that her authority was not to be regarded and that her sacraments were of little benefit. When this, coupled with a triumphalistic spirit of self-righteousness began to emerge and the havoc of split churches and divided communities developed, the real dangers were forcibly felt by all denominations. The disciplined charismatic, however, who values and appreciates diversity and pluralism, has contributed much in terms of joyous Christianity and generosity both financial and moral.

The alarming power of various sects to influence youth and young adults is another phenomenon that has noticeably diminished in recent years. A number of observers, among them Martin Marty, have said that in all probability this has been due to abuses and the inability to deliver what was promised. While the power of groups like The Children of God, The Way, the Unification Church of Sun Myung Moon and others like them are still to be contended with, the knowledge of their tactics has enabled both parents and youth to more ably and effectively confront them. Headlines are still made by deprogrammers like Ted Patrick and others who specialize in helping youth free themselves from the formidable power the cults exert and the return to the normalcy of family ties and community life. The Jonestown massacre in 1978 did much to stop the influence of cultism dead in its tracks.

A baffling problem every denomination and concerned citizen faces today is how to help those who are struggling with the effects of drug and mind-control substances. Some churches have developed groups of concerned parents to deal with the problem among youth, and here and there are groups organized to help adults, but for the mass of people there is little available help outside of government programs and private clinics. Unfortunately, the church does not have the expertise or facilities, particularly in the early stages of withdrawal therapy, to be of much help. The church is of great importance however, in the later stages of recovery when the spiritual disciplines and fellowship needs are crucial. There is much more intentional effort that needs to be done in this field if the church is to become more sensitive and helpful in this ever-growing problem of society.

Alcoholism, and the misery it brings to individuals and families, is another concern of the church. More and more the self-righteous approach of preaching about the evil (to the neglect of the persons involved) is being remedied. Alcoholics Anonymous and groups like Al-Anon are much more effective in rehabilitation and caring for people in meeting this problem than the church. These groups are to be commended and supported, but the church has a vital task to perform and in most United Methodist congregations an understanding compassion reaches out to help and strengthen in this ministry.

Currently the themes of religious groups are centering around religion and power politics as applied to the threat of nuclear war. The religious peace movement is crossing the lines that separate conservative and liberal ideologies. Billy Graham, at a Boston rally in 1982, alerted the nation to the perils of nuclear war, saying, "We are living at this moment on the very edge of the annihilation of the human race." The Methodist Board of Church and Society has long warned of this danger and has published many articles and recommended reading lists on the threat of nuclear war. Nearly every Annual Conference in 1983 dealt with the issue of nuclear war and the necessity to be about the business of peace-making in today's world. The issue of the controversy is not the need to work for peace, but the methods to achieve peace.

In late 1982, the *Reader's Digest* and in early 1983 the popular television program *Sixty-Minutes,* took deliberate aim at the World and National Council of Churches and the involvement of the United Methodist Church, alleging support of communist and guerrilla groups, particularly in Africa, South America and Central America. What many United Methodists began to realize in the midst of the assault, was how deeply the church was committed to making peace in the world. Methodists are a people committed to work for understanding, and a basis for communication, in a world that too frequently polarizes into opposing camps of bitterness and enmity without always knowing why. What amazed most people was the extent to which support at the grassroots recognized the efforts being made to do something to bring about peace and understanding among people of opposing views. Many people, as they reflected upon the two episodes, apparently were grateful someone was courageous and fearless enough to do something positive for peace. The peacemaker can make mistakes of judgment, and possibly some were made, that in the future can be rectified. Studies are currently being undertaken to prevent the misuse of aid, but the church's true commitment has always been to human need, never to violence. It is to this end that the people called Methodist have historically committed themselves as individuals and as a church.

It is safe to say that the technological age has brought into the realm of church efficiency and effectiveness two dazzling tools that, if properly utilized, will contribute much. The first is the computer. Computers are popular. For many years they were in the data processing departments of large corporations. They then moved to the desks of executives and secretaries, and now businesses of all sizes, large and small, could not function without them.

The breakthrough that made all this possible was the development of the microchip, a small chip of silicon that enable manufactures to build computers small in size and price, but powerful in computing and in the ability to store data. For several years large churches have had their computer office, but now small churches are discovering that they can economically have both the hardware and software to keep track of their membership, do mailing, write personalized letters to members, manage all the financial, inventory and attendance records, as well as file important data; thus eliminating the necessity for bulky filing systems. It is not hard to predict that the growing church of the future will be one that makes intelligent use of the computer.

The second amazing tool of the technological age in the eighties is cable television. Already churches are linked by cable and up-links to satellites that make possible broad ministries for untold millions of people. First Methodist Church, Shreveport, Louisiana, pioneered in this technology and has studios as well as the technical facilities to produce high quality religious programming. Several hours each week are dedicated to broadcasting not only to the surrounding communities, but with the capability of doing it worldwide. The great task is to develop programs that will be effective in meeting the interests and needs of people today.

Perhaps the greatest influence on what the church becomes, and what it will do in the future, hinges on what the seminaries of United Methodism are discovering about ministry. Since the time of John Wesley the motto has been, "Let us unite the two so long divided, knowledge and vital piety."

In 1973 a Readiness for Ministry Project was begun by the Association of Theological Schools. The aim was to determine if theological schools were really doing what they claimed to do, namely prepare their students for readiness in ministry. The fear was that there was too much mediocrity and amateurism instead of competency in the ministers they produced.

Among the definition of goals was that while worship and preaching were most important, no minister could do that effectively unless trust, understanding and communication skills were developed. Those who hold to the importance of a commitment to liberation of the oppressed, identification with the hungry and poor, and opposition to exploitation, are on target, but it becomes obvious, that if a minister is to become more than a functionary, there must be time given to the development of the inner life. As a result, the study showed that the ultimate task of preparing for ministry had to essentially focus on this development.

With the seminaries of United Methodism taking this seriously, the establishment of centers for Faith and Spiritual Formation may bring into being a generation of ministers portending a new church, a new age, and a new hope.

As we look into the future that the eighties will bring, and enter into the third century of Methodism, perhaps it may be as John Workman stated in the May 1980 issue of the *Interpreter,* that a significant "aspect of future-gazing is what we learn about ourselves in the process . . . and (that) for the United Methodist Church, the 1980s will be:

A TESTING TIME . . . whether . . . the denomination has 'the will and the leadership . . . to lift itself out of its present malaise.'

A TIGHTENING TIME . . . the United Methodist Church (will become) a leaner, 'tighter' church. Programming and the focus of mission will turn more from general agencies to annual conferences.

A RENEWING TIME . . . testing brings renewal . . . God is doing something creative in his Church, however disruptive or disconcerting it may seem. The 1980s will be a time of rediscovering identity . . . a time in which . . . United Methodism is stirred awake and with renewed vigor enters the challenge of a new 'decade of discipleship.'

A BONDING TIME . . . (when dialog will hopefully bring the various caucus groups together in a way that will reflect the strength of the denomination, rather than weakness.)"

United Methodists have done much in the shaping of American

thought, conscience, and values, and the church can look back with a measure of satisfaction on two centuries of obedience to the faith in the service of God and humanity. On the threshold of the third century, the United Methodist Church is present as a continuing force in the making of America.

Prepared by Gordon D. Casad

Index

Abbott, Benjamin, 82
Abolitionism, 209, 220, 225, 228, 292
Adams, John, 81
Addams, Jane, 401
Address to the Friends of Reform
  (Snethen), 199
African Methodist Episcopal Church,
  211, 216
African Methodist Episcopal Zion
  Church, 216-17, 353
Aguinaldo, Emilio, 333
Akron Plan, 317-18
Albright, Jacob, 279
Alcohol
  circuit rider peddlers, 355, 357-58
  dram drinking, 357
  early restrictions on, 357-58
  educational courses, 366-67, 370
  as a moral problem, 360
  newspaper advertisements, 359
  sales (1860-80), 359-60
  Wesley rule on, 359
  Women's Crusade against, 360-67
  See also Temperance movement
Alcoholism, 370
Alexander II, Czar, 376
Allen, Richard, 211-16
  ordained, 216
Allen, William, 169-70
Allen Street Memorial Church (New
  York City), 395-96
"Amazing Grace" (hymn), 90
American Board of Commissioners for
  Foreign Missions, 161
American Civil Liberties Union, 397
American Colonies
  disestablishment of Church of Eng-
    land, 27
  missionaries to, 15
  Wesley and, 14-15, 17
American Federation of Labor, 382,
  385
American Railway Union, 377
American Revolution, 14, 26, 43, 47,
  54, 132, 156, 203, 311, 330
  casualties, 44
  at Flatbush Heights, 18
  Loyalists, 15, 16, 18
  Negroes, 213
  Wesley Chapel and, 15-16, 18

Ames, Bishop Edward Raymond, 219-
  20, 244-45, 246, 249
  background of, 245
Anarchists (nineteenth century), 376
"And Are We Yet Alive?" (Wesley),
  109
Andrew, Bishop James Osgood, 172,
  220, 223-28, 229, 231, 232, 256
  background of, 223-24
Angell, Sir Norman, 426
Annual Conference (1771), 61
Annual Conference (1779), 37
Annual Conference (1784), 3, 23-42,
  52
  Asbury and, 26, 28-30, 33-42, 52
  autonomy issue, 23-32
  Christmas Conference, 41-42, 52,
    57, 58, 99, 105, 110, 213, 267, 413
  results of, 40-42
  Wesley and, 34-36, 38, 41, 42
Annual Conference (1787), 42
Annual Conference (1789), 13-21, 23
  address of allegiance, 13-21, 23
  on slavery, 20-21
Annual Conference (1799), 86
Annual Conference (1819), 55
Antinomianism, 10, 271
Anti-Saloon League, 5, 368-70
  founded, 355, 367
Aristotle, 53
Ark of Empire (Van Every), 47-48
Arnow, Harriet Simpson, 48-49
Asbury, Bishop Francis, 53-67, 102,
  106, 107, 194, 196, 205, 213,
  241, 259, 312
  American Revolution, 63-64
  Annual Conference (1784), 26, 28-
    30, 33-42, 52
  arrival in America, 61
  background of, 59-60
  on band idea, 75
  Barratt's Chapel meeting, 28-30
  on the *Calm Address*, 16-17
  camp meetings, 139, 141-43, 144,
    145
  class meetings, 71, 141
  consecrated, 3, 38-39, 40, 279
  death of, 53, 54, 189-90
  early preachings of, 60
  education of, 60
  on Great Revival, 139

Central Jurisdiction, 412–13, 416, 426
criticism of merger, 416–17
efforts to eliminate segregation, 413–16
membership, 352, 409, 411
Uniting Conference, 407–16, 425
Vietnam resolution, 410–11
Wesleyan religious beliefs and, 416–28
See also Methodist Church, The; Methodist Episcopal Church
United Nations, 351
United States Christian Commission, 339–40, 422
United States Constitution, 4, 11, 24, 51
United States Sanitary Commission, 339
United States Steel Corporation, 372, 383–90
strike of 1919, 384–90
University of Chicago, 323
University of Libby Prison, 419–20

Vanderbilt, Cornelius, 315
Vanderbilt University, 315–16
Van Every, Dale, 47–48
Van Lennep, A. O., 320
Vasey, Thomas, 28
Vazeille, Mrs., 101
Vietnam War, 351, 410, 411
Vincent, George, 325
Vincent, Bishop John Heyl, 318–20, 322–23, 324–25
Virginia Conference, 100–10
Virginia reel (dance), 49
Volstead Act, 371
Voltaire, 423

Wabash Avenue Methodist Church (Chicago), 397
Walker, Jesse, 152–53, 313
Walker, William, 153–54
Waller, John, 129–30
Ward, Harry F., 378–79, 397–98
Ware, Thomas, 34, 99
War of 1812, 207
Washington, George, 44, 45, 46, 190, 238
inauguration of, 15, 24
Methodist congratulatory address (1789), 13–21, 23, 51
Ohio inspection trip, 52
slavery petition to, 17–18

Watkins, Bishop William T., 93
Wayne, Anthony, 121
Webb, Captain Thomas, 80–81
Welch, Herbert, 379
Wesley, Charles, 31, 89, 109
Wesley, John, 2–3, 62, 69, 93, 119, 127, 128, 140, 175, 198, 200, 205, 268, 272, 284, 302, 303, 356, 371
Aldersgate meeting, 92
and American Colonies, 14–15, 17
Asbury and, 60, 61
autonomy issue, 26, 27, 28
Baltimore Conference (1784) and, 34–36, 38, 41
Christmas Conference pledge to, 42
class meeting idea, 69, 70, 73–74
doctrine of Holiness, 266–67
education of, 308
emphasis on preaching and reading, 3, 9–10
employment bureau, 391
frugality, 96
generosity of, 96–97
genius for government, 308–9
idea of perfection, 9
influence of, 14, 101
marriage of, 101
pilgrimage to Herrnhut, 92
publishing business, 309
rule on alcohol, 359
rule on pews, 33
on Webb, 81
Wesley, Mrs. John, 101
Wesley, Samuel, 92
Wesleyan Advocate (newspaper), 282
Wesleyan Methodist Connection of America, 210–11
Wesleyan Repository and Religious Intelligencer (publication), 196, 198
Wesleyan Service Guild, 352
Wesleyan University, 156, 222
Wesley Chapel (Cincinnati), 393–94
Wesley Chapel (New York City), 15–16
American Revolution and, 15–16, 18
christened, 81
Wesley Community Houses, 347
West, Thankful, 98
Westward movement, 43–52
Asbury on, 46
frontier life, 48–51
Indians and, 50, 51

Date Due
